The United Nations in Japan's Foreign and Security Policymaking, 1945-1992

National Security, Party Politics, and International Status

Harvard East Asian Monographs 257

THE UNITED NATIONS IN JAPAN'S FOREIGN AND SECURITY POLICYMAKING, 1945-1992

National Security, Party Politics, and International Status

LIANG PAN

Published by the Harvard University Asia Center
and distributed by Harvard University Press
Cambridge (Massachusetts) and London 2005

Printed in the United States of America

The Harvard University Asia Center publishes a monograph series and, in coordination with the Fairbank Center for East Asian Research, the Korea Institute, the Reischauer Institute of Japanese Studies, and other faculties and institutes, administers research projects designed to further scholarly understanding of China, Japan, Vietnam, Korea, and other Asian countries. The Center also sponsors projects addressing multidisciplinary and regional issues in Asia.

Library of Congress Cataloging-in-Publication Data

Pan, Liang.
    The United Nations in Japan's foreign and security policymaking, 1945-1992 : national security, party politics, and international status / Liang Pan.
        p. cm. -- (Harvard East Asian monographs ; 257)
    Includes bibliographical references and index.
    ISBN 0-674-01963-6 (hardcover : alk. paper)
        1. United Nations--Japan. 2. Japan--Foreign relations--1945- 3. National security--Japan. I. Title.
II. Series.
    JZ4997.5.J36P36 2006
    327.52009'045--dc22

                                                                                    2005028829

⊗ Printed on acid-free paper

Last figure below indicates year of this printing
13 12 11 10 09 08 07 06 05

To My Parents Pan Shi Yan and Liu Guang Ning

Acknowledgments

The origin of this study can be traced back to a question I came up with when taking an introductory course on international relations as a first-year graduate student in a Japanese university. During a class discussion on Japan's security stance in East Asia, we had a pretty serious debate on whether Japan's superior economic power would drive the country to search for military predominance in the international society. Before dismissing the class, the professor made a brief comment stating that Japan would not have to be a military superpower as long as the United Nations (UN) system still works to a certain degree. My Japanese classmates seemed to have little problem accepting this observation. But I remained puzzled. It was simply difficult for a foreign student and a newcomer to the field of Japanese foreign policy studies to figure out the causal relations between Japanese national security, which is already guaranteed by the military alliance with the United States, and the UN, which has been known for its weakness in terms of peacekeeping. Soon, the subject became the main focus of my research. I produced my master's thesis on it a year later, and that was followed by a Ph.D. dissertation, which became the basis for this book. During the process, the domain of the study also went through substantial changes. Beginning with a theoretical study dealing with the Japan-UN relationship in the late 1990s, the emphasis of the research gradually turned toward Japan's UN policymaking in the Cold War era as it became ever clearer that the government's attitude toward the UN was generated by something beyond international political trends in the aftermath of the Soviet empire's collapse. This book was produced as a result of this shift in focus.

Many individuals ranging from faculty members to fellow students contributed in helping me confirm the direction of the study throughout the exciting and sometimes frustrating days spent working on the project.

Words cannot express the debt of gratitude I owe to the following members of the Graduate School of International Political Economy at the University Tsukuba, where I spent six years, first as a research student and then as a Ph.D. candidate. Professor Hatano Sumio, my chief supervisor in the doctoral course, not only offered his precious guidance when I was preparing for the dissertation but deeply affected my academic career by being the model of a decent historian and mentor. This book was also completed under his encouragement and support. Professor Harald Kleinschmidt, another reader of the dissertation, significantly enriched my understanding of the meaning of as well as approaches to historical studies through hours of discussions on the subject at his office. I hope this book can at least partly answer some of the questions to which I was unable to respond properly then. Professor Satō Hideo graciously served as my advisor during the first three years of my study at Tsukuba. If he had not passed away so prematurely, I could have benefited more from his keen comments on my work. Acknowledgment is also made to Professor Tsujinaka Yutaka and Professor Ijiri Hidenori, who generously joined my dissertation reading committee and offered concrete advice regarding the revision of the early drafts. Outside Tsukuba, I am indebted to Professor Hosoya Chihiro, Professor Yamada Chūsei, and Professor Uchida Takeo for their cooperation and advice during my Ph.D. research.

The prototype of the current book was generated during the year when I was a postdoctoral fellow in the Reischauer Institute of Japanese Studies at Harvard University. This book would not have come into being without the academic and financial support extended by the institute. Among Harvard faculty members, I am particularly beholden to Professor Iriye Akira, who kindly agreed to let me join his classes in the History Department and consistently encouraged me to turn the dissertation into a book manuscript. His guidance and support proved extremely crucial during and after my stay at Harvard. My deep gratitude also goes to Professor Andrew Gordon, then Director of the Reischauer Institute, and the institute's staff for their efforts to maintain the liberal and productive environment from which all postdoctoral fellows including myself benefited. For their hospitality and encouragement, I wish to thank all visiting scholars of the institute and other postdoctoral fellows as well.

After finishing my study at the Reischauer Institute, I came back to Tsukuba to finalize this book project. During this period, I was fortunate to gain financial assistance from the Japan Society for the Promotion of Sciences, which allowed me to concentrate on the book manuscript without worrying too much about the high living cost in Japan. The Graduate School of Humanities and Social Sciences offered me the most ideal research conditions a junior scholar could ever expect. Alongside those who have been already mentioned, I would like to express my sincere gratitude to Professor Akaneya Tatsuo, Professor Shutō Motoko, and other faculty members of the Graduate School. In addition, I was invited to participate in various academic meetings and research groups outside the campus where I received comments and advice useful in improving the quality of the book manuscript. Professor Ishii Osamu, Professor Amakawa Akira, Professor Masuda Hiroshi, and Professor Hosoya Masahiro are due my deep gratitude in this regard. Last, but not least in any sense, I owe a great debt to the two anonymous readers of the book manuscript who were assigned by the Harvard Asia Center for their positive attitude toward the project and detailed suggestions regarding its further improvement.

It goes without saying that support and encouragement from seasoned scholars was essential to the development of the book project. But it would also have been very hard to keep working on the same subject for more than a decade without the assistance and friendship of many young scholars of my own generation. Despite their busy schedules, Satō Susumu and Miyagi Taizō took time to read all or parts of an early draft of the manuscript and shared with me their insights on the linkage between postwar Japan's bilateral and multilateral diplomacies. Nakajima Shingo, Takahashi Kazuhiro, Kurosaki Akira, Kanda Yutaka, Suzuki Hirokazu, Sairenji Hiroki, and Higuchi Toshihiro either gave me their constructive comments on certain parts of the manuscript or generously let me use valuable archival sources from their own research files. Tosh Minohara, Hosoya Yūichi, Ikeda Shintarō, Hamai Kazufumi, Lim Phaik Chean, and other members of the Postwar Diplomatic History Study Group have been both supportive colleagues and personal friends in the course of my research.

In the past few years, this project has been updated at least six times, and a number of individuals are valued for their contributions in editing or proofreading the manuscript at each stage of the study. Leslie Tkach, Casey Sedgman, and Shannon Morales offered their help in proofreading some portions of the original Ph.D. dissertation. Shannon also efficiently edited an early draft of the book manuscript. Cheryl Tucker of the Harvard University Asia Center Publications Office has always been supportive and patient in dealing with my questions, many of which were caused by my ignorance about the editing procedures of American publishers. I also thank Ann Klefstad for her contribution in the final copy editing process. It was a great pleasure working with all of them.

While the above individuals and institutions played a critical part in smoothing the process of this long project, the usual exoneration applies: none of those whom I have mentioned thus far should be held responsible in any way for the analyses I have presented in this book.

Finally, a special word of thanks to my family members: I thank my brother Pan Zheng, who was always the tallest and strongest guy in his classes in school, for making me understand the importance of settling conflicts at home in a peaceful way during the early days of my life, and for the spiritual support from him and his family (including my little niece) in the course of this project. My parents taught me how to enjoy good books, good music, and good movies. While surprised by my choice to pursue a career in the academic world, they have remained vital sources of encouragement ever since the very first day of my postgraduate study. This book is therefore dedicated to them.

About Japanese and Chinese Names

In this book, Japanese and Chinese names are rendered in their original style, with the family name preceding the given name.

Contents

Abbreviations

AA	Afro-Asian (Group)
ASG	Assistant Secretary General of the United Nations
CCD	Conference of the Committee on Disarmament
CCP	Chinese Communist Party
CGP	Clean Government Party (*aka* Komeito)
CLB	Cabinet Legislation Bureau
CPC	Committee for Program and Coordination
DLP	Democratic Liberal Party
DSP	Democratic Socialist Party
ECAFE	Economic Commission for Asia and the Far East
ECOSOC	Economic and Social Council
ENDC	Eighteen Nations Disarmament Committee
FASC	Foreign Affairs Study Committee
FLN	(Algerian) Front of National Liberation
G-18	Group of High-Level Intergovernmental Experts
Gensuikin	Japan Congress against A- and H-Bombs
Gensuikyō	Japan Council against A & H [atomic and hydrogen] Bombs
GNP	Gross National Product
ICJ	International Court of Justice
JCP	Japan Communist Party
JDA	Defense Agency
JSC	Joint Staff Council (of the SDF)

JSP	Japan Socialist Party
Kakkin	National Council for Peace and against Nuclear Weapons
LBP	Liberal Party
MOF	Ministry of Finance
MOFA	Ministry of Foreign Affairs
NATO	North Atlantic Treaty Organization
NDC	National Defense Council
NFZ	Nuclear Free Zone
NGO	Nongovernmental Organization
NNC	Non-Nuclear Conference
NPT	Nuclear Non-Proliferation Treaty
NSC	National Security Council
ODA	Official Development Assistance
ONUC	*Operation des Nations Units au Congo*
PCF	Peace Construction Force
PDP	People's Democratic Party
PHCF	Peace Homeland Construction Force
PPF	People's Police Force
PRC	People's Republic of China
ROK	Republic of Korea
SCAP	Supreme Commander for the Allied Powers
SDF	Self-Defense Forces
SDF Law	Law of Self-Defense Forces
SIS	Strengthening of International Security
SPSC	Security Policy Study Committee
SSD	UN Special Sessions on Disarmament (I, II, and III)
TDF	Territorial Defense Force
UAR	United Arab Republic
UK	United Kingdom
UN	United Nations
UNARH	United Nations Asian Regional Headquarters
UNDC	United Nations Disarmament Committee
UNEF	United Nations Emergency Force

UNESCO	United Nations Educational, Scientific and Cultural Organization
UNGOMAP	United Nations Good Offices Mission in Afghanistan and Pakistan
UNHCR	United Nations High Commissioner for Refugees
UNICEF	United Nations Children's Fund
UNIIMOG	United Nations Iran Iraq Military Observer Group
UNOGIL	United Nations Observer Group in Lebanon
UNPCB	United Nations Peace Cooperation Bill
UNRWA	United Nations Relief and Works Agency for Palestine Refugees in the Near East
UNSC	United Nations Security Council
UNTAC	United Nations Transitional Authority in Cambodia
USG	Undersecretary General of the United Nations
USSR	Union of Soviet Socialist Republics
WFP	World Food Plan
WHO	World Health Organization

The United Nations in Japan's Foreign and Security Policymaking, 1945-1992

National Security, Party Politics, and International Status

Introduction

In many ways, the year 1956 was a fresh starting point for postwar Japan's diplomacy. For the past decade, the country had borne witness to the most catastrophic change in its history since the mid-nineteenth century. The expansionist course the government adopted in the early 1930s led Japan to a miserable defeat in the Pacific War, which was followed by six years of foreign occupation. The 1951 San Francisco Peace Treaty initiated by Western allies restored Japan's independence but had only limited impact on the nation's isolation in the world community. Thus throughout the first half of the 1950s, Japan's reinstatement as a full player in international politics had continued to be Tokyo's foremost diplomatic goal. It was not until 1956 that the Japanese government's effort in this area began to pay off.

During the last few months of that year, as a result of Prime Minister Hatoyama Ichirō's legendary visit to Moscow, Japan reestablished its diplomatic relationship with the Union of Soviet Socialist Republics (the USSR), which had refused to sign the peace treaty five years earlier. The implication of the rapprochement, however, was not limited to the opening of diplomatic channels with nations on the other side of the Iron Curtain. Since 1952, Japan had been looking for a seat in the United Nations (the UN), only to be foiled by the USSR's obstinate opposition under the pretext that the state of war between the two countries was not yet over. All this ended in the wake of Hatoyama's visit. On December 18, after a break of some 23 years, Japan found itself once again standing alongside the majority of the international community in the headquarters of the world's biggest peace organization.

Aware of the necessity to adapt to this development, decision-makers inside the Japanese government went on to draft a new set of principles for the nation's diplomacy in early 1957. The result was a bluebook entitled "The Present Situation of Our Nation's Diplomacy" (*Waga gaikō no kinkyō*), in which three basic principles of Japan's foreign policy were outlined:

It is needless to say that the national policy of Japan is to establish and to maintain a peace based on freedom and justice and that this constitutes the fundamental aim of our foreign policy. Japan, who is now a member of the world community of nations, wishes to direct her efforts towards world peace by exercising her new right of voicing her opinions. The foundation of such diplomatic activities is laid on three principles—"the United Nations-centric policy," "cooperation with democratic nations," and "the maintenance of the position as a member of Asia."[1]

Despite the pacifist rhetoric, many policymakers and specialists both in and out of the government questioned the political feasibility of the three principles almost as soon as the bluebook was made public. For the next few years, officials at the Ministry of Foreign Affairs (MOFA) were forced to reiterate on various occasions that the three principles were mutually compatible and therefore could be pursued simultaneously. MOFA's argument was not entirely inaccurate. For more than four decades, the Japanese government conducted its foreign policy basically in accordance with some, if not all, of the principles. With the United States (US)-Japan Security Treaty as the core of its foreign policy, Japan closely associated itself with the Western democratic countries throughout the Cold War era. Likewise, though Japan's identity as an Asian state is a disputable topic domestically, the fact that relationships with countries such as Korea, China, and Indonesia always top Japan's diplomatic agenda demonstrates the significance of Asia in Japanese foreign policy. The only problem, however, is the first principle—the "UN-centric policy" or "UN centrism" (*kokuren chūshin shugi*), as MOFA officials dubbed it.

---

1. MOFA, "The Present Condition of Our Nation's Diplomacy," September 1957, FO371/133584, Reel 83, PRO, p. 7.

Unlike the case of the other two principles, by the early 1960s MOFA officials had started to implicitly deny the central role of the UN in Japan's foreign policymaking. In the annual diplomatic bluebooks, increasing space was devoted to emphasizing the inefficiency of the UN in protecting Japan's national interests. The term "UN centrism" was rarely mentioned after the mid-1970s. And when it did appear on occasion, as cynically noted by former UN Ambassador Saitō Shizuo, who was also one of the authors of the three principles, the term was simply used as a "pillow word" by politicians to impress upon the public that they were observing the nation's pacifist diplomatic course.[2]

While it is misleading to call the UN the center of Japan's diplomacy, it is equally inaccurate to completely rule out the significance of the organization in shaping the nation's foreign and security policies. As a matter of fact, the UN is ubiquitous in the diplomatic and political history of postwar Japan. The country has played an important role in buttressing the UN's finances and has ranked number two in the organization's donor list ever since the mid-1980s. It is one of the most frequently elected members of the UN Security Council (UNSC) and its representatives hold seats on all major UN committees. The Japanese government also harbors a longstanding dream of becoming a permanent member of the UNSC. Domestically, a well-functioning collective security system guaranteed by the UN is consistently treated as the ideal formula for Japan's national defense. And the government has officially maintained that its military alliance with the United States is a transitional measure before the UN's peacekeeping function begins to work—a position that was confirmed in the text of the US-Japan Security Treaty. Furthermore, the question of personnel cooperation with the UN in security areas has traditionally been a chief topic in policy debates between the ruling and opposition parties.

Now we have seen two images of Japan's policy toward the UN. On the one hand, there is a reluctant Japan who once enthusiastically announced that cooperation with the UN was the core of its foreign policy and then immediately began to water down the significance of the organization. On the other hand, we find a proactive Japan who is not only willing to extend considerable contributions to various missions of

---

2. Saitō, *Gaikō,* p. 45.

the UN but is also quite conscious of the connection between the organization and its national security interests. But which image reflects the reality of Japan's UN policy? If the UN is so important, why should Japan feel hesitant to emphasize the UN-centric principle? If the UN is inconsequential, why should Japan still be willing to uphold the foundation of the organization notwithstanding its extremely high costs? And more fundamentally, what exactly is Japan looking for from its relationship with the UN? This study aims at unraveling these puzzles from a historical viewpoint.

Research concerning the history of Japan's relationship with the UN is rare. The majority of current studies on postwar Japanese foreign policies focus on bilateral relations like the US-Japan alliance, or the Sino-Japan or Japan-Korea relationship. In contrast, among the small proportion of academic books or articles which have put Japan's UN policy under scrutiny, many were more interested in evaluating current Japanese policies or advising what should be done in the future than in analyzing what Japan has done for the past several decades. Others that did look back to history were inclined to either criticize Japan's policy in terms of ideological positions or narrowly concentrate on a specific policy area or a particular case without thorough background analysis. While they might bring certain aspects of a complicated story to light, what these studies reveal only serves to further stimulate, not satiate, the need to comprehend the whole picture of Japan's relationship with the UN in the postwar era.

Yet it may be unfair to chide previous authors for neglecting the significance of historical aspects of Japan's relationship with the UN. Until very recently, Japan's UN diplomacy was not a topic suitable for historical research due to the lack of firsthand documentary sources. The situation has only begun to change in the past few years as a large bulk of archives on this area have been released by the governments of the US, Japan, and the United Kingdom (UK). In addition, the publication of important primary sources of government leaders, senior bureaucrats, and politicians has further enriched the repertory of available materials. While a number of important documents are still locked in government storerooms, these days we are definitely in a much more comfortable position to study the background of Japan's behaviors during many critical UN incidents. In this book I attempt to tackle the contradictory images of Japan's UN policy through a careful account of these new materials.

The relative abundance of materials alone cannot guarantee the comprehensiveness of this study, however. Political scientist Kenneth Waltz noted in one of his classics that the formation of state foreign policy could be influenced by factors at different levels, ranging from the mentality of individual decision-makers to the overall international structure.[3] While having strong reservations about his argument that the international structure should always be the determinate factor in generating state behavior, I do agree that a comprehensive explanation of state foreign policy should take factors from various levels into account. Otherwise, we may be doomed to repeat the blind men's elephant type of research.

In this study, the word "comprehensive" does not mean "omnidirectional," as an encyclopedic survey covering every aspect of the relationship between Japan and the UN is not only technically impossible but would also be of little help in explaining the dynamism of Japan's policy. Instead, in the following chapters, I have focused on the role of the UN in postwar Japan's foreign policymaking in the political and security areas, which also make up the core of the UN's mission as a world peace organization. The comprehensiveness of this study is reflected in its approach; I will analyze the subject at three different levels—international political structure, domestic political structure, and the psychology of policymakers.

As the influence of both internal and external political factors in generating states' behavior in international spheres has been confirmed by numerous previous studies, I assume that most readers will not question my decision to focus on national security and party politics when tackling this subject. Like their colleagues all over the world, Japanese foreign policymakers are always under pressure to maintain the safety of their country as well as the stability of their political regime. What made this job even tougher for Japanese officials was the reality that in postwar Japan, national security and regime stability frequently turned out to be incompatible goals. Having lost its credit as a peace-loving country due to its prewar and wartime policies, Japan was forced to rebuild its national

---

3. Waltz, *Theory of International Politics.*

security without sufficient regular military forces. Based on their own suffering during wartime, the majority of the Japanese public, for their part, vigorously supported this barehanded defense policy imposed by the Allied Powers. But those inside the government and conservative parties were aware of the potential danger of lack of physical defensive power. Under Allied occupation, some of them, such as certain members of the cabinet and a number of senior MOFA officials, made secret plans to augment national defense through an intimate security bond with Western powers – in particular, the US.

While this may have been a rational option from a purely security viewpoint, it kindled a major domestic political clash that remains unsolved long after Japan regained its independence in 1952. With the endorsement of the mainstream of public opinion, most Japanese opposition parties refused to accept the conservative government's security policy of aligning Japan with the Western camp. In the eyes of many opposition leaders, a pro-Western or pro-American security stance would inevitably put Japan on the front line of the Cold War against the communist camp, and thereby expose the country to the prospect of another total war. Furthermore, the opposition feared that a close tie with Western nations might deepen Japan's isolation in the postwar world community by alienating the country from its Asian neighbors. Such concern was also shared by average citizens. As a result, ever since the early 1950s, there has been no consensus inside Japan regarding the nation's diplomatic and security strategies.

Despite this gap between the understanding of the government and that of the opposition, it is noteworthy that postwar Japan's foreign and security policymaking did not experience major difficulty regarding the country's international identity. As shown in the following chapters, since the late 1940s, Japanese foreign decision-makers have been impressively confident about their nation's identity as a powerful member of the Western camp (against the communist bloc) politically and an industrial power (different from the Third World) in the international economic arena. The real problem for the Japanese government, therefore, was not how to define Japan's international identity in a way that could be accepted by both the ruling and opposition parties, but how to avoid or lower the political risk caused by its choice to align with the Western industrial nations.

Such risk could be found at two levels. On the international level, given Japan's geopolitical position as a tiny island nation surrounded by big military powers in Asia and North America, as well as its increasing economic interdependence with the Third World, it was theoretically better for Japan to adopt a somewhat neutral stance in world affairs. But under the Cold War reality, authentic neutrality was highly impractical for an unarmed state with geopolitical importance to military superpowers. The Japanese government thus chose to cooperate with one of the superpowers for defensive reasons—a decision that only resolved half of the problem. The protection offered by one superpower could be accompanied by the danger of deteriorating relations with the other. The escalation of anti-Western sentiments in Third World nations, many of which were Japan's important trade partners, also deepened the complexity of the situation. The UN, despite its inability to solve these international problems, was at least useful in easing the tension caused by them.

On the domestic level, although the government was unwilling to make substantial compromises with the opposition, it had serious concerns about the response from the public mainstream, which was not ready to take sides in international conflicts. In other words, for the opposition, the public's desire to avoid the East-West or North-South dichotomy was an exploitable golden opportunity. In order to gain the upper hand in this partisan game, both government decision-makers and opposition leaders were prompted to find an effective way to make the public believe that they had made the most suitable choice to maintain Japan's military and economic security. In the following sections, I argue that a somewhat pro-UN stance helped the Japanese government and major political parties to meet these needs.

Moreover, discussions presented in this study indicate that the role of the UN in Japan's foreign and security policymaking was not confined to the framework of ongoing domestic or international political situations. In a much subtler, albeit no less important way, the UN exerted a far-reaching psychological impact on the formation of postwar Japan's stance in international arenas. In spite of Japan's remarkable achievements in the national economy field, Japanese foreign policymakers more or less shared the opinion that their nation did not occupy an honorable position in the world community. The Japanese view on international status largely reflected the nation's traditional understanding of international society coupled with its historical experience during and shortly after World War II. "[Since] Japanese feel a strong bond with the group to which they belong, they tend to focus keen concern on the social rank of their group," as political scientist Satō Seizaburō pointed out. "When these attitudes are directed toward international society, interstate relations similarly come to be viewed hierarchically, and the Japanese sense of belonging to the Japanese state makes them sensitive to the international status of their country."[4] The same explanation could be used to describe the mentality of decision-makers within the Japanese government. When leading Japan into the modern era, leaders of the Meiji Restoration declared in their very first diplomatic announcement that one fundamental object of the new empire's foreign policy was to "promote national prestige all around the world."[5] Throughout the prewar era, the term "first-class nation" (*ittōkoku*) was a cliché in the imperial government's documents and public statements. This aspiration to hold a seat in the top echelon of nations became even more urgent after Japan's defeat in World War II and its exclusion from postwar international affairs.

When the Pacific War broke out in the early 1940s, the Japanese Empire was enjoying its reputation as an influential member of the big powers' club due mainly to its military strength. However, that glorious period did not last long. Its defeat in World War II wiped away almost every diplomatic achievement the country had made thus far. And by the time Japan was ready to resume its international activities, it was no longer considered a great power. Yet postwar Japanese foreign policymakers were anything but oblivious to Japan's necessity for national prestige. This goal, to be sure, is not unique in comparison with the foreign policies of other nations. But again, in the case of Japanese foreign policy, it was not easy to achieve, because of both international and domestic politics. The need to boost national prestige and status could be fulfilled through many methods. Specifically, military buildup is a popular option in this regard. But owing to the debacle of the last

---

4. Satō Seizaburō, "The Foundations of Modern Japanese Foreign Policy," pp. 377-78.
5. Oka, *Meiji seiji shi,* pp. 102-3.

war and the restrictions imposed by the constitution, international status bolstered by a gigantic army, navy, and air force was an unrealistic scenario for Japanese diplomatic policymakers. This, in turn, created another delicate situation in the decision-making process whereby policymakers had to achieve their dreams of international prestige through extremely limited methods. The UN has also been utilized by Japanese policymakers to pursue this difficult mission.

In this study, I intend to illustrate how national security, domestic politics and psychological needs gave shape to the complicated and sometimes incongruous outcomes of Japan's policy toward the UN during the nearly five decades after the end of the last World War. Three independent variables—national security, party politics, and international status—bear on this. In regard to each variable, I will analyze a set of policymaking cases taken primarily from firsthand documentary sources. Part 1 of the book examines the correlation between Japan's UN diplomacy and national security. In this case, "national security" is used to indicate both the safety of Japanese territory and the stability of the international community in a broader sense. Part 2 takes the opposite angle by analyzing the formation of Japan's UN policy from the inside. In many previous studies, Japanese domestic politics has been interpreted in accordance with a bureaucrat-centric model. While the bureaucracy is no doubt very important, as indicated above, domestic political games concerning postwar Japan's foreign and security policy in fact comprise a very complicated story in which not only bureaucrats but also political parties and, under certain circumstances, civic activists or groups have had a crucial impact on government decisions. Thus, instead of singling out the role of certain actors (bureaucrats), I chose to address the bureaucratic influence under the more comprehensive framework of party politics, which covers interactions among government agencies, political parties, and other actors associated with these parties. The last part of the book handles the psychological aspect of Japan's UN policymaking. By examining Japan's energetic diplomatic campaign for higher status inside the UN, this part aims to elucidate the significance of national prestige in generating Japanese foreign policymakers' attitudes toward the UN.

In the end, it is not the purpose of this study to judge whether Japan was cooperative in dealing with UN-related issues or not. Instead, from a historical standpoint, the chapters offer a comprehensive analysis of the reasons behind the complexity of Japan's policy toward the UN. To put it another way, rather than making prescriptions on how to resolve problems that appear in Japan's UN policymaking, this book is designed to explain how these problems came into being and thereby substantially improve our understanding of the historical dynamics of Japan's relationship with the world's most important intergovernmental peace body.

PART I

The UN and Japan's Struggle for Peace and Security

❧ 1 ❧
Japan and the UN's Security Function
in the Early Postwar Era

It was one of the last days of World War II. A group of Japanese bureaucrats gathered in the headquarters of MOFA to watch a newsreel
of the Allied Powers summit held at Yalta earlier that year. Among
them was Nakayama Yoshihiro, then a junior officer at the Ministry's
Treaties Bureau. Fifty years later, having served as postwar Japan's representative to the Conference of the Committee on Disarmament
(CCD) in Geneva and as ambassador to France, Nakayama wrote an article commemorating the fiftieth anniversary of the end of the war for a
MOFA-sponsored journal, in which he vividly recollected what he had
seen on that gloomy day decades before.

> We saw the gallant [Franklin D.] Roosevelt, [Winston] Churchill and [Joseph]
> Stalin [on the screen]. It was beyond doubt that Roosevelt looked like a very
> sick man. But we could sense their firm spirit toward victory. It made us un-
> derstand that we had been driven into a corner of the world, put under a
> shabby and miserable state of isolation. It was the scene displayed there [on
> the newsreel] that moved the world. And we knew that we were doomed.[1]

As observed precisely by Nakayama and his colleagues, the Yalta Conference was an important arena where a host of subjects affecting the
fate of the world community were discussed. One of the decisions
made there was to begin the final process of establishing an international peace organization—the UN—as the core of the international
political and security order after the war.

---

1. Nakayama, "Senzen kara sengo e," pp. 16–17.

The UN was established by the Allied Powers as part of their scheme to maintain postwar international peace. But the idea of founding an international peace organization other than the ill-fated League of Nations was not shared solely by the victors of World War II. The Empire of Japan, one of the leading challengers of the Western powers, had picked up this idea as early as the mid-1930s after its representatives walked out of the League.[2] In 1943, when the Japanese military forces were rapidly losing their supremacy on the battlefield, senior policy-makers within the imperial government, under the leadership of Foreign Minister Shigemitsu Mamoru, drafted a plan to set up a peace organization in East Asia underlining the "equal" rights of states in the region. But the Allied Powers, which had also been toying with the idea of establishing a new international organization ever since the August 1941 meeting between Roosevelt and Churchill, moved faster. From August to October 1944, they assembled at Dumbarton Oaks in Washington, DC, to coordinate their policies regarding the proposed organization that would soon become known as the UN. And during the Yalta Conference the following February, most major agenda items for the establishment of the UN were resolved. In order to catch up with its enemies, Japan unveiled a counter-proposal in March 1945, envisaging a postwar international order supported by a set of multilateral security agencies at both regional and global levels.[3] But it was too late. Before this proposal was able to leave an imprint in actual foreign policy, Japan accepted its defeat in the Pacific War and was placed under occupation by the Allied forces.

The Japanese government's interests in the UN issue did not erode with the end of the war, although the rationale behind those interests changed. Rather than competing with the Western-dominated international system, Japan now studied its policy toward the UN based on grave concern for its own fate within a world community controlled by former enemies. The complicated response of Japanese officials to this dramatic change was revealed in a 1946 MOFA draft document:

---

2. Tobe, "Gaikō ni okeru shisōteki rikyo," p. 129.
3. Takenaka, "Kokusaihōgakusha," pp. 79–80; Hatano, *Taiheiyō sensō,* p. 206 and pp. 278–80.

Although the UN was initially set up for the sake of the fight against the Axis Powers, it has an ongoing purpose to maintain postwar peace. Thus, today, we shall not simply frown upon the UN but must determine our attitude toward the organization through deliberate considerations regarding the future of our country.[4]

The prime subject of such "deliberate considerations" was national security.

The Downfall of the UN-Centric Security Formula

In the early postwar era, given the reality that Japan had been completely demilitarized by the Allied forces, many Japanese believed that they should seek a guarantee from the UN—a peacekeeping organization whose major members participated in the occupation of Japan—for their nation's safety. This opinion was not limited to those outside the government. At least by the autumn of 1946, political leaders such as Prime Minister Yoshida Shigeru publicly remarked that the new Japanese constitution prohibited the right of belligerency because it assumed that in the event Japan was invaded the UN would come to Japan's rescue and punish the violator of world peace.[5] Many MOFA officials in charge of the preparation of future security policies held similar opinions. Ōno Katsumi, a division chief in the Ministry's General Affairs Bureau who would be responsible for the announcement of the UN-centrism principle a decade later, presented in an April 1946 report his "personal view" that postwar Japan should become a neutral state while leaving defense tasks to the UN.[6] Five months later, the Treaties Bureau, one of the most influential sections in the Ministry, produced a memorandum containing a similar reference to the possibil-

---

4. Treaties Bureau, "Kokusai rengō setsuritsu no ikisatsu" (The details of the establishment of the UN), 1946, UTL.

5. Statement made by Yoshida during the deliberation of the new Japanese constitution in the Imperial Diet, in Shimizu, *Chikujō Nihonkoku kenpō*, pp. 87–88.

6. Ōno, "Shin Nihon no kokuze to kokusai rengō kanyū mondai shiken (miteikō)" (A personal account of the national policy of the new Japan and question of admission to the UN, provisional draft), in B'0014, DRO.

ity that the UN might "insure our security."[7] Yet unlike the public's consistent endorsement of the UN-centric security formula, MOFA policymakers' enthusiasm regarding the feasibility of the UN's maintaining Japan's national security was short-lived.

In November 1945, a special committee was established within the Ministry to prepare for a peace treaty with the Allied Powers, and Japan's relation with the UN was one of the topics put under scrutiny. When the committee finished the first round of its study in May 1946, it issued a tentative report in which a formal affiliation with the UN was recommended. The report assumed that Japan could seek UN membership on the one hand while pursuing a "permanent neutral" stance in national security on the other.[8] A few months later, officers in the Treaties Bureau embarked on another policy survey focusing mainly on the outlook for Japan's acquiring a seat in the UN. It was in the course of this survey that policymakers began to foresee several problems indicating that a national security formula centered on an intimate relationship with the UN might in fact engender potential dangers to Japan's safety.

Aware of Japan's inferior status as a former Axis Power, MOFA officials were disturbed by the existence of Articles 53 and 107 of the UN charter. Usually referred to as the "Enemy States Clauses," Article 53 allows UN member states to take "enforcement action" against "any state which during the Second World War has been an enemy of any signatory" of the charter "without the authorization of the Security Council (UNSC)." Article 107, for its part, confirms that the charter shall not be used to "invalidate or preclude" action taken or authorized by a UN member against any enemy state during World War II "as a result of that war by the governments having responsibility for such action." Japanese officials apparently worried about these articles' justification of an invasion against their country. This concern was further stimulated by the 1945 Treaty of Alliance and Friendship signed between China (the Nationalist government) and the USSR in which both

---

7. Treaties Bureau, "Kokusai rengō sanka mondai" (The question of UN admission), September 1946, UTL.

8. MOFA Organizing Committee for the Peace Treaty Issue, "Daiichiji kenkyū hōkoku" (Report on the first round of research), May 1946, in Ōtake, *Sengo Nihon bōei mondai*, pp. 290–97.

parties affirmed their rights to take military action against Japan in the context of the UN charter.[9]

Even if Japan did not become a target of aggression, policymakers still had to face another potential danger caused by the give-and-take character of the UN security system. As a precondition to being protected by the UN's collective security arrangements, Japan had to become a UN member state. But as a member state, Japan would have the obligation to take part in military sanctions imposed by the UN against an outlaw nation and could thereby be automatically drawn into an international conflict among third parties. This seemed to conflict with the purpose for joining the organization in the eyes of some MOFA policy planners who believed that the UN should keep Japan out of any security disputes with other nations.[10]

A similar legal contradiction was found in the proposal to turn Japan into a permanent neutral state while holding a seat in the UN. When undertaking preliminary research on UN membership, officials in the foregoing committee for peace treaty studies had deemed that the incompatibility between the spirit of permanent neutrality and the active measures taken by the UN to contain aggression was "a problem that can be easily resolved."[11] But they soon discovered this problem to be more troublesome than it had seemed. The initial optimism regarding Japan's future UN membership as a permanent neutral state was inspired by Switzerland's experience of joining the League of Nations in the early 1920s without giving up its permanent neutral stance. What they did not know was that in March 1946 the Swiss government determined that unless substantial amendment could be made to the charter, there was no way to repeat in the UN what it had done in the League.

Last but not least, a fundamental problem was detected in the liability of the UN collective security system per se. MOFA policymakers lamented that although the UN acquired "teeth" by way of its ability to

---

9. Treaties Bureau, "Sūjikukoku to kokusai rengō" (The Axis Powers and the UN), August 13, 1946; Treaties Bureau, "Kokusai rengō sanka mondai," UTL.

10. Treaties Bureau, "Kokusai rengō ni yoru anzen hoshō no genkai (yōshi)" (The limitation of national security buttressed by the UN, outline), November 4, 1946, UTL.

11. Shimoda, "Kokusai rengō eno sanka mondai no kenkyū" (A study on admission to the UN), April 15, 1946, B'0010, DRO.

enact military sanctions against aggressors, such "teeth" were ineffective for Japan's self-defense. The reason for this, they observed, was that the only powers that were likely to threaten Japan's security were the permanent members of the UNSC (P5), who hold veto rights. If any of these five nations abused their veto power for aggressive purposes, the UN's peacekeeping capacity would be easily paralyzed, and this could in turn hamper the UN's usefulness in assisting Japan's resistance against big-power intervention. Given the existence of the aforementioned Sino-Soviet treaty, the Japanese government could not dismiss this grim scenario as merely a paranoid hypothesis.[12]

Among these problems, MOFA officials eventually judged that the menace of the Enemy States Clauses and the danger of being dragged into military conflicts as a UN member state might not be so serious. Regarding the former, they speculated that the Clauses' threat might gradually fade away once Japan joined the UN family and started warming its relationship with other member states. In respect to the latter, many thought that in practice, as a state without military forces, Japan's participation in UN coercive actions against aggression would be too limited to trigger hostile reactions from resisting states.[13]

The permanent neutrality problem was more formidable, as Japan had to make a choice between UN membership and permanent neutral status. But after the news of Switzerland's decision not to join the UN finally caught the attention of MOFA officials, the tide within the policymaking team changed. "We must not bind ourselves with the traditional concept of neutrality," a Treaties Bureau officer noted in July 1946. "We need to adopt a flexible foreign policy by taking advantage of the international situation, and we shall not feel hesitant to join the UN just because we have abolished the right of belligerency."[14] Two months later, the Bureau concluded—as did their Swiss colleagues—

---

12. Treaties Bureau, "Kokusai rengō setsuritsu no ikisatsu" and Treaties Bureau, "Kokusai rengō ni yoru anzen hoshō no genkai (miteikō)" (The limitation of national security buttressed by the UN, provisional draft), November 1946, UTL.

13. Ibid.; International Cooperation Division, "Kokusai rengō to Nihon" (The UN and Japan), July 1947, UTL.

14. Treaties Bureau, "Kōsenken hōki to chūritsu" (The abandonment of the right of belligerency and neutrality), July 1946, A'0392, DRO.

that considering the UN's strict regulations regarding the acceptance of the collective security obligations articulated in the charter, it was impossible for Japan to join the UN as a permanent neutral nation. By the end of the year, permanent neutrality became "the only obstacle" to Japan's bid for UN membership in the eyes of MOFA officials, and its attractiveness as a sound formula for national security further declined in the wake of the ongoing tension between Moscow and Washington.[15]

The real bottleneck of the UN-centric security proposal was the question concerning the vulnerability of the UN collective security function. It was the inability to find a practical solution to this problem that eventually forced Japanese decision-makers to seek out other scenarios. By early 1947, three alternatives—UN-centric security, a security arrangement with Western Pacific nations, and a security treaty with the US—sat on the policy discussion table.[16] The UN-centric proposal continued to be the basis for the discussion. Specifically, when officials could not reach an agreement on other options, they at least maintained the bottom line that reliance upon the UN was the ideal way to pursue national security. In the meantime, however, given the weakness of the UN system in the face of the big military powers' predominance, MOFA planners were increasingly open-minded toward the question of what Japan should do if the UN did not work.

One answer to this query was a Western Pacific security arrangement based on Article 52 of the UN charter.[17] The idea had been previously suggested by the MOFA committee of peace treaty studies as a component of the permanent neutrality plan. But starting in late 1946, offi-

---

15. Treaties Bureau, "Kokusai rengō sanka mondai."

16. For recent studies on this issue, see Watanabe, "Kōwa mondai to Nihon," pp. 26–35; Inoue, "Kokuren to sengo Nihon," pp. 194–97; N. Ikeda, "Senryōki gaimushō no anzen hoshō mondai kenkyū," pp. 54–56; Kusunoki, "Senryōka Nihon no anzen hoshō kōsō," pp. 17–24; Pan, "The Formation of Japan's UN Policy in the Early Postwar Era 1946–57," pp. 18–21; Sakaguchi, "Sengo Nihon no anzen hoshō to kokuren 1945–1952 nen," pp. 67–70.

17. According to Article 52, "(n)othing" in the UN charter "precludes the existence of regional arrangements or agencies for dealing with such matters relating to the maintenance of international peace and security as are appropriate for regional action, provided that such arrangements or agencies and their activities are consistent with the Purposes and Principles of the United Nations."

cials were inclined to consider it as an independent option for future defense policy. In theory, such a regional arrangement might have the effect of reinforcing Japan's position in the event of intervention from great powers like the P5, because it would allow its participants to take action before the UNSC began functioning. Yet policymakers also appreciated the difficulty of imagining that such a regional security system would come into being immediately after Japan's independence, since it was supposed to include all nations in the region with different, and sometimes contradictory, ideological and military backgrounds. Therefore, temporary security measures in a transitional period were still a necessity. In addition, even if the planned arrangement was ultimately concluded, there was no guarantee that none of the P5 members would nullify UN assistance of Japan's self-defense efforts at the regional level.[18] Under such circumstances, Japan would have to fight against the invaders outside the framework of the UN, and the promise made by other countries in the region to defend Japan would probably mean nothing but a "mere psychological consolation," as a Treaties Bureau officer sarcastically put it.[19]

The earnest need to have an effective security arrangement as soon as Japan's sovereignty was recovered made another alternative—a security pact with the US—more attractive. Due to the void of sufficient documentary sources, it is difficult to pinpoint the exact timing when the idea of the US-Japan security alliance surfaced. But evidence has demonstrated that by 1946, at least some officials in MOFA had already reckoned with it. In July of that year, Asakai Kōichirō, a senior MOFA officer then serving at the Central Liaison Office—a bureaucratic body for policy coordination with the US occupational authority—asked the State Department representative in Tokyo whether, since the UN might not be so efficient in maintaining Japan's national security, it would be possible for Japan to seek its safety from a "specific Allied Power."

---

18. The Policy Deliberation Committee, "Dai san kai kaigi giji yōroku" (The minutes of the third meeting), May 9, 1946, B'0014; MOFA, "Anzen hoshō mondai ni kansuru iken" (Comments on the security issues), June 12, 1946 and MOFA, "Gunbi teppaigo ni okeru keisatsuryoku oyobi kokunai kōku mondai ni kansuru iken" (Opinions regarding problems in the police forces and domestic aviation after disarmament), July 10, 1947, B'0008, DRO.
19. International Cooperation Division, "Kokuren to Nihon."

Given the identity of his counterpart, it was not difficult to determine which Allied Power Asakai was talking about.[20] In November, the Treaties Bureau registered the same opinion in a draft report, "The Limitation of the Security Guaranteed by the UN." Pondering potential methods by which Japan could avoid any damage brought about by a P5 member's abuse of veto power, the report inferred:

For instance, if we conclude an assistance treaty with the US (as long as it is not mutual, the treaty may forestall any troubles concerning violation of the constitution), we can utilize the collective self-defense rights of the two nations against an attack from the USSR until certain measures have been taken by the UNSC. . . . In this case, veto problems may not occur.[21]

In this report the US-Japan security treaty proposal was still considered alongside other regional multilateral security arrangements. But the escalation of the confrontation between the two blocs soon pushed the Japanese government in the direction of an exclusively bilateral security pact with the US. In March 1947, the deterioration of the situations in Turkey and Greece gave rise to the Truman Doctrine, indicating that the US was now ready to counter the penetration of international communist forces independently by whatever means were necessary. Six months later, Japanese Foreign Minister Ashida Hitoshi sent a "personal message" to Lieutenant General Robert Eichelberger—the commanding general of the Eighth US Army, stationed in Japan—in which he wrote that under the current international circumstances, the UN could "hardly be relied upon" as the means of preserving Japan's independence and security. As one of the "other alternatives conceivable," he proposed that "the conclusion of a specific agreement between Japan and the United States, by virtue of which the former's defense is entrusted in the hands of the latter," might deserve serious attention on both sides.[22]

One month after the handover of the Ashida Message, the Treaties Bureau revised its study on security policy options. While the review

---

20. Asakai, *Shoki tainichi senryō,* pp. 232–33; Nishimura, *Sanfuranshisuko heiwa jōyaku,* pp. 30–31.

21. Treaties Bureau, "Kokusai rengō ni yoru anzen hoshō no genkai (miteikō)."

22. Hitoshi Ashida, "Ashida nikki, September 24, 1947" in Ōtake, *Sengo Nihon bōei,* p. 307; text of Ashida's message to LG Eichelberger (English version), B'0008, DRO.

did not immediately lead to unwavering support for Ashida's proposal, it did make one point clear: the UN-centric scheme was no longer the basis for the government's security policy planning.[23]

The UN's Security Role in a Broader Sense

Did the Ashida Message mark the end of the UN's influence in postwar Japan's security and foreign policies? The answer is both "yes" and "no." The demise of the UN's collective security function as a reliable method of protecting Japanese territory from aggression demonstrated that from a narrowly defined security viewpoint, the "UN-centrism" slogan had lost its feasibility more than a decade before it was coined. Yet, in a much broader sense, the UN's role in Japan's national security design did not vanish in the aftermath of the Ashida Message. Apart from territorial security, the Japanese government viewed economic reconstruction as one of the most critical tasks for the nation's survival in the postwar international community. As early as April 1946, Shimoda Takezō, chief of the First Division of the Treaties Bureau, observed that having lost all armed forces, occupied territories, and colonies, Japan was unable to meet the minimum needs of the people for necessary provisions. The only way out of this impasse, according to Shimoda, was to take a course of "international cooperation" by joining the UN—if the organization could expand its mission to social and economic spheres. Shimoda's view was echoed by his colleague Ōno, who pointed out in his report that in order to draw the national economy back from the brink of collapse, Japan should adopt an "international dependence" policy by affiliating with the UN. Using his words, this policy was something that could influence the "fate of our country and the existence of our nation." All these arguments were more or less inherited in later policymaking studies.[24]

Besides economic security factors, some policy planners punctuated the role of the UN in long-term military security goals such as war

---

23. Treaties Bureau, "Sengo Nihon no anzenhoshō keitai (chūkan hōkoku)" (The security formula of postwar Japan, midterm report), October 25, 1947, B'0008, ibid.

24. Shimoda, "Kokusai rengō eno sanka"; Ōno, "Shin Nihon no kokuze."

prevention as well. In a July 1947, MOFA draft memorandum, the chief of the International Cooperation Division, Haga Shirō, contended:

Aggression will not abruptly occur. In most occasions, prior to aggression there will be conflicts or dangerous situations which can possibly be resolved by the UN's peace efforts. In addition, there are many other states that have similar misgivings [to aggression] as we do. If together we influence international opinion, even the big powers can be deterred. [Thus,] it is inappropriate to completely deny the value of the UN simply because of its perceived powerlessness.[25]

Presumably due to the need to concentrate on studies regarding the bilateral alliance with the US and the forthcoming peace treaty at that time, it would take another few years until the government could give more attention to this broader role of the UN in Japan's national security.

On September 8, 1951, the Japanese delegation led by Prime Minister Yoshida signed the Peace Treaty at the San Francisco Opera House— the same place where the ceremonial session for the inauguration of the UN was held five years earlier. Later that day, in a US military camp, Japan and the US concluded their first security treaty. Japan regained its status as a sovereign state, and the government no longer needed to worry about immediate military aggression against the country, because the security treaty allowed, albeit in a vague manner, US military forces to be utilized for "the security of Japan against armed attack from without."[26] On the basis of such a guarantee, it would not have been surprising to see Tokyo relinquish any security scheme in which the paralyzed UN might have a substantial role. But in reality, there were those within the government who perceived the issue in a rather different way.

Among other critical diplomatic items, Japan's relationship with the UN was put under further study in MOFA soon after the Peace Conference. In a policy guideline produced through these studies, officials defined the functions of the UN in three categories: "a security institu-

---

25. International Cooperation Bureau, "Kokuren no hanashi (miteikō)" (About the UN, provisional draft), July 1947, UTL.
26. Article 1 of the Security Treaty between Japan and the United States of America, September 8, 1951.

tion," "a town-meeting where all problems in the world are discussed," and "an institution to promote economic and social progress." There was a consensus that Japan should wholeheartedly cooperate with the UN in the last category. As for the second category, they suggested that at a certain stage after the peace treaty took effect the government might raise political problems such as peace arrangements with communist states which refused to sign the San Francisco Peace Treaty and the issue of the Northern Territories occupied by the USSR at "the UN town-meeting." Over the long term, they also suggested that Japan use the UN as "an arena for campaigns to demonstrate our benevolent and active international cooperation" and to "formulate an atmosphere of good faith and understanding [toward Japan] in international society." By contrast, discussions regarding the UN's function in the first category—national security—were somewhat fuzzy. Officials showed no hesitation in declaring that with the existence of the US-Japan military alliance, "there was no reason and necessity to request anything regarding our security from the UN." But at the same time, despite the consistent emphasis on the "non-political" or "technical" character of the government's UN policy, they did not entirely close the door on UN diplomacy of a more political hue. "If we do have any political requests for the UN," officials argued, "they must be the prevention of the Third World War and the reconciliation between the two camps led by the US and the USSR respectively."[27]

To some degree, the 1951 MOFA studies on the UN laid a foundation for the government's UN policy in the political and security spheres for the coming years. This was composed of understandings at two levels. At the first level, the UN was conceived as an arena or a "town-meeting" for international opinions where different political issues were discussed in an equal way. At the second level, the organization could be a war prevention machine free from the unhappy reality of the Cold War—a thought identical to that in Division Chief Haga's 1947 memorandum. These two tracks of understanding functioned not separately but interactively in shaping Japan's policy.

---

27. MOFA, "Heiwa jōyaku chōingo no gaikō seisaku shingi yōkō: Kokusai rengō ni kansuru gaikō" (Outline for the deliberation of diplomatic policies after the conclusion of the peace treaty: Diplomacy related to the UN), 1951, B'0014, DRO.

The idea of using the UN as a tribune of international opinion had its root in the "international democracy" (*kokusai minshushugi*) theme that initially appeared in the mid-1940s. Like many other Japanese political catchphrases, more often than not, "international democracy" was used by politicians and bureaucrats without a precise definition. A rare exception in this sense was a personal memo written by former Foreign Minister Shigemitsu in January 1946 before he was indicted for war crimes charges. According to Shigemitsu, international democracy was the extension of "domestic democracy" (which meant the acquisition of the status of a nation state). Under the rule of international democracy, all nations were supposed to have equal rights and be free from repression (colonialism or semi-colonialism) imposed by great powers. Shigemitsu viewed the postwar international order dominated by the US, the USSR and the UK as a "capitalistic" version of international democracy. The next stage of such international democracy would be "international socialism" (*kokusai shakaishugi*), in which a borderless international society would come into being. And Shigemitsu predicted that the establishment of the UN was the prelude of this international socialism.[28]

Shigemitsu was not the only Japanese diplomatic expert who related the UN to international democracy. Ōno, for example, presented a similar analysis in his 1946 memo. Compared to Shigemitsu's theory, Ōno's interest in this was formulated by a more practical concern. As a member of MOFA's security policy planning team, Ōno felt that small countries such as the disarmed Japan were threatened by the big nuclear powers in the postwar era. Japan's savior under this nuclear menace would be the UN, which he regarded as an institution that "embodies the principle of international democracy" through "the adoption of majority rule and the establishment of international military forces." By closely tying itself with such an international organization, he assumed, Japan might play an important role in "eliminating the arbitrariness of powerful nations" and thereby save itself from the depths of defeat.[29]

These personal accounts on the correlation between the ideal of international democracy and Japan's UN policy did not gain wide attention

---

28. Shigemitsu, *Zoku Shigemitsu Mamoru shuki*, pp. 415–18.
29. Ōno, "Shin Nihon no kokuze."

until the mid-1950s, when the government embarked on its endeavor to achieve UN membership. Instead of repeating their predecessors' arguments, which were made in a theoretical or idealistic context, MOFA officials in the 1950s took up this matter in light of Japan's experiences as a freshly independent member of the postwar international community. Questioning the desirability of completely binding Japan with the US in handling UN affairs, a 1955 memo prepared by an official at the newly established MOFA Bureau of International Cooperation read:

We should not neglect the point that we may naturally have different ideas than the US concerning the UN. I daresay the US would not be seriously disturbed if the UN no longer existed. But to our country, which is not a big power any more and has to steer its national course by counting on the good will of the international community, the existence of the UN as an arena for international democracy is indispensable. It goes without saying that we should continue to make the best use of our relations with the organization.[30]

Analyses linking the international democracy theme with the US-Japan relationship inevitably introduced the Cold War element into the government's UN policy research. If Japan wanted to have more freedom in using the UN to protect its interests as a "small nation," how should it deal with its Western allies, many of which were big powers? If Japan chose to stand with its anti-imperialist brothers, it could jeopardize its interests in the shadow of Moscow's international joint-front plot. If it decided to maintain its position as a humble rookie of the free world, then instead of an arena for "international democracy" the UN would probably mean nothing for Japan but a Cold War battlefield against the East and perhaps some of the radical small nations as well. Was that what was in the mind of Japanese policymakers when they were discussing the usefulness of the UN in 1955? It is difficult to find a quick answer to these questions unless we take a closer look at the second level of Japan's UN policy scheme—the use of the organization as a Cold War-proof shelter.

Just a few weeks after issuing the 1955 memo, the International Cooperation Bureau produced another long report on UN policies. This

---

30. First Division of the International Cooperation Bureau, "Waga kuni kokuren kamei no hōsaku ni kansuru ken" (The method of our country's admission to the UN), May 8, 1955, B'c040, DRO.

time, the Bureau devoted more space to figuring out the UN's role in the Cold War. Officials commented that the UN was not a "mere arena for the Cold War" since the two blocs did not found the organization in 1945 with clear foresight about their conflicts in the years ahead. Besides, under the current situation, while the UNSC was deadlocked due to the disputes among the P5, the UN's ability to "take considerable actions regarding issues that have no direct connection with the Cold War" was intact. Even in events related to the Cold War, such as what happened in Korea, the limited efforts made by the UN were "better than nothing." With these observations, the report concluded that as small neutral states proceeded to help the UN to restore its original security functions, it was worth embracing the hope that "the UN will continue to develop its status as both a tool for international democracy and an international agency transcending the Cold War."[31]

Such optimism was still alive at the time Japan was about to accede to the UN. In October 1956, one month before Japan obtained its membership, MOFA officials wrote in a document that considering the presence of ten communist nations at the UN General Assembly (UNGA), the UN was actually becoming a "shared forum where the two blocs are cooperating with each other." They thus recommended that the government improve relations with communist member states within this shared forum of the UN in accordance with the "objectives and principles of the charter, which superseded specific ideologies." Three months later, these words were reprinted in an official pamphlet commemorating Japan's admission to the UN. In addition, the pamphlet reminded the public that the time was opportune to resolve "crucial international issues . . . entirely within the framework of the UN" rather than other forums such as "summits of big powers or conferences of foreign ministers."[32]

---

31. First Division of the International Cooperation Bureau, "Kokuren kamei kōsaku ni kansuru shomondai" (Problems regarding admission to the UN), May 22, 1955, ibid.

32. First Division of the International Cooperation Bureau, "Kokuren kamei no igi ni tsuite" (The significance of joining the UN), October 10, 1956, B'0042, DRO; First Division of the Information and Culture Bureau, *Kokusai rengō gaikan.*

Indeed, it was quite amazing that the Japanese government was able to sustain this understanding of the UN's role in resolving international political and security disputes for so long (at least five years). Compared to the occupation era, Japanese policymakers in the 1950s saw no shortage of opportunities to test the feasibility of their ideas. In 1952, the government opened an observer's office in New York so that Japanese officials could watch and later have a limited hand in international diplomatic activities carried out within the UN. But whereas one might assume that seeing the confrontation between the US and the USSR within the UN with their own eyes would make Japanese policymakers lose their passion toward the organization, any such expectations proved false. A brief period of détente around the mid-1950s ameliorated the Cold War tension in New York and hence boosted Japan's expectations as to the UN's role in maintaining international peace.

The Brief Détente and Japan's Initial Policies

In August 1950, two months after the outbreak of the Korean War, the Soviets' boycott of the UNSC sessions (in protest of the Nationalist regime's occupation of the China seat) came to a halt. USSR Ambassador Yakob Malik returned to his seat in the UNSC chamber, albeit with a bundle of vetoes. The Council soon became crippled and so did the UNGA. Unable to recruit new members from neutral nations, the Assembly was torn apart by the face-off between the majority of Western or pro-Western states vis-à-vis a tiny but rigidly disciplined group of communist states ready to smash any proposal raised by their capitalist enemy. UN Secretary General Trygve Lie's painstaking efforts to make a breakthrough ended in his own resignation in 1953. The turmoil in the UN led major powers to move their negotiations to other venues. The Korean problem was forwarded to committees organized by the countries concerned, outside the auspices of the UN, and then the same was done in the Indochina case. Japanese policymakers were deeply upset by this trend. "When things like the Big Five Conference become reality," MOFA officials anticipated in early 1954, "Asian problems will probably be discussed outside the UN." While considering such a situation a "UN crisis," these officials still clung to a ray of hope that "sooner or later efforts will be made toward resolving these [international] problems inside the UN."[33]

What occurred in the subsequent years at least temporarily placated Japan's misgivings. After the death of Joseph Stalin in March 1953, the atmosphere surrounding the UN gradually changed. The USSR's new leader, Nikita Khrushchev, adopted a different strategy in regard to the UN. While the Soviets maintained their harsh anti-Western position at UN sessions, they now became more interested in preserving the organization for their own purposes. Representatives of the USSR started showing flexibility in working out package deals with the West on the admission of new member states, hoping that these deals could not only bring more socialist regimes into the UN system but increase the number of newly independent neutral states in the UN family, most of which were promising candidates to back up the Soviet offensive against the Western bloc. On the other side of the Iron Curtain, the victory of Dwight Eisenhower—a renowned supporter of the UN's collective security function—in the 1952 presidential election and the appointment of John F. Dulles—another UN veteran—as the secretary of state guaranteed Washington's adherence to its foreign policy of attaching great importance to the UN.[34] These developments considerably smoothed communication across the two camps on UN matters. While continuing to bandy words with each other in UN chambers, both at least began to recognize the value of UN diplomacy as a crucial tool in defending their national interests.

In the fall of 1956, Japan gained a precious chance to peek into this new phase of international politics within the UN. Ever since the 1948 military clash between Jewish and Muslim residents in Palestine, the Middle East had been a hot spot of turbulence. The 1952 Egyptian Revolution deepened the complexity of the situation. The leader of the revolution, Lieutenant Colonel Gamel Abdel Nasser, who was an assertive believer in Arab nationalism, launched a series of provocative policies to challenge Western powers' privileges in the region. In July 1956, in retaliation for the withdrawal of Western financial support to Egypt's Aswan

---

33. First Division of the International Cooperation Bureau, "Kokuren kamei mondai ni tsuite" (The admission to the UN), February 9, 1954, B'0040, DRO.
34. Ostrower, *The United Nations and the United States,* pp. 66–67.

Dam project, Nasser not only deepened his relationship with the Soviets but unilaterally declared the nationalization of the Suez Canal—a decision that frightened nations who depended on free access to the sea lane across the canal to transport critical commercial goods, fuel, and other resources. The canal's users subsequently held two conferences in London, but both ended without working out a solution that was acceptable to Nasser. The French and British—the traditional colonial powers dominating the Middle East—then raised the problem in the UNSC. Yet instead of waiting for the UN to resolve the crisis, the two secretly formed a coalition with Israel to plot an invasion of the canal area. By November, for the first time since the Korean War, the UN found itself in the unpleasant position of handling a regional military showdown instigated by big powers holding veto rights in the UNSC.[35]

Japan was not merely watching the crisis from the bench. It was invited to attend the two conferences of the canal users, and the Japanese Observer to the UN participated in the Afro-Asian (AA) Group's discussion on this issue. In the early stages of the conflict, opinions within the Japanese government split between two groups bearing pro-Western and pro-Asian nationalist tendencies, respectively. During the London conferences Foreign Minister Shigemitsu, a known anticommunist conservative, was interested in helping the Western allies contain Soviet penetration in the Middle East. But being an enthusiastic sympathizer of Asian nationalism (which he viewed as part of international democracy), he did not simply go along with the Western camp in scorning Nasser's radical cause. Instead, he advised the Egyptians to move the case into the UN, hoping the UN would "actively intervene in the situation and eliminate the threat of war."[36] When this issue did become part of the UNSC's agenda, the voice of the pro-Asian nationalist group within the Japanese government began to overwhelm that of its pro-Western counterparts.

Three weeks after the UNSC held its first meeting on the Suez crisis, Israeli troops attacked Egypt. The US, which was keen on augmenting the UN's authority in handling another international dispute—the Soviet invasion of Hungary—promptly responded to this emergency by

---

35. Meisler, *United Nations,* pp. 94–104.
36. Satō, "Reisen, kokuren, 'tōzai no kakehashi,'" pp. 8–10.

submitting a resolution to the Council calling for the withdrawal of the Israeli forces. But the UK and France spoiled Washington's move with their vetoes.[37] Japan considered the action of the two Western powers an intolerable abuse of their privileges. On November 16, Shigemitsu told the Diet in an unusually furious tone that "the two great [p]owers of Britain and France . . . have, by using the veto right in the face of opinions of first the United States and then the United Nations in general, and by resorting to direct military action, disregarded the long-fostered and universally accepted idea that force should not be used as an instrument of national policy, and are now the objects of loud and condemnatory criticism that their action tramples on the spirit of the United Nations and endangers its existence."[38] For whatever reasons, MOFA officials added some more radical expressions into the English translation of Shigemitsu's speech which was circulated among Western media and stirred up strong resentment in the British Foreign Office.[39]

Japan's outspoken stance was not limited to the Foreign Minister's provocative statements. Shortly before the Middle East situation became tense, Japan was granted a full membership within the AA Group in the UN regardless of the fact that its application for a UN seat was not yet approved. The first important assignment it received in the Group was to work with other AA states in searching for an effective solution to the Suez crisis. Japanese Observer to the UN Kase Toshikazu, one of Shigemitsu's closest disciples, eagerly devoted himself to this mission. Considering the sabotage by France and the UK, some UNSC members (Iran and Yugoslavia) proposed holding an emergency session at the UNGA based on the United for Peace Resolution, which had been devised by the US during the Korean War to avoid Soviet vetoes.

To enact this plan, it was necessary to gather the minimum seven votes at the UNSC so that a resolution for the emergency session could be adopted. The AA Group managed to secure six votes (including those of the US and USSR), but the seventh, which was supposed to be cast by the Chinese Nationalist delegate, remained uncertain. Kase took the responsi-

---

37. Meisler, *United Nations,* pp. 107–13.
38. Tokyo to London, No. 479, November 17, 1956, FO/371/121036, Reel 70, PRO.
39. Tokyo to London, No. 477, November 17, 1956; Morland to Dening, December 7, 1956, ibid.

bility of approaching Nationalist Chinese Ambassador Tsiang Ting Fu. Initially, Tsiang was reluctant to support the AA Group, which was generally antagonistic to the Nationalist government in Taiwan. But with Kase's persistence, he (presumably after consulting Taipei) switched his vote at the last minute.[40] Within a few days, the emergency session was summoned at the Assembly, where a resolution was adopted authorizing the Secretary General to send a UN force to the Canal Zone to separate the combating Egyptian and Israeli troops. The proposed UN force—later dubbed the UN Emergency Force (UNEF)—became the first of the UN Peacekeeping Forces that are deployed throughout the world now.[41]

Sensing the resentment on the British side, Kase shrewdly sent a courteous message to the UK ambassador in Tokyo, Esler Dening, to defend himself from the charge that he and his delegation were "taking part in making denunciatory statements" such as those emanating from the AA Group against the UK. Dening, however, was not moved. The British ambassador cautioned his colleague in New York that "if Japan thinks that she can gain anything by association with the Afro-Asian bloc she may exploit the possibilities."[42] Dening's unease might have been generated by the atmosphere in Tokyo. On several occasions British diplomats did find sympathetic views toward their country's policies in the Japanese capital. A Ministry of Finance (MOF) official, for example, was quoted as making a comment in front of UK embassy officials that "Britain's intervention in Suez is comparable to the Japanese intervention in Manchuria in 1932, which was similarly misunderstood."[43] A British officer wrote in a memo: "There is also a feeling abroad in some circles here—and Mr. Shigemitsu may well share it—that what we did was not so bad in itself, but that we had no right to do it in a manner which seemed to display so

---

40. Kase and Kiuchi, "Kokuren ni tsukai," pp. 77–78.

41. While the UN had dispatched a small number of unarmed military observers to oversee truces in conflicting areas before 1956, the UNEF was the first PKO force involving armed troops for more active missions.

42. Kase to Dening, November 16, 1956; Dening to Dixon, November 22, 1956, FO/371/121036, Reel 70, PRO.

43. British officers were by no means cheered up by such an argument, however, as they considered what Japan had done in Manchuria "sheer naked imperialism" and "the last thing we [British] would wish to encourage." See Chadwick to Far Eastern Department, November 6, 1956 and Selby to Mayall, December 5, 1956, ibid.

blatant a disregard for what other nations might think."[44] What upset British officials, nonetheless, was that these pro-UK sentiments did not represent the majority opinion in Japan. As admitted by most reports sent back to London, the embassy kept getting "bad press over Suez" and the Japanese public in general was apparently on the side of those who bluntly criticized the vetoes cast by the two big powers.[45]

In contrast to their irritated British counterparts, Japanese officials in charge of UN diplomacy felt relieved by the performance of the organization during the crisis. Four days after the passage of the UNEF resolution, Kase wired Shigemitsu:

While encountering a severe trial, it is fortunate that the UN is doing well in bearing it. In the interim, Secretary General [Dag] Hammarskjold's effort is winning the highest praise inside and outside the organization. And behind the applause, there is the undisputed fact that the UN is now speaking on behalf of the good faith of human beings. Any big power, no matter how mighty it is, will suffer a tremendous loss if it challenges the organization. The UN is different than the erstwhile League of Nations, which was ruled by the autocracy of big powers with a strong tinge of power politics. Under the influence of many small nations with the force of numbers and moral pressure toward big nations, the UN has made considerable progress in terms of international democracy.[46]

The small nations could use the UN to protect themselves from the exploitation of big powers. And as a shared forum where ideologically conflicting parties could work together, the world peace organization, supported by the spirit of international democracy, might also supersede the Cold War. With these dreams about a bright future for the UN, Japan took its seat in the General Assembly Hall as a full member state one month later.

---

44. Selby to Mayall, December 5, ibid.
45. Ibid.; Dening to Morland, November 22, 1956, ibid.
46. Kase to Shigemitsu, November 9, 1956, A'0377, DRO.

↬ 2 ↫
The Burgeoning Disillusion

On December 18, 1956, the UNGA adopted a resolution cosponsored by 51 nations to approve Japan's UN membership. On the same day, the Japanese government issued an official declaration, vowing to "not only faithfully obey the principles of international peace and justice based on the UN charter but also make contributions with other member states toward the construction of a better international society."[1] Japan's willingness and, more important, its ability to keep its word were soon to be tested in UN debates on a host of thorny political and security issues.

The Cold War Shadow

Almost from the moment Japan was first seated in the Assembly Hall, its expectations regarding the UN's broader security function faced serious challenges. Events taking place in the organization during the last four years of the 1950s led Japanese policymakers to realize that the idea of using the "shared forum" of the UN to ease the animosity between the two blocs was nothing more than a political fantasy.

Like many new member states, Japan was eager to demonstrate its will to discuss international security topics from the podium of the UN. The nuclear test ban was one of the initial policy areas chosen by the Japanese government for this purpose. As the only country in the world that had suffered two atomic bombings, the Japanese people in general

---

1. *Asahi shimbun,* December 19, 1957.

share an almost instinctive hatred of nuclear weapons. Such anti-nuclear sentiments escalated in 1954 in the aftermath of a US hydrogen bomb test in the Bikini Atoll, during which a Japanese fishing boat was fatally exposed to radioactive fallout.

The Japanese government's opposition to nuclear tests, on the other hand, was originally used as a "gesture" (borrowing the words of MOFA officials) to forestall the domestic left-wing opposition parties' strategy of mobilizing the public's anti-nuclear sentiments against the conservative regime's security alignment with the US. In the late 1950s, this stance was prompted by Prime Minister Kishi Nobusuke's daring attempt to snatch the initiative of the anti-nuclear movement back from the opposition through more proactive test ban endeavors in the international arena.[2] Inside the government, MOFA policymakers also believed that it was important to promote the test ban not merely for domestic political purposes but as part of the country's "independent diplomacy" (*jishu gaikō*), in order to reflect its view on international peace and security trends.[3] In 1957, Japan was ready to submit its own nuclear test ban proposal to the UN. The government took actions at two levels. On the bilateral level, Prime Minister Kishi dispatched a special envoy to London and New York to appeal for the suspension of pending nuclear tests. In the meantime, on the multilateral level, Japan invested enormous energy into activating nuclear-related discussions at the UN.

While they carried out their policies at both levels simultaneously, MOFA officials were fonder of the UN channel than of the bilateral approach. In the mid-1950s, although there was only one nuclear power in the communist camp, two Western nations—the US and the UK—were doing their utmost to refine their nuclear weapons, and the French also aspired to a seat in the nuclear club. Therefore, Japan's opposition to nuclear tests had the potential to impair the West's strategy to overwhelm the Soviet nuclear arsenal. MOFA hoped to ease, if not completely resolve, the dilemma by locating Japan's stance between that

---

2. For a very detailed and well-documented account of Kishi's strategy, see Higuchi, "Educating about the Fear."

3. MOFA, "Dai nijū kai kanjikai (shigatsu mikka) kiroku" (Record of the 20th executive meeting, April 3), April 3, 1957, C'0009, DRO; Sairenji, "Nihon no kaku jikken mondai e no taiō," pp. 6–7.

of the Americans, who stubbornly refused to stop testing, and that of the Soviets, who offered a comprehensive test ban plan but rejected a surveillance system. Japanese policymakers certainly did not contemplate affronting either Moscow or Washington. Yet they also understood that since a policy aimed at reducing nuclear weapons would offend the superpowers anyway, what Japan should do was to mitigate the damage incurred by that offense. Probably for this reason, MOFA judged that diplomacy at the multilateral level through the UN—the only forum where it could use the power of international opinion to press the nuclear giants—would have to take precedence over bilateral approaches.[4]

In early 1957, the Japanese delegation to the eleventh session of the UNGA submitted a resolution with Canada and Norway to restrict nuclear tests through a registration system. This was not a radical proposal; it only asked the nuclear weapon holders to report their tests to the UN, not to stop them at once. The Japanese government obviously believed that the registration system would be an acceptable scheme to break the standoff between the two military blocs on disarmament.[5] But this was overly optimistic. Considering the registration proposal a nuisance, delegates of the US, the UK, and France persuaded the UNGA to transfer the Japanese resolution to the Subcommittee of the UN Disarmament Committee (UNDC) in London for further discussion. This was a well-calculated move since, compared to the Assembly, the subcommittee was composed of a small number of UN member states; hence it was easier for the nuclear powers to manipulate the deliberations. The strategy worked. While it invited Japan to make "written comments" on its proposal, the subcommittee was unable to produce any substantial results concerning the issue. Japan's first nuclear test ban proposal at the UN was squelched without even being put to a vote.[6]

---

4. MOFA, ibid.; Sairenji, ibid., p. 7; Higuchi, "Kakujikken mondai to Nichibei kankei," pp. 112–13.

5. Edamura, "Kakuheiki ni taisuru Nihon gaikō no totta shisaku" (Measures taken in relation to Japan's diplomacy on nuclear weapon issues), August 1959, E-4a, Dōba Hajime monjo, PSI.

6. Higuchi, "Educating about the Fear," p. 136; Iguchi, *Nihon gaikōshi,* pp. 203–4.

Shortly before the twelfth session of the UNGA, Japanese officials waged another round of their offensive. In August 1957, they contacted the Americans to see whether they would be willing to make a deal with the Soviets on a test suspension pact without the participation of the British and the French, both of whom were more reluctant to regulate their nuclear experiments. But Washington's response was negative.[7] Having no other choice, on September 23 Japan submitted a draft resolution to the First Committee of the UNGA calling for a one-year suspension of nuclear weapon tests. The next day, Prime Minister Kishi sent messages to American, British, and Soviet leaders to ask for their support for Japan's proposal. By October 20, Kishi received replies from the three nations, though none contained quite what he had expected to see.

US officials had taken pains to dissuade Japan from submitting its proposal to the UN ever since the Japanese let them preview the draft, grumbling that while Japan's resolution reflected the sentiments of the Japanese people thoroughly, it failed to take the "general world situation" into consideration. Douglas MacArthur II, US ambassador to Tokyo, frankly told his Japanese counterparts that Washington was disappointed by Japan's draft, which seemed to him "close to what [the] USSR desired."[8] On September 15, the US government embarrassed Japan by announcing that it would start a new round of nuclear tests. Yet the shocking news did not alter Tokyo's stance in the UN. On the day when Japan was planning to present its draft resolution, the Americans concluded that "there might be little further" they could do to get the Japanese to take "a different course." Ten days later, President Eisenhower signed his official response to Kishi, a statement the Japanese described as indicating "no improvement from [the US's] previous policies."[9]

The second reply was from British Prime Minister Harold Macmillan, who was no less baffled than Eisenhower by Japan's appeal for a nuclear test ban. As a latecomer to the nuclear competition, the UK was earnestly catching up with the two superpowers in nuclear technologies

7. Memo of conversation, August 29, 1957, Box 12, Lot File 61D68, NA.

8. MacArthur to SAE, September 10, 1957; Lodge to SAE, September 12, 1957, both in Box 270, Lot File 58D133, NA.

9. Farley to Dulles, September 23, 1957, Box 12 Lot File 61D68, ibid.; MOFA, "Kokuren sōkai ni okeru ugoki," pp. 21–22.

and viewed Japan's request to cancel nuclear tests as a great obstacle to this effort. Trying to somehow soften Japan's attitude toward the Western nuclear disarmament proposals at the UN, the British government invited Japanese Foreign Minister Fujiyama Aiichirō to stop by London on his way to the UNGA.[10] Fujiyama did come, but with no intention to compromise. The British, unsurprisingly, went ahead and declared a continuation of their own nuclear tests. But unlike the US, which startled Tokyo with a sudden announcement, British leaders gave advance notice of their plan before the Japanese foreign minister headed for New York and thereby, in their words, "saved Fujiyama's face."[11] In his letter to Kishi, Macmillan reiterated that his government would not accept any test ban proposal short of a general disarmament agreement between the two blocs.

On October 19, the last and worst message—the one from Soviet Prime Minister Nikolai Bulganin—was delivered to Kishi's desk. Bulganin pointed out in his letter, described by MOFA officials as "a curious reply," that he was "satisfied to see" that Kishi shared Moscow's desire to conduct a nuclear test ban without links to other disarmament issues. Concerned about the grave influence of this message, the bewildered MOFA officials swiftly sent another letter to advise Bulganin that he might have "misunderstood" Japan's intention. The government also instructed Foreign Minister Fujiyama and Ambassador to the UN Matsudaira Kōtō to make explanatory statements at the Assembly, underlining that what Japan had recommended was a one-year test ban "parallel with" general disarmament negotiations and not without their continuation. This time, there was no response from Bulganin. Instead, Soviet Foreign Minister Andrei Gromyko published a letter in the widely circulated Japanese newspaper *Asahi shimbun*, claiming that the behavior of Fujiyama and Matsudaira at the UN was "inconsistent" with the spirit of Kishi's first message, and that the Japanese test ban draft resolution was actually no different from another one submitted by the Western nuclear powers.[12]

---

10. Mayal to Selby, October 3, 1957, FO 371/127531, Reel 78, PRO.
11. Morland to Lascelles, October 3, 1957, FO 371/127532, Reel 79, ibid.; "Kokuren sōkai ni okeru ugoki," p. 22.
12. Regarding Soviet reaction to Kishi's letter, see ibid., pp. 22–23; *Asahi shimbun,* October 28, 1957.

On November 6, the Japanese resolution was put to a vote. Needless to say, it was a diplomatic disaster. Among 81 members of the First Committee, only 18 gave their votes to Japan. The victors were two resolutions tabled by Belgium and 24 other Western powers (excluding Japan) that were adopted by wide margins of 70 and 57 ayes, respectively. After the vote, MOFA proclaimed that despite the loss of the battle, Japan would continue its efforts to promote nuclear disarmament by appealing to the "conscience of the UN member states, particularly the great powers."[13] Nevertheless, the political climate surrounding the UN made Japan's chances of getting its nuclear initiative passed extremely slim.

The Soviets had long been uneasy about the composition of the UNDC, in which five of the six members were from the Western bloc. On October 27, 1957, Soviet Foreign Minister Gromyko formally approached the UN Secretary General to ask for the establishment of a permanent committee for disarmament with the participation of all UN members to take the place of the current UN body on this field. When this suggestion failed to pass the First Committee, Soviet delegate Vassily Kuznetzov abruptly declared that the USSR would not attend UNDC sessions any more. Japan panicked. The UNDC was the sole occasion where Tokyo might exert influence over the nuclear policies of nations from the two Cold War blocs. Japanese policy planners could not afford to lose this forum. Throughout November, Japan joined Canada in efforts to talk the USSR out of the boycott while entreating other Western allies for possible concessions. The result was reflected in a resolution suggesting the expansion of the UNDC to 25 nations (in which nine were Socialist or neutral states). The resolution was adopted, but the Soviets were by no means satisfied.[14]

During the nine months before the next UNGA session, Japan continued its endeavor to preserve the UNDC. Japanese officials told the Soviets that if they wanted to come back to the committee, Japan was "ready to lend a hand."[15] They also dropped hints to the US that Japan

<hr />

13. MOFA, "Waga gunshuku teian hiketsu saru," pp. 8–11.

14. Ibid, pp. 11–16; Gaimushō hyakunenshi hensan iinkai, *Gaimushō no hyakunen,* pp. 914–15.

15. "Summary of the Japanese Government's Reply to the Soviet Note Verbale Dated 10 December, 1957," Box 40, Japan Post File, NA.

would like to see the "responsibility" for nuclear disarmament reside in the UN and any agreement reached outside the UN to require "confirmation" of the organization.[16] However, the US and USSR seemed to agree with each other that they would do better to resume their talks on nuclear weapons somewhere other than the vexatious UNDC. In November 1958, a resolution to form a new UNDC comprising all 82 UN member states was adopted at the thirteenth session of the UNGA. But this revised UNDC had no significant impact, since Washington and Moscow concluded an agreement at the same time to set up a disarmament committee in Geneva independent from the UN consisting of ten nations apportioned equally from the East and the West—and without the name of Japan. With its last hope for a place to carry out its nuclear disarmament scheme buried by the great powers' clandestine diplomacy, the Japanese government scrapped a draft test ban resolution prepared for the UNGA.[17] It never wrote a replacement. The only nuclear-related resolution Japan sponsored at this Assembly session was a statement that expressed support for the new committee in Geneva.[18]

Nuclear disarmament was not the only case in which Japan's passion to build a Cold War-proof UN collided with the interests of the big powers. In 1959, for example, the Japanese government was also forced into opposition to Washington's will when participating in the UNSC's investigation of the Laotian-Vietnamese border dispute: one of the ominous preludes to the Vietnam War.

As noted by former Deputy Secretary of State U. Alexis Johnson, in the late 1950s history, "in its curiously perverse way," had thrust the "quiet backwater" of Laos to the "center of the Cold War" in Southeast Asia.[19] Largely due to its unfortunate geographical location, the Laotians found that their territory always became a battlefield whenever Washington, Moscow, Beijing, or Hanoi decided to alter the military landscape of the area. In 1956, competing political factions within the country—including the Communist party (Pathet Lao) backed by the

---

16. "Disarmament," memo of conversation, February 28, 1958, Box 9, Lot File 61D68; Nuclear Test Suspension, memo of conversation, August 26, 1958, Box 25, Lot File 58D133, ibid.

17. Tokyo to Washington, August 27, 1958, Box 25, Lot File 58D133, ibid.

18. Gaimushō hyakunenshi hensan iinkai, *Gaimushō no hyakunen*, p. 919.

19. Johnson, *The Right Hand of Power*, p. 295.

North Vietnamese, the Chinese, and more remotely, the Soviets—agreed to form a coalition government. But the peace was short-lived. Two years later the Americans, who did not like the neutral character of the new regime, assisted Prime Minister Phoui Sananikone, a conservative anti-communist politician, to overthrow the coalition regime by driving the Pathet Lao out of the government. Phoui's action kindled an armed collision between the pro-American and Pathet Lao guerrillas, and intervention from the Vietminh to assist the latter escalated the turmoil.[20] In September 1959, the Laotian government reported to the UNSC that the nation had been attacked by considerable military forces from North Vietnam and asked the UN to dispatch an emergency force to the Laotian-Vietnamese border area. Fearing that Laos would be taken over by the communists and become another Korea, the US urged the UNSC to discuss the alleged invasion promptly.[21] The USSR, for its part, adamantly opposed any UN role in the conflict. But Soviet resistance was foiled by the US and other Council members, who tailored a draft procedural resolution to set up a UNSC fact-finding subcommittee on the Laotian case. As the charter prohibits the use of the veto on procedural issues, the resolution was easily adopted and a subcommittee team composed of officials from Japan and three other nonpermanent members was soon sent to Vientiane.[22]

The US gave strong emphasis to Japan's role in the UN subcommittee from the outset. The Japanese government, however, held different opinions.[23] Unlike the Americans, who eagerly tried to use the UN's presence to stop the penetration of the communists in Laos, the Japanese had little interest in taking advantage of the UN for Cold War purposes. As they saw it, their task in the subcommittee was to "prevent the US from taking too radical actions" so the situation could "calm down in an uneventful way."[24] Based on this policy, Shibusawa Shinichi, the Japanese representative to the subcommittee who also

---

20. Ibid., pp. 296–300.

21. Herring, *America's Longest War,* p. 78; Gaimushō hyakunenshi hensan iinkai, *Gaimushō no hyakunen,* p. 929.

22. Matsudaira to Fujiyama, September 6, 1959, A'0386, DRO.

23. Washington to Tokyo, September 6, 1959, Box 71, Japan Post File, NA.

24. Fujiyama to Matsudaira, September 7, 1959, A'0386, DRO.

served as the chief of the UN fact-finding team, faithfully maintained the objectiveness of his position.

Two days after arriving in Vientiane, Shibusawa reported to Tokyo that the Laotian government had greatly exaggerated the situation as part of its foreign propaganda and that he doubted the administrative capacity of the Phoui administration.[25] His suspicion was justified by the subsequent development of the investigation. The Laotians were not only unable to provide the UN team with sufficient evidence of the reported North Vietnamese invasion but they also failed or, more likely, were unwilling to support the team's fact-finding activities outside the nation's capital.[26] Likewise, the Americans, who eagerly intended to show the world that the alleged communist penetration did happen, were more interested in keeping the UN team in Laos as long as possible than in facilitating its mission.[27] Adhering to the original UNSC resolution, Japan declined to follow the US strategy. Rejecting strong pressure from Washington to extend the fact-finding team's mission, Shibusawa stuck to his belief that "it was most important for the prestige and the future of the UN" that the subcommittee should "complete [its] task promptly and effectively" without being sunk in the quagmire in Laos. He further angered the US when Washington received a report indicating that he and the Italian representative to the subcommittee had advised Phoui to restore peace through rapprochement with Hanoi and Beijing. Shibusawa later explained that it was the Italian who made the statement, but the US was not convinced of his innocence.[28]

---

25. Shibusawa to Shima (letter), September 17, 1959, ibid.

26. Beppu to Fujiyama, October 6, 1959; Kobayashi Toshihiko, "Kokuren Laos shōiinkai ni kansuru genchi shucchō hōkoku" (Report of an on-site trip regarding the UN's Laos subcommittee), October 15, 1959, ibid.

27. Tokyo to Washington, September 14, 1959, Box 71 and "Security Subcommittee on Laos," memo, September 18, 1959, Box 59, both in Japan Post File, NA.

28. Washington to Tokyo, September 19, 1959; Washington to Tokyo, October 10, 1959; Washington to Tokyo, October 15, 1959; Vientiane to Washington, November 24, 1959, all in Box 71, ibid.; Shima Shigenobu, "Laos mondai ni kanshi Beikoku yori mōshiire no ken" (The US request on the Laotian problem), October 19, 1959, A'0386, DRO.

In addition to Shibusawa's independent activities, Japan also blocked the US strategy in New York to continue the UN subcommittee's mission in Laos. Harboring reservations about the US plan, UN Secretary General Hammarskjold proposed replacing the current fact-finding subcommittee with a new investigative body firmly controlled by the UN. The US and other Western UNSC members flatly rejected this suggestion.[29] Instead of allying with the US, Japanese Ambassador Matsudaira, who was the president of the Council at this crucial moment, chose to support the Secretary General. While appreciating the necessity of maintaining the UN presence in Laos, Matsudaira observed that if the Western allies insisted on obtaining this goal by extending the mandate of the subcommittee, the UN's reputation would be severely hurt, as the Soviets might incite the majority of the UNGA to condemn the UNSC. On October 7, he visited Hammarskjold and suggested that in order to evade a possible collision between the West and the USSR in the UNSC, the Secretary General could use his discretion to form a new committee in Laos by himself without sending the case to the Council. Hammarskjold immediately embraced this idea. In accordance with the division of labor determined during the meeting, Matsudaira approached Soviet Ambassador Arkady Sobolev, while the Secretary General went to persuade the Americans. Perhaps finding the proposed UN committee under the control of the Secretary General more acceptable than the current subcommittee dominated by pro-Western states, the Soviets endorsed Matsudaira's plan.[30] Foreseeing the difficulty of persuading the majority of the UN to uphold the existence of the subcommittee, the Americans also reluctantly promised their support. In late November, with Harmmarskjold's visit to Laos followed by the dispatch of his own representative to Vientiane, the UN subcommittee led by Shibusawa wrapped up its activities with a final report indicating no evidence of a direct intervention from North Vietnamese troops.[31]

---

29. Matsudaira to Kishi, October 1, 1959, A'0386, ibid.

30. Kishi to Matsudaira, September 30, 1959; Matsudaira to Kishi, October 2, 1959; Matsudaira to Fujiyama, October 7, 1959, ibid.

31. Matsudaira to Fujiyama, October 8, 1959, ibid.; Washington to Tokyo, November 17, 1959, Box 71, Japan Post File, NA; MOFA, *Waga gaikō no kinkyō*, March 1960, pp. 48–49.

The Japanese government regards what it did at the UN during the nuclear disarmament discussions and its performance in handling the Laotian crisis as remarkable contributions of the country toward international peace. Indeed, Japan does have many reasons to feel proud of its performance. In both instances, it managed in one way or another to pursue policies relatively independent from the two Cold War blocs. On certain occasions, it even tried to induce the US and USSR to seek mutual compromise through peaceful negotiation at the UN. Yet judging from the consequences, it is questionable whether these efforts yielded the expected results. In the Laotian case, the tension in that country did not disappear after the withdrawal of the UN team. Instead of fulfilling its responsibility to the very end, Japan simply chose to pull out of renewed UN investigation activities in order to avoid further troubles with Washington. As for the nuclear test ban question, Japan was fooled by the Soviets and neglected by its Western allies—not to mention that the agenda itself was ultimately moved out of the UN, to Japan's great disappointment. In this sense, contrary to Japanese policy planners' hopes of seeing the UN act as a "shared forum" for peaceful dialogue between the two camps, what they had found by the end of 1959 was a countercurrent prevailing in both the Eastern and Western blocs to downplay the role of the UN in major political and security affairs. MOFA officials were aware of this reality and some of them deplored in early 1959 that the two blocs had run up against a "wall" in the UN "with no room for compromise."[32] Instead of renewing its effort to break this "wall" down, this time Japan began to change the direction of its UN policy.

In the annual Diplomatic Bluebook published in March 1960, the Japanese government laid out a revised explanation concerning the correlation between the nation's UN policy and the Cold War:

[O]ur country thinks that . . . it is necessary to utilize the UN's function as a peacekeeping institution under the current system and to patiently continue our endeavors to strengthen the organization for the amelioration and eradication of the so-called Cold War . . . Nevertheless, this does not necessarily mean that we should play a mediating role from a neutral stance concerning the Cold War problems in which the Eastern and the Western blocs' interests directly collide . . . Rather, issues in which we can play a special role within the UN are

---

32. MOFA, "Kokuren dai jūsan tsūjō sōkai owaru," p. 29.

those in relation to conflicting interests between Western European and AA nations.[33]

This statement contained two significant messages. First, it indicated that Japan was ready to take a firmer stance to defend the interests of the West within the UN (while not completely abandoning its belief regarding the anti-Cold War feature of the organization). Second, it reflected Japan's attachment to the UN's function in terms of resolving disputes between big and small nations within the international community. In other words, while it tried to dilute the idealistic cast of its aspiration toward a Cold War-proof UN, the government was not yet willing to give up another aspect of its hopes for the UN—the promotion of international democracy in relation with AA nations. But by the time these words were inserted in the Bluebook, Japan's policy for dealing with wrangles between Western and AA members of the UN was also entering a difficult stage.

The Shaky Bridge between the Orient and the Occident

Historian Iriye Akira once noted that "East" (i.e., Orient) and "West" (i.e., Occident) were the pivotal concepts within modern Japan's diplomatic thought.[34] From the early Meiji on, Japanese policymakers were forced to choose between diplomatic courses stressing either cooperation with Western industrial nations or Japan's special interest as an Asian power. Those in a position to conduct Japan's UN diplomacy in the mid-1950s were not immune to this choice. In fact, when the government was courting the AA states with its pro-Egypt stance during the Suez Canal crisis, Japanese officials had already noticed the potential rift between the attitudes of Japan and other AA Group members toward Western nations. Despite his struggle to save Egypt's face, Ambassador Kase reported in a telegram in November 1956 that the actions of some anti-British/French AA delegates in the UN showed "a little lack of prudence" and warned Tokyo that "serious consideration" regarding Japan's relationship with the group might be necessary in the near future.[35]

---

33. MOFA, *Waga gaikō no kinkyō,* March 1960, pp. 12–13.
34. Iriye, *Nihon no gaikō,* pp. 174–76.
35. Kase to Shigemitsu, November 7, 1956, A'0377, DRO.

The result of the government's "serious consideration" was made public weeks later. In his speech delivered at the UNGA upon Japan's admission to the UN, Foreign Minister Shigemitsu declared that since "the substance of Japan's political, economic and cultural life is the product of the fusion within the last century of the civilizations of the Orient and the Occident," Japan was "fully conscious" of its "great responsibilities" as a "bridge between the East and the West."[36] To put it differently, what the Japanese foreign minister proposed was a policy aimed at changing the zero-sum correlation between cooperation with the West and Japan's identity as an Asian nation to a positive-sum one.

In January 1957, a more detailed explanation of the "East-West bridge policy" was outlined in an article that appeared in a MOFA public relations journal. While claiming that Western industrial powers should take care to extend sufficient "sympathy and appreciation" to the nationalist movements in AA nations, the article also mentioned the importance of remaining alert to the "radicalization" of such movements. "Our country has suffered bitter defeats caused by radical nationalism," it read, "and therefore we are in a position to harbor serious interest in the healthy development of nationalism in AA nations." To this end, the author wrote, it was Japan's responsibility as "a country that most successfully combined the Eastern and Western civilizations" to play the role of "a bridge between the two sides."[37] Until the early 1960s, Japanese officials attempted to steer their nation's UN policies in the line of this lofty mission in at least three cases: the Suez Canal problem, the quest for Algerian independence, and the Lebanon crisis.

By the time the Japanese delegation set foot on the main stage of the UNGA, the first phase of the Suez crisis had already come to an end. The focus had shifted to the pullout of French, British, and Israeli forces in accordance with the spirit of a UN resolution passed in early November authorizing the stationing of a UN force in the canal area. After some mild resistance, the French and British left the canal by the end of 1956. The Israeli government, nonetheless, indicated that its troops would not move until Israel's security was guaranteed by the UN. Regarding this attitude as outrageous, the majority of AA Group

---

36. Kase to Takasaki, December 17, 1956, B'0042, ibid.
37. MOFA, "Nisso fukkō to wagakuni," pp. 39–40.

members called for a condemnation resolution or UN economic sanctions against Israel. The Israeli envoy in Tokyo turned to Japan for help. Some MOFA officials, such as Ambassador Tani Masayuki in Washington, insisted that Japan should refuse Israel"s request to serve as a go-between for the two sides because of the risk that Japan might offend both AA and Western nations.[38] The Japanese delegation in the UN took the opposite stance. Ambassador Kase generally followed the proactive line he had taken during the early stage of the crisis. In January 1957, he promised the Israeli delegate that although Japan did not want to be involved in the upheaval, it would "take every opportunity" to encourage the tendency toward a "constructive solution" of the problem within the AA Group.[39] Based on this policy, the Japanese UN mission refrained from supporting some AA states' plan to launch economic sanctions against Israel but kept in close contact with the US and the UN Secretary General in handling the problem. Within the AA Group, Japan mainly counted on a handful of pro-Western members. But it also took great pains in the meantime to protect its image as a fair judge before other AA members. For instance, Japanese delegates made it clear that "in any case" the Israeli troops' withdrawal from the Suez Canal area had to be "unconditional" and that Israel's reluctance to immediately leave the area was "a violation of the UN resolution."[40]

Despite the difficulty of upholding its identity as an Asian state and a Western ally simultaneously, Japan was spared in the Suez Canal case. In March 1957, the Israelis ultimately agreed to send their troops back home, thereby bringing the confrontation at the UN with the AA Group to an end before the latter could force the UN to take more coercive actions. Yet Japanese policy planners had no time to relax. The situation in the Suez Canal might have quieted down for a while, but even thornier conflicts in the Middle East and North Africa were just about to escalate.

During the first half of 1958, the UNSC was disturbed by reports from Lebanon and Jordan regarding an alleged military invasion by the United Arab Republic (UAR, formed upon the merger between Egypt

---

38. Tani to Shigemitsu, November 17, 1956, A'0377, DRO.
39. Kase to Kishi, January 16, 1957, ibid.
40. Kase to Kishi, January 30 and February 6, 1957, ibid.

and Syria) in their border areas. Frustrated by UAR President Nasser's antagonism against the West, the UN's inability to find evidence of the invasion, and the recent overthrow of a pro-Western monarchy in Iraq, the US and the UK declared that they might proceed to assist the Lebanese government through military means if necessary.

Having garnered a UNSC non-permanent membership six months earlier, Japan had taken part in the behind-the-scenes negotiations on the Lebanese matter from the moment it was brought up in the UNSC. Anticipating a possible military interference from the US, the Japanese government decided to act as a mediator between the Western allies and the UAR. Vice Foreign Minister Yamada Hisanari was the mastermind of this plan. He told the US ambassador to Tokyo that the Arab nationalist cause underlying Nasser's position on Lebanon should be respected, and he asked for the two sides to meet each other halfway. While the US was suspicious about a possible reconciliation with Nasser, the Japanese insisted that it could be more dangerous for the West if the UAR was forced to depend on the assistance of the Soviets for survival.[41] Within the UN, Ambassador Matsudaira, who succeeded Kase as Japan's permanent representative a year earlier, was also trying to deal with the situation from an objective viewpoint, which aroused serious concerns in the British and Lebanese governments.[42]

The landing of American and British troops on the Lebanese coast and in neighboring Jordan occurred at the time when Japanese officials were just about to step up their diplomatic efforts. Japan's initial response to the two Western powers' intervention was no different from that of other AA states supporting the UAR. Foreign Minister Fujiyama criticized the US military action as "pushing the Arab countries toward the communists." The Japanese ambassador in Cairo, Tsuchida Yutaka, went even further, referring to the two Western allies' behaviors as "aggression"—a statement that the British vowed the Japanese "should not be allowed to get away with" in the absence of a satisfactory explanation.[43]

---

41. Satō, "Reisen, kokuren," pp. 14–16.
42. UN Bureau, "Rasseru Eikoku taishi raidan no ken" (The visit of British Ambassador Lascelles), June 4, 1958, A'0384, DRO; Memos of conversation between Banna and MacArthur, June 2 and 4, 1958, Box 12, Lot File 61D68, NA.
43. For Japan's initial reaction, see Asakai to Fujiyama, July 30, 1958, A'0384, DRO; Tokyo to Washington, July 31, 1958, Box 40, Japan Post File, NA;

Back at the UNSC, Matsudaira was not as enthusiastic as some of his colleagues in condemning American and British unilateral actions. When discussing the emergent situation in the Council, he described the two big powers' behaviors as "inappropriate" and "regrettable." Yet in the meantime, he also indicated that his delegation was willing to accept a US proposal to replace American troops in Lebanon with a UN force. Matsudaira did not make the statement on his own authority. It was, in fact, based on an order from Tokyo, where many had begun to worry about a possible impairment of the US-Japan alliance after being pushed hard by the US on the Lebanon problem. But once Matsudaira aired Tokyo's new policy of endorsing the US, the government started feeling that this lukewarm position might make Japan lose its credit as a mediator between the AA and Western nations in the UN. Thus, within one day, MOFA forced Matsudaira to deliver a revised speech at the UNSC, which, while supporting the American proposal, contained more remarks criticizing the deployment of US forces.[44] In the meantime, following instructions from Tokyo, the Japanese delegation hammered out a draft resolution requiring the dispatch of UN forces without specific reference to the withdrawal of US troops—an attempt to let the Americans leave Lebanon in a dignified way. The US apparently was prepared to accept the resolution and started pressing the reluctant Lebanese to do the same.[45] But a Soviet veto killed the Japanese initiative and the issue was then transferred to a special UNGA session.[46]

During the General Assembly session, the Japanese mission led by Foreign Minister Fujiyama told the US that the final solution must encompass two elements—it must arrange for the US troops' withdrawal

---

"Translation of excerpts from Cairo's 'El Ahram' of Japanese Ambassador Tsuchida's pro-Nasser remarks and opportunities of trade with UAR," August 18, 1958 and London to Tokyo, August 23, 1958, FO 371/133584, Reel 83, PRO.

44. Satō, "Reisen, kokuren," p. 17–18; Murakami, "Kishi naikaku to Kokuren gaikō," p. 151; Bacon to Robertson, July 17, 1958, Box 3, Lot File 60D90, NA.

45. Iguchi, *Nihon gaikōshi*, pp. 57–58; New York to Washington, July 19, 1958 and Washington to Beirut, July 21, 1958, Fiche 8, FRUSF (1958–60), Vol. XI; "Memorandum of Conference with the President," July 21, 1958, DDE Diary Series, DDEL.

46. "Foreign Minister's Speech on [the] Middle East," July 28, 1958, FO 371/133584, Reel 83, PRO.

and it must be acceptable to the UAR.[47] The US delegation led by Secretary of State Dulles, in contrast, refused to take Nasser's interests into account and exerted tremendous pressure on the Japanese government to support an American-driven Norwegian resolution. But Fujiyama did not yield, pointing out that the Norwegian resolution did not specify a time limit for the American and British withdrawal from Lebanon and Jordan. In the end, an irritated Dulles made a last-ditch effort to draw a concession from Fujiyama by paying a personal visit to the latter's residence late at night on the eve of the vote. Once more, Fujiyama's answer was negative.[48]

Deliberations on the Lebanon crisis reached their final stage in the UNGA around August. Having found no explicit signs suggesting that the Middle East would become a Soviet sphere of influence, the Western allies, especially the US, lost interest in bearing the cost of stationing large forces in the region. The UAR, on the other hand, was prepared to make any deal with other UN members to get the American and British soldiers removed. Under these circumstances, though the Norwegian resolution failed to acquire the support of the AA states, it was incorporated into an Arab resolution, which was adopted unanimously by the Assembly. Following the resolution, the US and British forces left Lebanon by the end of November 1958 and a reinforced UN peacekeeping force (UNOGIL) was dispatched to the area.[49]

The Japanese government, as it had done in the Suez Canal crisis, had managed to defend its reputation as an honest UN negotiator during this conflict. "Except for the communist nations, only Foreign Minister Fujiyama and [West German] Chancellor [Konrad] Adenauer dared to clearly say no to Secretary Dulles," as a Japanese UN correspondent proudly recalled. Even those from the American side, includ-

---

47. Satō, "Reisen, kokuren," pp. 22–23; "Middle East Resolution," memo of conversation, August 14, 1958, Box 12, Lot File 61D68; "Declaration and Resolution," memo of conversation, August 17, 1958, Box 3, Lot File 60D90, NA.
48. Washington to Tokyo, August 20, 1958 and Tokyo to Washington, August 21, 1958, Box 40, Japan Post File, ibid; Ōmori, "Dokuritsu jūnen," pp. 50–51.
49. Cohen, *The Cambridge History of American Foreign Relations,* pp. 114–15; Ostrower, *The United Nations,* p. 88.

ing President Eisenhower, later evaluated highly Japan's behavior at the UN in relation to the Lebanon incident.[50]

Japan's performance during the Suez and Lebanon crises marked the climax of the government's effort to actively utilize its unique position as a Western ally in Asia to contribute to international peace through the UN. But these were the most and perhaps the only successful efforts of Japan in this regard during the first three decades of its UN membership. Unlike these crises, which were resolved within relatively short periods of time, most major political and security issues brought to the UN were discussed repeatedly within the General Assembly and the Security Council. It was in the course of those prolonged deliberations that the limitations of Japan's role in solving Oriental-Occidental wrangles became manifest. The Algerian independence question, in this sense, was a typical case that witnessed Japan's metamorphosis from an active self-appointed peacemaker to a grudging Western power estranged by the AA Group.

In November 1954, a group of local rebels later known as the Algerian Front of National Liberation (FLN) started a military campaign against the French colonial authorities in Algeria. The French government readily organized counterattacks with its army and air forces, but was unable to crush the rebellion. Rather, the rising casualties of military personnel and civilians brought severe damage to the stability of the French Fourth Republic. The issue was first taken up by the UNGA in 1955. But the French delegate, who denied the legitimacy of the organization in discussing this problem, walked out of the Assembly session. In 1956, the AA Group raised the issue again at the eleventh session of the UNGA. This time the French did not oppose its adoption on the UN agenda, on the condition that France would also have a chance to explain its own position.[51]

Before the committee session was summoned, French officials courted their Japanese colleagues in Paris, New York, and Tokyo in search of a friendly policy. But the results were anything but encourag-

---

50. Ōmori, "Dokuritsu jūnen," p. 51; Murakami, "Kishi naikaku to kokuren gaikō," p. 154.

51. UN Bureau, "Kokuren to Arujeria mondai" (The UN and the Algerian question), May 16, 1960, A'0318, DRO.

ing. Being one of the signatories of the 1955 Asian African (Bandung) Conference Final Communiqué, in which the self-determination of the Algerian people was endorsed, Japan judged it inexpedient to stand on the opposite side from the AA Group from the very beginning.[52] Ambassador Kase told French Foreign Minister Christian P. Pineau in February 1957 that in light of the Bandung Conference Communiqué, Japan would have to support the Algerian people's aspirations for self-determination. He asked France to reconsider its position on this issue by showing "statesmanship" in finding a "constructive" solution.[53] On February 12, Japan submitted a draft resolution regarding the issue to the First Committee with Thailand and the Philippines. Upon introducing the resolution, Kase made a passionate speech in which he asked the UN to take an active role in the Algerian question. "If we desire to save the flower of safety out of the danger of nettle," he said, "we must face the issue squarely and try to solve it—not evade it."[54] Despite France's reluctance concerning any UN resolution, the Assembly later adopted a resolution combining the Japanese-Thai-Philippine draft with a more modest one authored by the Latin American Group.

Resenting Japan's attitude, French officials straightforwardly told the Japanese envoy in Paris that they considered the Japanese UN delegation's position "perplexing" and "preferred not to see" Japan serve as a mediator between France and the FLN. A major French newspaper even labeled Japan as "France's real enemy."[55] Having been informed of French reactions, Kase promptly warned the government of the danger of giving the AA states the impression that Japan was simply working for its own interest. "Based on our principle of supporting and

---

52. UN Bureau, "Arujeria mondai no saikentō" (Reconsidering the Algerian question), May 12, 1958 and Chikaraishi Kentarō, "Arujeria mondai ni kanshi, zaikyō Furansu taishikan Do Rimerraku sanjikan to kaidan no ken" (The meeting with Counselor de Limairac of the French embassy in Tokyo regarding the Algerian problem), January 26, 1957, ibid.
53. Kase to Kishi, February 2, 1957, ibid.
54. "Statement of Ambassador Kase introducing the draft resolution of Japan, the Philippines and Thailand to the First Committee on February 12, 1957," ibid.
55. Furukaki to Kishi, February 13, 1957 and Furukaki to Kishi, February 20, 1957, ibid.

strengthening the UN," he remarked in a telegram, "we may have to take positions that will upset the West Europeans because this not only can gain the trust from AA states but will also eventually contribute to the interest of the West."[56]

Kase left his post shortly thereafter, but the Japanese delegation continued their efforts to search for a solution that could satisfy the Algerian requirement for self-determination without impairing France's prestige. In July 1957, it joined other AA nations in requesting the UN Secretariat to insert the Algerian issue into the Assembly's agenda.[57] Ambassador Matsudaira also closely worked with Iranian, Sudanese, Tunisian, and French delegates to keep the outcome of the discussion at the UNGA acceptable to major parties.[58] When Norway, Ireland, and Canada submitted a revised resolution aiming at softening the AA resolution in the First Committee, Japan firmly voted with the AA Group against it despite a US request for abstention.[59] On December 10, a resolution asking for a peaceful solution of the Algerian problem in accordance with the UN charter cosponsored by Japan and fourteen other nations passed the twelfth UNGA session.

For their cautious but efficient coordination among different member groups, the Japanese delegates received the appreciation of both AA states and the French representative.[60] Yet instead of reveling in their success, Japanese foreign policymakers' evaluation of their Algerian policy in the UN was rather cool at the end of the twelfth UNGA session. To those who had actively cooperated with AA delegates during the eleventh session, the outcome of the twelfth session was a "step backward." The final resolution cosponsored by Japan did not ask France to start an immediate "negotiation" with the Algerians, but merely suggested "pour parlers" between the two. Moreover, MOFA officials admitted that, facing the increasing consolidation of Western powers on the issue, Japan had been forced to jump on the bandwagon in the midst of the deliberations by keeping the Algerians at a dis-

---

56. Kase to Kishi, February 16, 1957, ibid.
57. First Division of the UN Bureau, "Dai jūni sōkai taisaku shiryō" (Materials for measures regarding the 12th UNGA), July 19, 1957, ibid.
58. Matsudaira to Fujiyama, November 27, 1957, ibid.
59. Matsudaira to Fujiyama, December 6, 1957, ibid.
60. Matsudaira to Fujiyama, December 6 and 10, 1957, ibid.

tance.[61] This subtle change of stance did not bring Japan any major trouble during the twelfth session thanks to the division of opinions within the AA Group. Yet it alerted Japanese decision-makers that their current policy within the UN might not be as workable in the long run as it used to be. In a policy report prepared for the forthcoming thirteenth UNGA session, officials claimed that their previous policy of mediating between France and the FLN while refraining from stimulating the hostile sentiments on both sides was somewhat "unreasonable" and had led to a "lack of consistency" among Japanese statements in the UN. They contended that a more aggressive response was necessary. The "appropriate way to go," they suggested, was to "coherently" criticize French policies from a "modest anti-colonialism" line while "speaking for the moderate sections of the [Algerian] rebellion forces." They also intended to "take the initiative to lead the AA Group in a unified direction" even though this could enrage French public opinion.[62] Nonetheless, within several months, Japanese officials would come to realize that a chance to test these bold proposals within the AA Group would never come.

Japan's attempt to take the lead in shaping the AA Group's attitude toward Algeria was challenged by the FLN in the early stage of the thirteenth session. Presumably due to its loss in recent battles coupled with French Prime Minister Charles De Gaulle's peace campaign, the FLN (and its AA supporters) sensed the need to deal France a heavy blow in the UN. In December 1958, seventeen members of the AA Group led by the UAR and Ghana drafted a resolution in the First Committee and earnestly pressed Japan to accept it.[63] Since the resolution set forth recognition of the FLN regime as a precondition for peace negotiations, the Japanese government, which did not have an official relationship with the Algerian rebels, found sponsoring it extremely difficult. Following its traditional strategy, Japan recommended a number of amendments to the resolution to dull the anti-French edge. But the reply of the majority of the AA Group was unexpectedly rigid. Conse-

---

61. First Division of the UN Bureau, "Arujeria mondai no saikentō," May 12, 1958, ibid.

62. Ibid.

63. Fujiyama to Japanese Envoys in AA nations, February 17, 1959, ibid.

quently, for the first time since the issue was brought into the UN, Japan abstained when the resolution was voted on in the committee.[64]

Though the AA resolution narrowly passed in the committee, it was eventually rejected in the plenary session by a margin of one vote. Japan, who again abstained, became the scapegoat for the loss. Senior officials from the FLN and the Saudi Arabian embassy visited MOFA for an explanation. Painstakingly reassuring the Algerians that nothing had changed in Japan's policy of being sympathetic to Algeria's fight for self-determination, MOFA policy planners tried to find a way out of this predicament.[65] In May 1959, officials from related sections of the Ministry held a joint meeting to search for a new strategy for the forthcoming Assembly. The result was not very fruitful. Most participants endorsed the plan to return to the pro-AA position Japan had taken at the eleventh session in 1957. But no one could tell what Japan should do if the AA Group rushed to a stance more radical than two years earlier. If this were the case, the meeting concluded, "we would again be forced to make a difficult decision."[66] This grim prediction proved quite accurate during the following years.

In the fourteenth UNGA session, the AA Group submitted two memoranda on the Algerian war to the UNSC. Japan refused to join other AA members in signing one of the memoranda, stressing that as a non-permanent member of the Council it had to take a neutral position. But this excuse brought Japan more troubles. In Tokyo, the French ambassador thanked MOFA, but in some Arab capitals, furious government leaders summoned Japanese envoys to convey protests against

---

64. Political Division of the UN Bureau, "Arujeria mondai hyōketsu no sai no wagahō taido ni tsuite" (Our attitude during the vote on the Algerian problem), January 28, 1959, ibid.

65. UN Bureau, "Arujeria kari seifu kyokutō daihyō Kiwan raidan no ken" (The visit of the Algerian government's Representative to the Far East, Kiouane), January 28, 1959; Middle and Near East Division of the European and Oceanic Affairs Bureau, "Kokuren ni okeru Arujeria mondai tōgi ni kansuru ken" (The UN deliberation on the Algerian problem), January 29, 1959, ibid.

66. Political Division of the UN Bureau, "Arujeria mondai ni taisuru wagahō no taido" (Our attitude toward the Algerian question), May 15, 1959, ibid.

Japan's unfriendly policy.[67] In New York, Ambassador Matsudaira was totally isolated within the AA Group. All he could do was either make negative comments on AA draft resolutions or lament before the few friendly delegates that pro-FLN Arab nationalism was "simply utilized as a tool for the USSR" and thereby "diverted the AA Group from the spirit of UN centrism."[68] From 1959, Japan refused to cosponsor any AA resolutions on the Algerian issues while abstaining in many cases during the votes. The FLN and the AA Group members also ceased to expect Japanese mediation for a peaceful solution. With the Algerian problem approaching its final stage, the only request from the group was for Japan to at least do "a little in general."[69] But Japanese officials seemed to have difficulty even playing such a minor role. In a December 1960 telegram asking for voting instruction, Matsudaira noted with dismay:

Though I think that it is not preferable to leave a record that we have done nothing to support the Algerians, whose chance for independence will probably come sometime . . . there was no room for us to draw out a compromising plan from the two [France and FLN] sides. We can do no more than explaining our position while avoiding offending the two.[70]

Six months later (a year before the French agreed to set Algeria free), Japan's outspoken UN ambassador, who had just retired from his post, spoke out in a closed-door lecture for a group of ruling Liberal Democratic Party (LDP) Diet members on what he had been unable to say in official documents: "The media's suggestion that we should serve as a bridge between the Orient and the Occident is nonsense; it is not so easy [to achieve]."[71]

---

67. Fujiyama to Kakitsubo, June 9, 1959; Matsudaira to Fujiyama, June 15, 1959; Fujiyama to Matsudaira, December 4, 1959, ibid.
68. Matsuno to Fujiyama, December 7, 1959; Fujiyama to Matsudaira and Furukaki, December 5, 1959; Matsudaira to Fujiyama, June 29, 1959, ibid.
69. Matsudaira to Kosaka, November 23, 1960, ibid.
70. Matsudaira to Kosaka, December 9, 1960, ibid.
71. Matsudaira, "Nihon no kokusaiteki chii to sekinin: Kokuren gaikō ni tsuite," p. 25.

✌ 3 ✌

The Turbulent Days

By all appearances, Japanese foreign policymakers, as they had done in the previous decade, treated the UN in a rather special way after 1960. The position of ambassador to the UN remained one of the most prestigious appointments inside MOFA. Throughout the history of postwar Japan, only three former foreign ministers have served in an overseas embassy after retirement. One of them, Okazaki Katsuo, who was the foreign minister of the Yoshida cabinet, was appointed in 1961 as ambassador to the UN. In the early 1960s, Japanese Prime Minister Ikeda Hayato even once considered adding a new member to his cabinet to focus on UN-related issues.[1] Similarly, on the lower level of MOFA's bureaucratic hierarchy, the UN was used as a place to enrich the experience of promising young diplomats. In fact, many senior MOFA officers who reached the top echelon in the Ministry had spent several years in the UN delegation in the earlier stages of their careers.

But regardless of the UN's attractiveness as a stage for highly sophisticated diplomatic games, Japan's UN policymaking was heading for a new age full of confusion and frustration. Having suffered the contradiction between their lofty expectations for the UN's peace functions and the reality of international politics in the 1950s, Japanese officials in charge of UN diplomacy in the 1960s and 1970s were well aware of the necessity to somehow bring their policies back down to earth. They no longer desired to use the UN to save the world from a military conflict between the two superpowers. Nor were they so confident about Japan's ability to be a

---

1. Drifte, *Japan's Quest for a Permanent Security Council Seat*, p. 16.

mediator to bridge the Orient and the Occident through the organization. Instead, a question heard widely during this period was whether joining or cooperating with the UN was worth the effort.

Most Japanese policymakers answered that question in the affirmative. Former UN Ambassador Okazaki in 1964 made the lucid remark that the lives of the hundred million Japanese people had to be supported by foreign trade, which could only be conducted in a peaceful international environment. Since the UN was reinforcing various aspects of its peacekeeping functions, he concluded, Japan could directly benefit through cooperation with the organization.[2] But what exactly could the UN do to guarantee this more peaceful environment? MOFA's UN Bureau director, Saitō Shizuo, provided an answer in a journal article published in the same year:

Since international disputes are just like skirmishes among human beings, they may embody harsh sentiments as well as misunderstandings. Therefore, considering both rational and emotional needs, a cooling-off period for reconsideration is necessary. And it is the UN that offers a place for this . . . The *raison d'être* of the organization is in this role.[3]

This thought of using the UN's moral influence to avoid international conflicts became more salient among officials and political leaders when the UN's reputation as a peacekeeping institution began to wane sharply in the late 1960s. In a 1969 public speech, the chairman of the LDP's Foreign Affairs Study Committee (FASC), Kosaka Zentarō, summarized the role of the UN as an "international salon," a place for "alleviating the dissatisfaction" of member states and a "registry office" for pooling different opinions concerning international disputes.[4] Likewise, in his article published in 1973, the chief of the Political Division of the UN Bureau, Owada Hisashi, called his readers' attention to the fact that during international conflicts, the nations concerned were accustomed to bringing their problems to the UN. "This phenomenon per se," he wrote, "is helpful for the sake of peace."[5]

---

2. Okazaki, "Kokusai rengō to Nihon," pp. 18–19.
3. Saitō, "Dai 18 kai kokuren sōkai," pp. 13–14.
4. Kosaka, "Wareware wa nani o kokuren ni kitai subeki ka," p. 37.
5. Owada, "Kokuren ni yoru heiwa iji to kokusai kyōryoku," pp. 22–23. For similar arguments made by MOFA officials during this period, see Nishibori,

Peaceful dialogue and international opinions were certainly significant in alleviating tensions among conflicting states. But during the two decades after 1960, it was not so easy for Japan to take advantage of this function of the UN—the two superpowers continued to treat the UN as an arena not for peace but for diplomatic warfare, and the smaller member states from the AA Group were disposed to turn the organization into an arena for opinions against Western industrial powers, including Japan.

A UN Transcending the Cold War or Serving It?

From the mid-1960s on, for the sake of their political and security interests, leading Cold War powers not only bypassed the UN during most important international negotiations but occasionally threatened the very existence of the UN system by taking drastic actions against their counterparts within the organization. Japan was distressed by this tendency. While they no longer considered the UN an organization that could "transcend" the Cold War, Japanese policymakers were equally unwilling to see a UN dominated by the Cold War.

In August 1960, newly appointed Foreign Minister Kosaka Zentarō remarked at a public gathering that although the UN was used by some nations as "a place for Cold War propaganda," the organization could somehow "neutralize" the "bipolarization" of international politics between the American and the Soviet camps.[6] What he witnessed at the UNGA a month later, however, was one of the most notorious moments of bipolar hostilities in Cold War history.

In May of that year, the pending Paris Summit between Eisenhower and Khrushchev was unilaterally called off by the Soviets due to the capture of an American U-2 spy plane in Russian territory. The so-

---

Japan Views the United Nations, p. 2; Aichi, "The United Nations and Japan's Position," p. 31.

6. "Hachigatsu jūshichinichi gaikō chishiki fukyūkai, kokusai rengō kyōkai, keieisha kyōkai, keizai dōyukai oyobi Kyōto shōkō kaigijo kyōsai ni yoru Kyōto kōenkai ni okeru Kosaka gaimu daijin no enzetsu," (The gathering for the diffusion of diplomatic knowledge on August 17: Foreign Minister Kosaka's speech at the lecture in Kyoto cosponsored by the Association for the UN, the Employers' Association, the Association of Corporate Executives, and the Kyoto Chamber of Commerce and Industry), August 17, 1960, A'0361, DRO.

called détente between the two superpowers had reached its limit. Cold Warriors began to flex their muscles for a new round of confrontation, and the upcoming UNGA would become the first battlefield. The immediate cause of the clash between the two blocs within the 1960 UNGA was the Congo crisis. Having been a Belgian colony for 75 years, the West African state of the Congo won its independence on June 30, 1960. But given the lack of a sufficient preparatory period coupled with the prevailing distrust among its leaders, the new state immediately fell into chaos. Without the permission of the Congolese government, Belgium shipped its troops back in early July to "restore order." In less than two weeks, at the request of Congolese leaders, the UNSC decided to dispatch an emergency force—Opération des Nations Units au Congo (ONUC)—to replace the Belgians. Anticipating that the ONUC might not let his government take charge of security within the country, the leftist Congolese Prime Minister Patrice Lumumba went to the Soviets for help—a move that deepened Washington's suspicion of his pro-communist penchant.

When Khrushchev arrived in New York in September, he had a plan to make the best use of the Congo crisis. In a virulent speech during the UNGA's general debate, Khrushchev attacked UN Secretary General Hammarskjold who, in his words, was engaging in some "dirty works" in the Congo. He then startled the members by declaring a proposal for a thorough "reform" of the UN system, including the resignation of Hammarskjold and the introduction of a so-called "troika" mechanism splitting the power of the Secretary General between three representatives, from the East, West, and neutral camps respectively. Although Hammarskjold heroically defended his post, the atmosphere of the Assembly curdled. During the rest of the Assembly session, the world would watch the thrust and parry among delegates from the two blocs, culminating in the legendary scene in which Khrushchev pounded the table with a shoe to interrupt the speech of his opponents.[7]

Japanese leaders did not conceal their resentment toward what was going on in New York. Foreign Minister Kosaka deplored that the 1960 UNGA "reflected the East-West struggle" and that "statements con-

---

7. Regarding the background of the fifteenth session, see Meisler, *United Nations*, pp. 121–22; Ostrower, *The United Nations*, pp. 94–97; Benton, *Soldiers for Peace*, pp. 101–7.

trary to the spirit of the UN charter tended to transform the UN from an organ for international cooperation into an arena for agitation and criticism by nations seeking to expand their influence among the new member nations." Prime Minister Ikeda aired similar concerns in the Diet.[8] In spite of these public statements, Japan did not immediately ally itself with the US and Hammarskjold at the UN. As early as October 1960, the chief of the Political Division of MOFA's UN Bureau, Takashima Masuo, observed in a journal article that although Hammarskjold bravely countered Khrushchev's troika plan, the UN Secretary General might have to "mollify his proactive stance somewhat" if the Soviets continued to refuse to cooperate with him. Ambassador to the Netherlands Miyazaki Akira, who also served as a Japanese delegate to the UNGA, even said on one occasion that "in order to save the UN" it might be necessary to discharge Hammarskjold because the latter was unable to obtain trust from both the Eastern and Western blocs simultaneously and hence had "lost his usefulness" as Secretary General.[9]

Just as MOFA officials were hesitating to take further steps to back up the UN Secretary General, their colleagues in the State Department were planning to incorporate Japan into US renewed efforts to overrule the Soviets on the Congo affair. In the first two months of 1961, senior officials at the US Embassy in Tokyo held meetings with Foreign Minister Kosaka and other MOFA counterparts time and again regarding the issue. The Japanese were asked to use their friendship with the AA group to sell Washington's new proposal to establish a "broadly based government" in the Congo under UN supervision rather than manipulated by left-wing factions supported by Moscow. The US government also declared its full support for Hammarskjold's suggestion of putting all Congolese military elements under UN control and expected Japan to follow suit. While remaining pessimistic about the consequence, Japanese policymakers agreed that a controversial peace proposal initiated by the UN was at least much more acceptable than the improve-

---

8. MOFA, "Gist of Foreign Policy Speech by Foreign Minister Kosaka before the 36th Extraordinary Session of the National Diet," October 21, 1960, FO 371/150567, Reel 94, PRO; MOFA, *Waga gaikō no kinkyō*, 1961, p. 297.

9. Takashima, "Kokuren kaiso, sono nerai," p. 35; Miyazaki to Kosaka, January 9, 1961, A'0387, DRO.

ment of the communist camp's influence in the Congo.[10] On February 17, Kosaka announced after the Cabinet meeting that Japan would "maintain its 'UN-first' diplomacy" and had "no intentions of supporting Soviet non-confidence moves against Hammarskjold." On the same day, MOFA informed the US embassy that the Japanese UN delegation would "work closely" with the Americans and would be "as helpful as possible in explaining to certain delegations the integrity and authority of the UN," as well as the "lack of legal status" of the leftist regime in the Congo.[11] Within a few weeks, this stance was reconfirmed at the highest level of the government.

In late February, Khrushchev suddenly issued a public letter to the heads of several foreign nations including Japanese Prime Minister Ikeda in which he accused Hammarskjold of collaborating with Western "colonialists" and brutally "murdering" Congolese Prime Minister Lumumba (who had been killed by domestic rivals early that month). The government quickly judged Khrushchev's letter to be "part of a Soviet effort to destroy the effectiveness of the UN and a propaganda effort to heighten rather than reduce tensions in Africa."[12] In his reply to Khrushchev, Ikeda commented that the Soviets had "arbitrarily" concluded that the UN had acted as a tool of colonialism in the Congo, a view with which the Japanese government did "not agree."[13] Defending the role of the UN, the Japanese prime minister pointed out that if there was room for improvement in the UN activities in the Congo, "all the member states must realize that such improvement can be made only through the fullest cooperation by all of them." For this reason, he adamantly rejected the troika scheme, arguing that "the reorganization of the UN Secretariat on the premise that the Secretary General should

---

10. Letter from MacArthur to Kosaka, February 6, 1961; Kosaka to Asakai, Ōno and Matsuhara, February 8, 1961; Middle East and African Affairs Division of the European and Oceanic Affairs Bureau, "Kongō ni okeru Berugī no katsudō ni kanshi zaikyō Bei taishikan yori no mōshiire no ken" (Request from the US Embassy in Tokyo regarding Belgium's activities in the Congo), February 27, 1961, all in A'0436, ibid.

11. Tokyo to Washington, February 17, 1961, Box 59, Japan Post File, NA.

12. Tokyo to Washington, March 2, 1961, Box 59, Japan Post File, NA.

13. For the full text of Ikeda's reply to Khrushchev, see Tokyo to Washington, March 15, 1961, ibid.

represent the interest of a particular group is a means of making the UN an instrument of policy of that particular group and will completely paralyze the functions of the UN and bring about its destruction." Satisfied with this unequivocal response, MOFA ordered the Japanese UN ambassador to circulate the text of Ikeda's letter among member states. Chief of the UN Bureau's Political Division Takashima, the very person who had cautiously responded to Khrushchev's attacks six months before, now appeared to be extremely confident when he assured US embassy officials in late March that Japan was "prepared to exert leadership" among AA states in "encouraging resistance to Soviet efforts to weaken the UN."[14]

Though there is little evidence that Japanese leaders actually exerted any crucial influence on AA states' attitude on the issue, they did try to turn the tables on the Soviets by mobilizing other Western countries to join a counteroffensive in the UN, sometimes behaving quite proactively. In July 1961, Kosaka told Italian Foreign Minister Antonio Segni that since the Soviets always raised "destructive proposals" in the UN, it was time for the UN side to "actively devise some counterproposals" so as to "drive the USSR into a difficult situation."[15] After the tragic death of Hammarskjold in August, Kosaka reiterated in a meeting with British Foreign Minister Alec Douglas-Home that "Japan was strongly opposed to the troika system" advocated by the Soviets. Furthermore, referring to the recent tension between the two blocs in Berlin, he suggested that "some use might be made of the UN forum in rallying public opinion" against the USSR "on the basis of self-determination."[16]

By the time Kosaka left Tokyo to attend the sixteenth session of the UNGA in September, Japan was already in the first row of an anti-Soviet united front. British officials reported that their Japanese friends were "determined to do what they can to make the Organization a

---

14. Tokyo to Washington, March 29, 1961, ibid; Kosaka to Matsudaira, March 7, 1961, A'0436, DRO.

15. Narita to Ikeda, July 14, 1961, A'0363, DRO.

16. "Record of Conversation between the Secretary of State and the Japanese Foreign Minister, Mr. Kosaka, at the Waldorf Astoria, New York on Friday, September 22, 1961," FO 371/158497, Reel 103, PRO.

more efficient one." The US Assistant Secretary of State for International Organization, Harlan Cleveland, even seriously considered Japan one of the "fire brigades" to snuff out Soviet propaganda at the UN.[17] But again, the Western allies had overestimated Japan's intention to join their Cold War crusade. The Japanese government might have wished to drive the Soviets into a "difficult" situation, but it certainly did not want to corner them; they did not want to force Moscow to repeat Japan's experience three decades before and leave the UN forever.

Saving the UN from Financial Crisis

Having failed to attain support for the troika scheme, the Soviets shifted the weight of their anti-UN campaign from the institutional sphere to the financial sphere. In view of its official position that the Peacekeeping Operation (PKO) deployed in the Congo contravened the UN charter, the USSR and its satellites refused to pick up the bill for the expense of the ONUC. (For slightly different reasons, Belgium and De Gaulle's France took the same action.) In December 1961, the UNGA passed a resolution to ask for the opinion of the International Court of Justice (ICJ) on this problem. Responding before the start of the seventeenth session of the Assembly, the ICJ declared in July 1962 that indeed the Soviets should pay, but the latter ignored the judgment. Meanwhile, the arrears of member states in terms of subscriptions to the UN regular budget increased to $93 million that year and the Secretariat, for the first time in the organization's history, had to issue $200 million in UN bonds in order to overcome this emergency situation.[18] In 1963, several resolutions concerning the UN's financial crisis were adopted at a special assembly and the eighteenth session, whereas the USSR still displayed no willingness to listen to international opinion.

The inflexible Soviet attitude deeply enraged the US government. In January 1964, the amount of the USSR's arrears had exceeded two years' worth of its designated contribution to the UN and therefore, accord-

---

17. "The Japanese Ministry of Foreign Affairs Fifth Annual Blue Book on Japan's Foreign Relations," minutes, September 12, 1961, FO 371/158483, Reel, 101, ibid.; "US Strategy at 16th General Assembly," memo from Cleveland to the President, July 24, 1961, Box 310, NS Files, JFKL.

18. MOFA, *Waga gaikō no kinkyō*, March 1962, pp. 55–56.

ing to Article 19 of the UN charter, raised the possibility that the Soviets would lose their right to vote in the UNGA. The US and the UK seized this opportunity to deal the USSR a *coup de grâce* by asking for the invocation of Article 19. The Soviets, in response, threatened to withdraw from the UN if this happened.

Until late 1964, the opinions of Japanese officials on this issue were divided. Some officials insisted that the government endorse severe punishment against the Soviets, whereas others gave higher priority to avoiding Soviet withdrawal, which could threaten the existence of the UN system.[19] The former position seems to have prevailed in the government at first. In official position papers, MOFA repeatedly contended that while it would be a disaster for Article 19 to be applied to the USSR, "the possibility that the USSR could avoid Article 19 would be even more disastrous" for the UN.[20] Accordingly, Japan agreed with the other big Western powers' view that Article 19 should be introduced automatically.[21]

However, when Japan was assigned by the UNGA chairman to a committee dealing with the arrears issue in the nineteenth session of the Assembly, its position changed. The members of this committee were all from the AA group, which believed that automatic application of the Article 19 could cause the USSR to walk out. Surrounded by fellow committee members with this opinion, Japan began to shift its objective from a prompt Soviet payment to the preservation of the UN system's integrity. Japanese UN Ambassador Matsui Akira became a leading member on the committee. He worked closely with the ambassadors of Afghanistan, Algeria, Jordan, Pakistan, and Nigeria in searching for a method through which the UNGA session could proceed "without voting" so that no decisions would have to be made concerning the USSR's voting right. They found a simple solution: have the Assembly concentrate on items not requiring a vote while postponing de-

---

19. New York to Washington, September 4, 1964, Box 1849, Subject-Numeric Files 1964–66, NA.

20. Division of Management at the UN Bureau, "Kokuren zaisei mondai" (The UN financial problem), August 2, 1963, A'0365; MOFA, "Kokuren kenshō dai 19 jō tekiyō mondai" (The application of Article 19 of the UN charter), 1964, A'427, DRO.

21. Cortazzi to Bentley, August 20, 1963, FO 371/170756, Reel 121, PRO.

liberations of all other issues.[22] In line with this idea, the nineteenth session of the Assembly became the only session since the establishment of the UN in which not a single item was put to a vote.

The 1964 Assembly was over, yet Article 19 continued to be a sword of Damocles, for the US did not want to let the Soviets go so easily. The nineteenth session was resumed in February 1965 to continue the efforts to resolve the UN financing problem. During the next six months, Japan and Nigeria hammered out a draft resolution suggesting the inapplicability of Article 19 to the ONUC budgetary issue and calling for resumption of the normal functioning of the UNGA and voluntary financial contributions from member states.[23] In order to pave the way for the enactment of the resolution, Japan took the initiative to make voluntary payments and used every chance to rally support from the US, the USSR, and the AA Group. Extremely reluctant at first, the US ultimately agreed to follow Japan's lead by shelving its proposal to raise Article 19 in the twentieth session. The AA Group also gave tacit consent to the resolution, which in turn left the Soviets no choice but to keep quiet.[24] Japan's unpretentious endeavor based on a neutral stance had contributed to the UN's survival in one of the most precarious American-Soviet encounters that the organization had endured.

The Vietnam War and the Matsui Letter

The Article 19 episode was a byproduct of the two superpowers' policy of bellicose bluff, which consistently tested the nerves of their counterparts. Throughout the East-West conflicts, Washington and Moscow acted like two verbose gunmen aiming their rifles at one another, exchanging dirty words but never pulling the triggers. They lost their temper from time to time. Yet on those occasions, instead of going af-

---

22. Kokuren kōhō sentā, ibid.; Iguchi, *Nihon gaikōshi*, pp. 81–82.

23. Matsui, "Kokuren gokanen no omoide," p. 46.

24. New York to Washington, June 18, July 23, August 12, 13, 18, 19, 20, 23 and 31, 1965, all in Reel 3, UN Files, LBJL; Political Division of the UN Bureau, "Daijin hōō yō, kokuren mondai" (For the use of the minister's trip to Europe: the UN problem), July 2, 1965, A'0387, DRO; Rome to Washington, July 30, 1965, Reel 39, DOS 1963–66; Tokyo to Washington, August 4, 1965, DDRS; Iguchi, *Nihon gaikōshi*, pp. 83–84.

ter the opponent directly, they would pick out one of the adherents of the other side as a scapegoat. This was the origin of many regional tensions during the Cold War era. The UN was by and large unreliable in resolving this type of military skirmish. But it was a useful forum in which to gain the sympathy of international opinion, in cases where the belligerents deemed this to be important. Thus, at a certain stage of each conflict, the big powers might introduce the issue to the UNSC, bandying words with each other on some condemnatory draft resolutions. When the resolutions at stake were killed by the veto of one side, the other would declare its moral victory and return to the battlefield. To most UN members, these ceremonial debates at the UNSC were painful moments. They knew that the two military giants were taking advantage of the UN. But if they refused to play supporting roles in these diplomatic shows, the two might cease to discuss their problems in New York at all and thereby cause the UN to lose even a symbolic role in international conflicts. In the mid-1960s, the Japanese government was caught in one such difficult occasion—the Vietnam War.

After the Gulf of Tonkin incident in August 1964, Japan was among those UN members who looked forward to seeing a UNSC meeting on the Vietnam problem.[25] Within a few months, Japanese expectations for the UN increased as the US mounted its request for Japan's assistance in the Vietnam operations. Japan was afraid of being regarded as America's close ally in the latter's military actions in Vietnam. In December, Prime Minister Satō Eisaku told US Ambassador to Tokyo Edwin O. Reischauer that it would be "easier" for Japan to send aid to Vietnam and Southeast Asia "if the UN could get involved in some way."[26]

Given the peace campaign initiated by the domestic left-wing opposition, Satō's pro-UN stance regarding the Vietnam issue was adopted mainly to avoid further trouble inside Japan. But this was not necessarily a timely choice in light of the international political situation. At the same time that Satō was considering using the UN card, the US government's talks with UN Secretary General U Thant on the Vietnam situation began to turn sour. By early 1965, the Lyndon B. Johnson ad-

---

25. "Record of the Secretary of State's Staff Meeting," August 5, 1964, FRUS (1964–68), Vol. I, p. 633.
26. Tokyo to Washington, December 29, 1964, Reel 38, DOS 1963–66.

ministration was convinced that it was not productive to discuss the Vietnam problem in the framework of the UN.[27] Meanwhile, within the Japanese government, opinions on this problem were divided. Japanese Ambassador to Washington Takeuchi Ryūji, who was much more familiar with the situation outside Japan, once told Secretary of State Dean Rusk that he thought Satō's proposal to aid Vietnam through the UN was "nonsense."[28]

In the absence of sufficient endorsement, the Satō administration had to look for other routes through which to channel its cooperation with the US in Vietnam. But before doing so, the prime minister still wanted to impress upon Washington that the UN option was Japan's favorite. On January 12, 1965, Satō informed President Johnson and Secretary of State Rusk during a meeting at the White House that although "unfortunately" Japan had to find other ways to assist the US military effort in Vietnam, Japan believed that "if certain things could be done under the auspices of the United Nations," the government "would have greater freedom to help." He made a similar statement before US Ambassador to the UN Adlai Stevenson when visiting the UN headquarters in New York.[29] The US, however, continued in 1965 to reject an active role for the UN in coping with the Vietnam problem. Under such circumstances, except for sporadic references to the importance of the UN's peace efforts, Japan had to maintain a low profile in handling the Vietnam agenda within the UN while starting to search for a mediator role through bilateral channels.[30] But a year later, when Washington did try to do something pertaining to Vietnam in the UN, Satō's foreign policy aides found out that a UN-centered Vietnam policy

---

27. Meisler, *United Nations*, pp. 160–62; Ostrower, *The United Nations*, pp. 118–19.

28. See "Prime Minister Satō's Visit; Bonin Islands; Japanese Temporary Agricultural Workers Program," memo of conversation, December 30, 1964, Reel 38, DOS 1963–66.

29. Washington to Tokyo, January 30, 1965, Reel 34, ibid.; "Current US-Japanese and World Problems," memo of conversation, January 12, 1965, Doc. 00437, NSA.

30. "Message to President Lyndon B. Johnson from Prime Minister Eisaku Satō," April 10, 1965, Doc. 00464, NSA; Tokyo to Washington, May 22, 1965, Reel 44 and "Soviet-Japanese Relations," memo of conversation, June 21, 1965, Reel 46, both in DOS 1963–66.

could actually bring Japan more troubles rather than keep it immune from them.

On January 30, 1966, the US government decided to renew its bombing of North Vietnam. To head off domestic and international criticism of this decision, the US announced that it was going to ask for a debate on the Vietnamese situation at the UNSC. Japan, which happened to be the president of the Council in February, was naturally selected to be the US's main partner in this strategy. When President Johnson asked Satō for his opinion one day before the official announcement, Satō promptly replied that he agreed with the US attempt to emphasize the role of the UN and pledged his "utmost efforts" so that the discussions at the UNSC would "achieve significant results."[31] But within a couple of days, Japanese UN Ambassador Matsui would realize that what the Americans expected him to do at the Council was nothing short of an impossible mission.

Two communist UNSC members, the USSR and Bulgaria, doggedly refused to take part in any discussion on this issue, for they thought the Vietnam problem could not be considered without the presence of Hanoi and Beijing. The AA members, on the other hand, were confused by the situation and were anything but enthusiastic about standing by the US.[32] Given such a desperate situation, Matsui, according to his coworkers, was "purposely cautious" to avoid being labeled a "US errand boy."[33] Initially, he intended to keep the discussion alive without a vote so as to evade a direct collision among conflicting Council members. But the US pressed him to put the agenda to a procedural vote on which a veto could not be used. The agenda was adopted, though the Soviets inevitably hardened their position.[34] Understanding that there would be no chance to work out a meaningful solution through public debates, Matsui adjourned the formal session and moved the agenda to

---

31. Washington to Tokyo, February 1, 1966, Reel 4, NS Asian & Pacific File (1963–69, first supplement), LBJL; Letter from Satō to LBJ, February 1, 1966, Doc. 00549, NSA.

32. New York to Washington, February 4, 1966, Box 3321, Subject-Numeric Files 1964–66, NA.

33. New York to Washington, February 5, 1966, ibid.

34. New York to Washington, February 3, 1966, ibid.; Kokuren kōhō sentā, *Nihon to kokuren*, p. 67.

informal consultation among member states. Once again, the US intervened and pushed Japan to take more "active" steps to ensure "control over" the consultation. This time, Matsui was determined not to yield to the American instruction. Opposing any proposal that might lead to acrimonious exchanges between the US and the USSR, Matsui and his delegation hoped that a resolution on the issue could pass the Council by consensus. But this proved to be difficult since the opinions of members concerned did not jell in the course of informal talks.[35] In the meantime, Western members such as France and the UK started to urge the US to stop discussion of the Vietnam issue in the Council because they were also worried about an American-Soviet showdown in the UN.[36] Japan shared these nations' concern but was unwilling to close the case without any results.

In hopes of preserving the UN's voice on the issue, Matsui made up his mind to take a daring step by following the French ambassador's advice to issue a "President's letter" for the record of the UN Secretariat. The Japanese delegation drafted the text of the letter with fairly ambitious contents, among which only two items survived after sounding out other members of the Council. First, the letter admitted the inability of the member states to reach an agreement on the issue. Second, it called for peaceful negotiations on the Vietnam conflict in an "appropriate forum." The ambiguous term "appropriate forum" was deliberately inserted by the Japanese. Though it could mean the Geneva Conference, the venue upon which the Soviet bloc insisted, the Japanese apparently also had the UN in their minds when using the term.[37]

The response of the Council members to the revised President's letter was flexible. The majority, including the US, silently accepted it. France and Mali declared their opposition but took no further actions.[38] The USSR also sent a message to Matsui to protest his letter. But Soviet Ambassador Nikolai Fedorenko, who had been consulted by the Japa-

---

35. Matsui, "Kokuren go kanen no omoide," pp. 43–44; New York to Washington, February 4, 1966, Box 3321, Subject-Numeric Files 1964–66, NA.

36. New York to Washington, February 16, 1966, ibid.

37. Kokuren kōhō sentā, *Nihon to kokuren*, p. 68; New York to Washington, February 17, 1966, ibid.

38. New York to Washington, February 21 and 24, 1966, ibid.; New York to Washington, February 26, 1966, Box 3306, Subject-Numeric Files 1964–66, NA.

nese all the while, was notably mild in dealing with this problem. Using the words of Matsui, Fedorenko's attitude was one of, "I like you and do not want to hurt you, so why don't you withdraw your letter?" When Matsui proceeded to submit his letter, Fedorenko did nothing to stop him.[39] This was the first time in UN history a UNSC president issued a letter of this sort, and it is one of very few pieces of written evidence that the organization did at least try something to prevent the bloodshed in Vietnam from escalating.

Coping with the Great Powers' Negligence

Japan was able to score some points during the Matsui letter incident because at least one of the superpowers did want to discuss the issue inside the UN. Unfortunately, this was not always the case during the Cold War era. The Vietnam War problem, for instance, was eventually negotiated and solved in an ad hoc body outside the UN. So were many other important issues, including nuclear disarmament, to which Japan had made a deep commitment during the 1950s.

As we have discussed in the last chapter, starting in the late 1950s the two main players of the Cold War began to agree that bogging themselves down in rhetorical fights over nuclear issues within the UN was not effective, and they were more likely to gain productive results through secret meetings somewhere else. This tendency became more and more conspicuous after 1960. Japan's response to this was by and large moderate. On one hand, Japan preferred to see frequent discussions of the disarmament problem within the framework of the UN, where it had more opportunity to play a significant role than in other US/Soviet-made international organs. On the other hand, sensing the menace posed by China's nuclear armament, the Japanese government was very conscious of its identity as a Western power and therefore refrained from any actions that could jeopardize the interests of the free world. Throughout the 1960s, Japan maintained that the best way to promote nuclear disarmament was a step-by-step format giving higher priority to the military balance between the two camps, a position widely shared in the West. Japan was not sympathetic toward idealistic appeals such as complete elimination of nuclear weapons or the estab-

---

39. Matsui, "Kokuren go kanen," p. 44.

lishment of a nuclear free zone (NFZ) in the Far East, as suggested by the Eastern bloc and neutral AA nations.[40] When resolutions containing these ideas were brought to the UNGA, the Japanese delegation usually refused to support them and on several occasions dauntlessly defended this "realistic" position before the AA Group.[41]

Pressed by the mood of détente between the two leading Cold War powers, Japan was more active in handling disarmament issues during the 1970s. It devoted itself to promoting resolutions on nuclear proliferation and NFZ.[42] It also submitted a treaty draft on the prohibition of chemical weapons to the CCD and brought this issue to the UNGA in 1974.[43] But again, none of these actions were taken at the expense of the interests of the Western bloc as a whole. Nor did they cause deviation from the step-by-step principle.

This type of moderate stance was also observed in Japan's handling of the nuclear test ban issue, which had given shape to a dramatic exchange of diplomatic messages among Tokyo, Washington, London, and Moscow in the 1950s. In the early 1960s, Prime Minister Ikeda and his aides from MOFA were extremely suspicious of the Soviets' sincerity in solving the test ban question and had grave concerns about China's nuclear weapons programs.[44] Outwardly, they opposed the reopening of nuclear tests conducted by either military bloc, largely for domestic reasons. But in reality, they did not feel obliged to maintain an equally rigid attitude toward the nuclear test policies of the two superpowers.[45] When informed by US President John F. Kennedy in June 1961 that Washington was considering reopening its tests, Ikeda simply

---

40. MOFA, "Ikeda sōri hōbei kaidan gidai (an)" (Topics for Prime Minister Ikeda's visit to the US, proposal), April 6, 1961, A'0361, ibid.; Nishibori, "Japan Views the United Nations," p. 7; Iguchi, *Nihon gaikōshi*, pp. 197–98.

41. New York to Washington, November 12, 1962, Box 1, Lot File 58D133, NA.

42. Office of Disarmament, MOFA, *Kokuren oyobi Juneibu gunshuku iinkai ni okeru gunshuku mondai ni tsuite no Nihonkoku daihyō no hatsugenshū (dai 6 shū)*, pp. 87–93; Kawabe, *Kokuren to Nihon*, pp. 86–87.

43. MOFA, *Waga gaikō no kinkyō*, 1975, pp. 323.

44. MOFA, "Ikeda sōri hōbei kaidan gidai (an)," April 6, 1961; MOFA, "Ikeda sōri hōbei dai go kai uchiawase," May 4, 1961, A'0361, DRO.

45. Ibid.; UN Bureau, "Gunshuku oyobi kakujikken chūshi mondai" (Disarmament and nuclear weapon test ban problems), undated, ibid.

replied that although it was impossible for him to publicly support the tests, he "appreciated" that the US had been "forced" to make such a decision due to the unconstructive position of the USSR. The Japanese prime minister even offered Kennedy a propaganda campaign led by his delegation at the UN to defend the Western camp's interest regarding this issue.[46] MOFA diplomats at the UN did not let their leader down. Four months later, despite Japan's ambiguous attitude toward the resumption of American nuclear tests, when Khrushchev announced a 50 - megaton H-bomb test as a result of Moscow's decision to terminate the suspension of its nuclear tests, Japanese Ambassador to the UN Okazaki readily tabled a draft resolution in the UNGA to express the "explosion of Japanese people's concern" and "resentment" toward the Soviets.[47]

The Japanese resolution passed the Assembly, albeit with no impact on Moscow's decision. This was not an unexpected outcome, but Japanese officials still seemed depressed. The deputy chief of Japan's UN delegation, Matsui Akira, recalled later that this was the first time he "sadly felt disillusioned over the UN's limitations."[48] For his government, what happened afterwards was even worse. Rather than resuming their talks within the UN, the US and the USSR repeated what they had done two years earlier by leaving the test ban question to a new independent agency, the Eighteen Nations Disarmament Committee (ENDC). In addition, the USSR made Japan pay the price for its anti-Soviet behavior by rejecting the latter's membership in the committee.[49]

After the Soviets resumed their nuclear tests, Japanese officials began to notice the need to refine their government's stance toward the two superpowers' competition on nuclear tests. Of course, they would not withhold their support for the US nuclear strategy against the USSR. But they became more circumspect when airing that endorsement. Some MOFA diplomats, for example, told the Americans that although

---

46. Shima Shigenobu, "Ikeda sōri, Kenedi daitōryō dai 3 ji (itomagoi) kaidan (denpō hokoku ni kaete)" (The third (farewell) meeting between Prime Minister Ikeda and President Kennedy, in place of telegram report), June 29, 1961, ibid; Higuchi, "Kakujikken mondai to Ikeda gaikō," p. 209.

47. MOFA, *Waga gaikō no kinkyō*, June 1962, pp. 25–26.

48. Kokuren kōhō sentā, *Nihon to kokuren*, pp. 55–56.

49. New York to Washington, December 11, 1961, Box 59, Japan Post Files, NA.

their government would like to adopt a position "as close to the US as politically possible," nuclear testing was an issue on which the two countries were "most widely separated."[50] A frequent excuse for Japan's different stance with the US was pressure from domestic opponents, which, as discussed in later chapters, was not entirely unfounded.[51]

For the rest of the 1960s, Japan used its expertise in seismology to develop nuclear test detection technologies within the UN. Its achievement in this area caught the attention of the international community shortly after its admission to the ENDC (which was soon expanded to become the CCD), when the Japanese delegation proposed to the committee in 1969 a resolution to forbid underground nuclear tests of a magnitude of 4.75 or higher. (The resolution, nevertheless, was rejected by the US and USSR.[52]) Japanese officials kept working on the test detection question in the 1970s. In August 1976, under Japan's sponsorship, a team of seismologists was set up in the CCD to discuss the possibility of establishing a worldwide network to detect nuclear tests.[53] Japan also cosponsored a number of resolutions at the UNGA urging further endeavors toward a test ban. All these activities emphasized the technical aspects of nuclear tests and usually exerted little influence on the ongoing negotiations between Moscow and Washington, which continued to be conducted on a bilateral basis without the UN's intervention.

The only occasion when Japan found the UN somewhat useful in protecting its security interests in regard to nuclear disarmament was on the Nuclear Non-Proliferation Treaty (NPT) question. Unlike the nuclear test ban diplomacy in the 1950s, which was shaped by domestic politics, the NPT issue had direct implications for Japan's national security. Since 1960, the Japanese government had been bothered by

50. New York to Washington, March 27, 1962, Box 96, ibid.; New York to Washington, August 24, 1962, Box 301, NS Files, JFKL.

51. Washington to Tokyo, September 4, 1962, Tokyo to Washington, September 5, 1962, Tokyo to Washington, September 12, 1962, Box 84; Tokyo to Washington, September 17, 1962, Box 96, all in Japan Post Files, NA.

52. Iguchi, *Nihon gaikōshi*, pp. 205–6; Akashi, "Japan in the United Nations," pp. 31–32; New York to Washington, November 15, 1965, UN Files, Reel 4, LBJL.

53. MOFA, *Waga gaikō no kinkyō*, Vol. 1, 1977, p. 277.

China's ambitious plan to join the nuclear club. MOFA officials devised a number of proposals, including the conclusion of a test ban agreement among current nuclear weapon powers and the establishment of an NFZ in the Far East encompassing China, so as to thwart Beijing's nuclear program. In the same vein, it also cooperated with Ireland in the UN to cosponsor a resolution on the nuclear weapon dissemination problem in 1960.[54] Ironically, however, after all these efforts failed with China's successful nuclear test in October 1964, the US and USSR achieved a belated agreement to stop the proliferation of nuclear weapons to other nations, among which Japan was also numbered.

The NPT proposal discussed among major nuclear powers was aimed at freezing the current configuration of nuclear weapons—a concept which was, noted a senior Japanese diplomat, "unequal from the very beginning," as most nations had been unable to build their nuclear arsenals by then.[55] Thus, during the process of treaty negotiation, those "have-nots" constantly asked the nuclear powers to scale down their own nuclear forces while publicly guaranteeing the security of non-nuclear nations. Among them, however, Japan behaved slightly differently from the others.

As a shrewd player of international power politics, the Japanese government did not believe that a multilateral agreement like the NPT would immediately liberate the country from the threat of nuclear attacks launched by Moscow or Beijing. To those working inside the government, the most practical mechanism to forestall such attacks was the nuclear protection, or "nuclear umbrella" as they called it, offered by the US.[56] In this sense, the NPT plan could even do harm to Japan's national interest if the concluded treaty contained certain regulations on non-nuclear nations' right to seek security assurance via bilateral arrangements. Moreover, having maintained the technical potential to develop its own nuclear forces, Japan held strong reservations about an earlier draft of the NPT produced by the Soviets and Americans in 1965

---

54. MOFA, "Gunshuku oyobi kakujikken chūshi mondai," 1961, A'0361, DRO.
55. Counselor's Office of the Asian Affairs Bureau, "Shōwa 42 nendo Ajia, Taiheiyō chiiki taishi kaigi giji yōroku" (Summary of the minutes of the 1967 annual conference of ambassadors to the Asian and Pacific area), September 9, 1967, p. 87, MOFAD.
56. Kurosaki, "Satō seiken no kakuseisaku to Amerika no 'kaku no kasa'," p. 79.

that aimed at maintaining the status quo among nuclear powers while paying little attention to the security of non-nuclear nations.[57] It also worried that the treaty might impair the right of non-nuclear nations to use nuclear technology for peaceful purposes.[58] But at the same time, Japan was unwilling to see the NPT effort spoiled because it feared this could encourage potential candidates for the nuclear club, including other Asian states, to speed up their nuclear efforts. Besides, Japanese policymakers understood that due to their country's reputation as the only member of the world community that had experienced nuclear attacks, they could not afford the political cost of rejecting an international nuclear agreement endorsed even by most nuclear powers.[59]

As a result, Japan's attitude toward the NPT was two-sided. On the one hand, it was eager to see the NPT plan accepted by most non-nuclear countries, in particular those with the potential to develop independent nuclear systems. On the other hand, it also intended to preserve as many potential rights for its own nuclear proposals as possible.[60] Japanese officials used the UN for both purposes. Unlike Japan, which enjoyed the safety guaranteed by the American nuclear umbrella, many other non-nuclear nations obtained no bilateral assurance from big powers and therefore were highly suspicious about the NPT idea, as it could easily expose their territories to future attacks from nuclear weapons holders. Fully aware of this concern, Japan was eager to supplement the treaty with a formal assurance of security for non-nuclear

---

57. Tokyo to Washington, November 19, 1965, Reel 44, DOS 1963–66.

58. New York to Washington, September 27, 1967, Box 3189, Subject-Numeric Files 1967–69, NA; Goulding to Denson, November 28, 1967, FCO 21/274, Reel 145, PRO; Iguchi, *Nihon gaikōshi*, pp. 206–14; Gaimushō hyakunenshi hensan iinkai, *Gaimushō*, pp. 1157–59.

59. MOFA, "Shiina gaimu daijin no Ōshū hōmon ni tsuite" (Foreign Minister Shiina's visit to Europe), 1966, A'427, DRO.

60. Commonwealth Affairs Division of the European and Oceanic Affairs Bureau, "Dai 5 kai Nichiei teiki kyōgi: daijin hatsugen kosshi" (The fifth Japanese-Anglo consultations: The gist of the minister's statement), October 14, 1966, ibid; Northeast Asian Affairs Division of the Asian Affairs Bureau, "Shōwa 43 nendo Ajia, Taiheiyō chiiki taishi kaigi giji yōroku" (Summary of the minutes of the 1968 annual conference of ambassadors to the Asian and Pacific area), October 1968, pp. 27–28, MOFAD; MOFA, *Waga gaikō no kinkyō*, 1966, pp. 66–68.

signatories. Such assurance, Japan insisted, should be authorized in the form of a UN (preferably UNSC) resolution. Furthermore, Japan was extremely critical of the lack of reference to the responsibilities of nuclear powers in the American and Soviet drafts of the treaty. One way to mollify this problem, Japanese officials suggested, was to insert a section in the preface of the treaty indicating that based on the spirit of the UN charter, nuclear weapon holders were prohibited from launching a nuclear attack against a non-nuclear nation.[61]

Though all these requirements were reflected in the final version of the NPT, Japan was still unsatisfied with the outcome of the pact. The reason was simple: The Japanese government felt its own right of utilizing nuclear power for nonmilitary purposes was not secured by the treaty. Once more, the UN provided Tokyo with a convenient podium from which to address this point. In 1966, Japan joined a number of countries in asking the UN to arrange a conference where non-nuclear nations could have their own discussions on the nonproliferation issue. And when the conference, formally named the Non-Nuclear Conference (NNC), was held in Geneva under the approval of the UNGA a month after the NPT's adoption, the Japanese delegation soon became one of the most active participants. The focal point of Japan's argument at the conference was the alleged unequal treatment between nuclear and non-nuclear nations regarding international surveillance of the peaceful use of nuclear energy. The Japanese representative strongly urged the establishment of a surveillance system under which nuclear energy programs of both nuclear and non-nuclear nations would be inspected by the International Atomic Energy Agency. In addition, Japan also asserted that the NPT was insufficient to guarantee that nuclear powers would indeed take actions to effectively reduce their nuclear armaments.[62]

The Japanese government was apparently proud of its performance at the NNC. In a semi-official history of Japan's UN diplomacy edited by MOFA officials, it was noted that "considering the active moves

---

61. "Visit to Japan," November 28, 1967, FCO 21/274, Reel 145, PRO; Gaimushō hyakunenshi hensan iinkai, *Gaimushō*, p. 1158; MOFA, *Waga gaikō no kinkyō*, 1969, p. 116; New York to Washington, September 22, 1967, Box 3189, Subject-Numeric Files 1967–69, NA.

62. Iguchi, *Nihon gaikōshi*, pp. 220–23.

made by Japan and West Germany—both were defeated in the last war and refrained from taking political actions thereafter—the NNC . . . is an international conference that deserves particular attention."[63] Unfortunately, however, this was not the position taken by the nuclear powers. Although Japan worked closely with some other Western non-nuclear nations in seeking a compromise resolution on non-proliferation that would be acceptable to all parties, the nuclear weapon holders found what was going on at the NNC to be nothing but irksome. The three nuclear powers that initiated the NPT talks refused to accept the view that their nuclear facilities should be treated in the same way as those in other countries. The US State Department claimed in a memorandum soon after the NNC was summoned that the conference was "flirting with unrealistic proposals for peaceful nuclear . . . explosives; ironclad guarantees for assurances against nuclear attack or threats; and sweeping commitments for nuclear disarmament." Convinced that the ongoing NNC lacked "focus and expertise," the department told the White House that it "strongly oppose[d] continuation of the conference" after its conclusion. The same opinion was directly conveyed to their Japanese colleagues in New York a month later.[64]

The nuclear powers' resistance made most of Japan's efforts at the NNC fruitless. But this result only intensified the feeling among Japanese government leaders, officials, and politicians that they were being forced by the great powers to swallow a treaty which had been composed without their full participation despite the enormous impact it had on Japan's security interests. The government did not sign the NPT until February 3, 1970—one month before the treaty came into effect. It then took another six years for the Diet to finally ratify the treaty.

Efforts to Revitalize the UN

Japan's policy toward the NPT was a unique case in that it pushed its own ideas through regardless of the reluctance of major Cold War powers. Yet like other cases we have discussed thus far, this one did

---

63. Ibid., p. 223.
64. MOFA, *Waga gaikō no kinkyō*, 1968, p. 152; "The 23rd United Nations General Assembly," September 22, 1968, Box 3178 and New York to Washington, November 6, 1968, Box 3206, both in Subject-Numeric Files 1967–69, NA.

not deviate from the normal policy pattern, in which Japan struggled to let the UN play certain roles in dealing with, if not solving, crucial international security affairs, only to find that the organization's voice was too faint before great military powers. But did Japan ever think about a more fundamental plan through which the UN's peace function per se could be augmented? The answer is yes, though the result was not encouraging.

During the last few years of the 1960s, Japan was impressively energetic in promoting various proposals to revitalize the UN's authority in security spheres. Starting in the early 1960s the Japanese government was attracted to the idea of reanimating the UN's peace function through channels other than the UNSC. One such channel was the magnification of the UN forces for peacekeeping purposes. In 1963, a group of Nordic nations put forth a proposal to set up reserve forces in UN member states for use in PKO. A year later, the USSR announced another plan to establish the permanent UN force which was postulated in the UN charter (Article 43) but had been foiled due to the East-West confrontation. Japan reacted positively to both ideas. In his 1964 UNGA speech, Foreign Minister Shiina Etsusaburō made concrete references to these plans, calling for the "prompt" establishment of a "permanent UN force" and for that force to later be "elevated" into a "UN peace force" in the course of "complete disarmament" among member states. Despite its praise for the plan, however, Japan had strong reservations regarding the Soviet proposal's emphasis on the UNSC's prerogative in commanding the force, since the P5's infighting could easily impede the force's operations. For this reason, it regarded the UN reserve force idea as a proposal to implement before the real UN force could be organized.[65]

Japan's intention to bypass the UNSC was reflected more articulately in Shiina's 1965 UNGA speech, where he unveiled a plan underlining the necessity of implementing the charter's provision for moving the UN's security duty out of the SC whenever the Council did not efficiently function. The Assembly, according to Shiina, must take more peacekeeping responsibilities on such occasions. Furthermore, the Japanese Foreign Minister recommended that the UN Secretary General be authorized to post "permanently" his representatives to each

---

65. MOFA, *Waga gaikō no kinkyō*, 1965, pp. 18–19.

site of international conflict or at least set up "roving institutions of some form" in the areas concerned. In a "given situation or dispute," rather than allowing the UNSC to decide everything, these representatives or institutions were supposed to pursue "certain peacekeeping activities" by request "either of the Security Council or the General Assembly."[66] In 1970, as one element of a new scheme named "Struggle for Peace," Shiina's successor Aichi Kiichi went further, suggesting that a section concerning PKO should be inserted into the UN charter.[67]

None of these intriguing proposals came to fruition, however. As we will find out in later chapters, the UN force plan was unfitted to the domestic political atmosphere in Japan. Prompted by the need to secure a permanent seat in an enlarged UNSC, some MOFA officials did propose to send Japanese personnel to participate in the PKO. But they were countered by political leaders, including some affiliated with the ruling LDP's leadership, who were averse to any attempt that might open the door to sending Japanese forces abroad. The proposal to shift the power from the Council to the Assembly did not leave a longstanding impact on Japan's UN diplomacy either. Again, the UNSC permanent membership bid was one reason, as it made the Japanese government give more attention to the reform of the Council than to reinforcement of the Assembly. But there was another important factor—the rise of the AA Group's influence in the UNGA—that made Japan's position increasingly difficult. And in the mid-1960s, the Assembly was no longer a comfortable place for Japanese delegates.

A "Moderate Mediator"

Japanese policymakers had no difficulty in figuring out the importance of using the UN to ease international tensions. But they ran into various troubles almost immediately when starting to handle tensions involving the AA Group and Western nations inside the UN. As newly independent nations flooded into the UN starting in 1960, the landscape of the organization rapidly changed. The Western camp no longer enjoyed the majority vote in the UNGA and was forced to increase the

---

66. UN Bureau, *Statements Delivered by Delegates of Japan during XIXth and XXth Regular Sessions of General Assembly, United Nations*, p. 36.
67. MOFA, *Waga gaikō no kinkyō*, 1971, p. 399.

number of seats designated to AA nations in the UNSC. Within the Japanese government, MOFA officials had difficulties viewing their country, a rising industrial power in the Western bloc, as one of the small, powerless nations like those in the AA Group. Instead, they shared the suspicions and disgust of many other Western big powers toward the political and economic backwardness of the AA nations. In May 1961, UN Bureau Director Tsuruoka Senjin reported to Prime Minister Ikeda that the AA Group was characterized by different races, a lack of common beliefs, and serious economic underdevelopment and therefore was unable to take any unified action within the UN.[68] A similar but harsher remark was found in a MOFA memo on UN policy prepared for Ikeda's visit to Washington that June:

> Rather than international cooperation, some radical nations in the AA Group are more interested in raising their international status and personal fame or national interests such as the occupation of advantageous positions in conflicts, or the expansion of technical assistance. For these purposes, there is a propensity within them to take the leadership of the group by controlling the atmosphere through emotional, unrealistic and radical arguments.[69]

In August, the government publicized its disagreement with the AA Group in the annual Diplomatic Bluebook: "If Japan's activities [at the UN] based on her fundamental policies result in a conflict with the positions of some of the Afro-Asian nations, so be it."[70] The idealistic aura in Japan's previous UN policies was no longer discernible, and the pragmatic need to protect Japan's own interests at the UN against unfriendly small nations began to outweigh the high-minded plea for "international democracy."

At first, the Japanese government did not take any concrete actions to either isolate radical members in the AA Group or closely ally itself with other Western states within the UN. Being an Asian member of the Western camp, Japan still tried to position itself somewhere in be-

---

68. MOFA, "Ikeda sōri hōbei dai go kai uchiawase."

69. UN Bureau, "Kokuren ni okeru AA shokoku taisaku" (Measures taken within the UN regarding the AA nations), March 1961, A'0361, DRO.

70. MOFA, *Waga gaikō no kinkyō*, August 1961, p. 10; the English translation was quoted from Overseas Public Relations Section, "Blue Book on Foreign Affairs Published," August 25, 1961, FO 371/158483, Reel 101, PRO.

tween. As noted by Japanese Embassy officials in Washington prior to Prime Minister Ikeda's 1961 visit to the US, Japan was willing to undertake the role of "mediator" between Western nations and the AA Group in the UN. Meanwhile, MOFA submitted a memorandum to the State Department urging the US to take note of the seriousness of the anti-Western tendency among the AA states in the UN. The memo made its point by emphasizing the Cold War element. It criticized the Soviet bloc's attempt to use issues of colonialism and racism to "sway Afro-Asians against the West" in the UN as part of its "global diplomatic offensive against the Free World." But instead of treating the AA Group as a follower of the Soviet bloc, the memo recommended that the West be "more flexible" in handling the AA nations in order to win their cooperation. Even in regard to the so-called "radical" members of the AA Group, the memo maintained that the West might need to make some compromise with these nations to avoid driving them into the "common front with the USSR." In sum, MOFA intended to highlight the importance of making the AA Group adopt a "realistic, moderate and fair" attitude at the UN and to reemphasize Japan's mediating role in such efforts.[71]

In 1962, the Japanese government went on to sell its new AA proposal to the British. In a memorandum for Anglo-Japanese policy consultations, MOFA elucidated that it was Japan's basic policy to play a role in the UN as a "moderating power" by "controlling" the "extreme opinions" of the AA Group, and thus contributing to "the settlement of [international] problems in a peaceful manner." But in order to fulfill this role, the memo proclaimed, it was "indispensable and important" for Japan to take a "fair and neutral" position "all the time."[72] In other words, while aware of the threat of the AA Group's provocative attitude toward the West, Japan was also alert to the danger of being too obedient to the West. The role as a "moderating power" or "mediator," in this context, was not a replication of the ambitious slogan of "a

---

71. "Afro-Asian Countries in the United Nations," and "Summary of United States and Japanese Positions Following Preliminary Discussions with the Japanese Embassy," June 16, 1961, in Box 125, NS Files, JFKL; MOFA, "Kokuren ni okeru AA shokoku taisaku."

72. "Second Meeting on Anglo-Japanese Co-operation in Africa," July 1962, FO 371/164973, Reel 110, PRO.

bridge across the Orient and the Occident," but was a proposal of a rather defensive nature.

A remarkable instance of Japan's mediation diplomacy in the UN took place in a regional conflict involving two Southeast Asian states. Since the early 1960s, the relationship between Indonesia and Malaysia (known as Malaya before September 1963) had been tense due to their disputes concerning territories included in the new Federation of Malaysia. This situation deteriorated further in 1962 when a riot occurred in Brunei, then a British protectorate geographically close to Indonesia. The problem later escalated into military confrontation between the two sides and violent attacks in Jakarta against diplomatic facilities of the UK, which was regarded as Malaysia's co-conspirator.

Ever since the issue came to light, the Japanese government had been looking for its appropriate role in calming down the two nations.[73] In 1963, Japan invited Indonesian President Achmad Sukarno and Malayan Prime Minister Rahman Putra to Tokyo for peace talks. In 1964, Prime Minister Ikeda arranged another summit for the two in Tokyo. During these meetings, Japan confined its role to that of an "assistant," not a "mediator," deliberately refraining from intervening in any substantive talks between the two countries. But this cautious attitude was replaced by a more proactive one after all diplomatic efforts failed and the Indonesians decided to walk out of the UN in January 1965, ostensibly because Malaysia obtained a non-permanent seat in the UNSC.

Japanese Prime Minister Satō was stunned by Sukarno's statements hinting his nation might have to leave the UN if Malaysia did acquire a seat at the UNSC. On January 5, before other UN members clarified their positions on the issue, Satō took an unusual move of cabling a personal message directly to Sukarno. The message, which was later described by an American diplomat as "a remarkable letter," was phrased in a unique way. Pointing out Japan's own "bitter experience" that "the withdrawal from the League of Nations led the Japanese nation into a series of great hardships," the Japanese leader urged the Indonesians to reconsider their decision and "thereby display the utmost statesmanship in overcoming minor differences for the attainment of greater common

---

73. Regarding Japan's mediation activities, see Yoshizawa, *Nihon gaikōshi dai 29 kan*, p. 309.

goals."[74] Besides the letter, from January 5 to 8, Japanese Ambassador to Indonesia Saitō Shizuo visited Sukarno almost every day to talk the latter out of taking the final step of withdrawal. Using his expertise on UN affairs, Saitō, the former director of MOFA's UN Bureau, suggested that instead of severing ties with the UN, the Indonesians might choose to "boycott" the proceedings of the organization by "walking out" of the Assembly hall during the period when Malaysia was serving as a UNSC member. Once Malaysia's one-year term ended, the Indonesian representative could then resume his full participation in UN activities. The Indonesian leader, however, made no sign of budging.[75]

Arguing that as a sovereign state his nation could not leave things half done, Sukarno flatly turned down Saitō's advice. In addition, alongside the UN main body, he also declared that he was going to put an end to Indonesia's relationships with a number of UN specialized agencies. The Japanese ambassador was disappointed, yet was willing to make one last bid to save Indonesia's UN seat for two reasons. Since it was difficult for Japan, a nation that officially adopted UN-centrism as a principle for its foreign policy, to maintain a close relationship with a non-member of the UN, Jakarta's withdrawal from the organization would unavoidably hamper Japan's diplomatic endeavors in Indonesia and Southeast Asia in general. Moreover, since Sukarno's decision was welcomed only by some communist states, Indonesia would find itself completely isolated once getting out of the UN. This situation would then push the country toward Asian communist powers, in particular China—the worst scenario Japan could ever imagine. Based on such observation, Saitō wired MOFA his proposal concerning Japan's policy in case the Indonesian president decided to fight to the bitter end. According to him, for the sake of smoothing Indonesia's comeback in the near future, as soon as the UNGA resumed in September that year, Japan must rally the AA group nations to table a draft joint resolution at the Assembly stating that after the "exceptional circumstances" (Malaysia's election to the UNSC) causing Indonesia's withdrawal no longer

---

74. Rangoon to Washington, January 21, 1965, Reel 38, DOS 1963–66; "Satō's Visit and His Regime," January 7, 1965, Doc. 00424, NASF; Personal message from Satō to Sukarno, January 15, 1965, MOFAD.
75. Saitō to Ōta, January 7, 1965, MOFAD.

existed, the UN should welcome the recovery of Jakarta's membership.[76]

Regardless of Saitō's efforts, bad news kept coming in. On January 7, Sukarno formally announced Indonesia's withdrawal from the UN. Four days later, he instructed the Indonesian ambassador in Tokyo to deliver his reply to Prime Minister Satō's personal message. Justifying his decision as an action "in order to give the sense of urgency" to all UN members to reorganize the UN "mentally and structurally fitting to the present-day requirements of the Comity of Nations," the Indonesian leader reiterated his will to leave the UN and viewed it "worth the while for the struggle for the greater ideals of peace, prosperity, social justice and the brotherhood of man."[77] On January 12, MOFA ordered Ambassador Saitō to hold off on taking any further actions aimed at restoring Indonesia's membership.[78]

While Japan was unable to forestall Jakarta's withdrawal, its cooperation with the UN in easing the regional tension caused by Sukarno's decision continued. It was clear that behind the anti-UN rhetoric, dispute with Malaysia was the real reason that gave rise to the clash between Indonesia and the UN. Fully understanding such background, UN Secretary General U Thant was eager to make a breakthrough on this issue. But because of the lack of an official relationship, the UN's role was limited. Japan, a nation which maintained intimate connections with both the UN and Indonesia, thus surfaced as an ideal mediator in the peace process. On January 14, during his meeting with Prime Minister Satō at the UN headquarters in New York, U Thant asked the Japanese government to provide its good offices starting with an ambassadorial meeting between the conflicting parties in Tokyo.[79] Satō readily responded to the request.

The Japanese government started its peace effort through the framework of an AA commission that had been set up through an earlier agreement between Malaysia and Indonesia. In April, Satō sent LDP Vice President Kawashima Shōjirō to Jakarta to attend a ceremony for the tenth anniversary of the Bandung Conference. The real

76. Saitō to Shiina, January 8, 1965, ibid.

77. Letter from Sukarno to Satō, January 11, 1965, ibid.

78. Saitō to Shiina, January 8, 1965; Tanaka to Saitō, January 12, 1965, ibid.

79. Matsui to Shiina, January 14, 1965, ibid.

purpose of the visit was to persuade Sukarno to accept the mediation of the AA commission. Having gained a vaguely positive response from the Indonesians, Kawashima turned to Malaysia for a gesture of compromise. The result of Kawashima's mission was a summit scheduled in early May in Tokyo. Malaysian Prime Minister Rahman arrived in Japan as promised, but Sukarno never appeared. Citing domestic reasons, the Indonesian president cancelled his trip at the last minute.[80]

While having no effect on Sukarno, Japan's mediation efforts paid off when General Suharto started challenging Sukarno's power in the aftermath of an aborted communist coup d'état the dawn of October 1, 1965. Supported by the army, Suharto and his followers were determined to entrench the country in a more pro-Western course and eager to restore Indonesia's seats in international organizations such as the UN, the International Monetary Fund (IMF), and the World Bank. These movements delighted Japan, which became one of the most influential advisors for the domestic and foreign policy planning of the Indonesian government after the coup. But since the situation was still fluid, Japanese leaders were wary of some potential hurdles that might force the Indonesians to slow down their efforts. When meeting with a senior Indonesian government mission in May 1966, Foreign Minister Shiina was anxious to know whether Sukarno, who remained the nominal head of state, had agreed to follow the policy of returning to the UN and other international organizations. Days later, Prime Minister Satō also expressed his concern to the mission that Moscow might blight the peace settlement between Indonesia and Malaysia, which was a prerequisite for the recovery of Indonesia's UN membership.[81]

The UN secretariat had similar fears. While hoping that Jakarta's return to the UN family could brighten the gloomy international situation

---

80. Yoshizawa, *Nihon gaikōshi*, pp. 309–10; Miyagi, *Sengo Ajia chitsujo no mosaku to Nihon*, pp. 129–39.

81. Division of Southeast Asia Affairs, "Hamenku Bono fukushushō no Shiina daijin to no kaidan yōroku" (Summary of a meeting between Deputy Prime Minister Hamengku Buwono and Foreign Minister Shiina), May 25, 1966 and Division of Southeast Asia Affairs, "Hamenku Bono fukushushō no Satō sōri to no kaidan yōroku" (Summary of a meeting between Deputy Prime Minister Hamengku Buwono and Prime Minister Satō), May 27, 1966, E'0054, DRO; Miyagi, *Sengo Ajia chitsujo no mosaku to Nihon*, pp. 225–26.

around the organization, UN officials worried that Indonesia's domestic situation as well as its confrontation with Malaysia might not allow the new leaders to move fast enough in the right direction. Japanese Ambassador Saitō, who by then was considered the most reliable source of information regarding Indonesia not only by his own government but by those of many western powers, was in a comfortable position to offer the UN his assistance. In May 1966, USG Jose Rolz-Bennett met Saitō in Tokyo and told the latter that as a member of UNSC and friend of Indonesia, Japan had the "dual capacity" to take the initiative to encourage Indonesia's recovery of its UN membership. Therefore, the UN would ask Saitō to inform the secretariat when he judged that the appropriate timing to let Indonesia return to the UN was coming. Upon receiving the Japanese ambassador's green light, the UN side would then start the procedure of restoring Indonesia's seat. Having pointed out that Japan should serve as a "bridge between Indonesia and the UN as well as the free world" on the eve of Indonesia's withdrawal, Saitō had no problem accepting the request.[82]

In May 1966, the Indonesian government normalized its relationship with Malaysia. Its resolve to resume Indonesia's duties as a UN member state remained unshaken as well. The only opponent inside the Indonesian government was President Sukarno. But in late August, it became apparent that his resistance was rapidly overwhelmed by the voices requiring the revitalization of a UN-cooperative stance.[83] In the interim, Ambassador Saitō maintained close contact with the new leaders, reassuring the latter that as soon as the Indonesians made up their minds Japan would make a "welcome appeal" in the UN.[84] On September 19, the Indonesian government officially asked for Japan's help in facilitating its return to the UN.[85] Ten days later, with the assistance of Japan and the Philippines, the Indonesian ambassador reappeared in the UNGA as if he had just returned from a long vacation. Despite having itself marched out of the largest prewar international peace body due to a bilateral conflict with an Asian state, Japan quietly lent a hand

---

82. Shiina to Matsui and Takamatsu, May 24, 1966; Saitō to Shiina, January 8, 1965, MOFAD.

83. Saitō to Shiina, August 9, 1966, ibid.

84. Saitō to Shiina, August 25, 1966, ibid.

85. Saitō to Shiina, September 19, 1966, ibid.

to recover the membership of another Asian state in the largest postwar international peace organization.

While Japan was able to play a relatively active diplomatic role in solving the Indonesian-Malaysian conflict by closely working with the UN, it was a singular case. The issue Japan tackled was political or security skirmishes between AA nations in which the US avoided any direct involvement. The UK (or to some degree, the whole British Commonwealth) was initially a target of the Indonesians because of its support for the Malaysians. But the US, which had to take care of its own business in Vietnam, was not enthusiastic about joining the old colonial powers' anti-Indonesia coalition. Such a lukewarm attitude was undoubtedly significant to Japan, who was extremely nervous about keeping the balance in its double-tiered status as an AA nation and an ally of Washington.

Also, the problem between Jakarta and Kuala Lumpur is a regional conflict with no substantial global overtones. Of course, Sukarno's intransigence did cause the first, and for the time being the only, withdrawal of a member state from the UN. Yet Indonesia's action drew almost no specific attention from the majority of UN members. In fact, when Sukarno ordered his delegates to leave the UN, most UN member states were concentrating on the much more urgent problem of applying Article 19 of the charter to the USSR and hence had no time to seriously discuss Indonesia's decision.[86] This, needless to say, created a cozy environment for Japan, which was loath to handle diplomatic issues under great pressure.

It was unfortunate that not all disputes considered within the UN during the 1960s and 1970s met these favorable conditions. As a matter of fact, more often than not, the UN and its member states were compelled to make tough decisions on formidable disputes that tangled the interests of the Oriental and Occidental powers. Japan's role in these cases was less impressive.

Jostled between the AA Group and the West

A classic example of Japan's inability to pursue the role of mediator was again related to Indonesia. Since the early 1950s, the Netherlands and Indonesia competed bitterly against each other for control over the is-

---

86. Kokuren kōhō sentā, *Nihon to kokuren*, pp. 62–63.

lands of West Irian (West New Guinea). The Indonesians claimed that the area at stake, which was then a Dutch colony, was part of its territory. The Dutch fought back in September 1961 by proposing a draft resolution at the UNGA to put West Irian under the management of an "international development authority," which only stirred up Jakarta's anger. Both sides approached Japan for help, but Tokyo's response was a far cry from that of an eager mediator. MOFA senior officials listened politely to the briefings of the two governments and then told them Japan's principal stance: first, the problem should be resolved through peaceful negotiations between the two parties concerned and second, Japan "should not directly involve itself in the conflict."[87]

The Japanese government had to decide its position on the Dutch resolution at the UN, nonetheless. Having failed to devise a solution that would not hurt anybody, the MOFA headquarters wired ambassadors in Indonesia, the Netherlands, Australia, the US, the UK, and the UN for advice. Within ten days, six telegrams with contradictory opinions reached Tokyo: two supported the Indonesians, one mentioned a possible mediation role, and three favored abstention from the vote.[88] The government chose the safest option: abstention. "Though this attitude looks inconsistent," wrote UN Ambassador Okazaki, one of the supporters of this option, "it cannot be helped considering the atmosphere of the UN at the moment."[89]

Japan kept the West Irian problem at a distance until early 1962 when the US altered its stance. In January that year, concerned about a possi-

---

87. Deputy vice foreign minister, "Nishi Nyūginia shori ni kansuru Oranda teian no ken" (Dutch proposal on the treatment of West New Guinea), September 22, 1961, A'0380, DRO; "Southeast Asia Division, "Nishi Irian mondai ni kansuru Kosaka gaimu daijin to Banban Sugen chū Nihon Indoneshia taishi to no kaidanroku" (Record of meeting between Foreign Minister Kosaka and Indonesian Ambassador in Japan Bambang Sugeng on the West Irian problem), January 12, 1962, A'0381, DRO.

88. Ōda to Kosaka, October 20, 1961; Ōno to Kosaka, October 21, 1961; Ōta to Kosaka, October 23, 1961; Asakai to Kosaka, October 25, 1961; Okazaki to Kosaka, October 31, 1961, all in A'0380, ibid.

89. Okazaki to Kosaka, October 31, 1961, ibid.; Western Europe Division, "Nishi Nyūginia kokusaika mondai (iii)" (The internationalization of the West New Guinean problem), November 29, 1961, A'0381, ibid.

ble Soviet intervention in the issue, the Kennedy administration ceased to support the Dutch and decided to push the two sides toward a quick solution through the mediation of the UN Secretary General. In the meantime, Washington also requested its allies, including Japan, to help talk the Indonesian government into this new proposal.[90] MOFA swiftly responded by recommending to the Indonesians that they give favorable consideration to Secretary General U Thant's mission. Six months later, it again suggested that the Japanese government "urge" the UN and concerned nations to redouble their efforts toward a peaceful solution of the problem. But before MOFA's activism could yield any concrete policy, the two conflicting parties reached an agreement with the mediation of the US and the UN. A "UN Temporary Executive Authority" was set up in West Irian and the Indonesians obtained a promise to take over the territory within a few years.[91] In the end, Japan left nothing but the record of three abstentions at the UNGA.

Five years later, Japan yet again failed to play a possible mediator role in another AA-related conflict taken up by the UN. When the Six-Day War between Egypt (then the UAR) and Israel broke out in June 1967, Japan was approaching the final stage of its term as a non-permanent UNSC member state. During the first round of the Council discussions on the war, the Japanese delegate proclaimed that it could only accept a UN resolution that was "neutral."[92] Such an ideal resolution, however, never took shape at the Council and the agenda was moved to an emergency UNGA session in which AA members supporting the UAR held the majority of votes. Unwilling to offend the Arab nations, the Japanese delegation intentionally alienated itself from the Western group and refused to discuss the issue with the Ameri-

90. Ostrower, *The United Nations*, pp. 113–14; Asia Bureau, "Nishi Irian mondai ni kansuru ken" (The West Irian problem), January 18, 1962, ibid.

91. Southeast Asia Division, "Nishi Irian mondai ni kansuru tai Indoneshia mōshiire no ken" (Request to Indonesia on the West Irian problem), January 20, 1962, "Nishi Irian mondai no keii" (The development of the West Irian problem), August 1, 1962, and "Nishi Irian no genjō" (Current situation of West Irian), December 10, 1962, all ibid.

92. Tokyo to Washington, June 9, 1967, Box 2242, Subject-Numeric Files 1967–69, NA.

cans.[93] On June 21, a government spokesman articulated that Japan would like to comply with any decisions expected to be reached by the forthcoming emergency Assembly session "without being hard pressed for any special judgment"—a position which, as confessed by a MOFA senior official later, committed Japan to "almost nothing."[94]

The Assembly ended up with a duel between a resolution submitted by non-aligned AA nations and another one cosponsored by the pro-Western Latin American Group. As usual, Japan found itself torn between the two sides. Rather than seeking a compromise, Japan chose an easier but slightly timeserving path: voting for both resolutions. The US promptly set out to press Tokyo "at the highest appropriate level"—the official meeting between Vice President Hubert Humphrey and Prime Minister Satō—to vote against the AA resolution. But the effort proved fruitless as Satō reiterated to Humphrey that his government needed to keep "neutral."[95] After the vote, Ambassador Matsui explained that Japan endorsed the AA resolution because territorial expansion was unacceptable and Israeli withdrawal from Egypt should be the prerequisite for peace, and the country supported the Latin American resolution as well since it "also provided basis for settlement."[96]

Japan's difficult time did not end with the two positive votes. The emergency Assembly session adjourned without offering any solution, and the case was sent back to the UNSC, where Japan, as a member of the Council, had less room to escape. In September, Japanese Foreign Minister Miki Takeo told US Ambassador to the UN Arthur Goldberg that Japan favored a plan to use Secretary General U Thant as a mediator in the Middle East crisis.[97] One month later, it turned out that it was the new Japanese ambassador to the UN, Tsuruoka Senjin, not U Thant, who was put in the position of conducting the mediation mission. As the President of the UNSC in October, Tsuruoka took no action regarding the Arab-Israeli conflict during the first few days of the

---

93. New York to Washington, June 23, 1967, ibid.

94. Tokyo to London, June 21, 1967 and Ellingworth to Pickles, June 30, 1967, both FCO 21/254, Reel 143, PRO.

95. Washington to Tokyo, June 29, 1967 and Tokyo to Washington, July 2, 1967, Box 3177, Subject-Numeric Files 1967–69, NA.

96. New York to Washington, July 6, 1967, Box 3203, ibid.

97. Tokyo to Washington, September 22, Box 3189, ibid.

month until Goldberg and his deputy Charles W. Yost came to the Japanese delegation's office for help in promoting a resolution drafted by the US and the UK.

Tsuruoka accepted the request and immediately arranged a session to discuss the draft resolution.[98] But as the Council entered into formal debates, he unilaterally brought Japan's active commitment to a halt. Like the emergency Assembly, the UNSC also became a stage for the showdown between a Western draft resolution and counterproposals advocated by the Arabs as well as the Latin Americans. The focal point of the controversy was a seemingly trivial problem. The Western resolution requested the "withdrawal of Israeli armed forces from territories occupied in the recent conflict" but it had to contend against another draft sponsored by the Arabs insisting that Israel "withdraw *all* its forces from *all* the territories of Jordan, Syria and the United Arab Republic occupied as a result of the recent conflict." The Arab nations tried to retain the term "all the territories," while the Western bloc contended that a single word "territories" was enough because it did not want to push the Israelis too hard. Naturally, the Council members asked for President Tsuruoka's coordination. However, having determined that it was not wise to intervene in the dispute, Tsuruoka adhered to an attitude which he dubbed "silentism" (*chinmoku shugi*).[99] Based on this stance, he flatly declined to serve as an arbitrator, arguing that since his mother tongue was Japanese, he found it better to leave the matter to other members from English-speaking nations.[100]

Though "silentism" might have been a comfortable strategy for Japan, the two authors of the West's resolution—Goldberg and British Ambassador Hugh M. Foot (Baron Caradon)—could not afford to watch the endless verbal battles at the Council from the back benches. In the wake of vigorous behind-the-scene consultations led by the two, Council members finally reached an agreement to adopt a draft that was later known as the famous UNSC Resolution 242 on the Middle East Conflict.[101] Tsuruoka was quite satisfied with Japan's policy during

---

98. Kokuren kōhō sentā, *Nihon to kokuren*, pp. 96–97.

99. Ibid., p. 101.

100. Ibid., p. 109.

101. Finger, *American Ambassadors at the UN*, pp. 184–85; Ostrower, *The United Nations*, pp. 122–23.

his presidency. While recognizing that the resolution sprang from "Japan's weakness, honesty and Council members' exhaustion," he later proudly remarked that Japan's "UN-centric diplomacy somehow made its mark" during that session and Japan's "impartial as well as unselfish pacifism was highly appreciated" by nations concerned.[102] This self-evaluation did not seem to be shared by other UNSC members, however. In a report to the British Foreign Office, an official of the UK delegation commented that although Tsuruoka "personally" made a "good impression," the Japanese mission as a whole preferred to "keep their heads down" in the debate on the Middle East. "This is probably the correct policy for them [the Japanese]," the official concluded, "but it has not allowed them to take the lead or make any really bold efforts to find compromise solutions."[103]

Japan was able to cleave to its noncommittal stance, or "silentism," on the Middle East agenda within the UN for another five years or so but not any longer. In October 1973, the Egyptians and Syrians waged a sudden attack against the Israeli fortifications along the Suez Canal. The Fourth Arab-Israeli War broke out. Japan, which just wrapped up its third term as a Council member months earlier, luckily avoided the risk of offending the Arabs and the Israelis (as well as the Soviets and the Americans behind them) during the heated UNSC debates on the war. Nonetheless, it was caught by surprise by a menacing side effect of the conflict: an oil sanction. After the Arabs threatened to stop exporting oil products to nations unfriendly to their cause, the Japanese government judged it necessary to do something to protect its oil supply. At the twenty-ninth UNGA session summoned immediately after the war, Japan cast a positive vote for an AA resolution granting UN Observer status to the Palestinian Liberation Organization (PLO). It also refused to join the Western bloc in voting against another resolution indicating that all natural resources in the Israeli-occupied Arab territories belonged to the Arabs.[104] Japan accompanied these actions with a state-

---

102. Kokuren kōhō sentā, *Nihon to kokuren*, pp. 101–2; MOFA, *Nihon gaikō 30 nen*, p. 71.

103. "Japanese role in the recent Security Council debates on the Middle East," January 3, 1968, FCO 21/254, Reel 143, PRO.

104. Ogata, "Nihon no kokuren gaikō no hensen," p. 287; Nagano, *Gaimushō kenkyū*, p. 208.

ment issued by Chief Cabinet Secretary Nikaidō Susumu announcing that the word "territory" in the UNSC Resolution 242 should mean "the whole territory occupied by Israel" in the recent war, thereby accepting the interpretation that Tsuruoka had refused to commit to in 1967 in keeping with his "silentism."[105]

But the AA nations wanted more. In November 1975, they introduced a more radical anti-Israeli resolution declaring that "Zionism is racism." Japanese UN Ambassador Saitō encouraged MOFA to ask for a postponement of the deliberation because Japan needed more time to study the "substantive" meaning of Zionism. The UNGA, however, had no time to wait. Japan thus proceeded to follow its old pattern during controversial votes, abstention, and became one of two members of the Western bloc (the other being Spain) that did not oppose this resolution.[106] In two years, Japan became categorized as one of the friendliest nations toward the Arabs at the UN. The policy change was amazingly swift, yet it was made not to resolve the wrangles among parties concerned in the area, but simply for the sake of the short-term security of Japan's precious energy supply.

The reluctance to take risks lessened Japan's interest in playing a mediator role during conflicts related to Asian states. But the damage dealt by this problem was still modest compared to the disaster caused by Japan's inability to balance political and economic interests when handling disputes between Western and African nations within the UN.

Targeted by the African Group

Unlike Asian issues, the African problem was a completely unfamiliar agenda to most Japanese foreign policymakers at the turn of the 1960s. When coining the catchphrase "a bridge between the East and the West" in the mid-1950s, few Japanese officials used the word "East" with both Asia and Africa in mind. But Africa became increasingly difficult to ignore as Japan witnessed events like the Egyptian-Israeli and French-Algerian conflicts in the UN. After the Congo incident, the ac-

---

105. Nagano, ibid., pp. 215–16.
106. Saitō, *Kokuren no mado kara*, p. 245; Kokuren kōhō sentā, *Nihon to kokuren*, p. 197.

celeration of decolonization movements in the area south of the Sahara (known as "Black Africa") became a popular topic in Japan as it did in other Western nations. Yet in contrast to their compassion for the suffering of Asian nations, many Japanese decision-makers were less sympathetic toward the course of former Western colonies in Africa. Ambassador to the UN Matsudaira, a France-educated diplomat who declared that he felt "more at home with educated Europeans," used to criticize the Africans and their behavior at the UN to the point of "indiscretion," as one of his European colleagues commented.[107] Matsudaira's boss, Foreign Minister Kosaka, also cynically told the British Foreign Minister in 1961 that he found the Africans were "slothful and slow" and "the UN should give them time to work things out."[108]

Despite the disgust toward the Africans, the Japanese government was aware of the urgency of softening newly independent African nations' positions toward the West. In the early 1960s, aiming at nurturing modest opinions, the Japanese UN delegation courted delegates of the so-called "Brazzaville Group" made up of former French and Belgian colonies in West Africa that were not so anti-Western as some African nations ("the Casablanca Group").[109] When working at the Delegation in New York, then Director of MOFA's UN Bureau Tsuruoka even voluntarily edited a French UN newspaper and delivered it every evening to French-speaking African UN delegates who had trouble understanding English information published by the Secretariat.[110]

In the meantime, Japan reinforced policy consultations with former colonial powers such as the UK. During these consultations, Japanese officials not only cooperated with Western allies in preventing the radicalization of African nations but also emphasized the necessity of making efforts to ease "the primary African grievances" such as economic

---

107. New York to London, June 21, 1961, FO 371/158493, Reel 102, PRO.

108. "Record of Conversation between the Secretary of State and the Japanese Foreign Minister, Mr. Kosaka, at the Waldorf Astoria, New York on Friday, September 22, 1961," FO 371/158497, Reel 103, PRO.

109. Tokyo to Washington, June 21, 1962, 033.9400/6–2162, Box 87, Subject-Numeric File 1960–63, NA.

110. Kokuren kōhō sentā, *Nihon to kokuren*, p. 92.

backwardness or colonialism.[111] Prime Minister Ikeda appeared to be extremely confident when mentioning the African problem during his 1962 visit to London. "There [is] for good or ill a lingering feeling of suspicion in Africa against the white nations," he told British Prime Minister Macmillan. He then relayed Japan's feeling that "as an Asian nation, closely tied to the major nations of the West, she could help to allay these lingering suspicions and act as a bridge between the West and Africa."[112] But at least inside the UN, Japan was never able to build that "bridge."

Beginning in the early 1960s, debates on three African issues—Portuguese colonies in Africa, the South Africa problem, and the conflict over independence for Southern Rhodesia—demanded tremendous energy on the part of the UN and its member states. The Portuguese colonies issue surfaced in the UN in November 1956 when the Portuguese government, in hopes of perpetually preserving its African colonies, denied that the status of these areas corresponded to that of the "non-self-governing territories" whose "administering powers" are obliged to assist the political and economic development there under the surveillance of the UN. The AA Group, then a minority faction in the UN, asked for the appointment of an ad hoc committee to investigate the non-self-governing problem among member states, but met strong resistance from Portugal and other Western allies. Japan joined the Western bloc in 1956 in voting against the ad hoc committee resolution not because it found the Portuguese position reasonable but because the proposed committee's investigation would be confined to new UN members like Portugal and Japan itself, which Tokyo considered discriminatory.[113] In 1957, however, to demonstrate its "UN-centric

---

111. Letter from Campbell to de la Mare, June 21, 1961, FO 371/158493, Reel 102; "Anglo-Japanese Co-operation in Africa," October 10, 1962, FO 371/164973, Reel 110, PRO.

112. "Record of conversation between the Prime Minister and the Prime Minister of Japan at Admiralty House at 3 pm on November 12, 1962," FO 371/164976, Reel 111, ibid.

113. MOFA, "Kenshō dai 11 shō no tekiyō mondai o meguru hi jichi chiiki no teigi yōso oyobi gensoku mondai to Porutogaru ryōdo mondai (dai 6, ketsuron no kan)" (The question of the principles and elements regarding the definition of the non-self-governing territories in relation to the application of Chapter

diplomacy," Japan refrained from opposing the establishment of the committee, though it refused to support the committee either. At the UN vote, Japan abstained on the AA resolution since it did not want the West to perceive a "drastic change" in the Japanese attitude.[114] While discontent with Portugal's uncooperative policy toward the UN, Japan continued to avoid voting for the ad hoc proposal for another few years based on bilateral concerns about its relationships with Portugal, Brazil (Portugal's biggest non-Western ally), and other Western nations. (At a certain point in the late 1950s, MOFA did once consider a possible Japanese mediation between the Portuguese and AA nations. Yet this was never acted upon.[115])

The shift in Japan's policy took place in conjunction with the change in US attitude. The Republican government had stood alongside Lisbon for five years. But the new Kennedy administration was ready to recognize the right of Portuguese colonies—specifically Angola—under the initiative of UN Ambassador Stevenson.[116] The first move was taken in a UNSC session on March 15, 1961, where the US delegation voted in favor of an AA resolution considering the recent disturbance in Angola a situation likely to endanger international peace and security and calling on the establishment of a subcommittee to investigate this case.[117] Though the resolution failed to pass the Council because of the abstention of most Western members, it was sufficient to alter Japan's position. Immediately after the vote, Japanese Ambassador Matsudaira wired Tokyo to ask for permission to sign a letter issued by the AA Group requesting the inclusion of the Angola problem in the UNGA's agenda. Probably understanding that this suggestion might not be compatible with the government's current policy, Matsudaira pointedly reminded MOFA that what the US delegate had done during the Council vote demonstrated Washington's intention to abandon its previous

---

XI of the charter as well as the Portuguese territory issue), undated, A'0277, DRO.

114. Fujiyama to Matsudaira, January 26, 1959, ibid.

115. MOFA, "Rokkakoku iinkai secchi an to kongo" (The proposal of establishing the six-nation commission and its future prospects), November 27, 1957, ibid.

116. Finger, *American Ambassadors*, p. 131.

117. UN Security Resolution S/4769, March 14, 1961, A'0277, DRO.

support of the Western colonial powers' position. "If we refuse to sign the letter," he warned, "we will have to face complete isolation from the AA Group," which welcomed the US stance while hardening attacks against uncooperative Western nations.[118] Without further argument, Tokyo followed Matsudaira's advice.

Japan's pro-AA policy on the Portuguese colony problem was short-lived, however, as the Americans swung back to their traditional stance around 1963. At first, Japanese officials tried to persuade the US to be tolerant of the AA Group's anti-Lisbon stance.[119] They also promised before the Portuguese that Japan could deter the Africans from choosing extreme measures at the UN.[120] Yet those positive actions quickly came to naught when the Japanese saw the American stance become increasingly rigid, whereas the AA nations showed no sign of compromising. What is worse, some African nations began to insert items into their anti-Portuguese resolutions that might hurt Japan's economic interest in the area.[121] In 1965, Japan adopted a strategy of abstaining on (or occasionally voting for) AA resolutions on this subject when they were put to a vote as a whole while casting negative votes on individual items when such resolutions were voted on item by item.[122] In doing so, it was able to keep a symbolic difference from other Western powers that usually voted against relevant resolutions in general, yet in the meantime to immunize itself from the risk of harming its own interests on concrete matters. The government stuck to this stance until all Portuguese colonies in Africa obtained their independence in 1975.

Japan's role during the UN debates on the Portuguese non-self-governing territories fell far short of serving as a bridge between the West and Africa as promised by Ikeda. But to most members of the AA Group, while Japan might not be considered a friend in this case, it

118. Matsudaira to Kosaka, March 16, 1961, ibid.
119. Okazaki to Kosaka, January 29, 1961, ibid.
120. Ōhira to Yoshida, September 11, 1962, ibid.
121. Shiina to Matsui, August 16, 1965, ibid.
122. For several examples, see Matsui, "Question of Portuguese Territories (Explanation of Vote) on 18 December 1965" and Tsuruoka, "Territories under Portuguese Administration (Explanation of Vote)," November 10, 1967, both in ibid.; MOFA, *Waga gaikō no kinkyō*, 1973, pp. 303–4; MOFA, *Waga gaikō no kinkyō*, 1974, p. 144.

was also not villainous enough to be treated as an enemy like Portugal, the UK, or France. In this sense, Japan's fate during the South African and the Southern Rhodesian disputes was much worse.

Discussion on the South Africa problem in the UN was first triggered by the South African government's refusal to put Namibia (then South West Africa)—which it took from Germany as a mandate after WWI—under the UN's international trusteeship system. Starting in 1947, this issue was routinely picked up by the Fourth Committee of the UNGA and the Trusteeship Council.[123] It also became the subject of a famous lawsuit at the ICJ. In 1952, South Africa again caught the attention of the UN when the nation's racially discriminatory policy, known as apartheid, was raised in the Assembly. For the subsequent four decades, the UN deliberations on these two issues made the white minority government in South Africa one of the world's most isolated political regimes.

Japan's initial attitude toward the South Africa problem at the UN was not necessarily unfriendly to the AA Group. In its 1957 maiden statement at the Special Political Committee of the UNGA, Japan solemnly declared that as a nation which had painstakingly opposed racial discrimination in the 1919 Paris Peace Conference and the League of Nations, it had no sympathy toward the South African government in this case. During the 1950s, such denunciations were sufficient to keep Japan in the mainstream of international opinion within the UN. Yet the atmosphere changed in the early 1960s when the AA nations, many of which were disposed to coerce the South African government to admit the equal right of black citizens, began to set the tone for the UN's voice. Japan had extreme difficulty adjusting to this new situation.

While Japan morally condemned the apartheid policy, South Africa was a remote nation for the Japanese both geographically and politically. Only when it considered the problem from an economic viewpoint did Japan feel a bit closer to that part of the world. By 1960, South Africa was already Japan's biggest market in the African continent, absorbing approximately $50 million worth of Japanese commodities every year.[124]

---

123. International Cooperation Bureau, "Kokuren ni okeru Nihon" (Japan in the UN), February 9, 1957, B'0042, DRO.

124. MOFA, "Nana aparutoheito ni kansuru Maraya renpō shushō mōshiire ni taisuru kaitōburi ni tsuite," (Our answer to the request from the prime minister

Around the same period, at the starting point of its legendary high economic growth, Japan's main items of export began shifting from light industrial products to higher value-added goods such as machinery and chemical products, which made the South African market even more alluring.[125] It was at this crucial moment that the AA Group required the Japanese government to join their crusade against South Africa. The request first came on a bilateral level. In July 1960, Malayan Prime Minister Rahman wrote to Japanese Prime Minister Ikeda to ask for the latter's endorsement of a proposal for a regional trade embargo against South Africa. A similar suggestion was made by India a few weeks later.[126] Worried about its own trade relationship with South Africa, Japan courteously declined the invitations while indicating that the UN should be the prime international body to cope with this situation.[127] But when the UN did intervene later that year, the Japanese government soon realized that the organization was not a comfortable arena that would allow Japan to maintain its tepid position pertaining to South Africa.

As noted by a MOFA official in 1965, Japan needed to keep a balance between two policy goals when handling its relations with South Africa: "the preservation of Japan's image among AA nations" and "economic national interests in terms of the South African market."[128] However, the active AA campaign designed to corner the South African authority within the UN made it impossible for the Japanese government to achieve those goals at one time. Shortly after the AA Group sharpened its attack against the South African government at the UN in 1962, the Japanese delegation maintained its traditional policy by supporting the spirit of the AA position while stressing the significance of using "peaceful means." Japanese officials even participated in an AA resolution drafting team, hoping they could foreclose radical actions from

---

of the Federation of Malaya on the apartheid in South Africa), August 16, 1960, A'0284, ibid.

125. Morikawa, *Minami Afurika to Nihon*, p. 22.

126. Rahaman to Ikeda, July 22, 1960 and Ikeda to Matsudaira, September 6, 1960, both in A'0284, DRO.

127. MOFA, "Nana aparutoheito ni kansuru Maraya renpō shushō mōshiire ni taisuru kaitōburi ni tsuite" and Ikeda to Rahaman, August 24, 1960, both in ibid.

128. Suzuki to Shiina, November 9, 1965, A'0274, ibid.

within the Group. The result, however, was disappointing.[129] Japan and the majority of AA nations locked horns on almost every concrete measure devised to press the South Africans to abolish apartheid. The AA Group wanted to level comprehensive economic sanctions at South Africa but Japan opposed the plan, as it was just about to renew trade negotiations with Pretoria. Many AA members also considered abandoning diplomatic ties with South Africa, whereas Japan found it unconstructive to completely estrange that regime. Unable to bridge the gap, the Japanese delegation stepped out of the team and ended up giving the only negative vote among Asian nations on a resolution to set up a "UNGA Special Committee Against Apartheid."[130]

In 1963, the AA Group continued to accelerate their offensive against South Africa within the UN. And the UN deliberation on the Namibian problem in 1965 hastened this trend. Japan, meanwhile, was still desperately searching for a strategy that could satisfy the AA nations while leaving Japanese economic interests in South Africa unscathed. Understanding that its intimate trade relations with South Africa were "a source of some embarrassment," the Japanese government raised its voice at the UN in criticizing the South African government's obstinate refusal to abandon apartheid. On one occasion, the Japanese UN delegate made a statement that was so prickly, it caused a protest by Pretoria.[131] Japan also sent checks to a number of UN foundations assisting black citizens in South Africa and Namibia. "If some $5,000 would somewhat appease the intensely critical attitude of the African nations toward Japan," UN Ambassador Matsui commented in his telegram asking for fund donations, "these could be the most efficient expenses."[132]

On the other hand, when it came to the submission of resolutions, Japan immediately returned to its original position as a grudging but tough negotiator trying to either remove or water down items it per-

---

129. MOFA, *Waga gaikō no kinkyō*, 1963, p. 40.
130. "Visit of Mr. Hōgen on Wednesday, September 4: South Africa and the Portuguese Territories," September 3, 1963, FO 371/170757, Reel 121, PRO.
131. Suzuki to Shiina, October 29, 1964, A'0284, DRO.
132. Matsui to Shiina, November 19, 1964, ibid.

ceived as too "radical" or "punitive."[133] Given the soaring amount of trade between the two nations, Japan firmly guarded the principle of protecting normal business from moral pressures.[134] Within MOFA, Consul General to Pretoria Suzuki Takashi warned the government that trade with South Africa should not be treated in a "thoughtless" way since trade promotion was an "indispensable condition" and "categorical imperative" for Japan's "survival and development."[135] Similar logic appeared in a 1965 official reply to UN Secretary General U Thant's questionnaire concerning regulation of trade with South Africa, in which Japan proclaimed that its imports from South Africa were mostly "indispensable" raw materials and the prohibition of such imports was "bound to have a considerably serious bearing on Japan's economy." Likewise, in terms of exports, the document reiterated that the loss of the South African market would have a "considerably severe bearing" on Japanese textile, heavy, and chemical industries, which were unable to find an alternative market.[136]

Japan's negative response was also buttressed by a legal argument based on the UN charter. According to Article 41 of the charter, it is the UNSC, not the UNGA, that "may decide what measures not involving the use of armed force are to be employed to give effect to its decisions" and "may call upon the members of the United Nations to apply such measures" including "complete or partial interruption of economic relations." Thus, whenever AA nations tried to pressure Japan at the Assembly to halt its business with South Africa, the Japanese delegation would instead ask them to forward the case to the Council.[137] After the AA nations did so, Japan would then use its outstanding

---

133. New York to Washington, September 19, 1963, Box 100, Japan Post Files, NA.

134. MOFA, "Nana seifu no aparutoheito seisaku ni kansuru tokubetsu iinkai ni kansuru ken" (The special committee on the South African government's apartheid policy), March 4, 1963, A'0283, DRO.

135. Suzuki, "Nana mondai ni kansuru waga kuni no seisaku ni tsuite" (Our nation's policy toward the South Africa problem), February 2, 1964, A'0284, ibid.

136. Matsui to Shiina, February 11, 1965, A'0283, ibid.

137. MOFA, *Waga gaikō no kinkyō*, 1966, p. 74; MOFA, *Waga gaikō no kinkyō*, 1968, p. 93; "Statement by Ambassador K. Chiba on the Question of South West Africa, at the Fourth Committee, on 8 November 1963" (Explanation of Vote on

negotiation skill to postpone the discussion at the Council.[138] Even though the agenda was eventually put on the table at a Council session, the situation would still be favorable to Japan since at least three of the P5 members with veto power—the US, the UK, and France—had similar trouble supporting sanctions or a rupture of economic ties with South Africa. In fact, the UNSC never issued a recommendation that could terminate Japan's economic connections with Pretoria.

The lack of a UN resolution authorizing trade embargo allowed Japan to continue its business with South Africa. But such a preferable situation never appeared in Japan's dealing with another knotty African issue: the Southern Rhodesia problem, which engendered a host of UNSC resolutions that were hard for Japan to swallow. As a self-governing dominion of the British Commonwealth, Southern Rhodesia was supposed to gain its independence by the end of 1965. Nevertheless, since the early 1960s, the cleavage of opinion between the UK government and the white minority-led Southern Rhodesian authority in Salisbury concerning the problem of including black majorities in the future regime cast an ominous cloud over the forthcoming independence. The controversy worsened after the British Labor Party led by Harold Wilson took office in 1964. The Wilson cabinet viewed the establishment of a new Rhodesian government consisting of both whites and blacks as a precondition for independence, whereas the Rhodesian leaders would only agree to a regime dominated by minority whites. Prime Minister Wilson considered this problem an internal conflict and desired to resolve it through bilateral negotiations. Southern Rhodesian Prime Minister Ian Smith, nevertheless, showed no room for bargaining and unilaterally declared independence in November 1965. The indignant UK had no choice but to define the government in Salisbury as a "rebel group against the Queen" and asked for the UN's help. On November 20, a UNSC session passed a resolution calling upon all mem-

---

Draft Resolution A/C. 4/L.777) and Tsuruoka to Miki, May 20, 1968, both in A'0274, ibid.

138. Africa Division of the Middle Eastern and African Affairs Bureau, "Dai 17 kai Afurika renrakukai kiroku" (Record of the 17th liaison conference on Africa), May 30, 1967, A'0274, ibid.

ber states "to do their utmost in order to break all economic relations with Southern Rhodesia."[139]

Japan's initial action in regard to the embargo consisted of no more than diplomatic gestures. Wary of suffering economic loss by moving too fast, Japan stressed at the Council that all UN members should take "united actions" in implementing the sanction.[140] It then took almost two weeks to make sure that other nations did faithfully enact the resolution. On December 3, MOFA belatedly announced its plan to stop exporting arms, oil, and petroleum products—all were specified by the Council resolution—to Southern Rhodesia.[141] Yet the announcement was ambiguous when referring to major trading items between the two countries. Japan promised that it would not buy Rhodesian tobacco in the future but refused to scrap the contracts Japanese companies had already signed. Furthermore, there was not a single word regarding iron ores and pig iron, the lion's share of Japan's imports from that country. This halfhearted response forced the Japanese government into a more difficult position when the British government began to push its allies—including Japan—to beef up their sanctions. The UK ambassador in Tokyo went to ask Prime Minister Satō for the latter's commitment to ban Southern Rhodesian sugars, iron commodities, chrome, and asbestos.[142] Satō showed a relatively cooperative attitude, but government officials chose to resist.

With the pretext that Japan's sugar imports were completely unregulated, MOFA and the Ministry of International Trade and Industry

---

139. "Resolution 217 (1965): Adopted by the Security Council at its 1265th meeting, on 20 November 1965," A'0310, ibid.

140. Political Division of the UN Bureau, "Rōdeshia no keizai seisai ni tsuite" (The economic sanctions on Rhodesia), December 18, 1965, A'0311, ibid.

141. MOFA, "Minami Rōdeshia ni taisuru waga kuni no hōshin ni tsuite" (Our country's policy toward Southern Rhodesia), December 3, 1965; Sterling Division of the Economic Bureau, African Division of the Middle Eastern and African Affairs Bureau, and the Political Division of the UN Bureau, "Minami Rōdeshia mondai ni kansuru gaimu daijin kaidan shiryō" (Materials on the Southern Rhodesian problem for the foreign minister's meeting), December 9, 1965, both in ibid.

142. African Division, "Waga kuni no tai Rōdeshia keizai seisai sochi" (Our country's sanction measures against Rhodesia), December 21, 1965, ibid.

(MITI) claimed that there was no way for the government to prevent trading companies from importing Rhodesian sugars based on contracts signed before independence was declared.[143] Regarding iron commodities, Japan made a concession to embargo pig irons while it refrained from taking similar actions against the iron ore that was more urgently needed by Japanese steel enterprises. MITI even told the media that since Japan had done enough to "save the UK's face," it was unnecessary to add iron ore to the sanction list.[144] As for asbestos and chromes, Japanese officials informed the British that the halt of chrome imports was "the most difficult" problem because the main alternative source would be the USSR.[145] The reason for the delay in the embargo of asbestos was more curious. In its instruction to the ambassador in London, MOFA explained that since the major importers of asbestos were small companies without a representative organization, the government had "no opportunity" to dissuade them from business with Rhodesia.[146]

To be sure, Japan was not the only Western power that had troubles in strengthening its embargo efforts. Nations like the US, France, Italy, West Germany, and the UK itself had all tried to evade the damage inflicted by the sanctions to their own businesses.[147] But because of the poor coordination among major businesses, MITI, and MOFA, Japan ultimately became the "biggest leak" (as noted by the British Foreign Office) among UN members (except for South Africa) in cutting trade ties with Salisbury.[148] As late as the first half of 1966, Japanese industries

---

143. "Satō no yunyū teishi ni tsuite" (The import of sugar), December 2, 1965 and Shiina to Shima, March 9, 1966.

144. "Tekkōseki nadono 'kinyū'" (The "embargo" on iron ores, etc.), March 3, 1966, ibid.; Shiina to Shima, May 13, 1966, A' 0310, ibid.

145. Shima to Shiina, March 16, 1966, A'0311, ibid.

146. Shiina to Shima, April 28, 1966, ibid.

147. Sterling Area Division, "Tai Minami Rōdeshia kyōseiteki keizai seisai ketsugi ni taisuru shuyō kakkoku no taido" (Major nations' attitudes toward the mandatory economic sanction against Southern Rhodesia), January 5, 1967, ibid.; Sterling Area Division, "Tai Minami Rōdeshia keizai seisai ni saishite no kikeiyakubun toriatsukai" (The treatment of signed contracts in the event of economic sanction against Southern Rhodesia), January 16, 1966, A'0310, ibid.

148. Shimoda, "Rōdeshia mondai ni kansuru zai kyō Eikoku taishi no Shimoda jikan to no kaidan yōshi" (Outline of the meeting between the British ambas-

continued to import a variety of commodities from Rhodesia.[149] And by the time Japan was finally forced to terminate its embarrassing trade connection with Salisbury in August 1968 in the aftermath of a UNSC resolution "mandating" (not "calling for") an overall economic sanction, it had become the biggest buyer of Southern Rhodesian goods in the world.[150]

The adoption of the new UNSC resolution was just the first act of the drama. Ever since 1967, the Japanese and British governments had been playing hide-and-seek as London charged Tokyo with cheating the international community by tolerating trade with Southern Rhodesia via a third nation. In a pattern typical of this game, officers of the British embassy frequently visited MOFA to report evidence of illegal shipments of Rhodesian goods to Japanese ports. MOFA officials usually promised investigation and forwarded the case to MITI. Several days later, MITI would inform the British via MOFA that the goods concerned were purchased with shipping documents and certificates of origin issued by nations other than Southern Rhodesia (Mozambique, for instance) and hence were not subject to the UN embargo.[151] The Japa-

---

sador in Tokyo and Vice Minister Shimoda on the Rhodesian problem), February 17, 1966, ibid.; *The Rhodesia Herald*, May 17, 1966 and Shima to Shiina, March 16, 1966, all in A'0311, ibid.

149. Sterling Area Division, "Sangatsu mikka no Rōdeshia renraku kaigi ni oite keizaikyoku stālingu chiiki ka ga nobeta kenkai" (Comments made by the Sterling Area Division of the Economic Bureau during the liaison conference on Rhodesia on March 3), March 8, 1966 and Shiina to Shima, June 10, 1966, ibid.; Miki to Tsuruoka, August 30, 1967 and Miki to Tsuruoka, January 18, 1968, both in A'0310, ibid.

150. Uomoto to Miki, June 19, 1968, A'0310, ibid.; MOFA, *Waga gaikō no kinkyō*, 1969, p. 97.

151. Sterling Area Division, "Zaikyō ei taishikan kara no tai Rōdeshia keizai seisai ni kansuru mōshiire" (Request made by the British embassy in Tokyo on economic sanctions against Rhodesia), September 21, 1967; African Division, "Mozanbiku shōgyō kaigijo hakkō no gensanchi shōmeisho ni tsuite" (The place of origin certificates issued by the Mozambique Chamber of Commerce and Industry), February 23, 1968; African Division, "Tai Rōdeshia keizai seisai ni tsuite" (Economic sanctions against Rhodesia), November 4, 1967, January 23, March 18 and April 2, 1968, all in A'0311, ibid.; "Anglo/Japanese Consultations (Item IV (A): African Affairs, Rhodesia)," November 1967, FCO 21/268,

nese UN ambassador claimed that even if the illegal trade behavior did take place, it was the third country, not Japan, that should take responsibility for the infraction of the UN resolution. While highly suspicious of such explanations, the British government (itself by no means innocent of using the same trick to resume the lucrative Rhodesian trade) could do nothing more than find another case with which to renew its protest.[152]

From an economic viewpoint, Japan's policies toward South Africa and Southern Rhodesia in the face of UN sanctions were quite successful, as Japanese enterprises at least maintained their presence in these two promising African markets with the assistance of the government. But such achievement was made at huge political cost. In neither case was Japan able to play even a tentative role as a moderator (not to mention a bridge) between the African and West European nations. On the contrary, Japan's primary concern about economic interests gave rise to negative feelings among the UN members. The Africans resented what they called Japan's "selfish trading purposes" in South Africa. At the UN Special Committee against Apartheid, African delegates denounced Japan's "humiliating" acceptance of a concession by the white minority government to treat Japanese citizens in South Africa as "white" and Japan's "arrogant flouting" of UN resolutions regarding racial discrimination.[153] Japanese trading companies and manufacturers were raised by name as prime collaborators with the Pretoria authority in the committee's report to the UNSC.[154] Similar condemnation was made by the

---

Reel 144; Wilkinson to Maitland, January 15, 1968, FCO 21/274, Reel 145; "Call by the Japanese Ambassador on the Secretary of State on 5 July, 1968," July 5, 1968, FCO 21/260, Reel 143, all in PRO; MOFA, *Waga gaikō no kinkyō*, 1972, p. 240; MOFA, *Waga gaikō no kinkyō*, 1975, p. 197.

152. Tsuruoka to Miki, June 4, 1968, A'0310; Sterling Area Division, "Shogaikoku no tai Minami Rōdeshia seisai no rikō jōkyō" (The situation regarding other nations' implementation of the sanctions against Southern Rhodesia), July 14, 1967, A'0311, DRO.

153. Hitomi to Ōhira, July 12, 1963, A'0283, ibid.

154. Political Division of the UN Bureau, "Aparutoheito tokubetsu iinkai no sōkai oyobi anpori ni taisuru hōkokusho teishutsu ni tsuite" (The plenary session of the Special Committee against Apartheid and the submission of its report to the UNSC), July 8, 1965, ibid.

UN's special commission in charge of the South West African problem.[155]

Japanese delegates at the UN sometimes became victims of African members' Japan-bashing. Ambassador Matsui, for instance, was cornered by Guinean Ambassador Achkar Marof at one session of the Assembly's Fourth Committee. In order to prove that Japan was actually sympathetic toward the cause of the Africans concerning apartheid, Matsui used a family story: that his father, former Foreign Minister Matsui Keishirō fought bravely at the 1919 Paris Peace Conference to insert an anti-racialism clause in the covenant of the League of Nations. But Marof shrugged off this desperate defense, simply telling Matsui that what he would like to know was not "history" but "reality."[156] Years later, another Japanese ambassador, Saitō, had an even more humiliating experience. At an official UN reception, Tanzanian Foreign Minister Salim Ahmad Salim emotionally questioned Saitō about Tokyo's increasing trade with South Africa before a roomful of guests. "While I tried hard to defend myself, I really felt slapped [by Salim] on the face," the seasoned Japanese ambassador bitterly recalled years later.[157]

Japan's reputation regarding the Southern Rhodesian issue was no less miserable. Owing to its aloofness toward the UNSC resolution recommending economic sanctions, Japan's Rhodesian trade was mentioned in a negative way not only by African officials but also by those of its Western allies. The British Foreign Office observed in a 1968 briefing memo that "Japan wished to do the absolute minimum to avoid international criticism with possible trade retaliation" by AA nations while continuing to "hope that a settlement may be obtained irrespective of whether it actually achieves our basic principles or not." In Tokyo, British Foreign Minister George A. Brown candidly told Foreign Minister Miki that Japanese companies were not being prevented from "seeking to frustrate the policy of sanctions" against Salisbury.[158]

---

155. Okazaki to Ōhira, September 11, 1962, ibid.

156. Kokuren kōhō sentā, *Nihon to kokuren*, p. 72.

157. Saitō, *Kokuren no mado kara*, p. 277; Kokuren kōhō sentā, *Nihon to Kokuren*, pp. 210–11.

158. "Visit of Japanese Foreign Minister 15 July, 1968: Rhodesia," FCO 21/277, Reel 143 and "Record of a Meeting between the Foreign Secretary and the

In 1966, UN Secretary General U Thant also joined the anti-Japanese chorus by issuing a report with concrete information about Japan's violation of the UNSC resolutions.[159] As usual, the fiercest protestor of Japan's policy was the African nations. In 1974, the Organization of African Unity (OAU) reproached Japan as the "most notorious" violator of the UN sanctions against Rhodesia.[160]

Dismissed by Both the Orient and the Occident

Beyond such criticisms, the most serious long-term impairment caused by Japan's ill-fated AA policy was the loss of its credit as a reliable partner in both the AA Group and the Western camp. In the early 1960s, Western powers such as the US and the UK had anticipated that Japan would be able to use its unique identity as an industrialized Oriental state to improve the position of the West in the UN.[161] These high hopes faded before long. As early as 1963, British policy planners found that Japan was the "odd man out" within the AA Group and that such an "odd position" had "conditioned" as well as "limited" the role it could play at the UN. They also observed that Japan had "little moral influence in the AA world" and was usually "unable" or "unwilling" to lead AA opinions.[162]

Japanese Foreign Minister at the Japanese Ministry of Foreign Affairs at 3 p.m. on Tuesday, 9 January, 1968," FCO 21/273, Reel 145, both in PRO.

159. *Nihon keizai shimbun*, May 18, 1966.

160. African Division, "OAU no tainichi hinan to sono hankyō (sono ichi)" (The OAU's criticism against Japan and its repercussion), June 18, 1968, A'0310, DRO.

161. "US Policy toward Japan," May 20, 1960, Doc. 00041, NSA; "Draft minutes from the Secretary of State to the Prime Minister on the question of a visit to Japan by the Prime Minister, December 1, 1960," FO 371/150581, Reel 96 and "Japanese Minister for Foreign Affairs: Meeting with the Secretary of State in New York and with the Lord Privy Seal on September 26," FO 371/165024, Reel 117, both in PRO; "Guidelines of US Policy toward Japan," May 3, 1961, Box 125, NS Files, JFKL.

162. "Japan and the United Nations," March 22, 1963 and "Briefs for the Secretary of State's Visit to Japan, March–April 1963," both in FO 371/170759, Reel 121, PRO.

The Americans, on the other hand, took a longer time to awake to the limitation of Japan's role in smoothing the relationships between the AA Group and the West. As late as the mid-1960s, the US government had no doubt that a "bridge" between the two sides would be built by the Japanese at the UN.[163] Ten years later, however, opinions in Washington became more divided. The US embassy in Tokyo still regarded Japan as "our most consistently helpful partner" at the UN. But in the eyes of those working in New York, like Ambassador Daniel P. Moynihan, who devoted himself to a lonely war against the AA Group in the UN, the Japanese UN delegation's performance was "disappointing" for its attachment to a policy of "avoidance of conflict" compounded by "a profound unwillingness to take sides."[164]

Western powers' negative accounts regarding Japan's UN policy were confined largely to words; the AA nations had moved a step further to display their dissatisfaction in actions, particularly during UN elections. Inflamed by Japan's friendship with South Africa, several African nations organized a noticeable protest in 1965 against Japanese candidature in a UNSC non-permanent member election.[165] Japan barely dodged this attack but remained the butt of opposition from the AA Group whenever it entered an important election.[166] The nightmare eventually arrived in November 1978 when Japan was humiliatingly defeated by Bangladesh, a small South Asian nation recently separated from Pakistan, in a UNSC non-permanent member election with a remarkably wide margin. This time, the Japanese not only failed to acquire the majority votes of African and non-aligned nations but could not win the support of Asian members, who refused to select Japan as the Group's unanimous candidate.[167]

---

163. "Implications of Evolving Nationalism for US Far Eastern Policies," February 4, 1965, Box 18, Papers of James C. Thomson Jr., JFKL.

164. Moynihan, *A Dangerous Place*, p. 125.

165. New York to Washington, USUN 200, July 29, 1965; Niamey to Washington, Niamey 53, September 13, 1965; New York to Washington, USUN 955, September 27, all in Box 3306, Subject-Numeric Files, 1964–66, NA.

166. Kawabe, *Kokuren to Nihon*, pp. 216–17.

167. Saitō, "Anpori senkyo haiboku riyū no bunseki," p. 19; Murata Kiyoaki, *Kokuren nikki*, p. 94.

The Japanese government tried its best to placate the public immediately after this shocking loss. Chief Cabinet Secretary Abe Shintarō
told the press that Japan would not change its foreign policy in the aftermath of this defeat.[168] Former Foreign Minister Kimura Toshio, who
was sent by the government to New York as an advisor for the election,
denied the alleged negative effect of the event on Japan's prestige at the
UN. Instead, he argued that the result should be "positively estimated"
since Bangladesh's triumph showed that "international democracy was
accomplished well" in the UN.[169] Though surprising, theoretically Kimura's statement might not be so wide of the mark. The only problem,
though, was that unlike Japan in the mid-1940s or 1950s, Japan in the
late 1970s was a universally recognized great power in the ironic position of defending itself at the UN before the surge of international democracy stirred up by the AA nations. Despite its efforts to hold back
the tide, as a MOFA official privately confessed, it was a westernized
Asian state that was "slowly being squeezed out of the AA Group"
while hopelessly watching the Africans "slipping away to the radical
left."[170]

---

168. *Asahi jānaru*, November 24, 1978, p. 7.

169. Kimura, "Saikentōki no Nihon gaikō," p. 42.

170. "Impressions Gained at the 22nd General Assembly of the United Nations," January 11, 1968, Box 3178, Subject-Numeric Files, 1967–69; "Atmospher-
ics at 27th UN General Assembly," December 27, 1972, Box 3175, Subject-
Numeric Files, 1970–73, both in NA.

๛ 4 ๛
Toward a New Trend?

At the turn of the 1980s, many Japanese government leaders and officials attempted to convince the public that Japan's foreign policy would be substantially different in the coming decade. The prime minister and MOFA senior policymakers vowed on various occasions that they would eradicate the "passive" image of Japanese diplomacy and invest more energy into making "international contributions" so the country could better fulfill its responsibility as a big power or a "helpful" member of the international community.[1] In the field of national security, they also started reshaping the nation's security policy in view of concepts beyond traditional territorial defense. In 1980, a policy advisory group organized under Prime Minister Ōhira Masayoshi's mandate issued a widely circulated paper calling for the reinforcement of Japan's "comprehensive security," a term that became one of the most popular political watchwords of the decade.

None of these thoughts had any immediate influence on Japan's attitude toward the UN, however. The idea of making an international contribution intertwined with the development of UN diplomacy in a rather marginal way. It brought progress in Japanese cooperation with the UN, but only on limited issues such as economic assistance for Indochinese refugees, concerning which Japan was long under pressure

---

1. Ōhira and Takemura, "80 nendai o hiraku," pp. 32–34; Sonota, *Sekai Nihon ai,* pp. 116–26; Gaimushō anzen hoshō seisaku kikaku iinkai (MOFA Security Policy Planning Council), undated document, pp. 12–13, E-10, Dōba Hajime monjo, PSI.

from Western allies for more "burden-sharing."[2] Theoretically, a comprehensive security policy that stressed the importance of pursuing national security through nonmilitary means fit the UN spirit in terms of resolving international conflicts in a peaceful way. Yet the supporters of this policy seemed to be uncertain about the UN's efficiency as a means of materializing their schemes. Most of them, including those serving in Ōhira's advisory group, avoided specific reference to the UN when discussing the mechanism of this idea. Among those who did occasionally mention the UN, some admitted that the organization could be one element of a comprehensive security policy, simply because it was an ideal place for friendly "dialogue" among conflicting nations—a view that MOFA officials had held since the early 1960s.[3] Others explored the possibility in the context of the comprehensive security concept of a closer tie between Japan and the UN in terms of peacekeeping, but on the premise that the UN's decision-making system must be more competent.[4] Consequently, Japan's UN diplomacy on political and security areas during the first two or three years of the 1980s could hardly be regarded as more active than that of the 1970s or the 1960s, specifically in view of the two traditional paradigms—the East-West conflict and the West-AA dichotomy.

As it had done ever since the mid-1960s, Japan adhered to its role as a moderate Western power during the Cold War fights within the UN in the early 1980s. It stood alongside the US and other Western allies to vote for resolutions at the UNGA asking for the withdrawal of Soviet forces from Afghanistan without taking a too provocative stance toward Moscow. For domestic reasons, Japan made several high-principled statements during the first two UN Special Sessions on Disarmament (SSD). In the actual voting, nonetheless, it showed no signs of altering its modest step-by-step disarmament plan and continued casting negative votes on draft resolutions presented by the nonaligned group and the Soviet bloc that required immediate abandonment of nuclear weapons. The Japanese delegation also joined the international

---

2. Ogata, "Nihon no kokuren gaikō no hensen," pp. 290–91; Ōta, "1980 nendai no Nihon gaikō," p. 14.

3. Ueki, *Nihon no seizon,* p. 166.

4. Sōgō anzen hoshō kenkyūkai, *Economisuto ga kaita sōgō anzen hoshō no kōzu,* pp. 205–6.

rally at the UN against the Vietnamese invasion of Cambodia. Yet again, in contrast to other Asian states such as members of the Association of Southeast Asian Nations (ASEAN) and China, it preferred to be relatively low-key in handling this problem.

Japan's relationship with the AA Group in the UN reflected a similar tendency. Having long lost its passion toward the romantic ideal of a bridge between the Orient and the Occident, Japan was basically an onlooker when the UN was searching for clues to resolve conflicts between Western and non-Western powers in areas like the Middle East (Iran and Lebanon) and Latin America (the Falkland Islands). As for Africa, MOFA officials still wrangled bitterly with the Third World in the UNGA over economic sanctions against South Africa while the government in Tokyo tacitly allowed Japanese industries to continue strengthening their business partnerships with Pretoria.[5]

Revamping the UN

Japan's UN diplomacy probably would have remained dormant for the rest of the 1980s if the US had not made its attack on the alleged inefficiency of the UN system. Since the late 1960s, the US government had been frustrated and to a certain degree frightened by the penetration of the Third World's influence within the UN, which generated an immensely strong anti-Western mood in the Assembly and other major bodies of the organization. In March 1970, the US cast its first veto in the UNSC against a draft resolution sponsored by African nations concerning Southern Rhodesia. In 1978, the US walked out of a UN special agency: the International Labor Organization (though it returned to its seat three years later). After Ronald Reagan entered the White House in January 1981, the US relationship with the UN reached its lowest point in postwar history. In 1984, Washington decided to withdraw from the United Nations Educational Scientific and Cultural Organization (UNESCO), one of the oldest UN special agencies and one that counted the US among its founders, accusing the organization of being overpoliticized and financially extravagant. The decision was carried

---

5. Regarding the amount of trade between Japan and South Africa in the early 1980s, see MOFA, *Waga gaikō no kinkyō,* 1980, p. 179; MOFA, *Waga gaikō no kinkyō,* 1981, p. 200; MOFA, *Waga gaikō no kinkyō,* 1982, p. 222.

out in 1985, followed by the withdrawal of the UK and Singapore a year later. The Republican-controlled Congress embarked on its own crusade against the UN, which culminated in the passage of the 1983 Kassenbaum Amendment and the 1985 Gramm-Rudman Act, holding back more than 50 percent of the US payment to the UN budget and many other UN-affiliated institutions. This, coupled with the accumulating Soviet arrears (approximately $205 million by 1986), drove the already fragile UN treasury to the brink of bankruptcy. The UN deficit skyrocketed from $17 million in the mid-1970s to $504 million by the end of 1985, and the US government announced plans to reduce its payment on its assessed contribution by another $112 million the following year.[6]

With the two biggest donors turning their back on the UN, Japan, which was ranked third (or second, if the payments of Ukraine and Belarus are excluded from that of the USSR) on the payment list, automatically became the last resort for the organization. The only question was Japan's will. There were several options available for Japanese policy planners. The easiest one would be a policy in line with the American one. Dissatisfied with the radical policies of the AA Group, as well as the asymmetry between its financial contribution and its inability to join the top echelon of the UN's power hierarchy, Japan had every reason to follow the US lead in the anti-UN campaign. If this had happened, the chances of the UN surviving would certainly have been much slimmer. Another alternative was to remain silent, shying away from any initiative to preserve the UN system. Though seemingly convenient, it also meant that Japan had to continue throwing away money via annual budgetary payments to prolong the life of the gigantic, paralyzed organization. The Japanese government took neither of these options, instead turning to the third and probably the boldest one: to help the UN reshape its administrative and financial mechanism.

MOFA senior officials ruled out the possibility of echoing US hostility against the UN from the outset. "The anti-UN trend among developed countries will lead to the collapse of the UN system," UN Bureau Director Nakahira Noboru warned in a November 1986 public lecture, "and this would conversely bring huge damage to Japan, which is heav-

---

6. Muller, *The Reform of the United Nations*, pp. 33–34.

ily relying on peace and international cooperation."[7] Ambassador Kuroda Mizuo, who served as permanent representative to the UN during the worst period of the organization's crisis, told his audience at a symposium in commemoration of the thirtieth anniversary of Japan's admission to the UN that he still believed in the urgency of "eliminating" the anti-UN tide as well as in the UN's "significant meaning" for "middle powers" like Japan, West Germany, and Nordic nations which "have faith in" the organization's peace missions.[8] Also present was Kuroda's predecessor, Ambassador Nishibori Masahiro, who made a more laconic reference to the subtle discrepancy between Japan's UN policy and those of other great powers:

As a nation that has to maintain a good relationship with all nations in the world . . . Japan's policy, specifically toward the UN, can differ from that of the US and USSR. We are in the position to do our utmost to protect, cultivate and reinforce the UN. And I think this is in our national interest.[9]

In spite of these high-minded remarks, it was obvious that the Japanese government did not relish taking over from the Americans the burden of being the UN's top sponsor. What Tokyo would have liked to do, according to another UN Bureau director, Kadota Shōzō, was to "encourage" the US to "return to its original resolution as the founding father of the UN to protect and nurture the organization for the sake of world peace and prosperity."[10] And the pivot of this policy was not to "protect" but to "reform" the UN or, as noted by MOFA officials, to "get rid of the superfluous flesh" of the UN so that the administrative and financial mechanism of the organization would become "healthier."[11]

Japan's reform package was made public at a very special time: the fortieth anniversary of the UN. Instead of the usual encomium on the UN's achievements, the message delivered by Japanese Foreign Minister Abe Shintarō at the general debate of the fortieth session of the

---

7. Nakahira, "Kongo no waga kuni gaikō to kokuren," p. 13.
8. Kokuren kōhō sentā, *Nihon to kokuren*, pp. 279–80.
9. Ibid., p. 251.
10. Kadota, "Kokuren to Nihon," p. 15.
11. Shuyō kokuren kikan taishi renraku kaigi, "Sekkyokuteki kokuren gaikō no suishin," p. 18; Nakahira, "Nihon to kokuren," p. 104.

UNGA sounded more like a checklist of the organization's failures. His tone was soft, but the words were harsh. "I am concerned that the United Nations system may be losing the unwavering support of peoples around the world," he told the audience, "[because many activities of the UN and its special agencies] are outdated, not urgently needed and even redundant." The "only" way that could make member states "gain the understanding of their peoples and continue their support of the United Nations for many years to come" was "a determined effort toward effective administrative and financial reform so that it can function more efficiently." The initial step of the effort Abe proposed on behalf of his government was the establishment of "a group of eminent persons for a more efficient United Nations," a group to be comprised of individuals from both developed and developing countries who would conduct a "thorough review of the administrative and financial operations" of the UN.[12]

In the last two months of 1985, the Japanese delegation worked with Canada and the Nordic nations to bring Abe's proposal to fruition in the form of a UN resolution. Though some African countries suspected that the plan's hidden goal was to diminish the UN, most member states were not opposed to Japan's initiative.[13] On December 18, the Assembly adopted a draft resolution that mandated the establishment of a "Group of High-Level Intergovernmental Experts" (G-18) to execute the plan.

Before the G-18 commenced its mission, a number of advisory groups on UN reform popped up within and outside the UN with the intent to sway the discussion in the forthcoming group sessions. When the G-18 members gathered in New York in February 1986, a huge pile of documents released by these groups was already there waiting for them. Even worse, most members at the G-18 were not well prepared to address the issues these documents raised. "We requested a vast amount of documentation that few of us had the time or even the desire to read," one member recalled years later, "and we spent a great deal of time in trying to understand just what our task was."[14] Having

---

12. MOFA, *Statements Delivered by Delegates of Japan During the Fortieth Session of the General Assembly of the United Nations,* pp. 16–19.

13. Saitō, "Kokuren kenjin kaigi to Nihon," p. 20.

14. Muller, *The Reform of the United Nations,* p. 47.

led the group into the process, now it was time for Japan to find the way out.

The primary problem for the Japanese government was the policy coordination between American and Third World members of the group. The relationship with the US was not so difficult to handle. The US was evidently consulted by Japan before Abe declared his proposal and was quite eager to see if the Japanese could succeed in streamlining the UN on its behalf. Shortly after Abe's announcement, the US delegation's enthusiastic promotion of Japan's draft resolution at the UNGA was so marked that it prompted the Japanese ambassador to request his American colleagues to "stay quiet for a while."[15] And this seems to have been the only discord between the two nations concerning G-18 affairs.

Communications with the Third World—African nations in particular—were far more painstaking. Apparently, fear of being overwhelmed by the Western members kept the African bloc vigilant about Japan's endeavor. It forced the Japanese delegation to revise a large portion of the original text of the draft resolution establishing the G-18.[16] After the adoption of the resolution, it again threatened to stay out of the G-18 until Japan persuaded other Western allies to allow an increased number of African members in the group. The Western members, who were used to expressing opinions as individuals, were extremely vulnerable in the face of the Africans' solidarity. The US and USSR, for their part, did little more than cling to their official positions while leaving Japan to confront the Africans. As the initiator of the group, Japan had no choice but to take on the role of a go-between.[17] After 67 closed-door sessions, the group finished its final report at the end of August 1986. Whether the 45-page report, which merely enumerated the sometimes contradictory opinions of group members, would be accepted by the UNGA was anybody's guess.

Before the UNGA deliberation started, Japan and some other group member states came up with an idea to use the president of the Assembly, Bangladesh Foreign Minister Humayun Rasheed Choudhury, who favored UN reform, to iron out negative opinions concerning the re-

---

15. Kokuren kōhō sentā, *Nihon to kokuren,* p. 284.
16. Ibid., pp. 284–85.
17. Saitō, "Kokuren kenjin kaigi to Nihon," pp. 24–25.

port.[18] In the general debate, Japanese Foreign Minister Kuranari Masashi littered his speech with all the positive expressions available to exhibit Japan's "wholehearted" support for the group's work. "None of the similar efforts to reform the United Nations in the past has produced as comprehensive and constructive a report as the one submitted by this group," he concluded.[19] The Africans almost immediately rejected that argument. The Ethiopian foreign minister upheld the view that the UN crisis was not "financial" but "essentially political." Calling the Assembly's attention to the lack of "consensus or evident agreement" in the group's report, the Tanzanian delegate swore that his government would "very strongly oppose any proposals" to establish a mechanism infringing upon the "equality of member states" or the prerogatives of the UN Secretary General, "no matter what they are called."[20]

In the face of such sharp confrontations, Japan understood that unless the report could be adopted by consensus, the reforms it proposed would never be ratified by the Third World. The biggest point at issue was the group's suggestion concerning the introduction of a consensus principle on UN budgetary matters.[21] The US, in accordance with the Kassenbaum Amendment, wanted to have weighted voting procedures, but this was not allowed by the charter. Other group members, specifically Japan, persuaded the US to accept the consensus principle, which did not require a vote. But this compromise met resistance by the Third World members, who did not want to relinquish their majority vote. The controversy was finally resolved after another round of arduous negotiations in which both sides agreed to transfer the budgetary discussion to the Assembly's Committee for Program and Coordination (CPC). The Third World accepted the proposal because the draft resolution based on the report reconfirmed the charter's spirit of deciding everything through votes; the Western donors were satisfied with the outcome as the draft also guaranteed that the CPC would take over the budgetary matters while maintaining its current

---

18. Saitō, "Kokuren gyōzaisei kaikaku no sono go," pp. 3–4.

19. Muller, *The Reform of the United Nations,* pp. 58–59.

20. Ibid., p. 76.

21. For a detailed account of this problem, see Saitō, "Kokuren gyōzaisei kaikaku no sono go," p. 4.

"convention" of making decisions based on consensus. A compromise was thus built upon these ambiguous terms. On December 19, 1986, the report passed the UNGA.

Needless to say, this was a happy ending for Japan. Japanese UN Ambassador Kikuchi Kiyoaki took the floor to offer his gratitude for the cooperation of both the advocates and opponents of the report, feeling "most gratified" that the "basic objectives" Japan had in setting up the G-18 had been "fully accepted" in the final resolution.[22] MOFA's Diplomatic Bluebook depicted the resolution as the "biggest achievement of this year's UNGA session" and an "epoch-making event in UN history."[23] In sharp contrast to this euphoric tone, the response of other nations, including those participating in the G-18, was much more cautious, if not negative. As noted by the US delegate, the resolution was simply the "beginning," not the "end," of the reform.[24] While welcoming the endeavors made by the G-18, the Reagan administration did not lift the restraints on the US payment to the UN budget until September 1988. In the interim, Japan still had to do the prodding during UN deliberations on financial problems.

The impact of Japanese efforts in the G-18 was probably more pronounced on Japan's own UN policy than on the UN's financial crisis per se. It was the first time since the late 1950s that Japan had voluntarily stepped forward to solve a sensitive contention between the AA Group and the Western bloc. The deadlock over the UN financial situation also reminded Japan how much it relied on a stable international environment, for which a universal peace organization like the UN was an essential ingredient. Above all, the experience of leading various nation groups almost single-handedly toward an agreement on one of the most intricate UN agenda items was a valuable warm-up for Japanese foreign policy planners, who would soon face the challenge of adjusting their policy to the renaissance of the UN's peacekeeping function in the aftermath of the renewed détente between the two superpowers.

---

22. MOFA, *Statements Delivered by Delegates of Japan during the Forty-first Session of the General Assembly of the United Nations*, p. 84.
23. MOFA, *Waga gaikō no kinkyō*, 1987, p. 241.
24. Muller, *The Reform of the United Nations*, p. 206.

The Restoration of the UN's Peace Function and the Takeshita Initiative

While the UN was struggling hard to wriggle out of its financial impasse, postwar international relations were approaching an historical turning point. After the death of three aging Soviet top leaders in less than three years, Mikhail Gorbachev became the head of the Kremlin in March 1985. During his six years in office, Gorbachev oversaw an unprecedented reform of Soviet domestic and foreign policies. Although his plan precipitated the downfall of the communist empire, the "new thinking" he introduced to Soviet diplomacy had a positive effect on the future of the UN. In 1987, as a step in its reassessment of the UN's peacekeeping functions, the Soviet government approved a payment of $197 million for peacekeeping operations (PKO) that it had been holding back for more than two decades. In New York, Soviet representatives were more cooperative than ever. Proposals for the peaceful solution of many prolonged international conflicts were raised and passed in the UNSC with the consensus of all member states, including the two superpowers. Gorbachev even started mentioning the possibility of strengthening the Military Staff Committee on the Council, an idea that had long been a defunct article of the UN charter.[25]

Having acquired a non-permanent seat in the UNSC in November 1986, Japan was in an advantageous position to sense these changes. The situation around the Council when Japan walked in was a unique one. As the USSR ceased to isolate itself, the mood among the P5 was the best it had been since the late 1940s. On the other hand, in addition to Japan, the Council's non-permanent members included West Germany and Italy, thereby coincidentally gathering in the center of the UN the three major Western powers with common historical backgrounds during World War II. And this trio of former allies turned out to be a leading force in the UNSC's struggle to resurrect peace in areas such as Iran and Iraq.

Japan's efforts at the UNSC received stronger endorsement from Tokyo after a cabinet headed by Prime Minister Takeshita Noboru was

---

25. The USSR had proposed a similar idea of establishing a permanent UN force in the 1960s as a tactic to shadow the lead of Western members on PKO issues. See Chapter 3.

inaugurated in November 1987. Unlike his predecessor, Nakasone Yasuhiro, Takeshita, who was a prominent master of domestic politics, was generally considered a novice of foreign policy. Perhaps with the aim of altering this image, the new prime minister eagerly looked for an opportunity to demonstrate his unknown talent in diplomacy. When he set out to form his first cabinet, Takeshita called the highest ranking MOFA bureaucrat—Administrative Vice Foreign Minister Murata Ryōhei—several times to discuss his idea about a new diplomatic scheme for the administration. The blueprint in his mind, "a Japan contributing to the world," was built around old LDP shibboleths and not creative in itself.[26] It was up to Murata and his men at MOFA to tailor this rough plan into an ambitious diplomatic course.

After more than forty staff meetings, MOFA drew up the proposal which made its debut in May 1988 when Takeshita delivered a speech at the Mansion House in London.[27] Entitled "International Cooperation Initiative," the proposal was made up of three pillars: "strengthening cooperation to achieve peace," "expanding official development assistance (ODA)," and "promoting international cultural exchange."[28] The second and third pillars contained no more than reconfirmations of previous policies; the first pillar, however, encompassed a number of new ideas.

A few weeks after Takeshita returned from Britain, Murata offered a concrete interpretation of the International Cooperation Initiative to a room of business leaders and former ambassadors. The focal points of the first pillar, according to him, were regional conflicts and disarmaments. "The strong power of the US and the USSR in setting a course for [regional] conflicts is declining," he stated. "Thus, besides the US and the USSR, nations like Japan, major European countries and under certain circumstances India, which hold considerable national power, must play a more important role than a decade ago in resolving regional disputes." In the same vein, referring to the recent progress in the negotiations between Washington and Moscow concerning nuclear and regular forces reduction, Murata implied that a consensus among Japan

---

26. Murata Ryōhei, Honma and Tabuchi, "'Kokuryoku' ni ōjita aratana bijon no keisei ni mukete," p. 14.

27. Ibid., p. 15.

28. MOFA, *Waga gaikō no kinkyō,* 1989, pp. 348–49.

and other Western allies on the need to make their voices heard on the big powers' talks was also behind Takeshita's proposal.[29] He provided no further information on how the government was going to accomplish these goals. But what happened henceforth indicated that a somewhat stronger UN would become the main vehicle for the Takeshita cabinet and its successors to carry out the plan.

In June 1988, Takeshita attended the opening debate of the third UN Special Session on Disarmament (SSD III), where he introduced his first plan based on the International Cooperation Initiative: the establishment of an "international nuclear test verification network" managed by the UN. An initial step toward this goal would be a UN conference held in Japan.[30] The proposed conference came about in spring 1989 with the participation of about 100 officials, experts, politicians, and nongovernmental organization (NGO) leaders from more than 30 nations. Two years later, under Japan's leadership, the UNGA adopted a draft resolution on a nuclear test verification system.[31]

The disarmament initiative was just a prelude to a string of new actions in the international security sphere. The core of Japan's plan pertained to regional conflicts, an area that the UN now took care of. A Japanese commitment to the UN's regional peace efforts was made in two dimensions: finance and personnel. As usual, the money came first. In order to ease the chronic shortfall of PKO budgets, Japan made a special voluntary donation of $20 million to the UN in March 1988, of which $15 million was immediately appropriated to the UN observation teams in Afghanistan and Pakistan (UNGOMAP), Iran, and Iraq (UNIIMOG).[32] Another voluntary payment of $60 million to the Office of United Nations High Commissioner for Refugees (UNHCR) and the World Food Plan (WFP) was pledged to strengthen the two UN special agencies' work of refugee relief in conflict areas. The Japanese ambassador to the UN, Kagami Hideo, also advised the UNGA that his government would do everything it could to help the countries suffering from armed disputes "to recover from the devastation of war, achieve eco-

---

29. Murata Ryōhei, "Kawariyuku kokusai jōsei to Nihon gaikō no kadai," pp. 16–22.

30. MOFA, *Waga gaikō no kinkyō,* 1989, p. 354.

31. Kawabe, *Kokuren to Nihon,* p. 107.

32. MOFA, *Waga gaikō no kinkyō,* 1989, p. 53 and p. 58.

nomic recovery and reconstruction, restore stability and improve the living standard of their peoples once the conflicts are ended."[33]

Financial contributions might be an expedient way for an economic superpower without immense military capacities to fulfill its international responsibilities, but it seemed that this time the Japanese government wanted to give the UN something more than money. Since the mid-1960s, MOFA officials had strenuously yet so far unsuccessfully promoted the dispatch of Japanese forces to PKO for reasons not necessarily confined to national security. Such efforts continued after the late 1970s. In April 1979, MOFA established a Security Policy Planning Council where councilors from each bureau of the Ministry could engage in monthly discussions on the nation's diplomatic and security stance. In a mid-term report publicized in July 1980, the members of the Council suggested that, apart from augmenting the security alliance with the US, it was important for Japan to make further contributions to the overall peace and stability of the world community. One way to fulfill this duty, they suggested, was the dispatch of personnel to the UN PKO. Two years later, the UN Bureau made a more concrete proposal for possible legislation to allow PKO cooperation.[34]

None of these plans, nor other similar suggestions, had an opportunity to be reflected in actual policies for most of the 1980s due to government leaders' hesitation to take up this sensitive issue. But when Takeshita looked to MOFA for an international cooperation plan, officials finally came up with a sound rationale to break the logjam.

Contending that the time was right for Japan to contribute not only money but people to the cause of securing international peace, MOFA took swift action to initiate cooperation with PKO in terms of personnel as part of Takeshita's plan.[35] Fearing domestic criticism, the government prudently avoided mentioning military participation in the PKO. What Japan intended to do at the moment, as noted by MOFA,

---

33. MOFA, *Statements Delivered by Delegates of Japan During the Forty-third Session of the General Assembly of the United Nations,* p. 12.
34. MOFA, "Gaimushō anpo seisaku kikakui bunsho," p. 112; Sairenji, "Nihon no kokuren heiwa iji katsudō sanka mondai," p. 39; Political Division of the UN Bureau, "Kokuren ni taisuru waga kuni kyōryoku no kyōka" (The reinforcement of our country's cooperation with the UN), July 26, 1982, MOFAD.
35. Murata Ryōhei, "Kawariyuku kokusai jōsei," p. 25.

was to share "sweat" not "blood" with other UN members.[36] In 1988, two MOFA officials were sent to UNGOMAP in Afghanistan and Pakistan and UNIIMOG in Iran and Iraq. Because of the officials' distinguished performance, both appointments were extended at the request of the UN. In October 1989, after the UN organized a mission to monitor Namibia's transition to independence (UNTAG), Japan took a braver step. Alongside a donation of $13.5 million, 31 Japanese officials were assigned to the mission. This was soon followed by another commitment to provide six observers to the UN election monitoring team in Nicaragua (ONUVEN), whose work would begin in February 1990.[37] From then on, the participation of civilian Japanese personnel in PKO became a routine element of the government's UN policy.

Peacekeeping Efforts in Cambodia

Besides direct cooperation with the UN, at times the Japanese government used other bilateral or multilateral frameworks to bolster its voice on regional security debates at the UN. The peace process in Cambodia was one such case. Surrounded by conflicting neighbors, Cambodia experienced numerous political and military interventions starting in the 1960s. The most recent one originated in the Vietnam War and accelerated after a fanatic self-styled communist regime called the Khmer Rouge came into power in 1975. After slaughtering Cambodian citizens for more than three years, the Khmer Rouge was forced into exile by Vietnam, whose troops stormed into Cambodia and established a pro-Vietnamese communist regime in 1978. Condemning the Vietnamese aggression, the majority of UN members, excluding the Soviet bloc, endorsed a resistance government composed of the Khmer Rouge and other opposition factions. Though the resistance government, officially called the Coalition Government of the Democratic Cambodia, fought a guerrilla war against the Vietnamese and their collaborators, the situation in Cambodia, like many other military skirmishes in the area before,

---

36. Murata Ryōhei, Honma and Tabuchi, " 'Kokuryoku' ni ōjita aratana bijon," p. 15.
37. Soeya, Heirich, and Shibata, *UN Peace-Keeping Operations: A Guide to Japanese Policies,* p. 18; MOFA, *Waga gaikō no kinkyō,* 1989, pp. 91–92.

became a quagmire, as none of the belligerents was able to gain the upper hand in the jungle.

Until the mid-1980s, Japan had taken a moderate stance with respect
to the Cambodian problem. Signs of increased assertiveness appeared
during Nakasone's time in office, as Japan began to offer detailed plans
for the postwar recovery of Cambodia's devastated economy. But the
low profile remained unchanged. Meanwhile, starting with a symbolic
meeting in 1987 between Prince Norodom Sihanouk (president of the
Coalition Government of the Democratic Cambodia backed by China,
the US, and other Western powers) and Hun Sen (prime minister of the
People's Republic of Kampuchea, which was known as the "Heng
Samrin regime," supported by the Vietnamese and the Soviets), the
warring parties in Cambodia gradually headed in the direction of peace
dialogues. In the spring of 1989, a peace conference attended by representatives of the four major Cambodian political factions and other
countries concerned was held in Paris.

Eagerly showing its determination to implement the Takeshita proposal, Japan managed to gain a seat at the Paris conference despite opposition from Vietnam.[38] Unfortunately, the peace conference achieved
no concrete results and was marred by nasty exchanges of personal attacks among current and former enemies. To Japan, what happened after the conference was even more damaging. Disillusioned by the inability of the Cambodian leaders to stop their bickering, Western
powers (especially the US and Australia) decided to hasten the peace
process in a classic way: negotiations among big powers, in this case,
the permanent members of the UNSC. While having no problem with
a more salient role for the UN, Japanese policymakers were extremely
nervous about such an arrangement. "Not belonging to the P5, Japan
was to be physically debarred from the doorway of the peace process,"
as Kōno Masaharu, then chief of the First Southeast Asian Division at
MOFA, put it.[39]

Kōno's boss, Deputy Vice Foreign Minister for Political Affairs Kuriyama Takakazu, shared the frustration. Faced with the P5's initiative,
Kuriyama ordered MOFA's Asian Affairs and UN Bureaus to undertake studies on what would be the best way to restore peace in Cambo-

---

38. Kōno, *Wahei kōsaku*, pp. 27–28.
39. Ibid., p. 38.

dia. Before long, two reports were handed in: The Asian Affairs Bureau proposed to work with the Cambodians to resolve their own problems with the assistance of the UN; the UN Bureau replicated the P5–centered idea. After a bitter argument between officers from the two bureaus at Kuriyama's office, the Asian Affairs Bureau's plan prevailed.[40] Although the Asian Bureau regarded their plan as a countermeasure to the dominance of the P5, Kuriyama had no illusion that Japan could outdo the big powers on this problem. He understood that the Cambodian conflicts would eventually end under the framework of the UN, that the P5 would impose their peace package on the parties involved, and that they would need Japan's money once the deal was done. Kuriyama upheld the Asian Bureau's idea not because he wanted to compete with the UN but because he needed to secure a role for Japan more significant than that of a financier in a P5–manipulated peace negotiation. "If Japan had not carried out its diplomacy [regarding Cambodia] proactively," he remarked later, "the US would not have felt it worthy to have serious policy talks with us even though we are allies."[41]

From the fall of 1989 to the spring of 1990, Kuriyama made several trips to Washington and Hanoi to sell the so-called Japanese Plan. At the same time, First Southeast Asian Division Chief Kōno flew to Phnom Penh to talk with senior officials of the Heng Samrin regime. The US, which considered the Phnom Penh authority a "puppet" of the Vietnamese, chafed at Japan's peace initiative. In Washington, Assistant Secretary of State for East Asian and Pacific Affairs Richard Solomon called the Japanese ambassador to protest MOFA's recent approach, which he thought might send the wrong signals to Phnom Penh and Hanoi and disrupt the P5's endeavor.[42] But the American resistance did not last long. Having been notified by Japanese officials that they would not simply "watch the game [the P5's negotiation] and then clean the stadium," the US softened its tone.[43] As predicted by Kuriyama, while Washington was probably annoyed by Japan's initiative, it could be disastrous if they failed to get Tokyo to take out its

---

40. Ibid., pp. 46–49.

41. Kuriyama, *Nichibei dōmei: Hyōryū kara no dakkyaku,* pp. 22–23.

42. Ibid., p. 23; Kōno, *Wahei kōsaku,* pp. 52–53.

43. Kōno, ibid., p. 56.

checkbook after the P5 worked out their solution. During the first half of 1990, the US government thus gave tacit consent to Japanese shuttle diplomacy until it reached its apex—a peace conference held in Tokyo with the participation of Thailand and all the belligerents of the Cambodian civil war.

The P5 did not sit idly by, of course. Beginning in January 1990, they quietly sped up their discussions in New York and Paris. On August 28, the five powers released a draft peace pact that became the basis for further negotiations in and outside the UN. In September, the UNSC adopted two resolutions supporting the P5's peace pact, while the Heng Samrin regime and its opponents continued to negotiate their terms for peace. In October 1991, in accordance with the two UNSC resolutions, delegates from 19 nations, including Japan, met in Paris to sign a comprehensive peace agreement for Cambodia. More than eleven years after Vietnamese troops occupied Phnom Penh, the upheaval in Cambodia reached its finale.

In the eyes of officials at the MOFA Asian Affairs Bureau, this outcome was by no means satisfactory. Despite all the passion the officials had for the Japanese Plan, the P5 eventually generated a peace treaty by themselves in a closed-door agreement. From the perspective of Japan's UN diplomacy, however, the result was more meaningful. MOFA had succeeded in reminding the P5, specifically the US, of Japan's potential to influence the situation in Cambodia. Throughout the P5's semi-clandestine diplomacy, Japan was put in a peculiar position. It had the opportunity to lay out its thoughts on the Cambodian problem through pre-consultations with the US whenever the P5 convened to prepare their draft for the peace pact. It was also invited along with a small group of nations to receive briefings regarding the progress made by the P5. American officials even told their Japanese colleagues that in relation to Cambodia, the US thought of Japan as "the sixth permanent member of the UNSC."[44] These words were by no means an exaggeration, as Japan started shouldering peacekeeping responsibilities in Cambodia that were heavier than most of the P5.

When the UN Secretariat was still busy preparing for its mission in Cambodia, it already became clear that Japan would play a role far more vital than that of a checkbook. In January 1992, the newly elected UN

---

44. Ibid., pp. 251–52.

Secretary General Boutros Boutros-Ghali designated a Japanese UN official, Undersecretary General (USG) Akashi Yasushi, as his special representative to lead the UN Transitional Authority in Cambodia (UNTAC): the largest and most ambitious PKO that the UN had ever conducted. Japanese Foreign Minister Watanabe Michio immediately called Akashi to offer him Japan's full-scale support. Akashi, on the other hand, informed Tokyo that the UN wanted to see Japanese assistance in both financial and personnel aspects. Regarding the latter, he made a specific reference to "police forces."[45] The Cambodians also spoke up. In January, Sihanouk told Japan Socialist Party (JSP) chairman Tanabe Makoto that his nation needed Japanese military forces' help in implementing the peace process. A more powerful appeal came from Prime Minister Hun Sen—the leader of the Heng Samrin regime, who had built an intimate relationship with MOFA. During his visit to Tokyo in March, Hun Sen asked Japanese political leaders to coordinate their views in order to make it possible to dispatch Japan's Self-Defense Forces (SDF) to the UNTAC, warning that the UN's inability to obtain sufficient troops for the Cambodian PKO would eventually "get the country mired in confusion" again.[46]

These external movements occurred just in time for the Japanese government, which had foreseen the possibility of sending personnel to cooperate with PKO in the Cambodian peace process years before and was currently struggling to get PKO legislation adopted.[47] Three months after Hun Sen's visit, the Law Concerning Cooperation for UN Peacekeeping Operations and Other Operations, which allowed the participation of SDF personnel in PKO for non-combat purposes, passed the Diet. In September, the first group of SDF officers arrived in Cambodia. By May 1993, more than 1,300 Japanese personnel had worked for the UNTAC, about half of whom (including 600 military engineers and eight observers) were from the SDF.[48]

---

45. Leitenberg, "The Participation of Japanese Military Forces," p. 21.

46. Ibid., pp. 22–23.

47. Suzuki, "Kokuren heiwa iji katsudō to Nihon," p. 6.

48. Soeya, Heirich and Shibata, *UN Peace-Keeping Operations,* p. 24.

The End of the Cold War

With the strengthening of Japan's engagement in the UN's peacekeeping mission came a notable change in the government's views of the UN's political and security function. By 1985, the main concern of Japanese leaders and officials was the UN's weakness in coping with military disputes and its own organizational crisis. The start of the new détente between the two Cold War leaders around 1986 and its impact on the UN's activities did instill a ray of hope, but the Japanese government remained cautious. While calling attention to the progress made by the UN in ending conflicts in Afghanistan, Iran, and Iraq, the 1989 edition of MOFA's Diplomatic Bluebook still concluded that whether these movements could "bring new dynamism to the UN" would have to be proven "through its activities in the future."[49] In 1991, the bluebook changed its tone, indicating that the UNSC was "gradually restoring its proper functions," paving the way for the "revitalization" of the organization.[50] A more positive prediction appeared in the 1992 edition: "[W]ith the end of the Cold War, it is clear that the role of the United Nations has become more important than ever, as signified by the efforts UN Peacekeeping Operations deployed worldwide are undertaking in trying to solve conflicts."[51] Vice Foreign Minister Owada Hisashi went even further to suggest the construction of an "international coalition" with the UN in its "center" to prevent any violation of the UN charter and challenge to the peaceful order of the world.[52] Since the announcement of the UN-centric principle in 1957, this was probably the most optimistic expectation aired by a senior Japanese policymaker in regard to the UN's security function.

The dramatic change in the international situation contributed to Japan's active cooperation with the UN in the political and security spheres from the mid-1980s on. But it was also noteworthy that this development did not automatically eliminate some of the dilemmas

---

49. MOFA, *Waga gaikō no kinkyō*, 1989, pp. 50–51.
50. MOFA, *Diplomatic Bluebook*, 1991, p. 78.
51. MOFA, *Diplomatic Bluebook*, 1992, p. 59.
52. Owada, "1992 nen no sekai jōsei to Nihon gaikō," p. 13.

that had baffled Japanese UN policy planners for decades. The collapse of the USSR discharged Japan from its awkward supporting role in the Western camp's diplomatic campaigns against Moscow and its satellites. Yet in the UN Japanese officials still faced the ghost of the Cold War. The confrontation's end did not wipe out the tension among holders of nuclear weapons, for instance. In the UN as well as the CCD, negotiations became even more protracted, as nuclear powers not only were unable to resolve problems among themselves but gradually lost their influence over nations who eagerly tried to join the nuclear club. Japan's record on this issue during the 1980s and the early 1990s was not as impressive as that of its PKO activities. Japanese policy toward the nuclear weapons test ban during this period reminded UN members of its active stance in the early days, but its overall position on the issue remained rigid. There was little evidence showing that Japan was willing to make any concessions on its basic disarmament principle, which underscored the balance of power among nuclear states (that is, the P5). Whether this attitude could be sustained in the post-Cold War era was not an easy question for the government to answer.

The same thing could be said about Japan's relationship with the AA or the Third World members of the UN. The Third World problem had not been high on the agenda of Japanese UN diplomacy since the early 1980s. Japan and the AA Group still did not see eye to eye on many issues raised in the UN, ranging from South Africa to the abandonment of nuclear weapons. The only difference was that, having been hit by the debt and food crises in the 1980s, most AA nations were economically too fragile to devote themselves to a diplomatic showdown with Japan, who had opportunely strengthened its ODA toward the Third World. The success of its financial strategy ushered in the most uneventful period of Japan's relationship with the AA states. But the temporary economic impasse in AA nations did not remove the existing political and security disputes among them. Nor did it prevent new conflicts from taking place, as exhibited by the sudden increase in regional conflicts and international terrorist activities. Without the backing of the two Cold War superpowers, states involved were more likely to bring these problems into the UN and thereby test the diplomatic sagacity of major members of the organization, including Japan. But at the moment when the red flag had just disappeared from the roof of the Kremlin, the Japanese government was hardly ready to meet such challenges. The international environment around the UN changed with the collapse of the USSR; the old problems left by the Cold War, however, perpetuated and would continue to motivate Japan's UN diplomacy in the years to come.

PART II

The UN and Japanese Party Politics

❧ 5 ❧
The UN and Domestic
Policies in the Occupation Era:
Developing a Security Formula

The UN, as the sole universal peacekeeping institution, may not have been entirely successful in preventing or resolving major international disputes during most of the Cold War era. Yet inside postwar Japan, the organization was undoubtedly one of the best defensive weapons during the relentless fighting among (and within) the nation's conservative and revolutionary parties on crucial political and security issues. In the international sphere, more often than not the UN was a source of conflict rather than a place to find resolution of conflicts. And the principles postulated in the UN charter were often criticized as too lofty and ambiguous to deal with complex international situations. On Japan's domestic political scene, however, these alleged shortcomings served to guarantee the popularity of the UN among politicians for half a century. The origin of such a paradox was found in the US-Japan military alliance—the foundation of postwar Japan's national security.

Putting the Security and Peace Treaties
into a UN Framework

During the winter of 1948, Japanese domestic politics underwent an important transition. In October, after the resignation of an unstable coalition government, the conservative Democratic Liberal Party (DLP) led by former diplomat Yoshida Shigeru made a comeback to become the ruling group in Japan's national politics. Winning a landslide victory in the Diet election the following January, the DLP became the first postwar ruling party to enjoy a clear majority in the House of Representatives (the Lower House).[1] Its competitors, ranging from the middle-of-the-road Democratic Party to the left-wing Japan Socialist Party (JSP), lost a large proportion of their seats. (The JSP was only able to secure about a quarter of the seats it had obtained in the last election.)Yoshida won the election, but this did not immediately mean that he and his party could also come out on top in another important campaign the coming year: the campaign for a formal peace arrangement for Japan.

Amid the turbulence of the Cold War, the year 1949 witnessed a series of historical events that changed the fate of the international community. On April 4, the US and its allies took a decisive step to block the threat of Soviet ground forces in West Europe: the formation of the North Atlantic Treaty Organization (NATO). In September, the USSR responded to the West's offensive by conducting a successful nuclear explosion. In the meantime, Moscow's comrade in East Asia, the Chinese Communist Party (CCP), exiled the American-sponsored Nationalist government from the nation's capital and established a new socialist regime, the People's Republic of China (PRC), in the world's most populous country on October 1. "The Chinese People have stood up," said CCP Chairman Mao Zedong at the PRC's commencement ceremony. But to the US, what had risen up was not the Chinese people but the threat of a chain reaction of communist penetration in the Asian continent. East Asia, which was an onlooker when the Truman Doctrine was declared two years earlier, rapidly grew into a second battlefield of the Cold War.

Leaving aside the sensational but somewhat belated debates on who had "lost China," US policy planners were compelled to protect what they still held in Asia. Nationalist China, the proposed defender of the postwar Asian order, had been unable to fulfill its duty because of prolonged civil wars. And Communist China now became the destroyer of such an order (at least in the eyes of the Americans). Japan, once the biggest military power in the Far East and currently a defeated nation under the exclusive occupation of the US, was Washington's choice as the alternate. But before being able to pursue the role of the West's prime collaborator, Japan first needed to take off its straitjacket—the

1. Kitaoka, *Jimintō,* pp. 43–44.

Allied occupation. In fact, the US had already started loosening its management of Japan around 1948 when the civil war on the Chinese mainland reached the tipping point. But with the hurdle of Soviet resistance to the conclusion of a peace treaty, the best the US authorities could do in Japan for the rest of the 1940s was to create a situation that was portrayed as "a de facto peace" or "a peace without a peace treaty."

The Communists' victory in 1949 prompted the US to make formal arrangements for a peace treaty concerning Japan. In September, the US and the UK agreed to cooperate with each other on affairs pertaining to the Japanese peace treaty. In January 1950, Secretary of State Dean G. Acheson told the Senate that the US government was going to make a peace settlement with Japan even without the USSR's endorsement. In May, President Harry S. Truman appointed John F. Dulles to take care of the treaty issues. The outbreak of the Korean War in late June did not delay the move toward the treaty's conclusion. Instead, the war strengthened the US conviction that an independent pro-Western Japan could offer the free world a much safer foothold in the Far East.[2] On September 14, Washington announced its decision to begin official talks with Tokyo on a peace treaty.

The Japanese government had been waiting for the green light for peace negotiations ever since the end of WWII, as we have already seen in Chapter 1. The US-led movement toward peace thus naturally garnered a positive response in Tokyo. In order to achieve an early independence, Japan had to decide its position on two critical problems: the format of the peace treaty and arrangements for the nation's security. The government already had its answers for both questions ready by the time the first US mission for the treaty talks arrived in Tokyo. As an astute politician who had spent decades in the Foreign Service, Prime Minister Yoshida had no illusion that the USSR would accept a peace proposal allowing Japan to remain in the Western bloc. The only possible way to acquire a quick independence, in his judgment, was to conclude a peace treaty exclusively with the Western allies. In doing so, Japan would automatically posit itself opposite the USSR and its geographically adjacent Asian comrades. Needless to say, such a choice would put enormous pressure on the question of Japan's national secu-

---

2. Sakamoto, *Nichibei dōmei no kizuna*, pp. 23–24; Nishimura Kumao, *Nihon gaikōshi 27*, pp. 62–64.

rity. Yoshida's idea for how to resolve this problem was to leave the nation's defense to the US, whose troops would continue to be stationed in Japan and be able to use military facilities within Japanese territory. To the Japanese government, this solution killed two birds with one stone. The presence of the US troops would substantially alleviate the government's burden of maintaining large military forces on its own, something which Yoshida thought his government was unprepared to do. Satisfied to see its military privileges secured, the US would also be more anxious to hasten the peace process. In May 1950, Yoshida sent one of his henchmen, Finance Minister Ikeda Hayato, to Washington and clandestinely conveyed this proposal to the US side.[3]

Yoshida's idea might have been the best for preserving the interests of the conservative regime and the free world. But before being adopted as a formal policy, it still had to deal with the complicated reaction of the nation's public opinion. The format of the peace treaty proved to be acceptable to the majority of the Japanese people. Until the Korean War most Japanese, specifically intellectuals, preferred an "overall peace" with all WWII allies to a "separate peace" with the Western bloc.[4] Nevertheless, what occurred in Korea during the last few months of 1950 seemed to convince the Japanese that an overall peace was extremely unlikely at the moment, as the two blocs were on the verge of an overall war. A September 1950 *Asahi shimbun* poll showed that only 21 percent of the Japanese people endorsed an overall peace, whereas those favoring a separate peace jumped from 21 percent ten months earlier to nearly 50 percent. Six months later, in a similar poll by another major daily newspaper, while supporters of the overall peace rebounded to a level of 57 percent, only 21 percent of the interviewees believed such a peace could be realized under the current circumstances.[5] In other words, while theoretically preferring an overall peace, most Japanese at least began to admit that if they wanted Japan's independence sooner, not later, they had to choose the other option. The shift was subtle and passive, but it was promising enough to sustain the Yoshida cabinet in the face of attacks from left-wing opponents championing an overall peace.

---

3. Miyazawa, *Tōkyō—Washinton no mitsudan*, pp. 52–56.
4. Yokota and Otaka, *Kokusai rengō to Nihon*, pp. 58–60.
5. Hirose, ed., *Tōyō daigaku shakaigaku kenkyūjo*, p. 22.

Compared to the separate peace, the government's US-centered security proposal was much more difficult to justify to the public. According to three public opinion polls undertaken during the fall of 1949, more than half of the Japanese people were willing to defend their country through methods other than a military alliance with a specific foreign power.[6] But, as had happened in the peace treaty case, the Korean War made many people change their minds. An August 1950 *Mainichi shimbun* poll, for example, demonstrated that cooperation with the US, which earned the support of some 44 percent of the interviewees, became the most favored option for national security.[7] Yet it seemed that the form of US-Japan security cooperation envisaged by ordinary people and that devised by the government were quite different. The government proposed to let the US forces remain on Japanese territory and maintain their own bases. The public, however, had no intention of going so far. In various polls undertaken by the press from late 1950 to early 1951, most answerers stated that they would allow the US forces to remain in Japan only "for a certain period," and they opposed the presence of US military bases.[8] It was the task of policymakers in MOFA and the Liberal Party (LBP; the DLP changed to this name in March 1950) to bridge this gap between the two sides.

Long before Yoshida offered his plan to Washington, the Japanese government, in particular MOFA, had already worked out a general proposal regarding Japan's future security policy based on military assistance from the US. Anticipating adverse public sentiment, MOFA originally attempted to confine the stationing of US troops to some small islands outside Japan proper.[9] But this idea lost its relevance upon the introduction of Yoshida's new plan to locate the US forces within the Japanese home islands. Now the government and the ruling party had to seek out a sound explanation by which to persuade the public to

---

6. Ibid., p. 23.
7. Nishihira, *Yoron chōsa ni yoru dōjidaishi*, p. 300.
8. Ibid.
9. Treaties Bureau, "Heiwa jōyaku kankei sagyō ni tsuite" (Operations regarding the peace treaty), December 28, 1949; Treaties Bureau, "Majoriti pīsu ni okeru anzen hoshō ni kansuru kihon hōshin an (kaitei ban)" (Draft proposal on the basic principles concerning security under a majority peace, revised version), December 3, 1949, B'0008, DRO.

accept the reality of having US military personnel and facilities in their country on a considerable scale notwithstanding the occupation's end. Soon it became clear that the UN would play a key role in the government's effort in this regard.

Considering the bent of public opinion, it was not surprising to see the government toy with the idea of using the UN to justify a security arrangement with Washington that included the stationing of US troops in Japan. By June 1950, the preferred alternative for future national security as reflected in public opinion polls was permanent neutrality—a policy that the Yoshida cabinet had no way of following. The second-best choice was a UN-centered security policy or a collective security system based on the UN charter.[10] A security scheme depending on the UN was virtually dismissed by the government in 1947 after the Ashida Letter incident (see Chapter 1). But as the UN's peace spirit was still widely regarded as the foundation for Japan's new constitution, the symbolic, if not substantive, usefulness of the organization in Japan's foreign policymaking did not completely disappear. The Korean War provided MOFA officials and LBP politicians a golden chance to re-package their security proposal under this UN framework.

Miyazawa Kiichi, then a young LBP Diet member and a top advisor to Finance Minister Ikeda, confessed years later that when he accompanied Ikeda to Washington to sell Yoshida's US-Japan security alliance proposal, he and his colleagues were not confident that they could gain sufficient domestic support. Just then, the Korean War broke out. "Then something called the 'UN forces' appeared for the first time in the world's history," he recalled, "and this undoubtedly forged a thought, which was more acceptable to the public both emotionally and practically, that Japan's security after the peace was protected not by the troops of the US but by those of the UN." Given the high support rate the UN-centered security proposal continued to enjoy in media polls after the war, Miyazawa and other party members now had a better idea about what they needed to do.[11]

Having received Yoshida's instruction to draft a Japanese proposal for the peace treaty, MOFA officials were also sensitive to the pro-UN

---

10. Hirose, *Tōyō daigaku shakaigaku*, p. 23.

11. Miyazawa, *Tōkyō to Washinton no mitsudan*, p. 59; Nishihira, *Yoron chōsa ni yoru dōjidaishi*, p. 247.

tendency among the public. Like LBP politicians, MOFA policy planners acknowledged the value of the UN in easing the public's apprehensions concerning a military alliance with the US. In the meantime, as professional diplomats, they were also sympathetic toward the public's so-called "allergy" to a security system dominated by the US and therefore hoped that the UN could somehow guarantee the equality of their nation's future relationship with Washington. But under the circumstances of the late 1940s, in hopes of achieving a quick peace and an earlier independence, MOFA officials had to give more attention to the UN's function of setting the public at ease than its possible role in balancing American predominance.

After President Truman's declaration of the commencement of formal peace talks with Japan, MOFA started its preparation of the peace treaty text in September 1950. On October 4, it delivered its first set of reports, code-named "Operation A" (*A sagyō*), to Yoshida. In these documents, MOFA officials echoed the prime minister's idea of maintaining national security through a US-Japan "special agreement" which, in their view, must be separated from the peace treaty so that the stationing of American troops in Japan would not be considered a principal condition for its independence. In addition, this bilateral security treaty with the US should be concluded within the framework of the UN charter.[12] "The [security agreement's] connection with the UN must be as intimate and concrete as possible," one of the documents read. "This is important from the political viewpoint as well as that of current public emotion."[13] A more detailed explanation was found in another memo meant to be handed to Washington:

It will be a tremendous contribution to the unification of public opinion if we could make it clear that the stationing of US troops in Japan is one component of the UN's security measures. The Japanese people were deeply impressed by the UN's efficient actions during the Korean War, even though it was an aggression against a non-UN member, and henceforth hold particularly strong

---

12. MOFA, "Taibei chinjutsu sho" (Briefing paper submitted to the US), October 4, 1950, in MOFA, ed., *Nihon gaikō bunsho: heiwa jōyaku teiketsu ni kansuru chōsho (dai 1 satsu),* pp. 660–61.

13. MOFA, "Beikoku no tainichi heiwa jōyaku an no kōsō ni taiōsuru waga hō yōbō hōshin (an)" (Principles of our request regarding the US draft proposal on the peace treaty with Japan, draft proposal), October 4, 1950, ibid., p. 650.

expectations toward a security guaranteed by the organization. . . . If we could clarify the correlation between the stationing of the US forces and the UN, even though the UN-guaranteed security means nothing but locating American troops on Japanese soil, this would appear to be the same as the fact that the UN forces saving the Republic of Korea (ROK) during the Korean War were actually American forces. We believe that the majority of the Japanese people will agree to uphold this [proposal].[14]

MOFA had come up with two options to enact this proposal. The "ideal way" would be a UNGA resolution stating that "the UN mandates the US to take appropriate measures to maintain Japan's security." If this proved unavailable, it would be necessary at the very least to characterize the security treaty on the basis of Article 51 of the UN charter, which admits the "inherent right of individual or collective self-defense if an armed attack occurs against a Member of the United Nations, until the Security Council has taken the measures necessary to maintain international peace and security."[15] Upon Yoshida's request, MOFA submitted a draft of the US-Japan Security Treaty (known as "Operation B" or *B sagyō*) on October 11 containing both options.[16]

Yoshida's response toward "Operation A" was not encouraging. "These worthless arguments are beneath notice," he scribbled on the cover of one MOFA report.[17] The impact of such unrelenting criticism on policymakers was enormous but not sufficient to alter their belief that the security treaty and the UN should be closely linked. The only concession they were willing to make was to concentrate on the Article 51 proposal while shelving the ideal option of requiring a UNGA resolution, which they knew was difficult to achieve.[18]

In a memo dated October 13, just two days after they heard Yoshida's criticism of Operation A, MOFA officials repeated their warnings that if there was no "discernible difference" between US troops stationed in Japan and the previous occupation forces, "disappointment

14. MOFA, "Taibei chinjutsu sho (an)," p. 661.
15. MOFA, "Beikoku no tainichi heiwa jōyaku an" (The US draft proposal on the peace treaty with Japan), p. 650.
16. MOFA, "Anzen hoshō ni kansuru Nichibei jōyaku an" (Draft proposal on the US-Japan treaty concerning security), October 11, 1950, ibid., p. 682.
17. Nishimura Kumao, *Nihon gaikōshi*, p. 81.
18. Sakamoto, *Nichibei dōmei no kizuna*, pp. 37–39.

and anti-American feelings would easily erupt from the Japanese people." One way to avoid this situation, the memo suggested, was "to insert provisions [into the security treaty] that the US forces are UN forces for the sake of Japan's security based on the UN charter."[19]

One of the best-organized interpretations of MOFA's plan in this respect was made by Nishimura Kumao (former director of the Treaties Bureau and the head of the Ministry's treaty draft team) in a book chapter published by an LDP think tank in the mid-1960s. According to Nishimura, he and his aides designed a treaty framework with four steps. First, "When the UN has determined that an aggressive act toward Japan has taken place, the US will take action to deal with the invasion." In the second step, since Japan has the right of individual self-defense granted by Article 51 of the UN charter, it can cooperate with the US to repel aggression through "any possible means." Then, Japan and the US would declare their rights to pursue "collective self-defense," again authorized by Article 51. Finally, the Japanese government would appeal to the public that in order to take responsibility for maintaining Japan's defense in accordance with the UN charter, it was necessary to locate US forces on Japanese territory. In sum, MOFA was going to depict the US-Japan Security Treaty as a legal mechanism for the two nations to fulfill their duties in preserving world peace based upon the principle of the UN charter. "There is no country whose people would welcome foreign troops to be stationed in their land," Nishimura acknowledged. "But if we had to create a security system accepting foreign military forces while keeping public resistance to its lowest level, it could be nothing more than the aforementioned four-step treaty formula."[20] Be that as it may, the US was not prepared to swallow a treaty governed to such an extent by Japan's domestic considerations.

On January 26, 1951, Special Presidential Representative Dulles arrived at Tokyo's Haneda Airport accompanied by Assistant Secretary of the Army Earl D. Johnson, US Minister to Tokyo John M. Allison, and other aides. A six-month-long diplomatic play between the two nations commenced. The negotiation (or "consultation," as Washington offi-

---

19. MOFA, "Heiwa jōyaku taian (an)" (Counterproposal on the peace treaty, draft proposal), October 13, 1950, B'0010, DRO.
20. Nishimura Kumao, "Nichibei anzen hoshō jōyaku no seiritsu jijō," pp. 207–8.

cially conceptualized it) was conducted in accordance with a topic list prepared by the US side covering thirteen items, which ran the gamut from territorial and security issues to fisheries and cultural relations.[21] For both sides, the security agenda was the most critical and energy-consuming part of the negotiations. Japan's initial position on this issue was summarized in a MOFA memo passed to Dulles on January 30, one day before the latter's second meeting with Yoshida. The statement was very brief: "(1) Japan will ensure internal security by herself; (2) As regards external security, the cooperation of the United Nations, and especially of the United States, is desired, through appropriate means; (3) Any arrangement for this purpose should be made apart from the peace treaty, as providing for cooperation for mutual security between Japan and America as equal partners."[22] Dulles's response was brief as well. Without mentioning the UN, he generally agreed that Japan needed to protect itself from external aggression to a considerable degree through a collective security system.[23] But within a few days, MOFA officials would come to realize that the US understanding of the connection between the UN and Japan's national defense was in fact totally different from theirs.

On February 1, MOFA submitted a memo titled, "Formula Concerning Japanese-American Cooperation for Their Mutual Security"—a duplication of Nishimura's four-step treaty proposal—to Dulles's aides.[24] The next day, a counterproposal was returned from the US side. This time, a short paragraph affirming "the inherent right of individual or collective self-defense" of the two treaty parties based on Article 51 of the UN charter was included, but there were still no words about the concrete correlation between the Article and the presence of the US troops and bases in Japan. Instead, the draft contained another new

---

21. "Suggested Agenda," undated, in MOFA, *Nihon gaikō bunsho: heiwa jōyaku no teiketsu ni kansuru chōsho (dai 2 satsu)*, p. 122.

22. MOFA, "1951 nen 1 gatsu 30 nichi senpō ni kōfu shita 'waga hō kenkai' (eibun)" ("Our comments" submitted to the US side on January 30, 1951, English), January 30, 1951, ibid., p. 145.

23. MOFA, "1951 nen 1 gatsu 31 nichi dai 2 ji kaidan memo" (Memorandum on the second meeting held on January 31, 1951), January 31, 1951, ibid., p. 148.

24. MOFA, "Formula Concerning Japanese-American Cooperation for Their Mutual Security," February 1, 1951, ibid., pp. 161–63.

section reading, "Both governments have agreed in the [t]reaty of peace that armed forces of the United States shall remain in the Japan area for this purpose [to preserve Japan's security and existence] until a superseding security arrangement acceptable to the United States government is adopted in pursuance of Article 43 [regarding the UN members' duty to offer military assistance to the UNSC's peace mission] or other appropriate Articles of the charter of the United Nations, or until other suitable arrangements are effected."[25]

On February 5, Ushiroku Torao, a member of the MOFA treaty draft team, sent a personal memo to Treaties Bureau Director Nishimura, claiming that the US proposal not only embodied no close connections with Article 51 but was instead a "naked US-Japanese alliance" devised before Japan was capable of taking actions according to Article 43. In addition, he reminded Nishimura that "a close tie between the US forces stationed in Japan and the UN should be acceptable for the US side and is necessary to secure the support of as many Japanese people as possible, or neutralize the opposition, toward this [security] treaty."[26]

Before Ushiroku's memo reached Nishimura's hands, MOFA senior planners had already laid this problem on the negotiation table. On February 6, the Dulles mission unveiled for Japanese officers a revised draft treaty. Except for the title—"Agreement Between the United States of America and Japan for Collective Self-Defense Made Pursuant to the Treaty of Peace Between Japan and the Allied Powers and the Provisions of Article 51 of the Charter of the United Nations"—Article 51 was found nowhere in the text of the draft.[27] Nishimura and Vice Foreign Minister Iguchi Sadao promptly questioned their American counterparts on this inconsistency. The US side, in return, pulled out a telling weapon: the Vandenberg Resolution.[28] In June 1948, the US Sen-

---

25. "Agreement Concerning Japanese-American Cooperation for Their Mutual Security," February 2, 1951, ibid., p. 175.

26. Ushiroku, "Ushiroku no ikensho" (Ushiroku's comment), February 5, 1951, ibid., p. 498.

27. "Agreement Between the United States of America and Japan for Collective Self-defense Made Pursuant to the Treaty of Peace between Japan and the Allied Powers and the Provisions of Article 51 of the Charter of the United Nations," February 6, 1951, ibid., p. 216.

28. Ibid., p. 70.

ate had adopted a resolution sponsored by Senator Arthur Vandenberg recommending that the president pursue a series of policy objectives based on the UN charter including the association of the US with "regional and other collective arrangements as are based on continuous and effective self-help and mutual aid, and as affect its national security."[29] Using this resolution, the Dulles mission contended that since postwar Japan was not constitutionally allowed to have military forces, it was not qualified to conclude a collective security treaty with the US based on Article 51, as it could not engage in "continuous and effective self-help and mutual aid."[30]

The Japanese side did not make further rebuttal during the meeting. But MOFA officials soon began to sense the seriousness of the problem. On February 7, the chief of the Treaties Division, Takahashi Michitoshi, forwarded Ushiroku's memo to Nishimura along with an attachment he wrote himself. Like Ushiroku, Takahashi expressed grave concern about the US draft devoid of any reference to Article 51. "Article 51 was the last line acceptable to us," he told Nishimura. "If we cannot even have this [Article 51], I do not think it [the treaty] can be justified."[31] The warning came a bit late, however. The meeting between Yoshida and Dulles on February 7 was the last one scheduled during the latter's stay in Tokyo. On February 11, the US mission left Japan to consult with other Allied powers about peace treaty matters. Before his departure, Dulles issued a statement in which he once again noted that "all regional or collective security arrangements of a definitive character, to which the United States becomes a party, must provide for 'continuous and effective self-help and mutual aid' by all of the [p]arties in accordance with the basic policy laid down by the 'Vandenberg' Senate Resolution."[32] The US stance seemed to be unyielding, but MOFA was not willing to give in.

---

29. "Resolution of the United States Senate ('Vandenberg Resolution')," June 11, 1948, ibid., p. 306.

30. Nishimura Kumao, *Nihon gaikōshi*, p. 94.

31. MOFA, *Nihon gaikō bunsho: heiwa jōyaku no teiketsu ni kansuru chōsho (dai 2 satsu)*, p. 499.

32. "Ambassador J. F. Dulles' Statement Issued Shortly Before His Departure for Manila," February 11, 1951, ibid., p. 282.

The recess of the Yoshida-Dulles talks gave Japanese policymakers the time they needed to carefully review the points at issue regarding the security treaty. On March 16, MOFA submitted to the State Department an English memo enumerating Japan's comments, in which the Article 51 problem was raised among seventeen items concerning the security treaty. The old argument was reiterated: "This [a]greement is considered a regional arrangement under Article 52 of the UN charter, while the military action by the United States armed forces in Japan is based on Article 51 of the same [c]harter." Therefore, "in order to clarify the relationship between this [a]greement [and] the UN [c]harter," a paragraph must be inserted into the preamble of the security treaty reading, "The United States, recognizing that an armed attack on Japan affects the peace and security of the Pacific area and of the United States, is presently willing to maintain certain of its armed forces in and about Japan" with the condition that Japan would also increasingly assume its own defense responsibility.[33] On April 4, MOFA received the answer: No. "Our suggestion for revision has been rejected as was expected," Nishimura noted in a memo that very day, "and now it becomes very clear that the title [of the treaty] . . . is not consonant with the text."[34]

Nishimura's judgment about the contradiction between the title and the text was accurate. Yet he and other MOFA negotiators made a strategic mistake when trying to reemphasize this point to their American counterparts. On April 16, Dulles returned to Tokyo to resume his talks with the Japanese government. Prime Minister Yoshida, who considered the security treaty a settled issue, had limited the topics of his meeting with the US side to other matters regarding the peace treaty.[35] MOFA officials, nevertheless, were eager to seize this chance to make a last-ditch bid for a satisfactory reply from the Americans on Article 51.[36]

On April 17, the MOFA treaty draft team persuaded Yoshida to let them present a memo concerning the gap between the title and the

---

33. MOFA, "The Japanese Government's Views and Requests on the Initiated Documents," March 16, 1951, ibid., p. 501.

34. Ibid., p. 541.

35. Yoshida Shigeru, *Kaisō jūnen dai 3 kan,* pp. 120–21.

36. MOFA, *Nihon gaikō bunsho: heiwa jōyaku no teiketsu ni kansuru chōsho (dai 2 satsu),* p. 458.

content of the US security treaty draft. MOFA first remarked in this memo that the American view related to the Vandenberg Resolution was "fully understood by the Japanese government." It went on to stress their conviction that Article 51 should be mentioned in the text even though Japan might not have sufficient military power for the time being. According to the original plan, the memo would be ended by pressing the Americans to reword the preamble of their draft in the context of Article 51. For some unknown reason, in the course of reviewing the memo draft shortly before its submission, MOFA officials added one sentence to the conclusion: "In case, however, it should prove impossible to alter the text of the Paragraph [of the Preamble] in question, it would seem necessary to reconsider the title of the present Agreement." This addition was superfluous to Japan, but to the US, it was a windfall.[37]

US officials accepted the memo on April 21 and politely promised to study it in Washington. There was no record indicating that the US made a formal reply to the memo. But it did answer Japan's question in an indirect way. On June 28, the State Department presented MOFA its updated draft for the security treaty with a much shorter title: "Security Agreement between the United States of America and Japan." US Minister Allison told Vice Foreign Minister Iguchi that the change was made "upon Japan's request."[38] In other words, of the two alternatives proposed in the MOFA memo, the US chose the easier one: altering the title.

During the last few months of the negotiations, MOFA officials were never able to revive the Article 51 question in relation to the text of the treaty. Meanwhile, they still felt the pressure of domestic public opinion. The interpretation of the treaty, in this schema, became their last hope. For the sake of aiding the ratification of the peace and security treaties, MOFA bureaucrats tailored an unofficial interpretation of the two treaties to distribute among Diet members. At the beginning of

---

37. MOFA, "Nichibei kyōtei an no seishitsu ni tsuite" (The character of the US-Japan agreement), April 4, 1951, ibid., p.602; MOFA, "Concerning the Character of the Proposed Japanese-American Agreement," April 20, 1951, ibid., p. 638.

38. MOFA, *Nihon gaikō bunsho: heiwa jōyaku no teiketsu ni kansuru chōsho (dai 3 satsu)*, p. 82.

the interpretation, they called the readers' attention to the points that, first, the security treaty was a "regional arrangement" as defined in the UN charter and second, as declared in the peace treaty, "any nation may enter into collective security arrangements."[39] Then, in contrast to the initial four-step proposal, they did not insist that the security treaty was a mutual arrangement in accordance with Article 51. Rather, the officials proclaimed that although Japan could not take the responsibility to defend the US as Article 51 postulates, US military actions taken for the sake of protecting Japan from foreign aggression were actually based on the Article. The logic was explained as follows:

In the event such an attack [against Japan] did occur, US forces in Japan will naturally retaliate at once. It is granted that [the] US can take military measures without first referring to the UNSC only by way of exercise of her inherent right of self-defense, as stated in Article 51 of the UN Charter. And such is the present case because an attack against Japan will constitute an attack against US forces stationed in Japan. Through exercising their own right of self-defense, they [US forces in Japan] contribute to the defense of Japan.[40]

Fujisaki Masato, who replaced Takahashi as chief of MOFA's Treaties Division, delivered the draft to his counterpart at the US mission, Richard B. Finn, for comments. Finn asked several questions that indicated he was bewildered by the passion Japan attached to the UN charter. Fujisaki's answer was lacking in novelty: "There is a strong interest among the Japanese people in the connection between the UN and the treaty."[41] But this time, the US did not corner Japan. A week later, Finn called Fujisaki to inform the latter that he thought the interpretation was "generally reasonable" and would forward it to the State Department.[42] No further contact ever came from the Americans on this issue. So long as the treaty text per se remained unscathed Washington did not much care about what the Japanese government might say to their people.

---

39. Ibid., p. 746.

40. MOFA, "Interpretation (3)," July 30, 1951, ibid., p. 747; Sakamoto, *Nichibei dōmei,* pp. 59–60.

41. MOFA, *Nihon gaikō bunsho: heiwa jōyaku no teiketsu ni kansuru chōsho (dai 3 satsu),* p. 748.

42. Ibid., p. 750.

The US government's tolerance hardly consoled Japanese officials, nonetheless. When recollecting the negotiations a decade later, the retired Nishimura was still haunted by a sense of failure:

In order to make the security treaty acceptable both externally and internally, we decided to articulate by any means possible that the security relationship between Japan and the US was congruent with the spirit of the UN charter— the constitution of international politics—and the principles of the Japanese constitution. The two nations had to agree that they established their special cooperation under the sacred banner of the UN and station the troops [in Japan] so as to efficiently fulfill their duties to this end. All paragraphs representing these thoughts were crossed out [from the treaty].[43]

The UN in the JSP's Counterproposal for Peace and Security

While the conservative government was unable to link the security treaty with the UN charter during diplomatic negotiations with the US, its fate in this regard was by no means worse than that of the opposition parties, many of which also tried hard to link their security platforms to the UN in one way or another.

The most influential domestic critic of the government's policies on the peace and security treaties was the JSP, which was the third biggest faction in the Diet in the early 1950s. With the backing of public opinion, the JSP held the position that a peace treaty must be concluded between Japan and all the Allied Powers concerned, including the USSR and China. It also opposed the idea of leaving Japan's security to a military alliance with a specific foreign nation, preferring demilitarized neutrality.[44] While none of these arguments matched the government's stance, the two sides had one point in common, at least outwardly: the emphasis on the UN.

Ever since its foundation in November 1945, the JSP consistently advocated Japan's participation in the UN. Furthermore, it was the first political party that declared in the Diet its endorsement of a direct link-

---

43. Nishimura Kumao, "Nichibei anzen hoshō jōyaku," p. 211.
44. Nihon kyōshokuin kumiai, *Kōwa mondai shiryō*, pp. 119–20.

age between the UN and Japan's security.[45] Yet as the left-wing factions of the party gradually gained power, the JSP's enthusiasm for the UN waned. In December 1949, it announced its general policy concerning the forthcoming peace negotiations, which gave higher priority to the neutral character of the Japanese constitution and required all Allied Powers to guarantee Japan's neutrality. Regarding the UN, on the other hand, the announcement simply mentioned that the party was "willing to" join the organization's collective security system while underscoring that this should not jeopardize Japan's neutral stance.[46]

But before JSP leaders could pursue this new policy, the Korean War pushed them back to the UN-centered course. Keeping an eye on the coming peace and security talks with the US, the LBP government, which had been skeptical about the UN's peace function, vowed to cooperate with the UN shortly after the UNSC voted to intervene in the Korean conflict. The JSP, for its part, took the position that although the majority of the UNSC viewed the North Koreans as invaders, the LBP cabinet's policy to actively cooperate with the UN forces in Korea was "imprudent," for this might embroil Japan in international disputes and hence violate the spirit of the constitution which prohibits war as a means of solving international conflicts.[47] At the same time, the party also began to acknowledge the difficulty of adhering to the neutrality scenario given the current international tension in East Asia. The abolition of the neutrality course was not a solution, since it would force the JSP to give up its status as a modest revolutionary party by aligning itself with the conservatives to support the West or joining the Communists to assist the East. What the party needed was a security formula that could make the current neutral policy look more practical.

The optimal way to reach this goal was found in the UN. In its new security scheme—"Theory and Practice toward Peace"—published in July 1950, JSP leaders insisted that the best means to defend the nation was to affiliate with the UN's collective security system while being exonerated of all duties unharmonious with the neutrality principle. On the other hand, they made a cunning amendment to the party's previ-

---

45. Nihon shakaitō seisaku shingikai, *Nihon shakaitō seisaku shiryō shūsei*, p. 10; Shimizu, *Chikujō Nihonkoku kenpō shingiroku dai 2 kan*, p. 92.
46. JSP, *Shiryō—Nihon shakaitō 50 nen*, p. 94.
47. Ibid., pp. 99–100.

ous platform, adopted in 1949. In the 1949 platform, UN collective security was intended to be a supplement to a strict neutral policy. The
updated scheme, on the contrary, denied such a correlation. "We must
step forward from the so-called permanent neutrality type of security
by making efforts to join the UN and receive the organization's global
collective security," as it read. "This means that we are not mere permanent neutralists but are supporters of global or overall collective security. People should understand that we are definitely not isolationists
or ignorant nationalists as labeled by some, but are progressive interna-
tionalists."[48]

JSP's theoretical campaign did not compel the government to draw
back from its proactive policy regarding Korea. In a white paper issued
on August 19, MOFA proclaimed that the UN "has swiftly come forward to take effective measures with the unanimous support of the
democratic world." Under such an emergency, it continued, the Japanese people needed to make a choice about the future security of their
nation:

Thus, we must choose between two courses: Either we abandon hopes of fully
achieving democracy in our country and bow to the communist world, or we
give the United Nations the strongest possible cooperation and, thereby, build
a peaceful and democratic Japan under United Nations' guarantee of security.
The war for democracy in Korea is nothing less than a war to protect democracy in Japan. Without giving today the United Nations forces, which are fighting in Korea, all possible cooperation, how can Japan assure her own security
for tomorrow?[49]

The escalation of the government's propaganda aroused JSP leaders'
vigilance to the danger of being viewed as reluctant concerning UN cooperation. Something had to be done. In late August, JSP Secretary
General Asanuma Inejirō, a member of the right-wing faction, started
hinting that the party might allow labor unions under its control to engage in "economic cooperation" with the UN's efforts in Korea.[50] On
September 7, Director of the JSP's Department of Foreign Affairs Sone

48. Nihon shakaitō seimu chōsakai (JSP Policy Affairs Research Council),
"Heiwa e no riron to jissen" (Theory and practice toward peace), July 1950,
Asanuma Inejirō monjo, NDL.
49. Public Information Division, *Our Position in the Korean Conflict*, pp. 14–15.
50. JSP, *Shiryō—Nihon shakaitō 50 nen*, p. 100.

Eki—a former diplomat and a right-wing faction leader—drafted a memo to local party units regarding UN cooperation. Denouncing North Korea's invasion of the South, the memo asked the party's supporters to embrace the UN resolutions on the Korean problem, not only "spiritually" but also through "actions" in fields such as manufacturing and transportation. With the security scheme freshly publicized in July, Sone had no difficulty justifying this recommendation. "As noted in 'Theory and Practice Toward Peace,' our neutral position means that we are not going to seek security through confrontational military alliances, nor are we satisfied with the so-called permanent neutrality; it indicates that we would like to count on the UN's global collective security system," he contended.[51]

Fearing that the right wing had made too many compromises with the government on UN cooperation, JSP left-wing leaders mounted a serious protest against Sone's argument. The party's Central Executive Council yielded at the last minute and canceled the distribution of the memo. But debate on the UN and the JSP's security policy continued. When Sone and his followers defended the legitimacy of collaborating with the UN, he obviously did not confine their discussion to the ongoing war in the Korean Peninsula. In the aborted memo, Sone had anticipated that if the UN's collective security functioned during the Korean conflict, the party's policy concerning a peace settlement upheld by security reliance on the UN would be proved realizable.[52] Nishimura Eiichi, another active member of the right-wing faction, presented a similar opinion in a personal note regarding the party's foreign policy. "In addition to our generous spiritual support for the UN's police activities against the North Korean invaders, we should voluntarily exhibit a cooperative attitude toward the economic mobilization in our country under the name of the UN forces and thereby advance the restoration of Japan's national and economic independence."[53] As the peace talks with the US were placed on the government's timetable,

---

51. JSP, "Heiwa undō to kokuren shiji no kankei ni tsuite" (The relationship between the peace movement and support of the UN), September 7, 1950, Asanuma Inejirō monjo, NDL.

52. Ibid.

53. Nishimura Eiichi, "Waga to tōmen no gaikō hōshin" (Our party's foreign policy at present), 1950, ibid.

these arguments laid the groundwork for discussions regarding the party's policy on the forthcoming peace.

Japan's path toward independence was also the JSP's path toward division. The right and left wings of the party never managed to find a common understanding on the peace issue. On the surface, the clash was stimulated by conflicting positions on the two treaties. The left wing opposed both the peace and security treaties, whereas the right wing decided to support the former while rejecting the latter. But this was just the tip of the iceberg. A more fundamental discrepancy was in the two sides' long-term visions regarding national security. Having discarded Sone's proposal, the JSP Central Executive Council reconfirmed the security policy line that had been issued in July 1950: the UN-centered neutrality scenario.[54] As an ideal as well as an ultimate goal, both right and left wings had no reservations about this formula. However, a transitional arrangement was necessary given the paralysis of the UN's collective security system under the Cold War. It was at this juncture that the two factions within the JSP seriously collided.

At one time after the Sone memo incident, some right-wing leaders indicated that they were ready to accept the stationing of UN forces or the existence of UN military bases on Japanese territory.[55] Presumably feeling this position to be too close to that of the government, around June 1951 the Central Committee—then strongly influenced by the right wing—began to emphasize that the party would not require the introduction of the UN forces into Japan before an armed attack against the country actually took place.[56] But Sone was unwilling to adopt a moderate stance. Instead, he came to prefer a regional security arrangement based on Articles 51 and 52 of the UN charter (which bore a curious similarity to MOFA's attempt to characterize the security treaty as a regional security arrangement).[57]

---

54. JSP, "Heiwa eno michi" (A path toward peace), October 1950, ibid.

55. Sone and Suzuki, "Waga anzen hoshō no michi" (Our security course), p. 13; Tanaka Hajime, "Tanaka Hajime an" (Tanaka Hajime's proposal), in JSP, *Jōhō tsūshin* (Information communication), June 1951, p. 32, ibid.

56. JSP, "Kokuren shiji ni kansuru tō no taido" (The party's attitude toward support of the UN), January 1951, ibid.

57. Sone, "Kōwa mondai ni kanshi dōshi shokun ni uttaeru" (An appeal to the comrades on the peace question), June 1951, p. 3, ibid.

Sone's idea was soon echoed by other members of the right wing. Nishimura asserted in his security proposal that in order to avoid a security "vacuum" after the peace, Japan had no choice but to join a regional arrangement permitted by the UN charter. On the condition that the two nations were placed in an "equal position," he also considered the US-Japan Security Treaty a "provisional agreement" for Japanese defense that was justified by the UN charter.[58] Hatano Kanae, another right-winger, also viewed the security treaty as the "only alternative" to take under current circumstances, while condemning the left wing's opposition to the treaty as originating in "misunderstanding of the spirit of the UN charter and the illusion of isolationist nationalism."[59] By early October when the party was deciding what its stance would be during the Diet's deliberation on the two treaties, most right-wingers seemed to agree that the security treaty was the single possible regional security arrangement for Japan at the moment.[60] But this position was totally inconsonant with that of the left-wingers.

The right wing connected Japan's safety with the survival of the liberal democratic world; the left wing deemed that a strict neutral policy would secure peace for their country. Also emphasizing the vital role of the UN as right-wingers did, the left-wingers looked at the connection between the organization and Japan's security from a different angle. Disavowing the option of the regional security arrangements stipulated in the UN charter, the left wing's foreign policy spokesman, Katsumata Seiichi, noted in April 1951 that such arrangements would function only when they served as supplementary institutions within the UN system. Otherwise, the regional security arrangements would become a military pact with a specific party in the event of international conflict and hence bring damage to the UN's peace function. To him and other left-wingers, given the existence of the anti-Japanese Sino-Soviet alliance,

---

58. Nishimura Eiichi, "Tainichi kōwa to waga tō no rekishiteki shimei" (The peace with Japan and our party's historical mission), pp. 6–7; JSP, "Chūō iinkai ni teiji sareta kōwa mondai ni taisuru shiryō" (Materials on the peace question submitted to the central committee), p. 15, ibid.

59. Hatano Kanae, "Heiwa, anpo ryō jōyaku ni taisuru taido" (Attitude toward the peace and security treaties), October 1, 1951, pp. 7–8, ibid.

60. JSP, "Chūō iinkai ni teiji sareta kōwa mondai ni taisuru shiryō,"p. 19.

the maintenance of a regional security treaty would inevitably lead Japan to a war with the communist bloc.[61]

Such a stance led the left-wing factions to take a much more reserved policy in handling concrete security matters. In the Korean case, left-wingers adamantly ruled out any substantial collaboration with the UN. Mutō Unjūrō, a left-wing member of the party's Diplomatic Committee, ridiculed Japan's UN cooperation as "illogical" and completely denied the legitimacy of the right wing's appeal to endorse UN forces in Korea. "The argument that Japan should not be a bystander during the Korean War is formulated by the judgment that Japan needs to make an advance payment to the UN, which is supposed to guarantee Japanese security after the peace conference," he remarked in a policy proposal. But it seemed to him that such a "payment" was "erroneous" because by giving up the right to militarize itself for self-defense, Japan had already saved other nations from concern about future Japanese aggression. If there was anything the Japanese government could do, according to him, it should be the maintenance of strict or even permanent neutrality, declining its duty to participate in the UN's military activities (including providing bases or allowing the passage of UN forces). Japan had nothing more to offer and it was the turn of the UN, whose member states endorsed the abolition of Japan's right of belligerency, to fulfill its promise to protect Japan from armed attacks.[62]

Similarly, the left wing also applied its policy on the Korean War to the security treaty case. In March 1951, JSP chairman Suzuki Mosaburō, the mastermind of the left wing, publicly denied the possibility of a power vacuum in Asia after the peace and suggested that rather than a bilateral treaty with the US, Japan should conclude "non-aggression pacts" with the USSR, China, the Oceania nations, and the Philippines "concurrent with the peace treaty." The proposal was immediately dismissed for its legal defect. A non-aggression pact premises sufficient military forces in each party—a condition that was prohibited by the

---

61. Katsumata, "Kōwa mondai to kōwa go no mondai to o kubetsu seyo" (Separate the peace problem from problems after the peace), pp. 92–93.
62. Mutō, "Kokuren kyōryoku no mondai ni tsuite (Mutō shian)" (The UN cooperation question, Mutō's personal proposal), Asanuma Inejirō monjo, NDL.

Japanese constitution.[63] Left-wing theorists' next attempt was to ask for the UNGA to take "concrete actions"—probably in the form of a resolution—to guarantee Japan's security after independence.[64] This proposal, which was hardly easier to implement than the non-aggression pacts scheme, was then replaced by a much vaguer one recommending that Japan's future security depend on the UN collective security mechanism without the stationing of foreign troops on Japanese territory. But regarding what security formula to adopt before the UN became able to take on such a responsibility, the left-wingers simply replied that this "must be decided by the free will of the Japanese people after independence."[65] In the end, postponement of a solution became the most viable answer for the left wing.

The difficult mission of narrowing the gap between the two wings on security policy was carried out by the JSP's Central Executive Council. On July 14, 1951, the Council announced the party's official comments on the Allied Powers' peace treaty draft and delivered them to US representatives in Tokyo five days later. The comments were mixtures of the left and right wing views. As the right wing always demanded, the Council emphasized Japan's right of individual and collective defense based on the UN charter. In a concession to the left wing, it confirmed that "the ways and means of defense should be decided on by the Japanese themselves of their own free will, after they have recovered complete independence," whereas the UN should "take concrete measures to guarantee security for Japan" through a UNGA decision so as to "cope with the situation immediately following the coming into effect of the peace treaty."[66] The reaction of the US was sneering. "To request that Japan's security be guaranteed by the United Nations implies a complete misunderstanding of what the UN is," Ambassador William J. Sebald forthrightly pointed out before a group of JSP representatives. "The UN is an organization of some 60 nations, and is not in a position to guarantee the security of any nation." The ambassador's

---

63. Tokyo to Washington, March 10 and 12, 1951, Reel 20, LOTF.
64. Katsumata, "Kōwa go no gaikō hōshin (an)" (Diplomatic principles after the peace), p. 4; JSP, *Jōhō tsūshin,* p. 30, Asanuma Inejirō monjo, NDL.
65. JSP, "Chūō iinkai ni teiji sareta kōwa mondai ni taisuru shiryō," pp. 15–16, ibid.
66. JSP, "On Draft Peace Treaty," July 14, 1951, Reel 13, LOTF.

alternative suggestion, on the other hand, was a familiar one: Japan's security could "be guaranteed by a collective security arrangement of some kind" such as the security treaty with the US.[67]

Sebald's negative response had no impact on the Executive Council's adherence to the UN-first policy, which was the last common ground respected by both right- and left-wing factions. By mid-October, the right wing began to retreat from its sympathetic position concerning the security treaty. Leading right-wingers announced that they would no longer support the treaty, ostensibly due to the bad "timing" (before independence) of its conclusion and the existence of certain "unequal" articles. The only part of their previous proposal that was preserved in this new position was the general demand for a "temporary security arrangement guaranteed by the UN charter."[68] The left-wingers seemed to have less difficulty accepting the right wing's revised attitude. Sharing the opinion that Japan should ultimately seek to secure its national security through the UN, left-wing spokesman Katsumata in fact remarked during a journal interview that he did not preclude the option of maintaining peace through "collaboration with other nations" after independence if this was decided by the free will of the Japanese people in an equal manner.[69]

Keeping the UN charter as the bottom line, the JSP was indeed quite successful in uniting the two factions under a joint campaign against the security treaty. Yet this success was offset by the party's failure to make a similar breakthrough concerning internal confrontations on the peace treaty. With the right wing tolerating the government's separate peace formula and the left wing insisting on an overall peace, the JSP eventually fell apart when the Central Executive Council voted by a very narrow margin to adopt the right wing's proposal. On October 26, the two wings of the party cast different votes on the peace treaty at

---

67. "Views of Social Party on Draft Peace Treaty," memorandum of conversation, July 19, 1951, ibid.

68. JSP, *Shiryō—Nihon shakaitō 50 nen,* p. 116; Asanuma, "Nihon no dokuritsu to heiwa to tō no tōitsu hoji no tame ni dōshi shokun ni uttau" (An appeal to the comrades for Japan's independence, peace and the maintenance of the party's unification), Asanuma Inejirō monjo, NDL.

69. Katsumata, "Yongensoku no jūyōsei wa izen to shite kawaranu," (The significance of the four principles remains unchanged), p. 146.

the Diet while observing their agreement to unanimously oppose the security treaty.

The JCP's Anti-UN Security Policy

If the security stances of the LBP and the JSP can be described as legitimizing their own policies through pro-UN gestures, the strategy of the Japan Communist Party (JCP)—another leading opponent of the conservative regime—was just the opposite. As part of its own policy regarding peace and Japan's future security, the JCP chose to strengthen its domestic status via an anti-UN stance.

When reinitiating its public activities in the aftermath of the Allied Powers' democratic reform, the JCP was no exception in welcoming a prominent role for the UN in both internal and external politics. "It is the combination of the UN charter and the World Federation of Trade Unions that represents the banner of the world's democratic peace system," the party noted in its first postwar platform issued in December 1945.[70] At the JCP's Fourth General Conference held the same month, Kamiyama Shigeo, a member of the party's Central Committee, proclaimed that "the reconstruction of the war-ruined Japan, the overall and thorough democratization, and Japan's true independence as well as participation in the International Peace Organization [a synonym of the UN at that time] were the most critical matters for all Japanese people."[71] In January 1946, Nosaka Sanzō, the chief of the JCP's wartime branch in exile in China, returned to Japan and published a joint declaration with the Central Committee, emphasizing that the "Japanese nation must overcome current trials and make indomitable endeavors to join the International Peace Organization."[72]

---

70. JCP, "Dai 4 kai taikai kōdō kōryō" (Practice platforms adopted at the fourth general conference), December 1, 1945, in Kamiyama, *Nihon kyōsantō sengo jūyō shiryōshū dai 1 kan*, p. 81.

71. Kamiyama, "Dai 4 kai to taikai ni okeru rōdō kumiai oyobi nōmin soshiki ni tsuite no hōkoku" (Report on the fourth general conference of the party regarding labor unions and farmers' organizations), December 1945, ibid., p. 85.

72. JCP, "Dōshi Nosaka to tō chūō iinkai no kyōdō seimei" (Joint communiqué between Comrade Nosaka and the party central committee), January 14, 1946, ibid., p. 98.

The JCP's rhetorical friendship with the UN became vulnerable when exposed to the unpredictable international situation, however. As the relationship between the USSR and the Western-dominated UN went sour, the JCP gradually turned its back on the organization. By early 1950, the party was the sole Japanese political party inimical to the UN. This change was reflected in the JCP's policy toward peace and security affairs. When the party declared its first policy guidelines on the coming peace in August 1948, it still mentioned Japan's affiliation with the UN. But there was not a single word about the UN in its second declaration concerning this question, released in June 1949.[73] On the contrary, nervous about the JSP right wing's pro-UN policy concerning Japan's security after peace, the JCP headquarters circulated a directive full of reproaches against its competitors' UN cooperation in February 1950. "Under the disguise of UN cooperation," the directive charged, "Japanese reactionary factions receive the imperialists' collective security, actively collaborate with anti-communist, anti-Soviet, colonialist aggression, and play a role in dividing the international labor front." From the JCP's standpoint, plainly aired in the directive, those "reactionary" elements, including JSP right-wingers and a number of labor unions following their orders, were "subordinate to American imperialism in the name of UN-dependent security."[74]

Strong pressures from both the LBP and the JSP in favor of UN cooperation after the outbreak of the Korean War further isolated the JCP in the domestic political arena. Such isolation in turn fortified its antipathy toward the UN. The party's new peace policy called the LBP's appeal for sovereignty restoration and UN-centered security a conspiracy to "revitalize militarism, repress internal revolution and drive Japanese people to join the mercenary troops to suppress the liberation of Asian nations."[75] In a document drafted in October 1950, all

---

73. Nihon kyōshokuin kumiai, *Kōwa mondai shiryō*, pp. 117–19.

74. JCP, "Nihon kyōsantō no tōmen no kihonteki kōdō hōshin" (Basic principles of JCP's present activities), February 1950, in *Chika sennyū no taisei o totonoeta Nihon kyōsantō no bunkenshū (zokuhen)*, pp. 656–60.

75. JCP, "Sensō to eikyū senryō tandoku kōwa hantai, jiyū to heiwa to dokuritsu no zenmen kōwa no tame ni" (Against the unilateral peace for war and permanent occupation, fighting for the overall peace), September 27, 1950, ibid., pp. 422–25.

the JCP's foes, in particular the US, the LBP, and the JSP, were criticized for their UN policies:

[T]he proposed peace with Japan means cooperation with the UN and the provision of bases to the UN police force. Political parties from the LBP to the JSP have betrayed our national interests by following policies of a certain imperialist [the US] while attempting to resurrect militarism. Officials of parties ranging from the LBP to the JSP are paving the way toward making our country a war base and turning our people into slaves and human bullets through their behavior in the name of UN cooperation.[76]

Needless to say, if cooperation with the UN could be so vicious, the party would not put up with its penetration in the nation's political life, as it demonstrated in a local election report in January 1951: "Whenever someone wants to make speeches on UN collaboration or anti-communism, we will join the masses to concentrate our protests and use the pressure of the masses to smash such speeches."[77] As this hostility toward UN cooperation became heated, the UN itself was not immune from its flying sparks either. Up until then, while denouncing other parties' UN cooperation, the JCP had shied away from directly challenging the authority of the UN as an international peace institution. But this propensity was no longer discernible during the Korean War. "The current operation of the UN is blatantly violating the spirit of the UN charter, ignoring the principle of consensus among major powers, and is attempting to resolve everything simply through unilateral majority votes," a JCP representative said at the Diet in November 1951. "Consequently, we have to say that the UN is not an organization for world peace but is utilized as a tool to legitimize wars."[78]

The anti-UN strategy did not bring the JCP any benefit during domestic political tussles regarding the peace arrangements. The party seemed to plunge itself into a formidable situation by running counter to the pro-UN sentiments of the public at the outset. The motive be-

---

76. JCP, "Kikanshi katsudō ni tsuite" (Activities of the party organ), October 15, 1950, ibid., pp. 400–1.
77. JCP, "Zenmen kōwa to jiyūtō datō de taishū o tōitsu sensen ni soshiki—Chiba tōitsu senkyo no kichō na kyōkun" (Mobilizing the masses under the united front through overall peace and overthrowing of the LBP—the valuable lesson of the unified election in Chiba), January 1, 1951, ibid., p. 426.
78. Yokota and Otaka, *Nihon to kokusai rengō*, p. 65.

hind this action may not have necessarily been irrational given the fact that the conservative cabinet's policy to dilute domestic confrontation on the peace issue through UN cooperation had begun to gain momentum. If JCP leaders had been capable of changing the tide of public opinion, this strategy would still have had a chance to succeed. But the JCP in the early 1950s was the worst candidate to pursue such a difficult task. Infighting within the party was as bad as in any of its rivals. Party policymaking was under the surveillance of Moscow and Beijing, who had no good feelings toward the UN. Moreover, most party leaders were banished from public posts (including the Diet), and party-affiliated agencies had been made illegal in June 1950 in the so-called Red Purge by the Supreme Commander for the Allied Powers (SCAP). Against such a bleak backdrop, the foregoing condemnations made by JCP leaders regarding the UN's alleged crimes constituted perhaps the only remaining method to remind domestic constituencies of the JCP's independent political stance.

The Triumph of the Conservative Coalition

With the JSP crippled and the JCP suffocated, the Yoshida cabinet felt assured of its ability to settle the peace and security arrangements. In the November 1950 issue of the LBP's party organ, the chairman of the party's General Council, Hoshijima Nirō, even had the latitude to satirize his JSP colleagues who were in the midst of an internal melee regarding UN cooperation: "Since the JSP also said that it would 'give consideration to anything necessary to the UN force's police activities,' if troops belonging to the UN instead of to a specific nation would like to be stationed in Okinawa, Aomori or other areas for the sake of peace in East Asia, why shouldn't we be happy to welcome them?"[79]

In theory, LBP leaders' high-handed attitude seemed premature, as they still had to obtain the support of the People's Democratic Party (PDP)—the biggest conservative opposition party in the Diet. But practically speaking, this was not a big deal for the ruling party. Also belonging to the conservative camp, the PDP endorsed a positive role for the UN in Japanese security. The party's stance toward the UN was concisely outlined in its answer to a press questionnaire conducted

---

79. Hoshijima, "Kōwa kaigi o mae ni shite," p. 16.

soon after the Korean War. It said first that Japan's cooperation with the UN in Korea should not be limited to the [economic] activities currently requested by the organization; next, that it had been difficult for Japan to maintain neutrality in the Korean conflict; and concluded by stating that Japan should accept UN requirements concerning the provision of military bases.[80] At the party's annual conference held in January 1951, the PDP reaffirmed its position that Japan's security after the peace must be guaranteed by the UN collective security system.[81] Some members of the party also stepped forward to suggest that Japan's future security be protected "by a UN police force composed of Japanese soldiers."[82]

None of these policies posed a problem for the LBP. After several rounds of behind-the-scenes talk, the two parties' deal on the peace and security treaties was complete. (Certain PDP members felt the two treaties were not fair enough to Japan, yet their grumbles were outweighed by the majority, who basically backed up the government.[83]) Yielding to the PDP's demands, Prime Minister Yoshida made official reports on the peace and security negotiations with the US at an extraordinary session of the Diet in August 1951, an action that he had been resisting, ostensibly due to the need to protect diplomatic secrets. Before the session, Yoshida, who was notorious for his haughtiness, paid an unusual visit to PDP president Tomabechi Gizō to ask for the latter's cooperation during the peace process. In return for these gestures of courtesy, the PDP promised to stay on the side of the government.

When Yoshida took a seat at the San Francisco Opera House—the chamber for the peace conference—in September, the makeup of his delegation was nearly perfect from a domestic political point of view. Behind him, there were not only his protégés from the ruling LBP but two leaders from the conservative opposition: PDP president Tomabechi and president Tokugawa Muneyoshi of the Ryokufūkai (or "the

---

80. Yokota and Otaka, *Nihon to kokusai rengō,* pp. 75–77.

81. *Tōyō keizai shinpō,* February 3, 1951, p. 14.

82. Tokonami Tokuji, "Jiei mondai ni taisuru minshutō no taido (fukushi kokka de kanzen dokuritsu o) Tokonami shian" (JDP's attitude toward self-defense, complete independence through a welfare nation, Tokonami's personal proposal), October 1951, Ashida Hitoshi monjo, NDL.

83. Masuda, *Masuda Kaneshichi kaisōroku,* pp. 193–223.

Green Wind Party," a moderate opposition faction in the Upper House). In the gallery, one could find another unexpected guest, former Prime Minister Katayama Tetsu, a JSP right-winger who joined a group of LBP politicians to attend the Conference as an informal "observer." A month later, the peace treaty passed the Diet by a comfortable margin.[84]

The security treaty, on the other hand, aroused more criticism but not enough to nip the US-Japan alliance in the bud. Despite the opposition from JSP left-wingers, the Communists, and several members of other parties, the treaty earned more than two-thirds of the votes in both the Upper and Lower Houses.[85] Until the very end of the Diet deliberations, government and LBP leaders clung tenaciously to the position they had repeated so many times. As one LBP member put it in an Upper House session, "in the Far East as well as the world we would like to contribute to world peace through the UN. Yet as it may take some time until we can join the UN, we have concluded the security treaty which, therefore, should be characterized as a supplementary arrangement before acquiring admittance to the UN."[86] But the UN's collective security mechanism has never been able to function. The "supplementary" bilateral arrangement with the US has actually served as the de facto foundation for Japan's national security in the decades that have followed.

---

84. The peace treaty received 307 ayes (47 nays) in the Lower House and 219 ayes (45 nays) in the Upper House.

85. The security treaty was adopted in the two houses with votes of 289 to 71 and 147 to 76, respectively.

86. "Dai 12 kai kokkai sangiin honkaigiroku dai 20 gō" (Proceedings of the 12th Diet Session Plenary Session, Upper House, No. 20), November 18, 1951, NDL.

The UN: A Political Panacea (1)

Japan's domestic political landscape changed rapidly after 1951. In the conservative camp, prewar politicians purged by SCAP made their comeback to the political arena and began to threaten the existence of the postwar leaders who filled Yoshida's LBP cabinet. Desperately attempting to remain in power, Yoshida answered the old conservatives' challenge with confrontations that caused two dissolutions of the Diet in six months between August 1952 and March 1953. After these efforts ended in failure, Yoshida reluctantly stepped down in December 1954. The new cabinet, led by Japan Democratic Party (JDP) President Hatoyama, strove to draw Japan back to a more nationalistic course. While unsuccessful in attaining contention-fraught goals such as revising the constitution, a document that he and his party saw as an American imposition, Hatoyama did make some essential progress in foreign affairs, including normalizing relations with the USSR and joining the UN. His endeavor to unify the conservative camp also bore fruit in November 1955 when the JDP and the LBP merged to become the Liberal Democratic Party (LDP).

The situation on the opposition side was complicated. The JSP split into two separate socialist parties, differentiated by the media as the Left Socialist Party (LSP) and the Right Socialist Party (RSP), after the bitter infighting on the peace and security treaties in 1951. Both the LSP and the RSP succeeded in increasing their seats in the Diet during the first half of the 1950s. Like their conservative rivals, the two also reunited in 1955 and became the largest opposition party until the mid-1990s. The JCP experienced more twists and turns. Its influence on

Japanese politics suffered a traumatic setback at the turn of the 1950s. Having been banned by the SCAP in 1950, the party was literally an outcast from the nation's political scene, holding no seats in the Lower House and barely keeping three members in the Upper House. Major JCP leaders fled to Beijing. The remaining JCP organs within Japan were either torn apart by different factions or barred from political activities. The party began to rebuild its organization after 1955, but it was unable to resume normal operations until 1958, when a new leadership under Miyamoto Kenji and Nosaka was established.

The political scene for the opposition camp became even more intricate after the late 1950s with the appearance of two self-styled "middle-of-the-road" parties: the Democratic Socialist Party (DSP) and the Clean Government Party (CGP, or Kōmeitō). The DSP was the offspring of a final showdown between the right-wing and left-wing factions of the JSP in 1959. The CGP, on the other hand, was initially founded in 1961 as the Clean Government League (CGL, or Kōmeikai)—a political branch of an influential Buddhist group, the Sōka Gakkai ("The Value-Adding Society")—and changed to its current name in 1964. Though the party officially cut its ties with the Sōka Gakkai in the early 1970s, it remains the only Japanese political party whose supporters are generally religious believers. Compared to the gigantic JSP, neither the DSP nor the CGP was capable of posing a threat to the ruling LDP independently. But by switching back and forth to form coalitions with the two biggest parties, their ability to exercise a deciding vote during elections or on certain policy issues could not be underestimated.

Apart from the realignment of political parties, the nation as a whole also entered a new epoch after the San Francisco Peace Conference. Boosted by US "special procurement" during the Korean War, economic rehabilitation had been going smoothly since the early 1950s. In 1956, the Economic Planning Agency made a proud and symbolic declaration that with Japan's impressive economic achievements, it was no longer in the "postwar" stage. But such forward-looking judgment only applied to the nation's economy. On the political scene, Japan was still coming to grips with the negative legacies of the last war, particularly in the fields of diplomacy and national security, where the UN continued to serve the needs of the government, the ruling party and the opposition parties in one way or another.

Domestic Controversies over China and AA Policies

Throughout the Cold War period, the conservative regime maintained its pro-US/Western stance in managing foreign affairs, while the opposition seized every tiny opportunity to condemn the government's lack of independence from the Americans. Until the early 1970s, this led the two sides to clash on a number of major diplomatic issues, two of which—Japan's policies toward the AA nations and China—were closely connected to the UN.

The conservative party was put on the defensive regarding the AA problem. The slogan of "serving as a bridge" between the AA Group and the West was misleading in light of Japan's position as a member of the Western camp. Specifically, within the UN, where the AA nations continued gaining influence, Japanese delegates could do nothing more than repeat official principles: While sympathetic to the course of the AA Group, Japan wished that the members of the group could choose more modest or constructive means to accomplish their goals at the UN. But as we have seen in Chapters 2 and 3, the AA nations were not in a position to take Japan's advice, just as Japan could not easily go along with the AA nations' anti-Western policies. The impasse led to an unsurprising scene in the domestic sphere: The government generally handled the AA issue at the UN in a way that it considered necessary for Japan's interests, neglecting the opposition's condemnations of how it followed America so closely. And the opposition parties welcomed such negligence because it provided abundant opportunities for them to attack the ruling conservatives in the Diet and other public venues.

The correlation between the UN and the government's China policy was more complex. After the establishment of the PRC in 1949, Beijing consistently asserted that it was the sole legal government in China (including the island of Taiwan) and therefore must be allowed to take the Chinese seat at the UN over from the Nationalist government of Chiang Kai-shek, who fled to Taiwan in 1949. While supported by the Soviet bloc and some AA states like India and Egypt, this demand was refused by the West, in particular the US, which considered the PRC an aggressive nation and a threat to the UN as well as to international peace.

After Japan acceded to the UN in 1956, it had to clarify its attitude on this problem. The LDP government unhesitatingly stood with Western allies to shut the PRC out of the UN, a decision that seemed natural for a member of the free world. A PRC without a seat at the UN was also a preferable situation for the conservative regime for domestic reasons. Under strong pressure from Washington, the Yoshida cabinet chose not to maintain official relations with the PRC, instead concluding a peace treaty with the Nationalist government in 1952. Though this might have been the only possible choice for a Japan whose hands were tied by its reliance on the US for its security, the government's decision was opposed not only by the left-wing progressives but by a certain portion of the public, who deemed that a normal relationship with one of their biggest neighbors was indispensable in view of Japan's own interests. The ruling party thus earnestly needed a sound rationalization by which to defend its China policy. Anticommunism was not a useful card, as the majority of Japanese people were reluctant to get deeply involved in the Cold War. The Chinese military threat to Japan's national defense had been an effective reason during the early 1950s when the memory of the Korean War was still fresh, but it lost persuasiveness after the mid-1950s as the communist states started their peace offensives. The PRC's confrontation with the UN, however, was a perpetually safe excuse for the Japanese government, given the public's longstanding aspirations regarding the UN.

During the last days of the Yoshida administration, LBP leaders had already used "UN cooperation" to legitimize their policy toward the PRC. In 1954, Foreign Minister Okazaki Katsuo stated in the Diet that as long as Beijing continued to be designated as an "aggressor state" by the UN, Japan should not actively pursue the normalization of relations between the two countries.[1] This position was maintained by all conservative cabinets for the remainder of the 1950s. "As international rela-

---

1. "Dai 19 kai kokkai sangiin gaimu iinkaigiroku dai 22 gō" (Proceedings of the 19th Diet Session Committee on Foreign Affairs, Upper House, No. 22), April 16, 1954 and "Dai 19 kai kokkai shūgiin gaimu iinkaigiroku dai 58 gō" (Proceedings of the 19th Diet Session Committee on Foreign Affairs, Lower House, No. 58), September 14, 1954, both in NDL.

tions are centered around the UN, the current situation does not allow us to change our policies toward the Chinese Communists," said Foreign Minister Shigemitsu in 1956.[2] After Japan joined the UN a few months later, Shigemitsu's successor, Kishi Nobusuke, explained this point more confidently: "We have determined our international course as a UN member state, whereas the Chinese Communists still do not participate in the UN and have not been recognized by many states. With this situation in mind, I find it is premature for us to normalize relations with the Chinese Communists." On Kishi's initiative, MOFA inserted this position into the 1957 Diplomatic Bluebook.[3]

The Ikeda cabinet inaugurated in July 1960 was more flexible in associating with the PRC than its predecessors. Non-governmental trade with Beijing thrived, and the government became more tolerant of the escalation in informal communications between LDP politicians and Chinese leaders. But the détente did not go so far as the resumption of official ties. Washington was still nervous about Beijing's antagonism, and such caution was echoed by several influential LDP members who continued to endorse a closer relationship with Taipei. By the middle of the 1960s, the government came up with a UN-centered method to balance its willingness to improve relations somewhat with the PRC and the current situation that restricted its efforts.

In January 1964, France became the first major Western power after the UK to establish diplomatic relations with the PRC. Japan, which had been faithfully following the anti-PRC principle of the Western bloc, was shocked by this news. Shortly after the issue was brought up in the Diet, Prime Minister Ikeda started arguing that although his government had not yet recognized the PRC, it had to face the existence of "over 600 million people together with that regime in the Chinese mainland" and take "independent measures" on this issue "within the

---

2. "Dai 24 kai kokkai shūgiin gaimu iinkaigiroku dai 58 gō" (Proceedings of the 24th Diet Session Committee on Foreign Affairs, Lower House, No. 58), May 28, 1956, ibid.

3. "Dai 26 kai kokkai shūgiin honkaigiroku dai 4 gō" (Proceedings of the 26th Diet Session Plenary Session, Lower House, No. 4), February 24, 1957, ibid.; Chen, *Sengo Nihon no Chūgoku seisaku—1950 nendai higashi Ajia kokusai seiji no bunmyaku,* pp. 201–2; MOFA, *Waga gaikō no kinkyō 1957,* pp. 44–45.

UN in conjunction with international movements."[4] At first, members of opposition parties seemed unable to figure out the meaning of this statement. But the puzzle was soon cleared up by Ikeda's foreign minister, Ōhira Masayoshi, who told a JSP member of the Lower House in February that since the government gave higher priority to its UN diplomacy it might have to "make a grave decision" regarding its relations with the PRC in the event that the "Chinese Communist regime is accepted into the UN with the blessing of the world."[5]

Ōhira's statement was a double-edged sword. While sounding similar to previous remarks made by the ruling party linking the normalization issue with the UN seat, the statement did not stop with using the UN as an excuse to decline a normal relationship with the PRC. Rather, it referred to the possibility of recognizing the PRC once the latter was able to get into the UN. More trickily, this seemingly positive stance would actually bring no immediate change to the Chinese representation in the UN, since the Ikeda government had successfully assisted the US in finding an efficient method to block any attempt among UN member states to immediately create a seat for Beijing. Throughout the 1950s, the Western camp depended on a so-called moratorium resolution to freeze discussions on the Chinese representation issue at the UNGA. However, with pro-Beijing member states gaining power inside the Assembly, support for the moratorium resolution declined sharply starting in the late 1950s. The Ikeda government actually preferred a "one China, one Taiwan" formula at the UN, which was at the moment opposed by both the PRC and Chiang's Nationalist government. Until this formula could eventually be accepted by the two sides, Ikeda and his foreign policy aides had to find another way to at least keep the Nationalist government seated in the UN. In order to do so, Ambassador to the UN Okazaki helped the US devise an elaborate proposal in 1961 to replace the moratorium resolution. Drawing on Article 18 of the UN

---

4. "Dai 46 kai kokkai sangiin honkaigiroku dai 4 gō" (Proceedings of the 46th Diet Session Plenary Session, Upper House, No. 4), January 23, 1964; "Dai 46 kai kokkai shūgiin yosan iinkaigiroku dai 7 gō" (Proceedings of the 46th Diet Session Budget Committee, Lower House, No. 7), February 4, 1964, ibid.

5. "Dai 46 kai kokkai shūgiin gaimu iinkaigiroku dai 6 gō" (Proceedings of the 46th Diet Session Committee on Foreign Affairs, Lower House, No. 6), February 12, 1964, ibid.

charter, the proposal insisted that all decisions concerning China's representation be considered an "important question" and therefore require "a two-thirds majority of the members present and voting" at the UNGA. It was immediately adopted by the Western members and served as a sturdy breakwater to shut out demands for the PRC's membership for the rest of the decade.[6]

After taking over as LDP president and prime minister in 1964, Satō followed the UN-centered strategy explored by Ikeda and Ōhira, albeit in a half-hearted manner. The Satō cabinet inherited Ōhira's argument that the PRC's admission to the UN must be blessed by the international community, while refusing to regard UN membership as a barometer for normalizing Sino-Japan relations. Satō was not ignorant of the implication of UN representation on Tokyo's relationship with Beijing. "If the Chinese Communists were admitted to the UN," he warned Secretary of State Rusk during his visit to the US in January 1965, "the pressure for recognition within Japan would build up and be very difficult for the Japanese government to manage." But instead of preparing for this scenario, Satō was convinced that such a situation must be "put off into the future as long as possible."[7]

Satō's wariness of a quick recognition of the PRC was to some degree whipped up by the latter's nuclear plan and increasingly hostile attitude to Japan's conservative regime. His strategy to delay the recognition by raising the hurdle for Beijing's membership at the UN, nonetheless, went against the tide, as more and more nations switched diplomatic recognition from Taipei to Beijing. In the 1970 UNGA, those supporting the "important question" resolution became the minority among UN member states for the first time since 1961. The Nationalist government's seat was secured that year, since the negative votes against the important issue resolution did not reach the two-third requirement, but there was no doubt that the PRC's admission was just a question of time. Yet the Satō cabinet decided to back Taipei's presence at the UN for at least another year. Even after President Richard Nixon's sudden announcement that he would visit Beijing, Satō still

---

6. Kosaka, *Giin gaikō 40 nen watashi no rirekisho,* p. 69; Kokuren kōhō sentā, *Nihon to Kokuren,* pp. 71–72.

7. Ishii, Gabe and Miyasato, *Amerika gasshūkoku tainichi seisaku bunsho shūsei dai 9 ki Nichibei gaikō bōei mondai 1965 nen dai 9 kan,* p. 183.

chose to cosponsor two draft resolutions at the 1971 UNGA asserting that the expulsion of Taipei (not the admission of Beijing) was an "important question" according to the charter, and proposing UN membership for both the PRC and Taiwan. It is unclear why Satō was so anxious to defend the Nationalist government. He might have been concerned about the anti-PRC tendency of the US Congress, where Okinawa's reversion to Japan was under deliberation. Or perhaps he would have simply felt guilty if he discarded the Generalissimo in Taiwan, who had been generous to the Japanese troops and civilians stuck in mainland China after the end of WWII. For whatever reasons, however, it was a decision made with the worst possible timing.

The two draft resolutions were unable to preserve the Nationalist government's seat in the Assembly in late October, and the opposition forced the LDP government to take responsibility. This time, Satō returned to Ikeda's UN-centered principle and declared that since the UN had recognized the PRC as the sole legal representative of the Chinese people, his government would like to negotiate with Beijing for a normal diplomatic relationship.[8] He also told the Americans that with the PRC's appearance in the UN his government had no choice but to recognize Beijing, and that Japan's peace treaty with Taipei "will be resolved in the process of normalization."[9] Satō was never able to implement this new policy. Distrusted by Chinese leaders, he had to leave this work to his successor, Tanaka Kakuei.

The Chinese representation issue cost Satō his premiership, but many government officials did not regret their UN-first stance toward the PRC. As MOFA began to consider ending the hostile relationship with Beijing in early 1972, Deputy Vice Foreign Minister Hōgen Shinsaku told a group of Japanese ambassadors that he still felt Japan "did the right thing" in defending Taiwan's seat at the UN. "[The Nationalist government] was very appreciative of the position taken by Japan on

---

8. "Dai 67 kai kokkai shūgiin yosan iinkaigiroku dai 5 gō" (Proceedings of the 67th Diet Session Budget Committee, Lower House, No. 5), October 29, 1971; "Dai 67 kai kokkai sangiin yosan iinkaigiroku dai 4 gō" (Proceedings of the 67th Diet Session Budget Committee, Upper House, No. 4), November 4, 1971, NDL.

9. "Meeting with Eisaku Satō, Japanese Prime Minister, on Thursday, January 6, 1972 at 1:30 p.m. at San Clemente," January 6, 1972, Box 925, NSC Files, NPM.

this issue," he reportedly said, "and thus had much less reason to complain about Japan's attitudes today."[10] Satō's UN Ambassador, Nakagawa Tōru, held a similar opinion and commented after his retirement that although the loss of Taipei's seat in the UN "was a fatal wound for the Satō cabinet, it had little negative influence on Japan in general." In Nakagawa's view, what the Japanese had done at the UN in 1971 was simply to fight a ceremonial battle before breaking with the Nationalist government that they had been supporting for so many years.[11]

Like the government, the opposition parties also went through many trials and tribulations when deciding their positions on the AA and China problem at the UN. As the biggest progressive party, the JSP did not miss any opportunity to attack the government's UN policy regarding AA nations. During the 1950s the party tried to press the government to reinforce Japan's official affiliation with the AA Group at the UN. After the government unsurprisingly took a completely different course, JSP leaders started criticizing the conservative leaders' lack of independence in the international sphere.

By the mid-1960s, it was clear that the UN was incapable of resolving most of the critical issues involving the interests of AA states. The Vietnam War escalated without UN intervention. The PRC was showing more and more animosity toward the UN, and Indonesia—Beijing's biggest ally in Southeast Asia—walked out of the organization in 1965. The JSP's faith in the UN was shaken by these events. Some party members started to echo the anti-UN policy of Beijing and Moscow. Resentment against the "lack of justice" of the organization in handling AA issues became all the more marked in the party's official documents. But disappointment over the UN's performance in defending AA nations' interests did not lead the JSP to an anti-UN position. While some radical AA members turned their backs on the UN, it was undeniable that the influence of the AA Group as a whole rose rapidly with the participation of newly independent nations beginning in the early 1960s. This created a favorable situation for precipitating the PRC's admission to the UN—another major issue for the JSP, which had been incensed

10. Bangkok to Washington, April 24, 1972, Box 2405, Subject-Numeric File 1970–73, NA. The author thanks Mr. Kanda Yutaka for bringing this document to his attention.

11. Kokuren kōhō sentā, *Nihon to kokuren no 30 nen,* p. 132.

by the government's decision to support the Chinese Nationalists at the UN. Consequently, from the mid-1960s, the party began to hold the view that it would continue to support the UN while pressing for greater influence of AA nations through admitting the membership of the PRC.[12]

Along with the JSP, two "middle-of-the road" opposition parties also attempted to take advantage of the perplexity of the government's AA policy at the UN during the 1960s. Established by a group of right-wing members who split off from the JSP in January 1960, the DSP always showed two faces in public: that of a believer in democratic socialism and that of a stubborn, anti-communist, nationalistic player in domestic politics. Its attitude regarding the AA issue at the UN epitomized the coexistence of these two identities. Embracing an "independent and autonomous diplomacy" on the international stage, the DSP was an active critic of the LDP regime's "follow America" policy in dealing with the AA Group's proper rights. It also strongly supported more economic aid from industrial nations to the AA Group through UN agencies.[13] But when it came to the Chinese representation issue, the party's conservative side differentiated its policy from those of other progressive parties.

DSP leaders felt no affinity toward the PRC, which they viewed as an "expansionist" state. They agreed with the LDP that the PRC's membership was an important question deserving prudent handling at the UNGA (though they thought Japan did not have to cosponsor the important question resolution). Probably feeling this position to be too close to the conservative regime, the party later shifted toward the "one

---

12. JSP, *Nihon shakaitō seisaku shiryō shūsei,* p. 217 and p. 495; Yamaguchi Fusao, "Shakaitō gaikō rosen o jiko hihan suru," p. 118.

13. "Dai 37 kai kokkai shūgiin honkaigiroku dai 3 gō" (Proceedings of the 37th Diet Session Plenary Session, Lower House, No. 3), October 21, 1960, "Dai 38 kai kokkai shūgiin yosan iinkaigiroku dai 8 gō" (Proceedings of the 38th Diet Session Budget Committee, Lower House, No. 8), February 10, 1961, "Dai 41 kai kokkai shūgiin yosan iinkaigiroku dai 1 gō" (Proceedings of the 41st Diet Session Budget Committee, Lower House, No. 1), August 20, 1962, "Dai 63 kai kokkai shūgiin honkaigiroku dai 24 gō" (Proceedings of the 63rd Diet Session Plenary Session, Lower House, No. 24), May 7, 1970, all in NDL; Kamijō, "Minshatō kihonseisaku no hensen," pp. 50–51; "Eki Sone Explains Democratic Socialist Party Foreign Policy," October 12, 1960, Reel 32, DOS 1960–63.

China one Taiwan" formula, contending that although the PRC may be entitled to a membership, Taiwan's fate must be determined by the Taiwanese people based on the self-determination principle of the UN. And the normalization of relations with China had to wait until this problem was resolved within the UN. The DSP firmly stood by this policy until the important question formula was defeated in the UNGA. On October 30, 1971, four days after the PRC acquired its seat at the UN, the party declared that it recognized Beijing as the sole legal representative of China. Moreover, unlike the Satō cabinet, which had merely asked for negotiations, the DSP unilaterally abandoned the "one China one Taiwan" formula by admitting that Taiwan was part of the PRC. The following April, the PRC, which had been refusing formal contact with the DSP, invited party chairman Kasuga Kazuyuki to visit Beijing. The DSP's UN-first China policy thus had a better end than that of the ruling LDP. [14]

As a major religious party in postwar Japan, the CGP's political stance was anything but articulate in the first place. The party's platforms in the early days contained many Buddhist thoughts that were difficult for ordinary constituents to understand. The core of its policy ideal was called "*ōbutsu myōgō,*" which meant to combine politics with the merciful Buddhist philosophies so that a highly civilized society cherishing individual happiness and social prosperity could come into being.[15] During the first few years of its history, the CGP's policies produced by this doctrine were usually ambiguous and lacking in substance. Foreign policy was no exception in this sense.

After the party set out to acquire seats in the Lower House in May 1964, it started sensing the urgency to put more lucid policy plans before the public. Party policymakers were not going to abandon the Buddhist principles, but rather fasten these principles to actual policy

---

14. DSP, *Minshatō sanjūgo shūnen shi,* pp. 194–95 and p. 204; Kamijō, "Minshatō kihon seisaku no hensen," pp. 50–51; External Affairs Division of the National Police Agency, "Gensuibaku kinshi Nihon kyōgikai hōchū daihyōdan ni taisuru Ryō Shōshi, Kaku Matsujaku no danwa ni tsuite" (Statements made by Liao Chengzhi and Guo Moruo before the delegation of the Japan Council against A & H Bombs to China), June 1961, C'0009, DRO.

15. Policy Studies Bureau, CGL, *Yakushin suru kōmeikai no seisaku,* pp. 18–20.

issues through some new political concepts. Based on the belief that the *ōbutsu myōgō* ideal must be realized worldwide, the CGP (then called the CGL) argued in early 1964 that Japan's foreign policy should be pursued according to a spirit of global nationalism—a concept indicating that all nations in the world were in actuality one united body and therefore must pursue their individual interests in a harmonious way.[16] One of the most important channels through which this thought could be enacted was the UN. "Promotion of UN diplomacy" was among the five pillars of the CGL's foreign policy from 1964 on. From the CGL's viewpoint, the UN was an international organization that reflected the "one world" thought coincident with the global nationalism theme. In this schema, the rise of the AA Group in the UN was not necessarily a promising sign because it would accelerate the multipolarization trend in international society. But for domestic reasons, the party still stressed the significance of cooperating with the AA nations within the UN, arguing that the bias caused by the government's pro-American position needed to be corrected before it could work on the one world ideal.[17]

By the same token, the CGP also dealt with the Chinese UN representation problem in line with its global nationalism principles. Although the party never supported the government's effort to keep the PRC out of the UN, it was at one time reserved about replacing Taipei with Beijing and favored a "two Chinas" solution.[18] But foreseeing the failure of the strategy to isolate the PRC, the CGP readily changed this policy. In September 1968, Sōka Gakkai chairman Ikeda Daisaku, the spiritual leader of the CGP, indicated at a gathering of young party members that it was time to apply global nationalism to Japan's China policy by normalizing relations with the PRC and resolving China's UN representation issue. In January 1969, the CGP announced six principles for rapprochement with Beijing, including promoting PRC's admission to the UN and accepting the one China formula that treated the Taiwan

---

16. "Dai 46 kai kokkai sangiin honkaigiroku dai 5 gō"(Proceedings of the 46th Diet Session Plenary Session, Upper House, No. 5), January 24, 1964 and "Dai 46 kai kokkai sangiin honkaigiroku dai 24 gō" (Proceedings of the 46th Diet Session Plenary Session, Upper House, No. 24), May 25, 1964, NDL.
17. Policy Studies Bureau, CGL, *Yakushin suru kōmeikai no seisaku*, p. 155–56 and pp. 159–60.
18. Ibid., p. 165.

problem as China's domestic affair.[19] This new China policy not only made the CGP the first non-progressive political party that held an official channel to the top PRC leaders but encouraged the party to stand firm in opposing the government's cooperation with the US on the important question resolution. By 1971, the CGP and the JSP were in fact the most vocal supporters for the PRC's UN seat within the Japanese domestic scene.

The JCP was perhaps the only one of postwar Japan's opposition parties that did not share a positive attitude toward the UN. As during the Occupation era, the party's UN policy since the early 1950s had been both negative and ambivalent. The JCP was the only party that opposed the government's application for UN membership in 1952 because it thought the US was using Japan's seat at the UN as a "tool for propaganda."[20] After Japan joined the UN in 1956, the party's UN policy became more or less pragmatic. Like their colleagues from other opposition parties, JCP Diet members enjoyed exposing the government's awkward relations with the AA Group at the UN. When discussing certain AA issues such as those related to Korea, they had no problem borrowing the UN charter to justify their accusation of the conservative regime's policies.[21] But at the same time, the progress made by the AA Group within the UN did not change the party's view that the US was taking advantage of the UN for the sake of its imperialist foreign policy. "The UN's true nature as a *bourgeois* parliament is good enough for the US to use the organization as a voting machine," an article appearing in the January 1964 issue of the JCP organ read,

---

19. Ishihara Iwane, *Kōmeitō no seiji, kokkai kisha no me*, pp. 150–51 and pp. 176–87.
20. Yokota and Otaka, *Kokusai rengō to Nihon*, pp. 95–96; "Dai 13 kai kokkai shūgiin gaimu iinkaigiroku dai 23 gō" (Proceedings of the 13th Diet Session Committee on Foreign Affairs, Lower House, No. 23), May 7, 1952, NDL.
21. "Dai 28 kai kokkai sangiin honkaigiroku dai 18 gō" (Proceedings of the 28th Diet Session Plenary Session, Upper House, No. 18), March 31, 1958, "Dai 36 kai kokkai sangiin honkaigiroku dai 5 gō" (Proceedings of the 36th Diet Session Plenary Session, Upper House, No. 5), October 23, 1960, "Dai 40 kai kokkai shūgiin gaimu iinkaigiroku dai 16 gō" (Proceedings of the 40th Diet Session Committee on Foreign Affairs, Lower House, No. 16), March 24, 1962, "Dai 43 kai kokkai sangiin honkaigiroku dai 9 gō" (Proceedings of the 43rd Diet Session Plenary Session, Upper House, No. 9), January 26, 1963, NDL.

"and the expectation that the UN is no longer an American voting machine because of the participation of newly independent nations from Africa and elsewhere has produced a great illusion."[22] In April 1965, the party's daily newspaper *Akahata* ("The Red Flag") even issued a long editorial calling for the "eradication of illusions toward the current UN by disclosing the reality of the organization" before the Japanese people.[23]

While verbally dismissing the public's pro-UN sentiment as an "illusion," the JCP did not return to the radical anti-UN path it had taken in the early 1950s. In fact, one month before the publication of the *Akahata* editorial, the party's Central Committee had already decided to opt for a more flexible course aimed at "democratic reform of the UN" rather than the abolition of the organization. As the major component of this "democratic reform," the party supported the PRC's UN seat, a stance maintained even after its bitter collision with the CCP in 1966. It also required the withdrawal of UN forces from Korea while attributing the responsibility for the instability of the peninsula to the US instead of the UN. Finally, it asked for reconsideration of the composition of UN councils, committees, and the Secretariat so that the voice of the communist bloc and the AA and Latin American Groups could be more fairly reflected.[24] Despite its antipathy toward a US-dominated UN, the JCP also could not resist the temptation to use the increasing influence of the AA nations inside the organization.

PKO and an Overseas Mission for SDF

Concerning the China and AA problems, the government and the ruling parties used the UN for defensive purposes, whereas the opposition saw the UN principles as effective offensive weapons to attack, or at least embarrass, the conservatives. In the security sphere, the situation

---

22. Kameda, "Amerika teikokushugi no nimen seisaku—sono ikutsuka no tokuchō," pp. 88–89.

23. JCP, "Kokuren no genjitsu to Nihon jinmin no tōsō," p. 90.

24. Ibid.; Ikeda Ichirō, "Kokuren de sōten to sareta Chūgoku daihyōken mondai," p. 246; JCP, "Anpo jōyaku hantai to Okinawa henkan o mezasu, zen minshu seiryoku no tōitsu to, minshu rengō seifu no taigai seisaku," p. 115; JCP, "Nihon no heiwa to chūritsu, shin no dokuritsu o kachitoru," p. 32.

was more equal for both sides. The conclusion of the 1951 US-Japan Se-curity Treaty was a triumph for the conservative LBP regime, yet it did little to discourage the opposition from continuing their criticism of the nation's security formula. It was anything but difficult to point out the defects of the government's current policy, which left national defense almost entirely to a foreign power, automatically bound Japan with the Western camp in the Cold War face-off, and prohibited the resumption of political as well as business ties with some important neighboring na-tions. To offer a workable alternative, nevertheless, was a formidable mission. Both ruling and opposition parties shared experiences of this.

While contending that a security arrangement with the US was the best option for the time being, many leaders of Yoshida's LBP avoided suggesting that their country would be restricted by such a policy for-ever. Instead, they dropped hints indicating their unease about Japan's inability to take full responsibility for its national defense. "Without the natural upsurge of people's willingness to protect their nation, rearma-ment is impossible," LBP Secretary General Hayashi Jōji told a journal reporter in November 1952. "If rearmament becomes necessary as the result of the escalation of people's love of their motherland, then the issue of revising the constitution to this end would surface." The only factor preventing all these from taking place, in his words, was the "economic reality at present."[25]

Two years later, a nationalist branch (headed by former president Hatoyama) of the LBP organized a committee for the revision of the constitution. In September 1954, the committee, officially named the Constitutional Investigation Council, publicized its draft for a new con-stitution. One of the most substantial changes was made in the security-related articles. In contrast to the current constitution, which prohibits Japan's right to maintain military forces, the Council recommended the establishment of a "national defense force" (albeit on a modest scale) and the articulation of the Japanese people's "duty of national defense." It also proposed to replace the constitution's articles renouncing war in general with articles only rejecting "war for aggressive purposes," and it attempted to articulate people's "rights and duties in the event of war or a state of national emergency." At the same time, the authors of the draft did not forget to add some liberal or even cosmopolitan color to

---

25. Hayashi, "Sekai no jiyū kokka to tomoni," p. 114.

their proposal. The collective security concept of the UN charter was utilized for this sake. The preamble to the proposed constitution thus proclaimed that in a spirit of international cooperation, Japan should prohibit aggressive wars and would like to join the "International Peace Organization as well as the collective security system."[26]

The ruling conservative party's course to alter Japan's security stance through constitutional revision was further refined after Hatoyama became prime minister and president of the JDP. Hatoyama was the first postwar Japanese prime minister who publicly (in the Diet) aired his opposition to the constitution because it forbade military forces. When the JDP and the LBP merged to form the LDP in November 1955, requests concerning rearmament and the revision of the constitution were written into the new ruling party's policy guidelines. So was support for the UN. As part of the mission to "maintain a self-defense structure," the guidelines read, Japan must "participate in the UN and strengthen the collective security system."

The ruling party's strategy to bind its rearmament effort with an official endorsement of the UN's collective security principle was by and large a smart choice. The Korean War and the escalation of military conflicts in areas like the Taiwan Strait and Indochina had brought back a sense of insecurity to the Japanese people in the early 1950s. Public opinion polls conducted in this period indicated that the idea of Japan possessing its own national military forces via the revision of the constitution enjoyed stable support from a majority of the people.[27] Meanwhile, although they admitted the importance of rearmament, most Japanese people also seemed to agree that their national defense could only be realized with the assistance of an international arrangement. Presumably due to the government's propaganda on the role of the UN forces in Korea, many expected that the UN would take such a responsibility. A 1953 opinion poll undertaken by the Prime Minister's Office, for instance, showed that nearly half of all Japanese thought their country's security could be assured if it was seated in the UN.[28]

---

26. LBP, "Jiyūtō, kenpō kaiseian o happyō," pp. 58–59.
27. Hirose, *Tōyō daigaku shakaigaku kenkyūjo*, pp. 29–31.
28. Nihon kōhō kyōkai, *Sōrifu, kokuritsu yoron chōsajo, yoron chōsa hōkokusho, dai 7 kan*, pp. 494–95.

However, the combination of rearmament and UN cooperation no longer fit the domestic situation after 1955. Though the UN generally maintained its popularity, as the Eastern and Western camps gradually eased the tension between them and the domestic peace movement regained its momentum, the option of revising the constitution rapidly lost its attractiveness to the Japanese public. The approval rate for rearmament and constitutional amendment in various polls declined from about 50 percent in 1952 to little more than 20 percent in 1958.[29] Besides the lack of public support, the ruling party was unable to secure two-thirds of the seats in both the Upper and Lower Houses. Because any change to the constitution must be initiated by the Diet "through a concurring vote of two thirds or more" in the two Houses and should be approved through a "special referendum" requiring "an affirmative vote of a majority of all votes" cast by the Japanese people, the chance of the LDP achieving its goal in the foreseeable future was extremely remote.

Unwilling to abandon its dream of an independent defense system, the Hatoyama cabinet set up a committee to "investigate," if not immediately revise, the constitution. But the LDP took no further step in this regard after the committee submitted its final report sympathetic to the revision in 1964. Instead, the ruling party and the government apparently reached an agreement that if it was impossible to move forward, they should at least not draw back from the current position. Beginning in the mid-1950s, the LDP began to give more attention to defending the legitimacy of the US-Japan alliance before the public and the opposition. Its strategy was not a new one. Like what the LBP and MOFA did when concluding the security and peace treaties, the LDP turned to the UN's collective security concept for the legal basis of military collaboration with the US.

In September 1957, Japan and the US exchanged memoranda stressing the compatibility between the UN charter and the security treaty. This action meant nothing substantial to those at the State Department, the Pentagon, or the White House. But it undoubtedly had important psychological and political implications for the Japanese side. Specifically, regarding domestic politics, the memoranda gave rise to a liberal and, in some degree, idealistic tinge to US-Japanese security coopera-

---

29. Hirose, *Tōyō daigaku shakaigaku kenkyūjo*, pp. 32–34.

tion that was useful in forestalling criticism from the opposition parties.[30] The LDP leadership wasted no time in cultivating this effect.

In the spring of 1959, after the US and Japanese governments entered into formal negotiations on the revision of the security treaty, the LDP produced several policy papers in which it requested, among other things, that the new treaty should not allow the use of military force for any purpose incompatible with the UN's principles, while admitting Japan's right of individual and collective security based on Article 51 of the UN charter.[31] These arguments served as a prelude to the LDP's official position on this issue, which was publicized under the name of the party's Diplomatic Investigation Committee in the same year. "If all nations determined their behavior in accordance with the principles of the UN charter, there would be no problems," the position read. "In reality, however, international politics is not so easy and . . . the UN, currently, is incapable of preventing violations of peace from occurring." For nations trying desperately to maintain their security and independence in such a perilous world, therefore, the establishment of a collective security system with other friendly nations as postulated in the UN charter was nothing but a "natural" and "necessary" action.[32]

As we saw in the last chapter, these observations were generally duplicated from the Yoshida cabinet's stance on the security treaty and hence were familiar to both the public and the opposition. Yet on the heels of the exchange of memoranda between Tokyo and Washington, the same words obviously carried greater weight compared to nine years earlier. Throughout the 1960s, the UN was a faithful guardian of the US-Japan military alliance, especially when the two nations had to decide whether they should terminate the new security treaty in 1970.[33] Even after the automatic extension of the treaty, the fragility of the UN's peacekeeping function continued to offer the LDP government sound grounds for preserving the military alliance with the US. The weakness of the UN was mentioned in the government's first Defense Whitepaper in 1970 to justify Japan's need to invoke its right of individual or collective self-defense against armed attacks from the outside. In

---

30. Sakamoto, *Nichibei dōmei no kizuna,* p. 186.
31. LDP, *Jiyū minshutō shi,* pp. 588–91.
32. Ibid., p. 596.
33. Ibid., p. 628.

1973, a similar section was incorporated into the final version of the LDP's revised draft for the constitution.[34]

The defensive effect in terms of evading criticism was not necessarily the sole rationale that encouraged the LDP government to highlight the correlations between the UN and its security policies. Some members of the party also favored a closer tie with the UN for a more proactive purpose—creating an international role for the SDF. The SDF was prohibited from pursuing overseas missions almost as soon as it was founded. When the Law of Self-Defense Forces (the SDF Law) was adopted in June 1954, the members of the Diet took action to pass a resolution forbidding the dispatch of the SDF outside of Japanese territory. But within the LDP and various government agencies, there seemed to be no firm consensus regarding how tightly this resolution should be explained and applied. The SDF's Joint Staff Council (JSC), for instance, contended in a 1955 assessment that Japan must expand the front line of its defense to areas like Sakhalin, the Kurile Islands, or South Korea and should "seriously consider" a basic proposal to send its forces overseas.[35]

In May 1957, this problem caused controversy among LDP leaders when they were deliberating a draft of the government's Basic Principles for National Defense. Composed of brief items reflecting current policy on defense, the document was not supposed to arouse any sensational debates within or outside the government and the ruling party. But when the original draft was forwarded to the Executive Committee of the National Defense Council (NDC) for comments, LDP members of the committee were unable to unify their opinions on one item related to UN cooperation.

In the mid-1950s, the SDF held a positive view of Japan's relationship with the UN. In a 1956 policy paper, the JSC noted that without any illusions about the UN's security function under the Cold War, collaboration with the UN might still be the only vehicle through which Japan could contribute to world peace. And it also described the UN charter's principle of maintaining peace not only with words but

---

34. Ibid., pp. 678–79.

35. Secretariat of the Joint Staff Council, "Shoyō bōeiryoku no kentō" (Study on required defense forces), March 31, 1955, B-4, Dōba Hajime monjo, PSI.

through actions as a "modern spirit" that Japan should uphold.[36] Similar understandings appeared in the NDC's draft for basic defense principles. The draft indicated that Japan must "actively support the UN's activities" and "contribute to peace in the Far East as well as the world." This paragraph caught the attention of some senior LDP members at the Council's Executive Committee. "What is the meaning of 'active support' and how far can we go in this respect?" asked one member. This was followed by another comment: "Our concern after reading it [the draft] was that it may have an overtone of sending troops overseas." These suspicions were immediately rebutted by other members who felt that the paragraph was "meaningful" and hence should not be deleted.[37] Unable to work out a compromise in the Executive Committee, the problem was transferred to Prime Minister Kishi, who was also the chairman of the NDC. While having no problem with "active support" to the UN, Kishi agreed that contributing to peace in the Far East and the world could carry the danger of overseas military deployment. Upon his instruction, the NDC submitted another draft, in which reference to Japan's active role in maintaining peace in the Far East and the world was dropped. Nevertheless, the draft retained the paragraph concerning UN cooperation, though the wording was changed from "actively support" to "support."[38]

The compromised version of the principles did not completely eliminate the tug-of-war among LDP leaders in relation to the overseas dispatch of SDF. In addition to the main text, the NDC also drafted an official interpretation for these principles, reiterating that Japanese cooperation with the UN would be conducted within the framework of the constitution and therefore could not involve military actions beyond the limit of self-defense, such as sending troops to a foreign na-

---

36. Secretariat of the Joint Staff Council, "Chūritsu seisaku no gunjiteki kanōsei" (The military feasibility of a neutral policy), October 22, 1956, ibid.

37. NDC, "Kokubō no kihon hōshin shingi, kanjikai" (Deliberation of the basic principles for national defense, the executive committee), April 30, 1957, E-2b, ibid.

38. NDC, "Kokubō no kihon hōshin no shingi" (Deliberation of the basic principles for national defense), May 2, 1957, ibid.

tion.[39] This proposal again chafed some members of the NDC's Executive Committee. Kodaki Hin, an LDP member then serving as director general of the Defense Agency (JDA), complained that the interpretation was "a little bit weak." Mizuta Mikio, another influential LDP politician who was Kishi's finance minister, asked the government to remove the section prohibiting military cooperation with the UN from the interpretation.[40]

Despite the dissent of certain conservative politicians, the government published the Basic Principles of National Defense in accordance with the NDC's revised version—a mild statement leaving little room for the dispatch of Japanese troops abroad. But those who hoped for a larger military role for the SDF did not easily abandon their beliefs. When phrasing the text of the Basic Principles of National Defense, government and LDP policy planners considered the problem of SDF overseas missions in relation to what was considered the ideal type of UN force proposed by the UN charter. Sending the SDF to such a UN force was hardly a realistic option from the outset since the latter may be used to conduct combat missions, which are prohibited by Japan's constitution. Nevertheless, the weakness of the UN's security function offered a window for those favoring the SDF's presence in a different type of international peace mission—the PKO forces.

Because of the UN's inability to organize a formal UN force during the Cold War, a UN peacekeeping force specializing in surveillance and maintaining order was created in 1956 after the Suez Crisis and soon became a widely used method to partially fulfill the UN's duty in handling international conflicts. The Lebanon crisis in 1958 was the first international security event that made Japanese officials and LDP politicians seriously dwell on the option of using SDF personnel as part of a UN PKO force. In late July of that year, UN Secretary General Hammarskjold passed a *note verbale* to the Japanese government requesting the dispatch of ten SDF officers to join the PKO observation group in

---

39. NDC, "'Kokubō no kihon hōshin' no kaisetsu" (Interpretation of the "basic principles for national defense"), 1957, ibid.
40. NDC, "Kokubō no kihon hōshin no kaisetsu shingi, kanjikai" (Deliberation of the interpretation of the basic principles for national defense, the executive committee), May 20, 1957, ibid.

Lebanon.[41] Before the UN had made this formal request, JDA policy-makers, led by General Director and LDP cabinet member Satō Gisen, had already put forth a plan to send SDF soldiers to the PKO in Lebanon in the name of "training," as the SDF Law did not forbid overseas dispatch of SDF personnel for training purposes.[42] MOFA, for its part, also felt obliged to cooperate with the PKO, yet it preferred to send SDF officers under the guise of diplomats in hopes of evading legal conflicts with the opposition.[43] But when the issue was taken up in the cabinet meeting, many conservative leaders appeared to be unsure about the desirability of touching upon this sensitive issue and preferred to let the proposal rest for the time being. Yielding to the negative opinions, on July 30 the government declined the UN's request to contribute SDF officers to the PKO mission in Lebanon.[44]

Though Tokyo had chosen to play it safe in Lebanon, as noted by officials from MOFA and the JDA, the general question of SDF assignment in PKO still remained "open for future decision."[45] Domestic debate on Japan's cooperation with PKO was rekindled in February 1961 when Ambassador to the UN Matsudaira told a group of LDP politicians that it was time to send SDF to the UN's peacekeeping forces in the Congo. Outside Japan, the US government also gave certain attention to this matter when considering a boost in Japan's national defense buildup in the early 1960s.[46] Secretary of State Rusk, for instance, said at a State Department internal meeting in December 1963 that supplying SDF personnel for UN PKO "might be a neat gimmick to permit the Japanese to get around the political obstacle to their developing a larger defense force." But it took another year or two before

---

41. Message from Hammarskjold, July 27, 1957, MOFAD.

42. Tokyo to Washington, July 19, 1958, Box 40, Japan Post Files, NA.

43. Treaties Bureau, "Jieitai no kokuren kanshidan sanka ni kansuru hōritsujō no shomondai" (Legal problems with the SDF's participation in the UN observation group), July 31, 1958.

44. Tokyo to Washington, July 29, 1958, Box 40, Japan Post Files, NA; Fujiyama to Matsudaira, July 30, 1958, MOFAD; Murakami, "Kishi naikaku to kokuren gaikō," pp. 154–55.

45. Tokyo to Washington, July 29, 1958, Box 40, Japan Post Files, NA.

46. Pan, "Amerika no tainichi seisaku ni okeru kokuren heiwa iji katsudō sanka mondai," pp. 4–6.

the members of the Japanese ruling party started reconsidering the use-fulness of this "gimmick."[47]

On June 19, 1960, the new US-Japan Security Treaty was ratified in the Diet. LDP leaders, nevertheless, had not been completely liberated from their concerns regarding national security, for they still had to face one last hurdle: the need to make a decision by 1970 on whether the treaty should be extended. In April 1962, the party set up a Security Policy Study Committee (SPSC) to search for an efficient policy on the matter. Rather than stabilizing the existing security arrangement with the US, the members of the committee, many of whom were recruited from hawkish nationalistic factions of the party, decided to use this opportunity to create a more independent defense system upheld by a strong military force that could be deployed outside Japan proper. The UN PKO would have a big role to play in this plan.

During the first few years after its commencement, the SPSC showed no specific interest in UN affairs. It was not until 1964, when discussions on the PKO issue were rekindled within the government, that the committee's attitude began to change. In April 1966, the SPSC summoned officials from MOFA and the Cabinet Legislation Bureau (CLB) to discuss the correlations between the Japanese constitution and the UN's peacekeeping functions. Both MOFA and the CLB had already embarked on their own studies concerning domestic legislation on PKO cooperation before sitting down for the meeting.[48] The focus of the SPSC's study, however, was slightly different from that of the bureaucrats.

Compared to MOFA and the CLB, who considered the issue from the standpoint of strengthening the UN peacekeeping function and Japan's international status, what attracted the SPSC was the possibility of using the UN PKO to dodge the domestic barrier for the SDF's overseas deployment. Hence, during the meeting SPSC members repeatedly questioned whether there would be a solid legal basis to separate "police missions" from "military missions" and justify the dispatching of SDF to the former. They also asked MOFA and CLB officials to confirm that if Japan were going to organize a "UN standby force" for

---

47. "Japanese Forces for UN Peace-Keeping Operations," memo from Hilsman to Bacon, December 3, 1963, Box 6, Roger Hilsman Papers, JFKL.

48. See Chapter 9.

purposes such as "public peace and order" or "social welfare," this would not be considered a violation of the constitution. One member even raised the possibility that Japanese citizens might join UN forces as "volunteer soldiers" through the coordination of a "special agency" other than the government.[49]

Two weeks after its meeting with MOFA and the CLB, the committee circulated a draft report within the LDP as a trial balloon to test the ruling party's reaction to their audacious design for the nation's security. The draft, issued under the name of SPSC Chairman Hoshina Zenshirō (a former Imperial Navy admiral), suggested amending the security treaty so that it could be extended for another ten years and be ratified every five years after that. It also recommended that the government deploy, if not produce, nuclear weapons in Japanese territory, set up a Ministry of Defense, introduce anti-espionage legislation and, more important, establish a regular defensive military force to supplant the current SDF. Specifically regarding the last suggestion, the committee proposed a new Article 9 for the constitution: "For the sake of its own security, Japan may obtain a defensive military force with a mission to cooperate with an international peace organization, in particular the UN."[50]

Aside from the opposition parties and the media, many LDP faction leaders were among the most vehement critics of the SPSC draft proposal. The main target of their criticism was the thought of extending the security treaty only for a fixed term, because this would force the government to revise the treaty and thus run the risk of repeating the political catastrophe of 1960 caused by the conclusion of the current treaty. Members of the party's Foreign Affairs Study Committee (FASC) also felt uncomfortable with the "strong militarily confrontational tendency" of the draft and demanded more emphasis on the "diplomatic"

---

49. MOFA and CLB, "Kokuren keisatsu gun oyobi taikigun kōsō ni tsuite" (Proposals on UN police and standby forces), April 22, 1966, in Watanabe Yōzō and Okakura, *Nichibei anpo jōyaku sono kaisetsu to shiryō,* pp. 201–11.

50. "Nichibei anpo jōyaku mondai o chūshin to shita kakutō no gaikō bōei seisaku" (Each party's diplomatic and defense policies particularly in relation to the US-Japan Security Treaty), undated, Wada Hiroo monjo, NDL; Ikei and Horie, *Nihon no seitō to gaikō seisaku kokusaiteki genjitsu to no rakusa,* pp. 20–21.

aspects of national security.[51] The item of making military contributions to the UN was taken up in this connection. In the same month that the SPSC proposal was issued, former Foreign Minister Kosaka, then vice chairman of FASC, published a journal article expressing different views on the feasibility of military cooperation with the UN. While endorsing the dispatch of Japanese military specialists under the status of "MOFA officers" to participate in PKO for "fact-finding" purposes, Kosaka argued that the SDF troops must confine their duty to the maintenance of national security and therefore should not be sent to any PKO mission other than the UN force proposed by Article 43 of the charter. "Since the UN force postulated in the charter does not exist nowadays," he contended, "it is appropriate for us to cautiously avoid misleading statements on this issue."[52]

Facing criticism from their own colleagues, SPSC members had no choice but to go through the same process as the NDC had done nine years earlier to search for a compromise. But they were unwilling to concede more than minor amendments. In late June, a revised draft titled "Interim Report on Our National Security" was made public. The report largely preserved the idea of extending the security treaty for a fixed term, whereas the wordings of other controversial sections like the nuclear weapons issue and anti-espionage legislation were softened. Proposals concerning the UN were rearranged into a section named "Cooperation with UN PKO" underlining the compatibility between the idea of contributing Japanese staff to UN forces and the constitution: "It cannot be called a violation of the constitution to dispatch personnel to UN forces on the basis of a request from the UN if such forces do not have the duty of military actions but rather bear the purpose of maintenance of order and stabilization of people's livelihood." Moreover, without mentioning the necessity of revising Article 9 of the constitution, the committee also maintained its position on the UN standby force.[53]

---

51. "Nichibei anpo jōyaku mondai o chūshin to shita kakutō no gaikō bōei seisaku," ibid.

52. Kosaka, "Waga kuni no kokuren kyōryoku no sho mondai," p. 24.

53. SPSC, "Waga kuni no anzen hoshō ni kansuru chūkan hōkoku" (Midterm report on our country's security), June 1966, in Watanabe Yōzō and Okakura, *Nichibei anpo jōyaku,* pp. 148–62; Tokyo to Washington, "LDP Study on Japa-

The SPSC Interim Report was far from satisfactory in the eyes of its critics within the LDP. With the tenth anniversary of the security treaty approaching, the second wave of criticism naturally zeroed in on the treaty extension problem. Fearing further troubles at this crucial juncture, the LDP leadership reshuffled the composition of the SPSC in 1967. A year later, the new SPSC recommended an automatic extension format for the security treaty.[54] But the SDF's cooperation with UN PKO remained a controversial subject among LDP politicians.

Mainstream faction members, including Prime Minister Satō, consistently denied the feasibility of the SDF's participation in PKO, whereas nationalistic party members showed no intention of backing off. "When the time is ripe, I personally believe that we should revise the SDF Law so as to conduct this sort of cooperation [with UN's peace surveillance missions]," said JDA Director General Nakasone Yasuhiro, an outspoken LDP nationalist, at the Upper House in April 1970.[55] Though Nakasone described this remark as a "personal opinion," he had no shortage of like-minded comrades.

In July 1973, the SPSC published a report on Japanese security policy during the 1970s that not only reiterated the necessity of joining UN PKO but also treated this idea as part of a "basic proposal for a self-defense buildup." The possibility of a UN standby force was no longer mentioned. Instead, the report laid out a more realistic scenario: sending regular SDF troops to take part in PKO. The authors of the report deftly chose a narrow interpretation concerning the constitutional restriction on SDF by pointing out that the constitution only prohibited dispatching SDF personnel abroad for combat missions. "If a UN police force has been established through due procedures to conduct non-combat surveillance, or in the future if a UN police force has been managed by the organization in a ideal way," they asserted, "the partici-

---

nese Security," June 21, 1966, in Reel 32, DOS 1963–66; Ikei and Horie, *Nihon no seitō to gaikō seisaku,* p. 21.

54. Tokyo to Washington, "LDP on 'Automatic Extension' of Security Treaty," June 13, 1968, Box 1561, Subject-Numeric Files 1967–69, NA; Ikei and Horie, *Nihon no seitō to gaikō seisaku,* pp. 22–24.

55. "Dai 63 kai kokkai shūgiin naikaku iinkaigiroku 18 gō" (Proceedings of the 63rd Diet Session Committee on Cabinet, Lower House, No. 18), April 23, 1970, NDL.

pation of SDF in these forces is not entirely forbidden by the constitution."[56]

It was unclear to what extent the SPSC report represented the ruling party's position in general, particularly given the fact that many influential leaders had aired completely different opinions. Even nationalistic leaders understood that with intricate legislative barriers like the amendment of the SDF Law (if not the constitution per se) there was a long way to go before SDF personnel could march under the UN banner. Some of them, such as JDA Director General Nishimura Naomi, attempted to evade domestic hurdles by searching for options to send SDF troops overseas through channels other than UN PKO.[57] Another two decades would be required for the party to reach a consensus that, if there were to be any overseas dispatch of the SDF, it must take place through the UN.

The UN and the Opposition's Alternative Security Scheme

Domestic political restrictions made the LDP unable to realize its dream of giving Japan a self-dependent security scheme based on a revised constitution. Thus, as the second-best choice, the government and LDP leaders had to stick with the current defense system offered by the security treaty, while continuing to look for a larger security role for the SDF. The opposition parties, on the other hand, were not so lucky because they did not have a current policy to rely on and were always under pressure to produce an alternative plan that looked more attractive than the government's policy in the eyes of the public.

Ever since the end of WWII, one of the major battlefields between the ruling and opposition camps in Japanese domestic politics has been the competition to offer long-term plans for the nation's security. The ruling conservatives' performance in this regard during the last few years of the occupation was unimpressive. The opposition parties, as we have already seen, fared hardly better and lost the battle with the LBP on the peace and security treaties in 1951. The result of the San Francisco Peace Conference had pressed the progressive opposition

---

56. SPSC, "Waga kuni no anzen hoshō seisaku," pp. 50–51.

57. Nishimura speech text, October 11, 1971, FCO 21/912, Reel 161, PRO.

leaders to intensify their campaign against US-Japan security cooperation. To be sure, the opposition had never stopped exposing the flaws
of the government's security policy. But what they most earnestly
needed was not material for criticism but sound counterproposals, specifically in relation to the two keystones of the conservative regime's
defense policy—the security treaty and the SDF. The idealistic UN
spirit, once again, came in handy when opposition leaders moved in
such a direction.

Until 1955, the two JSPs—the ruling conservatives' prime competitor—agreed that a military alliance with the US was not an acceptable
way to pursue national defense. But they clearly had different views on
what a preferable security formula would be when protesting against
the government's policy.

Under sensational slogans like "Young men, don't take up guns
again!" the LSP campaigned for its belief that Japan's security could
only be guaranteed if it disarmed itself while maintaining equally
friendly relationships with all nations belonging to both camps in the
Asian Pacific area. The best way to achieve this goal, according to the
party, was to adopt a "demilitarized neutral policy." Two major steps
were necessary in line with this scheme. First, the current security treaty
with the US must be abandoned, as must the Sino-Soviet Treaty for
Friendship and Mutual Assistance. After these conditions were fulfilled,
as a "third force" independent from the two blocs, the disarmed Japan
would declare its neutrality and sign treaties with the US, the USSR, the
PRC, and other Asian states leading to the establishment of a "New
Locarno Pact" in Asia—an idea inspired by Churchill's suggestion to
create a European security system similar to the 1925 Locarno Pact that
had symbolized the brief period of peace in Europe after WWI.[58] The
party cautiously differentiated this plan from the regional collective
security arrangements illustrated in the UN charter. To many left-
wing leaders, military pacts concluded among Western allies were actually part of the US strategy to offend "a particular group of nations"
under the "cloak of regional collective security." Thus, they argued that

---

58. LSP, "1952 nen no zenshin: Nihon shakaitō undō hōshin sho narabini shin
gaikō hōshin to heiwa undō" (Progress in 1952: The JSP's principles for activities, new diplomatic policies and peace movement), 1952, Asanuma Inejirō
monjo, NDL.

the New Locarno Pact they proposed was not a regional collective security pact (like the US-Japan Security Treaty) against a third party but a "nonaggression" arrangement with the nations concerned.[59]

Like the security treaty, the SDF was also not immune from being abolished in the LSP's policy blueprint. Shortly after the foundation of the SDF in 1954, the party's Policy Planning Council drafted a plan to dissolve this "unconstitutional" military force and replace it with a so-called Peace Construction Force (PCF) specializing in disaster relief, natural resource exploration, and infrastructure building. And the party hinted that this plan must be treated separately from the dissolution of the SDF, thus excluding the possibility of transferring SDF members to the PCF.[60]

Compared to the thoroughly anti-conservative stance of the LSP's proposal, the RSP's security policy was much more modest and even shared some common ground with that of the government. Harboring grave concerns about a possible Soviet invasion of Japan, the party supported Japan's identity as a member of the Western camp and dismissed the LSP's disarmed neutrality scheme as one that would leave the nation defenseless. As an alternative, the RSP based its security proposal on the UN collective security system from the very beginning and suggested that Japan's national security must ultimately be guaranteed by the UN. Like the ruling party, the RSP agreed that since the UN was unable to fulfill this duty for the time being, it was unwise to "entirely" reject a regional collective security arrangement legitimized by the UN charter. The US-Japan Security Treaty, therefore, need not be "abandoned" but should be subjected to "revision" so that certain unequal articles could be eliminated.[61]

---

59. LSP, "1954 nendo tō undō hōshin sōan" (Draft proposal of principles for activities in the year 1954), December 26, 1953, ibid.

60. JSP, *Shiryō—Nihon shakaitō 50 nen,* pp. 139–40.

61. Katō Kanjū, "Kōwa jōyaku kaisei no yōbō" (Request for the revision of the peace treaty), June 4, 1952; RSP, "Nihon shakaitō to saigunbi mondō" (Questions and answers on the JSP and rearmament), March 22, 1953; RSP Policy Council, "Heiwa, anzen hoshō oyobi jiei ni kansuru hōshin (an)" (Principles on peace, security and self-defense, draft proposal), December 28, 1953, all in Asanuma Inejirō monjo, NDL.

The RSP's attitude toward rearmament was also more tolerant than the LSP. In contrast to the LSP's demilitarization policy, the RSP was sympathetic to the idea of maintaining a defense force of a certain scale to deal with foreign aggression. While disagreeing with the government's policy on the SDF, it did not rule out the need to establish a small military force with purely self-defensive missions. Once the Cold War was over, the party even pondered, as did the government, collaboration with a "UN police force" founded neatly on the basis of the UN charter.[62]

Notwithstanding these differences in concrete policies, domestic politics soon made the split too costly for the two JSPs. As the gap between the total seats held by the LSP and RSP in the Diet and those of the ruling LBP became distinctively narrower after the first two Lower House elections in the 1950s, the two parties started searching for means to bring the division to an end.[63] In October 1953, they publicized their respective principles for reunification, and before long, members of both sides began to hold meetings to discuss this problem.[64] National defense was a thorny item during these talks, as it had been in the process of splitting years earlier. But compelled by the common need to build up a more efficient structure to fight against the conservatives, leaders of the two parties acted more realistically this time.

The united JSP's security platform, unveiled at a 1955 special assembly for reunification, was the fruit of compromise. The right wing's emphasis on Japan's role as a Western ally disappeared from the party's security principles, whereas the left wing's favorite catchphrase—"neutrality"—was diluted to an aspiration to keep good relations with "all nations from a standpoint independent from either bloc" of the Cold War. The UN, one of the few items causing no substantial controversies, served as an adhesive agent. The two sides agreed that Japan must eventually look to the UN's collective security function for its national defense. Before such an ideal UN-centered system could be established, the New Locarno Pact favored by the left wing would be the common ground for a transitional defense formula. The two JSPs had

---

62. Ibid.
63. Iokibe, *Seijishi II: Nihon seiji gaikōshi*, pp. 132–33.
64. JSP, *Shiryō—Nihon shakaitō 50 nen*, pp. 154–55.

some trouble in settling on the correlation between the New Locarno Pact and the US-Japan Security Treaty. The LSP insisted that the liquidation of the security treaty be a precondition for the pact, whereas the RSP thought the conclusion of the pact must go first. The two eventually came up with a seemingly fair way to resolve the problem: They inserted a fuzzy item into the unified JSP's platform postulating that the security treaty was to be abolished "in correspondence with" the New Locarno Pact.[65]

The RSP made more concessions in regard to the security treaty issue. This, however, was partially compensated for by the LSP's compromise on rearmament and the SDF. Concerning the former, the two parties determined that they would oppose rearmament "at present," which left room for the right wing to preserve its idea of a limited self-defense force in the future. As for the latter, the LSP not only basically followed the RSP's line to "gradually" reduce the scale of the SDF but also promised to "support a UN police force when the perfection of the UN mechanism and global disarmament are achieved."[66]

Although the 1955 platform of the unified JSP was a masterpiece of mutual compromise, it was unable to guide the party very long. During the last few years of the 1950s, as the Kishi cabinet entered negotiations for a new security treaty with the US, left-wing factions rapidly gained power within the JSP—a tendency that was further accelerated after the departure of several major right-wing leaders in October 1959. This change naturally had an effect on the party's security policy. In late 1958, echoing the appeal for neutrality from Soviet and Chinese leaders, the left wing persuaded the party's Central Committee to officially reinstate "neutralism" or "positive neutralism" in the center of the JSP's security scheme.[67] Rather than waiting for the conclusion of a New Locarno Pact, the left wing-dominated JSP now demanded the immediate abandonment of the security treaty and planned to replace the SDF with a "Peace Homeland Construction Force (PHCF)"—a proposal similar to the former LSP's PCF plan—as soon as the party came into power.[68]

---

65. Sone, "Foreign Policy of the Japan Socialist Party," pp. 22–23.
66. JSP, *Nihon shakaitō seisaku shiryō shūsei*, pp. 74–75.
67. Stockwin, *The Japanese Socialist Party and Neutralism*, p. 87.
68. JSP, *Shiryō—Nihon shakaitō 50 nen*, pp. 93–97.

The demilitarized neutral policy had made its way back to center stage with only one exception: the connection with the UN. JSP leaders, especially those belonging to the left wing, did not always feel comfortable using the UN's collective security concept insofar as the LDP government continued to characterize the security treaty as a regional security arrangement based on the UN charter. But they were equally unwilling to entirely isolate their security policy from the framework of the UN, which was traditionally one of the public's favorite options for national defense. The JSP policymakers' solution to the dilemma was to create their own interpretation of the close relations between the UN principle and the party's security proposal.

This strategy was first used to deal with the new security treaty question in 1960. Flatly rejecting the government's position that the treaty was concluded due to the inefficiency of the current UN system, JSP leaders attempted to convince the public that their party was the real faithful follower of the UN's peace ideals. "The UN is the most crucial element for the peace and security of both Japan and the world," a 1960 JSP public document read. "It may be true, as the LDP claimed, that the UN at present does not sufficiently function . . . but participation in the American military bloc is not the right thing to do."[69] The party also went further to demonstrate how the security treaty was incompatible with the UN's peaceful spirit.

Although the UN charter admits the rights of collective and individual self-defense for its members, there is a legal problem on the Japanese side if it ever tries to fully utilize these rights. If invaded by a foreign state, Japan is undoubtedly entitled to use its individual self-defense right to resist the aggression. But in terms of the collective self-defense right that permits a nation to take military actions in response to a foreign attack originally launched against a third party, Japan is totally handcuffed by its constitution, which prohibits the use of military force to resolve international disputes. The government is inclined to take the view that while legally having a collective self-defense right, Japan shall not actually exercise such a right in pursuing national defense. Actions taken on the Japanese side in accordance with the security treaty, there-

---

69. JSP, "Anpo jōyaku kaitei ni tsuite: Jimintō no kenkai ni kanren shite" (The revision of the security treaty: regarding the LDP's opinions), 1960, Asanuma Inejirō monjo, NDL.

fore, are based on "individual" rather than "collective" self-defense rights.[70] The JSP, nevertheless, rejected this official position.

Categorizing the treaty as a "mutual defense" pact like NATO arrangements, the party accused the LDP government and its American counterparts of plotting to use the collective self-defense right to fight against specific "potential enemy states" (such as the PRC and the USSR). Such a treaty, the JSP determined, was an "abuse" of the UN charter. Instead of using Article 51 of the charter concerning regional collective security arrangements, the party found the legal basis for this charge in Article 2 regarding the peaceful solution of international disputes and the prohibition of the threat or use of military force against the territorial integrity or political independence of other nations. By turning to this article, the JSP easily reached the conclusion it needed: The LDP's security treaty infringed upon the UN charter, whereas the nonaggression collective security pact proposed by the JSP was a formula "in harmony with the charter," for it neither served any military bloc nor was designed to compete with any other nation.[71]

By reemphasizing the similarities in spirit between the UN charter and the JSP's security proposal, the party put itself in an advantageous position to counter the conservative regime's pro-UN strategy. But with JSP leaders adamantly opposed to the regional collective security system proposed by Article 51 of the charter, an awkward situation became more and more salient: The party supported the UN charter's pacifist ideals on the one hand while refusing to adopt the security formula recommended by the charter on the other. Until the late 1960s, the nonaggression collective security treaty with the US, the USSR, the PRC, and later a united Korea constantly served as the JSP's standard counterproposal to the US-Japan Security Treaty. It was incorporated into the party's "Long-Term Political and Economic Plan" in 1961; the 1964 party platform, "A Path to Socialism in Japan"; and the 1968 security platform "A Path Toward Demilitarization and Peaceful Neutral-

---

70. Satō Isao, "Dai kyū jō no seifu kaishaku no kiseki to ronten (ge)," pp. 40–42.

71. JSP, "Mondai no shōten o sorasu Jimintō" (LDP turning away from the focal point of the issue), June 11, 1960; JSP, "Shin anpo jōyaku fushōnin sengen" (Declaration of non-recognition of the new security treaty), June 19, 1960, both in Asanuma Inejirō monjo, NDL.

ity." However, the linkage between this proposal and the collective security idea of the UN remained unclear. The party diligently refrained from using terms such as "collective security" or "regional security" that could remind people of Article 51 of the UN charter.[72] One JSP member even stated in the Diet that Article 51 was illegally inserted into the charter draft by the US and therefore must be deleted during charter revision.[73] After all, it was up to the party to decide which part of the UN charter must be played up or played down in its policy plans.

From a domestic political standpoint, the JSP's selective use of the UN as a prop in its campaign was undoubtedly a crafty tactic against the LDP. But it was also a cause of infighting when members of the party's policymaking team held different opinions as to whether or when such a tactic should be employed. In the 1960s, this type of problem occurred when policy staff proposed amending the JSP's position on another crucial security issue, the SDF.

Since the late 1950s, the JSP's official plan to resolve the SDF problem had been to dissolve the SDF and replace it with an unarmed PHCF. But as the international tension around Japan continued to intensify, the plan for an immediate abandonment of military forces for self-defense appeared too radical even in the views of some JSP policymakers like the chairman of the party's Diplomatic and Defense Committee, Ishibashi Masashi. Based on his experience of giving lectures at various SDF training programs, Ishibashi was suspicious about the practicality of the SDF dissolution proposal and believed that a more persuasive plan was necessary in the current situation. After five years of research, he made the first bid to streamline the party's SDF policy in 1966.[74]

In April that year, Ishibashi circulated a policy draft titled "The Formula to Transfer JSP Security Policy" (later known as the "Ishibashi Plan") at the party's Policy Planning Council, in which he dismissed the

---

72. JSP, *Nihon shakaitō seisaku shiryō shūsei*, pp. 190–91, pp. 494–95 and p. 519.

73. "Dai 48 kai kokkai shūgiin gaimu iinkaigiroku dai 14 gō" (Proceedings of the 48th Diet Session Committee on Foreign Affairs, Lower House, No. 14), April 9, 1965 and "Dai 48 kai kokkai shūgiin gaimu iinkaigiroku dai 17 gō" (Proceedings of the 48th Diet Session Committee on Foreign Affairs, Lower House, No. 17), April 23, 1965, both NDL.

74. Ishibashi, *"Gojugo nen taisei" uchigawa kara no shōgen*, pp. 112–13.

current policy to completely abolish the SDF. According to his plan, after the JSP came into power, the SDF would first be downgraded to a more modest force called "the People's Police Force" (PPF). The party would then further scale down the PPF based on four conditions: the stability of the JSP regime, the government's ability to efficiently control the PPF, the amelioration of the international environment, and the support of public opinion. Only when all four conditions were met would the PPF be transformed into a completely unarmed force. The traditional PHCF idea, on the other hand, was preserved in the plan, though it was not an alternative to the SDF but just one separate proposal during the process. Finally, regarding the concern about national defense under an unarmed police force, Ishibashi turned to the UN. He hinted that in the long run, the best way to maintain the security of all nations, including Japan, was to rely on a UN police force in which Japanese people could participate. While currently the UN might not be able to function as the charter had anticipated, he believed that the organization was heading in such a direction because of the rise of AA member states and the possible restoration of the PRC's membership.[75]

The Ishibashi Plan was a giant leap from the JSP's traditional policy with respect to the SDF. Yet the party leadership controlled by left-wing factions was unable to immediately accept it. Specifically bothered by the cautious steps designed for a phased SDF reduction, left-wing leaders suspected Ishibashi of contemplating acknowledging the present existence of military forces. They also strongly opposed the close relationship between the unarmed PPF and the UN police force, worrying that this would blur the party's opposition to the LDP's proposal to use UN PKO as a starting point for sending the SDF overseas.[76] It

---

75. The only reservation he made was that if Japanese citizens were going to join such a UN police force, it would be "preferable" for them to do this "individually rather than in the form of military units." JSP, *Nihon shakaitō seisaku shiryō shūsei,* pp. 506–8; "The Ishibashi Defense Plan," memo of conversation, June 6, 1966 and "The Japan Socialist Party's Draft Policy Proposal on Defense and Security," June 8, 1966, both in Reel 32, DOS 1963–66; "Shakaitō no anzen hoshō seisaku (an)" (Draft plan on the JSP's security policy), Ishibashi Masashi monjo, NDL.

76. Williams to Pickles, July 8, 1966, FO 371/187115, Reel 140, PRO; Ishibashi, *"Gojūgo nen taisei" uchigawa kara no shōgen,* pp. 112–17; "Nichibei anpo jōyaku

took almost three years for the party to coordinate its position on this issue. Starting in August 1966, the JSP produced at least three compromised plans, into which Ishibashi's original ideas were incorporated little by little. But facing the government's inclination to automatically extend the security treaty, the party's supporters became impatient. Local party representatives' demand for a more clear-cut answer to the conservative camp's challenge concerning the SDF put a heavy strain on the JSP leadership. In December 1969, just a few days before the last general election prior to the tenth anniversary of the security treaty, the JSP Central Committee finally decided to let Ishibashi publicize his plan in a party journal that was then circulated to all party organizations.[77] While still refusing to accept any proposal to send the SDF overseas via the UN track, the JSP could not avoid adopting a double standard by ensconcing its alternative plan on defense forces into a UN-related framework.

During the 1960s and early 1970s, the JSP was not the only opposition party that took advantage of the UN in legitimizing security policies. Two newly founded parties, the DSP and the CGP, were actually more enthusiastic in exploring the potential of the UN.

Inheriting the tradition of the former RSP, DSP policy planners exhibited a strong tendency to emphasize their party's passion toward the UN when handling security issues. Under the leadership of Chairman Nishio Suehiro, the DSP's major concern in the early 1960s was to plant its defense policy somewhere between the policies of the LDP and the JSP so that it could be freed from the conservative vs. progressive impasse in this area and thereby move closer to the throne of the ruling party. But like what happened in other parties, before a desirable policy could be found, the DSP also first needed to unify the opinions of its own members on two fundamental defense problems: the security treaty and the SDF.

---

mondai o chūshin to shita kakutō no gaikō bōei seisaku," Wada Hiroo monjo, NDL.

77. Murasawa, "Seisaku shōiinkai hōkoku," p. 260; JSP, *Nihon shakaitō seisaku shiryō shūsei,* pp. 513–21; JSP, "Toward Peace and Security for Japan," August 31, FO 371/187080, Reel 137, PRO; Ishibashi, *"Gojūgo nen taisei,"* p. 117; Ishibashi, "Hibusō chūritsu kenpō o sekai no kenpō ni," pp. 24–37.

When deciding the party's provisional platform in 1960, the DSP leadership was already tormented by these two problems. Influential members, including Nishio and Sone, supported the US-Japan alliance and the idea of having a military force for self-defense. Yet there were many moderate leaders who still held a position close to that of the JSP. As a result, the party issued a security policy draft in which different opinions were sheltered under a common set of expectations with regard to the UN. It agreed that Japan must depend on the UN's peace-keeping function for its national defense. Until the UN was ready to shoulder such a responsibility, a regional collective security arrangement was necessary. Unlike the LDP, the DSP did not consider the current security treaty a satisfactory regional collective security format. But neither did it concur with the JSP's recommendation to abrogate the treaty immediately. The path the party agreed on was to "gradually" abandon the treaty without destroying the security balance between the East and the West. The party also did not accept the SDF as an appropriate self-defense force and felt it must be reorganized to fulfill the requirement for only "minimum" self-defense needs.[78]

The DSP's moderate members did not feel comfortable even with the security position of the provisional platform. As the party began to draft a definitive version for the platform in 1961, they rehashed their demands for a further modest security policy. Their stance was so firm that the mainstream leaders had little choice but to make more concessions. Reference to regional collective security arrangements disappeared in the final platform, for the two sides failed to reach a consensus on whether its preferred security formula for the nation should be collective security or "non-aligned neutrality." The party's position on the security treaty was unchanged, whereas its policy on military force was tightened. The term "minimum measures for self-defense" was altered to "minimum measures to protect the nation" because moderate members thought "self-defense" might collide with Article 9 of the constitution. Aside from these changes, however, the UN was still ubiquitous in the platform, which promised to support UN reinforcement and the establishment of a UN police force so that the organiza-

---

78. Ikei and Horie, *Nihon no seitō to gaikō seisaku,* pp. 32–33; Kamijō, "Minshatō kihon seisaku no hensen," pp. 48–49; "Social Democratic Party Draft Foreign Policy Statement," December 29, 1959, Reel 1, DOS 1960–63.

tion could move forward toward an ideal "world nation." In November 1961, the DSP Central Executive Committee issued a supplementary declaration to clarify the correlations among the "minimum measures to protect the nation," the constitution, and the UN charter. While using the charter to legitimize Japan's right for self-defense until the UN could take actions to nullify military aggressions against Japanese territory, the declaration also stated that Japan's defense force must never be used to "launch preemptive attacks under the name of self-defense or unlimitedly expand counterattacks neglecting UN resolutions."[79]

Political bargaining among DSP members on national security continued for another few years despite the issuance of the platform. But with conservative members firmly holding key posts in the party's leadership, the DSP's overall defense policy shifted gradually to the right. Bit by bit, the nebulous position on collective security and neutrality gave way to a more forthright stance favoring the collective security scheme. "While each state must choose a defense formula by itself," the party stated in its 1963 defense proposal, "our principle is to strengthen UN-centered collective security while philosophically rejecting neutrality."[80] In 1966, the DSP formally declared that it had decided to ask for "revision," not "gradual abandonment," of the security treaty, again taking shelter under the UN: "As an independent state responsible to the nation and its people and as a member of the international community, it is our duty to maintain autonomous defense measures to protect our nation and deter foreign aggressions, and to conclude regional collective security arrangements admitted by the UN charter with other nations as a complement for self-defense."[81] For the three decades that followed, the party never deviated much from this position, which had no substantial differences from that of the LDP.

A more drastic change took place in the party's policy on military forces and the SDF. Though the 1960 DSP provisional platform suggested a reduction in the SDF, a national police force in charge of do-

---

79. Satō Hiroyuki, *Nihon no seitō kōryō,* pp. 46–52 and pp. 273–74; Wada, "'Jiei' no hyōgen o kaeta tō kōryō," pp. 100–101.

80. DSP, "Bōei to anzen hoshō narabini heiwa no tame no hōsaku," July 25, 1963, p. 15.

81. DSP, "Anzen hoshō to bōei ni kansuru waga tō no kihon hōshin," October 12, 1966, p. 15.

mestic order as depicted by the JSP was definitely not the ideal out-come for the DSP's "minimum self-defense force." In actuality, the party became increasingly interested in seeking a more proactive role for a Japanese military force in maintaining international peace. If such a tendency had appeared as part of the party's SDF policy, it would probably have been nipped in the bud for ignoring the constitutional prohibition on overseas military deployment. But the DSP shrewdly staved off this risk by linking its proposal with the party's longstanding wish to "magnify the UN mechanism," in particular the peacekeeping function.

The DSP originally opposed the idea of sending Japanese personnel to participate in UN PKO. And in February 1961 when UN Ambassador Matsudaira was reported to have urged Japan's participation in the PKO in the Congo, it had joined the JSP and the JCP to warn of the dangerous connection between PKO cooperation and the dispatch of Japanese troops abroad.[82] In less than two years, however, the party shifted its position in the opposite direction. In January 1963, the DSP stated in its annual foreign policy draft that it would promote the establishment of a UN police force and might support Japan's participation in such a force at a time when "progress has been made in disarmament among nations."[83] This idea was fleshed out in a security policy proposal published six months later, in which the party discussed concrete plans to strengthen the UN by authorizing interventions by the UNSC and UNGA in international conflicts and sending police forces to PKO missions. The proposal repeated the suggestion to found a "standing UN police force" in the long run and required all military forces to be either abrogated or transferred to that UN force when it was established.[84]

The Nordic nations' movement to build up a UN standby force around 1964 further stimulated the DSP's passion toward Japan's role in

---

82. "Dai 38 kai kokkai sangiin honkaigiroku dai 9 gō" (Proceedings of the 38th Diet Session Plenary Session, Upper House, No. 9), February 24, 1961 and "Dai 39 kai kokkai sangiin gaimu iinkaigiroku dai 6 gō" (Proceedings of the 39th Diet Session Committee on Foreign Affairs, Upper House, No. 6), October 24, 1961, both in NDL; Kōzai, *Kokuren no heiwa iji katsudō*, p. 490.
83. DSP, "Shōwa sanjūhachi nendo gaikō seisaku," p. 140.
84. DSP, "Bōei to anzen hoshō narabini heiwa no tame no hōsaku," p. 16.

UN PKO. Citing the Nordic nations' standby force plans, DSP members cornered government leaders at the Diet in an effort to induce the latter to make positive remarks on Japanese personnel cooperation with PKO.[85] At first, these DSP members still admitted that coordination with the constitution and the SDF Law might be necessary for such cooperation. But before long, they started playing down the legal barriers for Japan's joining in PKO. "Although Japan has adopted a UN-centric policy, it seems to me that the government would not like to make sacrifices to promote the UN-centric diplomacy," a DSP member grilled Foreign Minister Shiina at a Diet session in March 1965. "If Japan really believes in pacifism, it should be more active in handling the UN police force problem, which would cause no trouble regarding the constitution."[86]

As the government showed no sign of following the DSP in addressing this sensitive topic, an ironic phenomenon surfaced in Diet debate after the mid-1960s. Politicians from the DSP, an opposition party that characterized itself as middle-of-the-road, enthusiastically worked to persuade the supposedly more hawkish LDP leaders to let Japanese military officers take part in overseas missions of UN PKO. On several occasions, DSP members even tried to remind their conservative counterparts of loopholes in current legislation that could be used to avoid domestic troubles if the government was going to make a breakthrough on this issue.[87] At least in relation to the domain of the SDF's mission, the DSP obviously held a far more ambitious plan than the ruling LDP.

---

85. "Dai 47 kai kokkai shūgiin yosan iinkaigiroku dai 6 gō" (Proceedings of the 47th Diet Session Budget Committee, Lower House, No. 6), December 4, 1964, NDL.

86. Kōzai, *Kokuren no heiwa iji katsudō*, p. 492.

87. "Dai 55 kai kokkai shūgiin gaimu iinkaigiroku dai 12 gō" (Proceedings of the 55th Diet Session Committee on Foreign Affairs, Lower House, No. 12), June 14, 1964, "Dai 55 kai kokkai shūgiin naikaku iinkaigiroku dai 28 gō" (Proceedings of the 55th Diet Session Committee on Cabinet, Lower House, No. 28), July 5, 1967, "Dai 63 kai kokkai shūgiin honkaigiroku dai 13 gō" (Proceedings of the 63rd Diet Session Plenary Session, Lower House, No. 13), March 26, 1970, "Dai 68 kai kokkai shūgiin yosan iinkaigiroku dai 8 gō" (Proceedings of the 68th Diet Session Budget Committee, Lower House, No. 8), March 2, 1972, and "Dai 76 kai kokkai shūgiin naikaku iinkaigiroku dai 10 gō" (Proceedings of the

If the UN could be described as a neutralizer that mollified the DSP's nationalistic image, the organization's function in the CGP's security schemes was more like a magnet that absorbed vague policy fragments into a perceivably unified framework. Like its foreign policy, the security stance of the CGL, the CGP's predecessor, was in no sense clearly articulated during the early days of the party. The CGL protested the conservative ruling party's move toward revising the constitution and exhibited a deep abhorrence of nuclear weapons, reiterating that those trying to wage a nuclear war must "be sentenced to death." But despite these passionate statements, the CGL had never offered concrete plans regarding the path that the nation must take either to defend itself or to maintain international peace.[88]

After deciding to seek seats in the more influential Lower House, the CGP rapidly moved its interest from constructing an idealistic society to what it could do to reinforce national defense under the current situation. And it was during this change that the party began to view the UN's collective security mechanism as a realistic policy alternative to the government's defense policy. At a special party convention held in June 1966—five months before a general election—the CGP announced its new security proposal. Maintaining the position that a so-called global nationalistic society was the ideal formula for international security, the proposal acknowledged that before such a society could become a reality it was crucial to strengthen the UN's security function and hasten the establishment of a "UN police force to maintain the world order." With this understanding, all regional collective security arrangements including NATO and the US-Japan Security Treaty must be "gradually" abrogated. The SDF would be "maintained for the time being" and would eventually be dissolved once the UN police force started functioning and an "Asian Branch" of the force was set up in Japan. Individual SDF members, at the same time, would have to make a choice to either join the UN force or find work in the private sector.[89]

76th Diet Session Committee on Cabinet, Lower House, No. 10), December 16, 1975, NDL.

88. Ikei and Horie, *Nihon no seitō to gaikō seisaku,* pp. 63–64.

89. CGP, "'Heiwa e no michi' anzen hoshō" ("The path toward peace" security), July 1966, Wada Hiroo monjo, NDL.

The 1966 security proposal was the most substantial defense plan drafted thus far by the CGP, but it was still insufficient, as it did not present any concrete thoughts on a security formula for the transitional stage between the security treaty/SDF system and the UN-centered collective security system. Both the JSP and the DSP had faced similar problems in the past. The former decided to count on collective nonaggression pacts with neighboring powers, a small police force, and the unarmed PHCF. The latter chose to generally preserve the security treaty and the SDF while using collaboration with UN PKO to rebut charges of copying the government's policy. Vacillating between the two socialist parties, the CGP needed another two years until it was able to find its own policy, namely a "complete neutrality" (or "equidistant complete neutrality") scheme emphasizing active diplomatic, not military, cooperation with the UN.

The "complete neutrality" scheme made its debut in April 1968 when the CGP unveiled a rough proposal of its procedure to gradually abrogate the security treaty.[90] Eight months later, it appeared in a refined draft of the proposal that was adopted as the party's security plan for the 1970s. The proposal divided Japan's national security into three stages. The first stage was the current security treaty system. This was to be replaced by complete neutrality in the second stage, in which the nation would keep neutral in international affairs while making positive efforts to create a peaceful international environment. In this stage, the CGP planned to take sequential steps such as removing US bases or refusing a self-defense buildup so that the security treaty would exist in name only and lose its *raison d'être*. In addition, the nation's safety under the complete neutrality system would be guaranteed by both diplomatic and minimum defense measures. Diplomatically, such actions, including establishing a nonaggression system in the Asian Pacific, introducing a "UN Asian Regional Headquarters" (UNARH) to Japan, and normalizing relations with the PRC, were indispensable. These would be strengthened by transforming the SDF into a "Territorial Defense Force" (TDF) with less powerful equipment and stricter civilian control. When all these goals were achieved, Japan would then reach the final

---

90. Ikei and Horie, *Nihon no seitō to gaikō seisaku,* pp. 70–72.

stage of its security efforts: a "universal collective security system" in which the TDF would be assigned to a UN police force.[91]

The complete neutrality scheme filled several theoretical blanks left by the 1966 security proposal. But CGP leaders did not stop at picturing scenarios. To them, it was more critical to show the public that the party's plan was not only attractive as an idea but also workable as a policy. Among the measures listed in the 1968 proposal, no evidence demonstrated that the CGP ever treated the promotion of nonaggression arrangements among Asian Pacific states—a proposal originally issued by the JSP—as anything beyond a political watchword. The party's role in the normalization of Sino-Japan relations was remarkable. Yet again, the CGP was neither the first nor the only political party in Japan to come up with the idea of smoothing relations with Beijing. And its motivation for tackling this issue was also far more complicated than concerns about national defense.

In contrast, the UNARH plan was the only measure that was initially devised by the CGP itself. The plan was directly linked with the phased dissolution of the security treaty, the cornerstone of the complete neutrality scheme from the outset. When announcing the UNARH plan in a press conference on January 6, 1969, CGP chairman Takeiri Yoshikatsu characterized it as "part of the preconditions to gradually discard the security treaty." The proposed headquarters would be set up as a "permanent supplementary agency of the UNGA and UNSC" specializing in fact-finding, mediation, and arbitration missions whenever a military conflict occurred in Asia. The Secretariat of UNARH should be located in Japan and would be led by one of the USGs of the UN.[92]

In February, the CGP embarked on a campaign both in Japan and abroad to promote this plan. Domestically, party leaders used the occasion of Diet debate to solicit a government promise for the necessary assistance, and Takeiri formally asked Prime Minister Satō to obtain the endorsement of the US when the latter visited Washington in November. The party also discussed the issue with other opposition parties in order to add a supra-partisan hue to the plan. The early response to

---

91. Ishihara Iwane, *Kōmeitō no seiji,* pp. 149–53; CGP, "Nichibei anpo taisei no dankaiteki kaishō no hōto," pp. 366–67.

92. Watanabe Ichirō, "Kokuren Ajia honbu secchi no igi　sono hassō to gutaisaku o ronzu," pp. 52–54.

these efforts, though, was lukewarm at best. The LDP government officially showed their "respect" for the CGP's intention, though officials at the policymaking level thought the plan per se was "impractical" and Satō made no reference to the plan in his talks with American leaders.[93]

With the extension of the security treaty only a few months away, the CGP was not going to slow down its campaign regardless of the indifference of its domestic competitors. In October, Takeiri wrote a letter to UN Secretary General U Thant to sell the UNARH proposal. U Thant's reply, which arrived in November, was courteous and, unsurprisingly, contained no substantial commitment. But the fact that the Secretary General responded to the request had positive effects on the CGP's campaign within Japan.[94]

The party escalated its offensive toward the LDP after 1970. Government leaders shied away from positive comments at first but soon gave up as their CGP counterparts began to cite U Thant's message in Diet sessions. In March, both Prime Minister Satō and Foreign Minister Aichi expressed their willingness to cooperate with the CGP to realize the UNARH plan. As a symbolic gesture, Satō told U Thant when the latter visited Tokyo in early April that he would like to see "something similar" to the UNARH located in Japan. Takeiri also gained an opportunity to discuss the issue with U Thant in person during the Secretary General's stay.[95] While U Thant remained cautious, the CGP seemed to

---

93. Adachi, *Shinsei suru kōmeitō,* pp. 144–46; "Dai 61 kai kokkai shūgiin honkaigiroku dai 4 gō" (Proceedings of the 61st Diet Session Plenary Session, Lower House, No. 4), January 30, 1969 and "Dai 61 kai kokkai shūgiin gaimu iinkaigiroku dai 2 gō" (Proceedings of the 61st Diet Session Committee on Foreign Affairs, Lower House, No. 2), February 17, 1969, NDL; Ishihara Iwane, *Kōmeitō no seiji,* p. 215; New York to Washington, March 29, 1969, Box 3207, Subject-Numeric Files 1967–69, NA.

94. Watanabe Ichirō, "'Kokuren Ajia honbu' secchi no igi," pp. 22–23.

95. "Dai 63 kai kokkai shūgiin yosan iinkai dai ni bunkakaigiroku dai 1 gō" (Proceedings of the 63rd Diet Session Second Subcommittee of the Budget Committee, Lower House, No. 1), March 11, 1970 and "Dai 63 kai kokkai sangiin yosan iinkai dai 1 gō" (Proceedings of the 63rd Diet Session Budget Committee, Upper House, No. 1), April 13, 1970, NDL; Adachi, *Shinsei suru kōmeitō,* pp. 147–48; Policy Division of the UN Bureau, "Satō sōri, U Tan kokuren jimusōchō kaidan kiroku" (Record of meeting between Prime Minister Satō and UN Secretary General U Thant), April 20, 1970, pp. 6–7, MOFAD.

be quite satisfied with the plan's ramifications. Until the party switched its policy from phased abolishment to immediate dissolution of the security treaty in 1973, the UNARH was a regular topic in the CGP's defense policy drafts, Diet statements, and propaganda articles, notwithstanding the fact that the chance of the UN implementing this proposal was next to zero.[96] To the party, what ultimately mattered was not the successful establishment of a UN regional headquarters on Japanese territory but the public impression that the CGP had the ability to pursue its own security proposal at this critical moment of the government's automatic renewal of the security treaty.

The practicality of various security schemes was an issue confronted by all the parties, not only by the ruling and opposition parties that more or less admitted the merit of a democratic political system. The JCP, a party that aimed at entirely reconstructing the nation's political life based on Marxist-Leninist ideologies, faced the same problem. And despite its willingness, the party also had to ask for the UN's help when coping with this issue.

Being one of the two biggest progressive parties, the JCP persistently required the immediate abrogation of both the US-Japan Security Treaty and the SDF. Around the late 1950s, JCP leaders tried to use the UN charter to deny the legitimacy of the security treaty. Both the JCP and the government emphasized Articles 51 and 52 of the UN charter in their arguments. The LDP government contended that the security treaty was a regional security arrangement that was permitted under Article 52 and concluded by exercising the collective self-defense right mentioned in Article 51. In contrast, the JCP called the security treaty a violation of both articles. According to the party, Article 51, which admits the use of the right of collective self-defense before the UNSC is able to take action, was a "single exceptional" case in the charter, which originally denied collective self-defense activities without the explicit

---

96. Rōyama and Yano, "72 nen ni okeru Nihon no sentaku," p. 31; Terasawa, Kuroyanagi and Nakagawa, "Kokuren Ajia Kyokutō chiiki honbu no secchi o isoge," pp. 38–45; "Dai 71 kai kokkai sangiin honkaigiroku dai 4 gō" (Proceedings of the 71st Diet Session Plenary Session, Upper House, No. 4), January 31, 1973, "Dai 71 kai kokkai sangiin hōmu iinkaigiroku dai 22 gō" (Proceedings of the 71st Diet Session Committee on Justice, Upper House, No. 22), September 18, 1973, NDL.

permission of the UN. Therefore, in the JCP's view, it was illegal to combine Article 51 with other articles in the charter, including Article 52, which, again based on the party's explanation, only justified regional security arrangements that were directly under the control of the UN.[97]

On the other hand, since the mid-1950s, the JCP's own security scheme had basically contained two steps. First, the party would abolish the security treaty and the SDF—the alleged real threat toward Japan's safety—while choosing a neutral position in international society. In the second stage, the party would take the necessary measures to reinforce Japan's neutrality and would maintain minimal self-defense forces that could not carry out aggressive missions. Probably due to the need to dilute this policy's overtones of rearmament, the party's attitude toward the SDF was strict. It confirmed that the SDF must be dissolved once and for all without a chance of being dispatched to UN PKO missions. Though it did not rule out the possibility of revising the constitution in the future, the party also emphasized that under the current constitution it would not encourage rearmament.[98]

These arguments were similar to those adopted by the JSP, but with one difference: The JCP was more open to the concept of a regional collective security arrangement than the JSP. As early as the mid-1950s, the JCP was already an ardent supporter of the Soviet proposal to include Japan in a regional collective security arrangement among Asian Pacific nations under the endorsement of the UN.[99] While this position blurred in the early 1960s because of the deterioration of the party's relationship with Moscow, it reemerged in the late 1960s when the JCP was pondering the policy plan with which to confront the government's attempt to extend the security treaty. The plan publicized in the Diet in June 1968 proposed that after the abandonment of the security treaty, Japan must make efforts to create a "real collective security system" in

---

97. Ueda Seikichi, "Shūdan anzen hoshō to gunji dōmei Nichibei anpo jōyaku to kokuren kenshō gojūichi jō narabini gojūni jō," pp. 51–54.

98. JCP, "Nihon no shin no anzen o mamoru tame ni Nihon kyōsantō no anzen hoshō seisaku," pp. 95–97

99. "Dai 25 kai sangiin honkaigiroku dai 11 gō" (Proceedings of the 25th Diet Session Plenary Session, Upper House, No. 11), December 5, 1956 and "Dai 32 kai kokkai sangiin honkaigiroku dai 5 gō" (Proceedings of the 32nd Diet Session Plenary Session, Upper House, No. 5), June 27, 1959, NDL.

place of the current military blocs in the world. As one element of this new system, a regional collective security arrangement incorporating all nations in the Asian Pacific area would be established. In addition, the party declared that at the time the UN was able to conduct its collective security mission based on the charter, Japan might participate in UN "sanctions against aggressors" through "non-military means."[100]

The 1968 security plan offered a fairly articulate picture of what the JCP was going to do to prevent aggression from happening, but it did not recommend any methods that could be used to defend Japan in the event the nation was actually invaded. Insisting that no threat of war could become a reality under an efficient neutrality system, the JSP had grown accustomed to avoiding this topic. The JCP took a slightly different stance. In the wake of its triumph in the 1972 general election, when the JCP became the second biggest player in the opposition camp, the party started dreaming about taking office by forming a "democratic coalition government." With itself as a candidate for the seat of ruling party in this proposed government, the JCP became more willing to take every possible security scenario into account. In 1973, the party issued its platform for the coalition government in which it stated that in a situation of actual aggression, the government would allow its people to conduct "autonomous resistance" and would mobilize "police forces" to fight against the invaders.[101] While sounding brave, the proposal was hardly logical for a nation facing an invasion by full-fledged, foreign military forces. Presumably having sensed this weakness, in 1974, the party quietly inserted a brief sentence into the previous year's platform: "It is for certain that [in the event of a pressing aggression] we will also ask for the UN's collective actions based on the charter"—a statement that acquiesced in the role of the world peace organization as the last resort in the JCP's defense plan.[102]

---

100. JCP, "Nihon no chūritsuka to anzen hoshō ni tsuite no Nihon kyōsantō no kōsō," pp. 42–44.

101. JCP, *Nihon kyōsantō no rokujū nen 1922–1982,* pp. 300–301, pp. 319–20; Nishizawa, "Kyōsantō no anpo, gaikō seisaku no yūisei Nihon no shinro to sono sōten," p. 74.

102. JCP, "Sangiin senkyo de no sōten to Nihon kyōsantō no yondai kihon seisaku," p. 67.

✧ 7 ✧

The UN: A Political Panacea (2)

The last fifteen years of the Cold War marked the uneasiest period in the history of the UN, but from the domestic standpoint it was an exciting era, as the UN's role in bargaining among Japanese political parties became increasingly salient. Major parties continued to use the UN in defending their conflicting proposals for the nation's foreign and security policies. The UN-centric principle was still the standard tool for the LDP to legitimize military cooperation with the US. The opposition parties kept competing among themselves in offering alternative diplomatic and security proposals that supposedly observed the UN principles more closely than the government's policy. However, for Japanese political leaders, the function of the UN after the mid-1970s was no longer limited to justifying controversial policy schemes in public documents and statements. They became ever more aware of the pressure to respond to the changes in the domestic and international environments not through eloquent arguments but with substantive actions.

SSD and the Opposition Parties' Coalition Dreams

The opposition parties were swifter than the ruling LDP in adapting themselves to the new situation. With the establishment of the DSP and the CGP, the LDP and JSP domination of domestic politics reached its end. The LDP's clout began to deteriorate in the late 1960s due to a string of political scandals that culminated with the arrest of former Prime Minister Tanaka in 1976 on a charge of taking bribes from private American and Japanese corporations (the Lockheed Scandal).

But the ruling conservatives' unpopularity did not boost the influence of the opposition parties. Moving fast to the left, the JSP alienated itself from many constituents who preferred a neutral stance in ideological debates. The three smaller opposition parties—the DSP, the CGP and the JCP—were somehow able to reinforce their power by depriving the JSP and the LDP of the support of undecided voters, yet none of them was strong enough to challenge the ruling party's leadership. By the mid-1970s, major players in the opposition camp found themselves in an ironic position. Despite the unprecedented weakness of their conservative foe, the opposition parties' prospects of taking power remained slim.

For opposition leaders, one way to end the LDP's preponderance was to form a coalition government. As a traditional gimmick in the world of party politics, the act of forming a coalition was by no means unfamiliar to postwar Japanese politicians. Faithfully following the classic teaching that the enemy's enemy is a friend, Japanese political parties formed a number of coalition cabinets in the late 1940s. The strategy became less attractive after 1955 when a partisan framework anchored by the LDP and the JSP reached full bloom. But the multipolarization of the domestic political scene during the 1970s once again pushed the opposition parties toward the idea of a coalition government. Among left-wing opposition parties, the JSP issued a "People's Coalition Government" proposal in 1970, which was followed by the JCP's "Democratic Coalition Government" proposal three years later. The anticommunist DSP and CGP also published their own "Middle-of-the-Road Progressive Coalition Government" proposals, respectively, in 1972 and 1976. Nevertheless, the existence of various plans did not mean the coalition could readily materialize. Except for the common aspiration to the throne of the ruling party, the opposition parties actually had little to share with each other. Their policies on many critical agendas were widely divided, to say nothing of the severe collision of interests regarding the lineup of the new government (for instance, should the JCP be invited to join?).

With the establishment of the coalition government still remote, the opposition parties had to concentrate on forging a tentative united front, or "joint struggle" (*kyōtō*) as they called it, in selected policy areas. And one such area was nuclear disarmament, which regained attention at the center of the nation's security debate in the 1970s in the aftermath of certain developments at the UN.

Japan was morally sensitive about any policy agenda that related to nuclear weapons. In Chapters 2 and 3, we examined the government's position on this topic, which was predicated upon Japan's identity as a Western ally instead of as a victim of nuclear attacks. But what was going on inside the opposition camp? At first sight, the opposition parties seemed to be far more anxious about saving the world from the threat of nuclear war. As early as the mid-1950s, the JSP and the JCP had already managed to mobilize domestic antinuclear armament campaigns of sizable scale under the command of a civic organization called the Japan Council against A & H [atomic and hydrogen] Bombs (Gensuikyō).

Japan's antinuclear movement achieved remarkable developments starting in the mid-1950s when the nuclear disarmament issues were discussed under the framework of the UN. But the UN's authority in handling nuclear affairs was shattered in the late 1950s by the big powers' attempt to move disarmament talks to the CCD or other bilateral settings from which Japan and many other non-nuclear developing nations were excluded. This shift was a fatal turning point in Japan's domestic antinuclear campaign. Insofar as the two nuclear superpowers were willing to conduct their negotiations inside the UN, it was easier for Japanese opposition parties to work together in pressing the government to encourage the peace process within the organization. Yet when the UN cushion no longer functioned and disarmament became an issue directly determined by the superpowers, Japan's antinuclear movement began to crack along old ideological boundaries. Unhappy about the progressive parties' domination, the right-wing factions withdrew from Gensuikyō in 1959. Four years later, the remaining JSP members also left Gensuikyō after a bitter debate on whether the USSR's nuclear tests were as evil as those carried out by the US. The once united front then split into three separate bodies: the JCP's Gensuikyō, the JSP's Japan Congress against A- and H-Bombs (Gensuikin), and a DSP-affiliated National Council for Peace and against Nuclear Weapons (Kakkin).

The infighting among antinuclear groups lasted for more than a decade until the trend toward a coalition government made opposition leaders question the desirability of the schism. In June 1974, the CGP submitted a proposal to the main opposition parties and civic organizations under their control calling for the reunification of antinuclear campaigns "beyond ideologies and what happened in the past."[1] The appeal was a rational attempt by the CGP, which was established with a strong antinuclear weapon stance but remained a minor player in the nation's antinuclear movement, to expand its influence. It was not so easy, however, for major opposition parties like the JSP and the JCP to bury the hatchet right away. Indeed, as part of their coalition strategies, the JSP and the JCP did try to unify their movements in 1975, though the negotiation produced no meaningful results.[2] The two were simply not yet ready to forget the barriers that had torn the movement apart ten years earlier.

Just as domestic efforts toward a joint struggle against nuclear armaments were about to end in vain, something occurred at the UN that changed the tide. Having remained idle since the late 1950s, the UN returned to center stage of the global disarmament process in 1976 when a draft resolution sponsored by nonaligned powers regarding a Special Session on Disarmament (SSD) passed the UNGA. Although the UN had held several special sessions before then, it was the first time that such a session was summoned to discuss disarmament topics. Many member states from the Third World hoped that the session could lead to the establishment of a World Disarmament Conference in the UN as a counterpart to the CCD, which was dominated by big powers. Japanese opposition parties, especially the progressives, were also heartened by the news, since they predicted that the SSD would be a good opportunity to weaken the government's position on nuclear issues while bolstering the influence of Japanese antinuclear movements in international society.

The JCP acted swiftly. After its view of the role of the UN had changed around the late 1960s, the party quietly intensified its relationship with the organization. In November 1974, it took the unusual action of sending a Gensuikyō delegation to the UN headquarters in New York. A year later, Gensuikyō became a member of the UN's NGO

---

1. Asai, "Kaku haizetsu e aratana ketsui o!—ima koso gentaiken o wasurezu kokusai yoron no kesshū o," p. 84.
2. Kawamura, "Tōitsu mondai o meguru byūron," pp. 43–44.

committee for disarmament.[3] Having obtained the recognition of the UN, the JCP and Gensuikyō were then in a fairly comfortable position for setting in motion a united antinuclear campaign under the aegis of the world's biggest peace organization.

In September 1976, as soon as the nonaligned powers decided to submit the draft resolution on the SSD at the UNGA, JCP chairman Miyamoto told the leaders of the General Council of Trade Unions of Japan (Sōhyō)—a labor union controlled by the JSP—that his party would continue to seek for reunification of the antinuclear movements prior to the opening of the SSD.[4] Unwilling to take the onus of ruining an antinuclear campaign arranged by the UN, the JSP, Sohyō, and Gensuikin agreed to join the JCP and Gensuikyō in organizing a nationwide movement to support the forthcoming SSD and in sending a unified delegation to attend the special session. In March 1977, Gensuikin and Gensuikyō signed an agreement to make efforts to call a truce and reunite their domestic activities. As a gesture to show good will, the two also held a joint international conference of antinuclear organizations for the first time since the early 1960s.

The symbolic cooperation between the two leading progressive parties soon became a catalyst for an even wider joint struggle among opposition parties. According to the JCP-JSP agreement, their joint struggle would be carried out in two stages. In the initial stage, they would stir up the antinuclear atmosphere within Japan through a large signature-collecting campaign. Then, after the SSD was summoned, the two would send these signatures together with a mixed delegation to the UN headquarters, where they intended to turn the Japanese campaign into a worldwide one.

Seeing the big two make up their minds to work together, other smaller organizations affiliated with the DSP and the CGP followed suit. In order to forestall internal skirmishes, a board with representatives from Gensuikyō, Gensuikin, Kakkin and another neutral organization was assigned to coordinate the activities of the civic delegation to the SSD. Each organization was to take responsibility for recruiting its own members to the delegation according to the quota determined by

---

3. JCP, "Kokuren honbu to Amerika kakuchi o tazunete," pp. 142–43; Kaneko, "Gensuikin undō tōitsu e no dōhyō," p. 17.

4. Kaneko, ibid., p. 22.

the board. But applications poured in, and when the Japanese NGO delegation ultimately departed for New York, it was composed of nearly 500 members. Since some of the members, including several atomic bomb victims and a ninety-two–year-old activist, were physically unfit for such a long trip, the organizing board had to dispatch a medical team with the mission. The result of the signature-collecting was even more amazing. Approximately 17 million signatures were collected within less than six months and another 3 million were added to the list during the first two weeks after the opening session of the SSD in May 1978.[5]

The government and the ruling LDP were somewhat overshadowed by this joint struggle. Once the agreement was finalized, the relevant opposition parties quickly embarked on a rally at the national legislature against the government. Their prime target was Foreign Minister Sonoda Sunao. As a leader of a liberal faction, Sonoda maintained an image as an independent dove within the ruling party. In the early days of his political career, he was one of the few non-progressive Diet members who chose to abstain rather than voting for the security treaty in 1951. Years later, he was also among a group of young politicians who had the guts to challenge the conservative leadership's rigid diplomatic stance by visiting the USSR and the PRC. The opposition developed a sophisticated strategy to seduce this unique figure into cooperating with them. Rather than attempting to get him in hot water as they usually did to government officials, opposition members used a softer but no less effective way to conquer the foreign minister in the Diet. During the three months before the special session, whenever Sonoda appeared at a Diet session, he was surrounded by opposition leaders. Some of them reminded him of the importance of showing flexibility on the coming SSD. Others indicated that they expected the assistance of Sonoda's statesmanship in bringing the Japanese people's voice into the UN. Even the JCP members—routinely merciless critics of the LDP— behaved modestly when questioning the foreign minister.[6]

---

5. Sekiguchi, "NGO to kongo no gensuikin undō no kadai," pp. 123–24.
6. "Dai 84 kai kokkai shūgiin naikaku iinkaigiroku dai 6 gō" (Proceedings of the 84th Diet Session Committee on Cabinet, Lower House, No. 6), February 28, 1978, "Dai 84 kai kokkai shūgiin gaimu iinkaigiroku dai 9 gō" (Proceedings of the 84th Diet Session Committee on Foreign Affairs, Lower House, No. 9),

While parroting the official line initially, Sonoda was unable to hold his defensive stance very long and wound up echoing the opposition parties' cause. He promised to press the UN Secretariat to allow NGO leaders to deliver their opinions in New York, and he agreed to mention Japan's three "Non-Nuclear Principles" (Japan will not maintain, produce, or introduce nuclear weapons) at the SSD despite the desire of many of his conservative colleagues to loosen the government's nuclear regulations. Sonoda also accepted the opposition's request to incorporate another two issues into his SSD speech: the achievement of total and comprehensive disarmament, and the establishment of NFZs in appropriate areas for the sake of preventing nuclear proliferation.[7] Both issues were emphasized by the Third World nations and had been previously viewed by Japanese officials as either unrealistic or carrying a risk of tipping the balance of power among nuclear weapons holders. The opposition was certainly pleased by these crucial compromises. When Sonoda showed up at the Lower House after returning from New York, opposition members applauded him for his "straightforward" performance at the SSD.[8] The applause, however, came at a high cost for the government, as Sonoda's SSD speech became a bible for the opposition, who frequently quoted it when attacking the LDP's nuclear policies.[9]

March 29, 1978, "Dai 84 kai kokkai shūgiin gaimu iinkaigiroku dai 15 gō" (Proceedings of the 84th Diet Session Committee on Foreign Affairs, Lower House, No. 15), April 19, 1978, "Dai 84 kai kokkai sangiin gaimu iinkaigiroku dai 22 gō" (Proceedings of the 84th Diet Session, Upper House, No. 22), May 25, 1978, all in NDL.

7. "Dai 84 kai kokkai shūgiin gaimu iinkaigiroku dai 9 gō" (Proceedings of the 84th Diet Session Committee on Foreign Affairs, Lower House, No. 9), March 29, 1978, ibid.; Public Information and Culture Bureau, *Kokuren gunshuku tokubetsu sōkai,* pp. 3–4 and pp. 17–25.

8. "Dai 84 kai kokkai shūgiin gaimu iinkaigiroku dai 22 gō" (Proceedings of the 84th Diet Session Committee on Foreign Affairs, Lower House, No. 22), June 2, 1978, NDL.

9. "Dai 87 kai kokkai shūgiin honkaigiroku dai 21 gō" (Proceedings of the 87th Diet Session Plenary Session, Lower House, No. 21), April 26, 1979, "Dai 93 kai kokkai shūgiin anzen hoshō tokubetsu iinkaigiroku dai 2 gō" (Proceedings of the 93rd Diet Session Special Committee on Security, Lower House, No. 2), October 21, 1980, "Dai 93 kai kokkai sangiin anzen hoshō oyobi Okinawa

The achievement of the Japanese opposition parties' joint struggle during the first SSD (SSD I) was remarkable. Having made their debut on the international stage, the morale of antinuclear groups with various partisan backgrounds was at an all-time high. The conservative ruling party, by contrast, was completely on the defensive. Naturally enough, opposition leaders decided to further cultivate this favorable situation.[10] Again, they gained help from the UN. When the nonaligned nations proposed the SSD to the UNGA, many of them hoped that the special session could end the domination of the CCD in Geneva, which was co-chaired by the two nuclear superpowers, and thus restore the authority of the UN in handling disarmament issues. Although the big powers did not like the idea of turning the SSD into a permanent UN agency, the majority of UN member states agreed at SSD I that they must meet in 1982 to hold a second SSD (SSD II) so that the UN could be kept posted about recent developments in the field of disarmament.

The Japanese opposition parties' strategy during SSD II was by and large consistent with their experience four years earlier. Gensuikyō, Gensuikin and a number of smaller antinuclear groups started a new round of joint struggle. Activists belonging to these groups again set out to collect signatures from citizens and farmers all over the country. Presumably due to the fact that the CGP, the DSP and some religious groups also conducted similar signature-collection activities, the movement ended with some 80 million signatures altogether—more than seven times what had been collected in 1978. As the number of signatures skyrocketed, the scale of the Japanese NGO delegation to SSD II

---

hoppō mondai ni kansuru chōsakaigiroku dai 5 gō" (Proceedings of the 93rd Diet Session Investigation Committee on Security, Okinawa and Northern Territory Affairs, Upper House, No. 5), November 14, 1980, "Dai 94 kai kokkai shūgiin naikaku iinkaigiroku dai 5 gō" (Proceedings of the 94th Diet Session Committee on Cabinet, Lower House, No. 5), April 9, 1981, "Dai 95 kai kokkai sangiin honkaigiroku dai 5 gō" (Proceedings of the 95th Diet Session Plenary Session, Upper House, No. 5), October 2, 1981, "Dai 95 kai kokkai shūgiin gaimu iinkaigiroku dai 1 gō" (Proceedings of the 95th Diet Session Committee on Foreign Affairs, Lower House, No. 1), October 15, 1981, ibid.

10. Sekiguchi, "NGO to kongo no gensuikin undō no kadai," p. 132; Tanuma, Yoshida Yoshikiyo and Tachiki, "Kokuren gunshuku tokubetsu sōkai to Nihon no gensuikin undō," pp. 150–53.

also swelled. Eventually, more than 1,200 activists registered to join the delegation. Many members actually carried the signatures collected by their groups to New York and forced the UN Secretariat to arrange a ceremony where they could directly hand the signatures over to the Secretary General.[11]

Back in the Diet, opposition parties renewed their tactic of urging government leaders to show more sympathy toward disarmament. This time both Prime Minister Suzuki Zenkō and Foreign Minister Sakurauchi Yoshio seemed to be more resolute in defending the conservatives' policy. Yet neither of them intended to meet the challenge of the united opposition front with a hawkish stance. The prime minister actually went to New York and made a speech at the special session. Before the trip, he also invited representatives of civic groups to his office to discuss the Japanese delegation's position.[12] While these gestures did not lead to any substantive concession on the side of the government, they at least indicated that LDP leaders were not going to entirely pull back from the liberal line set by Sonoda at SSD I.

The Japanese opposition parties' joint struggle during SSD I and II was a fruitful experiment in coalition politics. For the JSP and the JCP, the struggle offered them an optimal stage on which to demonstrate

---

11. Sekiguchi, "Ikanishite kaku gunshuku o tassei suru ka," pp. 28–30; Yamashita, "Hitorihitori no fujin ga jikakushite tachiagaru," pp. 19–24; JCP, *Nihon kyōsantō no rokujūnen,* p. 486; Yoshida Yasuhiko, *Kokuren Kōhōkan,* pp. 70–71.

12. "Dai 96 kai kokkai shūgiin yosan iinkaigiroku dai 8 gō" (Proceedings of the 96th Diet Session Budget Committee, Lower House, No. 8), February 9, 1982, "Dai 96 kai kokkai sangiin yosan iinkaigiroku dai 5 gō" (Proceedings of the 96th Diet Session Budget Committee, Upper House, No. 4), March 11, 1982, "Dai 96 kai kokkai shūgiin naikaku iinkaigiroku dai 4 gō" (Proceedings of the 96th Diet Session Committee on Cabinet, Lower House, No. 4), March 18, 1982, "Dai 96 kai kokkai sangiin yosan iinkaigiroku dai 15 gō" (Proceedings of the 96th Diet Session Budget Committee, Upper House, No. 15), March 26, 1982, "Dai 96 kai kokkai sangiin gaimu iinkaigiroku dai 3 gō" (Proceedings of the 96th Diet Session Committee on Foreign Affairs, Upper House, No. 3), April 1, 1982, "Dai 96 kai kokkai sangiin yosan iinkaigiroku dai 19 gō" (Proceedings of the 96th Diet Session Budget Committee, Upper House, No. 19), April 3, 1982, "Dai 96 kai kokkai shūgiin gaimu iinkaigiroku dai 10 gō" (Proceedings of the 96th Diet Session Committee on Foreign Affairs, Lower House, No. 10), April 21, 1982, all in NDL.

their political influence in front of the constituents who were getting tired of the old-fashioned progressive vs. conservative competition. Through participating in policy coordination among various civic groups and activists, middle-of-the-road parties like the CGP and the DSP were also able to find their own seats at the center of the nation's antinuclear movement, which had been long dominated by the progressive parties. Thus, at least in the eyes of outsiders, the united antinuclear front had created a win-win situation for all opposition parties. Nevertheless, this state did not last very long, as the opposition parties became interested in how to win more than their partners.

While agreeing to temporarily cooperate before SSD I, the JCP and the JSP had never seriously tackled the problems that caused the split in their antinuclear movements in 1963. With the Gensuikyō under their control, JCP leaders were confident about the survival of their party's influence in the course of reunification of the movement. They insisted that a new organization be set up to replace existing groups including Gensuikyō and the JSP's Gensuikin and promised that once such a unified organization was forged, it would be entitled to all privileges or status which Gensuikyō had obtained from the UN and other international agencies. JCP chairman Miyamoto also emphasized that political parties should guarantee the independence of the civic movement.[13]

These ideas sounded fair and attractive, but they did not assuage the concerns of other parties, specifically the JSP. Given the Gensuikyō's predominance in terms of organizational scale, it would undoubtedly become the biggest faction within the new organization. And Gensuikyō's eagerness to stress its own nuclear policies at international NGO conferences furthered the distrust by its domestic competitors.[14] In addition, considering the JCP's exquisite skill in penetrating civic groups, the promise regarding the new organization's independence was by no means reliable. As a matter of fact, one direct reason JSP members had left Gensuikyō in 1963 was that the supposedly nonpartisan organization had been totally controlled by JCP supporters.

The lack of mutual trust between the two biggest partners of the joint struggle was already manifest before SSD I. Japanese Ambassador

---

13. Kaneko, "Gensuikin undō tōitsu e no dōhyō," pp. 24–26; Miyamoto, "Kakuheiki kinshi wa shōbi no kyū," p. 273.
14. Sekiguchi, "NGO to kongo no gensuikin undō no kadai," p. 121.

to the UN Abe Isao was reportedly being badgered by Gensuikyō and Gensuikin representatives, both of whom demanded an opportunity to make a speech at the Assembly Hall. Foreign Minister Sonoda also had to request that members of the NGO delegation stop their infighting before they left for New York.[15]

The internal controversies escalated during the interim period between the two special sessions. Having passively allowed the lead of the JCP and Gensuikyō at SSD I, the JSP and Gensuikin began their endeavor to draw the tide back to the non-Communist side. To counter the JCP's drive to fortify Gensuikyō's position as the sole orthodox antinuclear group, the JSP organized a series of separate events aimed at using the SSD II to improve its own image as a leading power in promoting Japan's nuclear disarmament effort. In March 1982, JSP chairman Asukata Ichio toured four European countries to sell the party's proposal to establish NFZs in the Asian Pacific area. The NFZ proposal had been a main component of the JSP's nuclear policy for more than two decades.[16] By raising such a long-cherished agenda just three months before SSD II, the party hoped to create an antinuclear fad with JSP markings.

The SSD question was a primary topic in the chairman's talks with European socialist leaders during the trip and remained in the forefront after the delegation returned to Japan.[17] In mid-May, for the first time in its history, the JSP hosted an international conference on nuclear disarmament in Tokyo with the presence of left-wing politicians from 26 nations. The purpose of the conference, according to the party's official interpretation, was to secure the success of the coming SSD II. Yet no representative from the JCP, the JSP's joint struggle partner prior to the special session, could be seen in the gathering.[18]

The JSP was not the only opposition party that tried to keep its distance from the JCP during the joint struggle. The CGP and the DSP

---

15. Isomura, "Gunshuku, kakkin o mezashite," p. 82; Watanabe Ryōjirō, *Sonoda Sunao gaimu, kōsei daijin nitteihyō,* p. 44.

16. Kawakami, "Kakugunshuku to hikaku busōchitai secchi no suishin o," p. 43.

17. JSP, "Asukata hōōdan kaidan, komyunike," pp. 195–210 and pp. 213–22; JSP, Mission to Europe, "Hankaku, gunshuku no tatakai no kyōka o," pp. 188–89.

18. Asukata, "Hikaku heiwa chitai secchi o suishin shiyō," p. 14; JSP, *Shiryō— Nihon shakaitō 50 nen,* pp. 738–39.

also refused to merge their activities under the JCP's united organization proposal. While sending representatives to the coordination board of the Japanese NGO delegation to SSD I, the two were less active during the special session than their progressive partners. The CGP joined the JSP to table a draft resolution at the Lower House calling for more efforts on nuclear disarmament, yet the party's role in other domestic campaigns was not so conspicuous.[19] Likewise, the DSP showed little interest in the sensational mass movements. Except for endorsing the plan of turning the SSD into a permanent UN organ, the party's policy toward the special session was extremely similar to that of the government.[20] As Gensuikyō's performance during SSD I seemed to be allowing the progressives, specifically the JCP, to take the credit for the success of domestic disarmament campaigns, the two parties started reconsidering their strategies.

The CGP took the initiative to solidify the collaboration among anti-JCP parties. Criticizing the JCP's pro-USSR nuclear policy, the CGP's National Conference adopted a proposal in December 1981 to collect ten million signatures to support the party's own stance on disarmament issues before SSD II. In January 1982, the CGP established two liaison offices with Sōhyō and the DSP-backed Japanese Confederation of Labor (Dōmei) to coordinate their activities before SSD II. The party's Central Executive Committee also instructed its nationwide branches to push local legislatures to pass antinuclear resolutions so that a similar resolution could be submitted to the Diet. The DSP responded positively to these initiatives. In February, the two invited the New Liberal Club and the Socialist Democratic Federation, which had recently split from the LDP and the JSP, respectively, to form a non-progressive coalition in dealing with SSD II-related affairs.[21] As a result, unlike the joint struggle during SSD I, which was manipulated by the two progressive giants, the united opposition front for SSD II was in fact composed of three rather independent campaigns mobilized by the JCP, the JSP, and the middle-of-the-road parties.

19. Watanabe Ichirō, "Gaikō ni okeru risō to genjitsu," pp. 51–53.
20. DSP, "1978 nendo gaikō hōshin," p. 195.
21. Watanabe Ichirō, "Issenman shomei undō ni atatte," pp. 14–20; Watanabe Ichirō, "Hankaku, gunshuku undō to kōmeitō no tatakai," p. 67; DSP, "Kakugunshuku to anzenhoshō o ikani hakaru ka," pp. 24–26.

Behind the upsurge of cooperation among non-Communist opposition parties was the JCP's frustration. Feeling uneasy about the coalition movement between the CGP and the DSP, JCP leaders had been eager to court the JSP to join their side. And this need became more and more urgent as SSD II was approaching.[22] To their disappointment, the JSP remained cool toward the idea of forging a unified antinuclear organization with the JCP and Gensuikyō. As a matter of fact, JSP leaders seemed more enthusiastic about consolidating its ties with the CGP and the DSP, both of which were firmly opposed to the JCP.[23] The JCP was certainly not happy about such indifference. Yet insofar as Gensuikin and Sōhyō remained inside the nominal joint struggle for the SSD, there was nothing it could do other than venting its anger by occasionally pointing out the JSP's "error" in the party's journal.

The result of SSD II was in one sense humiliating to the JCP. Since the Reagan administration did not wish to lay out the welcome mat for so many Japanese communists and their sympathizers in the UN compound, the State Department singled out more than 200 members of Gensuikyō and other pro-JCP groups from the jumbo Japan NGO mission and refused to grant them a visa. The JCP's sit-ins in front of the US embassy had no effect in changing the latter's policy. In the end, the party could only send many of its supporters to attend NGO demos outside the US whereas representatives from the JSP and anticommunist organizations were busy advertising themselves in New York.[24]

The JCP's passion for using the UN to weaken the conservative regime's position on nuclear disarmament did not decline after SSD II. Rather, the US's discriminatory policy reinforced the party's belief in the necessity to unify domestic antinuclear groups through the channel of the SSD. "While it is not right to overestimate the UN, neither is it appropriate to underestimate it," a senior JCP officer commented after

---

22. Kaneko, Nakajima and Niihara, "Kakuheiki o meguru jōsei to kakuheiki kinshi undō," pp. 38–39, p. 50; Ide, "Kakuheiki haizetsu eno michi," p. 64; Tsugawa, "Gensuikin undō tōitsu no honryū to shōgai," pp. 74–75.

23. JSP, "Kakushin bundan ni te o kasu Nihon kyōsantō no dokuzenshugi," pp. 86–95.

24. Ueda Kōichirō, Kaneko and Tanuma, "Jidai yurugasu hankaku undō no nami," pp. 109–12.

the visa episode. "Above all, this is a problem regarding how to connect [SSD] with the people's movement."[25] But it became crystal clear that there was no willingness among other opposition parties to allow the birth of a JCP-led "people's movement."

In May 1984, without the participation of the JCP, JSP Secretary General Tanabe Makoto, former Prime Minister Miki Takeo and politicians from the CGP declared the establishment of a supra-partisan committee on peace and nuclear disarmament.[26] The JSP-sponsored Sōhyō also refused to join disarmament demos where pro-JCP groups displayed their flags.[27] In the same year, the DSP and Dōmei left the joint struggle with the JCP. Two years later, the withdrawal of the JSP, Sōhyō and Gensuikin ultimately ended the nominal united front of all groups in opposition against the government's nuclear policy.[28]

Inflamed by these incidents, the JCP leadership fired Gensuikyō's top officials, who supported a united front with Sōhyō, and ordered the party's propaganda apparatus to tone up public criticism of the JSP's "obstruction" in antinuclear campaigns.[29] Meanwhile, the JCP also began to look for new allies outside the country. And the new partner turned out to be an old friend. In December 1984, JCP chairman Miyamoto visited Moscow, where he signed a joint communiqué with the Soviet Communist Party concerning the cooperation between the two sides on nuclear disarmament issues.[30]

By the time SSD III was held in May 1988, Japanese opposition parties were not in the mood to have any kind of joint struggle. Each of them still invested considerable energies in organizing campaigns to support the special session: Signature-collecting movements, international symposia and public demonstrations again appeared on street corners around the country. But the relationship between the JCP and other opposition

---

25. Ibid., p. 110.
26. Tomizuka, "Hankaku, gunshuku, heiwa: kōdōsuru nijūni nin iinkai," pp. 22–30.
27. Nishitani, "Gensuikin undō wa dō arubeki ka," pp. 83–84.
28. Narita, Takebayashi, "Nakasone naikaku, shakōmin no bika wa hankaku heiwa undō o bōgaisuru," p. 53.
29. Kaneko, "Gensuikin undō no tōmensuru kihon mondai," pp. 39–40; Komori, "Gensuikin undō o henshitsu saseru bunretsu rosen," pp. 26–34.
30. JCP, "Kyōdō seimei," pp. 53–55.

groups was reaching the freezing point.[31] And the government no longer needed to be nervous when the NGO delegation with its hundreds of activists flooded into New York.

The SSD stimulated the policy coalition movements among Japanese opposition groups in the late 1970s. But the movement was soon thwarted by the opposition parties' distrust of each other (especially between the JCP and other parties). The failure, however, did not bring an end to the UN's influence on Japanese domestic politics. When the world entered the last decade of the century, another UN decision significantly reshaped the political game among Japanese parties regarding security policymaking. Similar to the SSD case, coalition-forming was once more a key element. Yet in this case, the ruling LDP, instead of the opposition, would take the lead.

The UN and the PKO Legislation

On August 2, 1990, the world was astounded by the CNN breaking news reporting Iraq's invasion of Kuwait that morning. The UN reacted quickly. On August 6, UNSC members adopted a resolution mandating an economic embargo against Iraq until its military forces pulled out from Kuwait. In Japan, the government also responded instantaneously, announcing its own economic sanction on Baghdad an entire day before the UNSC's decision. Probably deeming that what must be done had been done, Japanese leaders took a wait-and-see attitude from mid-August on, hoping the Iraqis would obediently follow the instruction of the UN resolution.[32] But circumstances took an unexpected turn. Stubbornly rejecting the intervention of the UN, Iraqi President Saddam Hussein put the whole territory of Kuwait under his control and declared sovereignty over the tiny kingdom by the end of August. The US and other Western allies, in response, decided to expel the Iraqi troops from Kuwait with an iron fist—a multinational coalition force.

---

31. Kaneko, "INF zenpai jōyakugo no sekai no hankaku, heiwa undō no hōkō," pp. 40–41; Arakawa, "Hankaku heiwa no kyōdō o kyohisuru bōgaisha," pp. 126–135; JSP, "1988 nendo undō hōshin," p. 26.
32. Watanabe Akio and Mikuriya, *Shushō kantei no ketsudani,* p. 65.

For constitutional reasons, Japan (and Germany as well) had diffi-culty devoting combatants directly to the coalition force. The Japanese government hence gave higher priorities to financial and material con-tributions to the coalition's military operation. But the US was less than satisfied to watch its most affluent ally merely write checks while American soldiers risked their lives. About the end of August, US offi-cials started dropping hints to their Japanese friends that what Wash-ington needed might be something more than cash. US Ambassador in Tokyo Michael H. Armacost urged a number of senior policymakers within the LDP government "to think of ways in which Japan could perform noncombat duties in the Gulf region so that it would be seen as an active participant in the broad multilateral effort that was taking shape."[33] While Armacost later tried to avoid exaggerating his role dur-ing the event, he and his colleagues' activities undoubtedly applied strong pressures on the Japanese leaders. Around early October, the ruling party and the government found themselves facing the toughest security decision that a postwar Japanese administration had ever en-countered: whether or not Japan should send its military personnel (that is, the SDF) to the coalition force in the Middle East.

The legitimacy of sending SDF on an overseas mission was always a sensitive topic in Japan's domestic political debate. To recap, opinions among the ruling and opposition parties were traditionally divided into three groups. The pro-dispatch group represented by the DSP distin-guished the dispatch of SDF to the UN PKO from other overseas mis-sions for pure combat purposes. While ruling out the possibility of the latter, it viewed the former as not only legal but necessary in terms of making contributions to the UN's peace efforts. This argument was dismissed by the anti-dispatch group, which included the JSP, the JCP and the CGP. To these parties, dispatching SDF to PKO was nothing more than another deftly devised pretext to revive Japan's status as a leading military power. Standing between the two was the ambiguous group led by the ruling LDP. Many LDP members were sympathetic to the pro-dispatch group. Yet given that the resistance from the opposi-tion and the public opinion behind it were not something that could be easily ignored, the party leadership was less than enthusiastic about

---

33. Armacost, *Friends or Rivals? The Insider's Account of US-Japan Relations,* p. 101.

sticking their necks out for the precarious security idea of deploying Japanese soldiers outside the country.

Certain changes became visible in each of those groups after the late 1970s. First of all, the boundary between the pro-dispatch DSP and the ambiguous LDP blurred. The DSP's forward-looking stance on the SDF's engagement in an international mission like PKO did not suffer any setback in the 1980s. In November 1980, a DSP security policy committee presided over by party chairman Sasaki Ryōsaku made a reference to the PKO cooperation problem in its final report.[34] "Without violating the constitution," the report read, "we must consider cooperating with the UN's ceasefire surveillance teams and dispatching medical teams to PKO based on our duty as a UN member state." In 1981, under the party's request, another policy research panel (chaired by a pro-DSP scholar) produced a proposal which devoted much space to the idea of making "military contributions" to PKO in the form of SDF officials and equipment.[35] Presumably concerned about legal barriers and its official stance as an opposition party to defend the constitution, the DSP leadership generally maintained the less provocative line suggested in the 1980 report during the subsequent years. It welcomed contributions of personnel to PKO while respecting the regulations imposed by the constitution—a position that began to be shared by the LDP in the late 1980s.[36]

---

34. DSP, "Heiwa to anzen hoshō mondai ni tsuite no shinpojiumu kanren shiryō," p. 35.

35. Anzen hoshō kenkyūkai, "Nihon no anzen hoshō seisaku," pp. 173–75.

36. DSP, *Minshatō seisaku handobukku,* p. 90; DSP, "Minshatō no kangae wa kō da," p. 29; "Dai 96 kai kokkai sangiin gaimu iinkaigiroku dai 13 gō" (Proceedings of the 96th Diet Session Committee on Foreign Affairs, Upper House, No 13), July 6, 1982, "Dai 101 kai kokkai sangiin gaikō sōgō anzen hoshō ni kansuru chōsa tokubetsu iinkai gaikō mondai shōiinkaigiroku dai 9 gō" (Proceedings of the 101st Diet Session Subcommittee on Foreign Affairs of the Special Investigation Committee on Foreign Affairs and Comprehensive Security, Upper House, No. 9), August 1, 1984, "Dai 102 kai kokkai shūgiin gaimu iinkaigiroku dai 14 gō" (Proceedings of the 102nd Diet Session Committee on Foreign Affairs, Lower House, No. 14), May 22, 1985, "Dai 109 kai kokkai shūgiin Okinawa oyobi hoppō mondai ni kansuru tokubetsu iinkaigiroku dai 4 gō" (Proceedings of the 109th Diet Session Special Committee on Okinawa and Northern Territory Affairs, Lower House, No. 4), September 11, 1987, NDL.

Despite some party members' appeal for the contribution of SDF officers to PKO, the LDP leadership continued to resist these pressures during the early 1980s by emphasizing domestic legal barriers, specifically the SDF Law. However, this prudent attitude began cracking in the second half of the decade. As the relationship between the two superpowers warmed up again in the mid-1980s, the LDP government started reconsidering the possibility of Japan playing a more prominent part in international security affairs. One initial chance came in 1987 when the US approached Japan to request the dispatch of SDF minesweepers to the Persian Gulf area in the aftermath of the truce between Iran and Iraq. Prime Minister Nakasone was inclined to accept this offer. But the idea was shot down by one of his top aides, Chief Cabinet Secretary Gotōda Masaharu, who was convinced that the appearance of SDF battleships in the Middle East would ultimately lead to the collapse of postwar Japan's peaceful security policy.[37]

This episode was just the prelude to a series of new impulses toward stepping up Japan's international cooperation in the form of not only money and goods but also people. In September 1987, the Diet passed legislation called the "International Emergency Assistance Team Act" permitting staffers from the Fire Defense and Maritime Safety Agencies to conduct overseas missions during natural disasters. A year later, the reinforcement of personnel contributions to the UN's peacekeeping efforts was eventually written into Prime Minister Takeshita's International Cooperation Plan.[38]

During the same period, the anti-dispatch group was also undergoing certain changes. Fluctuating between the JSP and the DSP, the CGP's security policy was on shaky ground by the early 1980s. In 1979 and 1980, the party concluded two coalition agreements with the JSP and the DSP, respectively. Noticing that their coalition partners did not see eye to eye on national security and SDF affairs, CGP policymakers had to tailor the relevant sections in these agreements by playing with words or nuances while refraining from articulating their own ideas.[39] But such intelligence did not bring their party the expected benefits during the election. The opposition parties, including the CGP, suf-

---

37. Gotōda, *Sei to kan,* pp. 185–87.
38. See Chapter 4.
39. Ikei and Horie, *Nihon no seitō to gaikō seisaku,* pp. 86–87.

fered a humiliating defeat in the 1980 Upper and Lower House elections, allowing the LDP to recover its comfortable majority in both Houses. Although CGP leaders swore that they would not give up the coalition plans after the election, many of them understood that it was time to stop sitting on the fence.[40]

In October 1980, the CGP publicized a revised security and defense scheme at its annual conference. The scheme registered a distinct inclination toward the right. Rather than accentuating the difference with the government, the scheme was written with the understanding that the security policies of the opposition and the ruling party must be made upon "common ground" because the public would not welcome a total change in this crucial field. In the scheme, maintaining the US-Japan security relationship was treated as more significant than the future abolition of the security treaty. The proposal of replacing the SDF with a modest TDF was retracted, and a plan to reform SDF into a "constitutional" force was put forth.[41] Dispatching the SDF to a foreign land was still a taboo, though the drafters of the scheme left the following words: "We do not refuse to make contributions or assistance within the domain of the Japanese constitution in the event that a sanction resolution has been adopted by the UNSC through due procedures or the occurrence of an aggression is evident according to the common standard of the international community."[42] Until the 1990 Gulf crisis, the CGP had never approved any proposal that authorized the SDF's participation in a UN mission. But it also continued to serve as a dedicated supporter of the UN by offering plans to strengthen the UN's function. Diet members belonging to the party also occasionally aired "personal" opinions that Japan might contribute nonmilitary experts to PKO.[43]

---

40. Yano, "Kongo no tatakai no hōkōsei ni tsuite," pp. 20–21.
41. Yano and Ichikawa, "Ima tōnai de rongi shiteiru koto," p. 83; Ichikawa, "Shin anzen hoshō seisaku 20 mon 20 tō," pp. 40–41.
42. CGP, "Kōmeitō no anzen hoshō seisaku," p. 56.
43. CGP, "Kōmeitō no gaikō seisaku," p. 58; CGP, *Ningen shugi 'chūdō shugi' no atarashii sentaku,* pp. 141–142; "Dai 102 kai kokkai sangiin gaikō sōgō anzen hoshō ni kansuru chōsa tokubetsu iinkai gaikō mondai shōiinkaigiroku dai 3 gō" (Proceedings of the 102nd Diet Session Subcommittee on Foreign Affairs of the Special Investigation Committee on Foreign Affairs and Comprehensive

The CGP's coalition counterpart, the JSP, went through a similar process in gearing their security policy toward the trends in international and domestic politics. After signing the coalition pact with the CGP in 1979, the JSP made piecemeal amendments to its defense policy in order to preserve the harmonious mood between the two parties. Following the CGP's status quo policy, the JSP also ceased to require an immediate abolishment of the security treaty and started talking about abandoning the treaty through "negotiation" under the appropriate international environment.[44] Meanwhile, the SDF problem seemed more difficult to handle, since the JSP was known as a ruthless attacker of the unconstitutionality of the force, whereas the CGP was reluctant to deny the SDF's constitutionality. But as the CGP slipped to the right after its defeat in the 1980 election, the JSP decided to do all it could to save the coalition. In 1983, upon chairman Ishibashi Masashi's instruction, the JSP made a sudden announcement admitting that the SDF was an "unconstitutional military force established by due legal procedures" and thus needed to be treated in a "realistic" way.[45] The statement was a compromise reaching only halfway to the CGP's position, but it was sufficient to assure colleagues on the other side that the JSP's SDF policy might not be so different from theirs.

All these movements had the side effect of pushing JSP members to ponder many security-related agendas from different angles. The party's arguments on Japan's personnel participation in UN peacekeeping activities were one such example. At a Lower House session held in June 1982, JSP Diet member Yokomichi Takahiro remarked that to make Japan's UN cooperation more efficient it was necessary to draw a line between personnel contribution to PKO and dispatching the SDF overseas. One way to do this, he suggested, would be participation in

---

Security, Upper House, No. 3), May 29, 1985 and "Dai 102 kai kokkai sangiin gaikō sōgō anzen hoshō ni kansuru chōsa tokubetsu iinkai gaikō mondai shōi-inkaigiroku dai 5 gō" (Proceedings of the 102nd Diet Session Subcommittee on Foreign Affairs of the Special Investigation Committee on Foreign Affairs and Comprehensive Security, Upper House, No. 5), June 12, 1985, NDL.

44. JSP, *Shiryō—Nihon shakaitō no 50 nen,* pp. 655–56 and pp. 670–73; Hayase, "Hankyō yatō no anpo seisaku no hensen," pp. 88–89.

45. Tatebayashi, "Jieitai o ikani kaishō suru ka" pp. 26–27; JSP, *Nihon shakaitō seisaku shiryō shūsei,* pp. 1231–1234.

nonmilitary aspects of PKO such as through a "UN Cooperation Bill."[46] Three years later, at an Upper House special committee on comprehensive security issues, a JSP representative once again hinted that as long as the SDF was excluded, his party would not oppose plans to send civilian experts to join PKO on logistical or medical missions.[47]

The only member of the anti-dispatch group that did not change its attitude was the JCP. The JCP became more accepting of the UN starting in the late 1960s. Party leaders and theorists conducted very careful analysis of each paragraph of the UN charter to prove that the government blatantly ignored the UN spirit by substituting a military alliance with the US for the collective security principles.[48] On the other hand, however, the JCP pointed out that the respect paid to the charter should not be used to legitimize cooperation with military actions mandated by the UN for peacekeeping purposes. This was not because the party was antagonistic to PKO, as JCP leaders asserted, but due to the understanding that the Japanese constitution prohibited the nation from involvement in military operations outside its territory.[49] Though

---

46. "Dai 96 kai kokkai shūgiin yosan iinkaigiroku dai 22 gō" (Proceedings of the 96th Diet Session Budget Committee, Lower House, No. 22), June 25, 1982, NDL.

47. "Dai 102 kai kokkai sangiin gaikō sōgō anzen hoshō ni kansuru chōsa tokubetsu iinkai gaikō mondai shōiinkaigiroku dai 3 gō" (Proceedings of the 102nd Diet Session Subcommittee on Foreign Affairs of the Special Investigation Committee on Foreign Affairs and Comprehensive Security, Upper House, No. 3), May 29, 1985 and "Dai 104 kai kokkai sangiin gaikō sōgō anzen hoshō ni kansuru chōsa tokubetsu iinkai gaikō mondai shōiinkaigiroku dai 1 gō" (Proceedings of the 102nd Diet Session Subcommittee on Foreign Affairs of the Special Investigation Committee on Foreign Affairs and Comprehensive Security, Upper House, No. 1), February 14, 1986, ibid.

48. Ueda Kōichirō, "'Sangiin senkyo no sōten to Nihon kyōsantō no seisaku' no tokuchō to kihonten," pp. 21–22; Yoshioka, "Nihon no shin no anzen hoshō no michi," pp. 13–14; JCP, "Shin no heiwa kōryō no tameni," pp. 57–58; JCP, "Hidōmei chūritsu, jiei no seisaku kōsō Nihon no heiwa to anzen o hoshō suru michi," p. 96.

49. "Dai 102 kai kokkai sangiin gaikō sōgō anzen hoshō ni kansuru chōsa tokubetsu iinkai gaikō mondai shōiinkaigiroku dai 5 gō" (Proceedings of the 102nd Diet Session Subcommittee on Foreign Affairs of the Special Investiga-

this position sounded similar to that of the JSP or even the CGP, it was implemented far more strictly. Sending the SDF was, of course, out of the question. In addition, the JCP treated all UN peacekeeping efforts as military actions and thereby demurred to any kind of PKO contribution "no matter whether it is made by sending civilians, money or equipment."[50]

In sum, by the summer of 1990, save for the JCP, it was no longer appropriate to assign the attitudes among Japanese political parties regarding personnel contributions to international security spheres to the categories of positive, neutral, or negative groups. The LDP and the DSP reached a consensus that it was desirable at least to have Japanese personnel in UN PKO. To them, the only question left was how such cooperation should be carried out. While still wary of the SDF's involvement, the CGP and the JSP also became flexible. Though taking alarm at any move toward using SDF troops, the two were more or less tolerant of nonmilitary personnel contributions if they were conducted for the UN's mission. This was the domestic situation when the US and other Western allies started testing Japan's resolve to join them in punishing Saddam Hussein's Iraq.

For many years, Japan's response to the West's expectations during the 1990 Gulf crisis was branded by the media as "too little, too late." Kaifu Toshiki, then prime minister and LDP president, is usually pictured as the epitome of a weak leader who had lost himself and his political vision during the chaotic post-Cold War era. Now more than a decade has passed since the Iraqis were driven out of Kuwait, and new materials on the issue have become available. It is the time for us to retrace the decision-making process within the Japanese government and the ruling party during those turbulent days so that we can piece together a more concrete story that goes beyond impressionistic judgments.

---

tion Committee on Foreign Affairs and Comprehensive Security, Upper House, No. 5), June 12, 1985, NDL.

50. "Dai 102 kai kokkai sangiin gaikō sōgō anzen hoshō ni kansuru chōsa tokubetsu iinkai gaikō mondai shōiinkaigiroku dai 3 gō" (Proceedings of the 102nd Diet Session Subcommittee on Foreign Affairs of the Special Investigation Committee on Foreign Affairs and Comprehensive Security, Upper House, No. 3), May 29, 1985, ibid.; Yamane, "Jieitai kaigai hahei eno shōdō," p. 104.

Prime Minister Kaifu might not have been the most brilliant conservative politician of his generation, but he was definitely not so dull as to be unaware of the urgency of meeting the US request for a contribution of personnel to the coalition force. Having the experience of organizing the Japanese Overseas Cooperation Volunteers (JOCV) program, Kaifu was in fact a well-known expert in terms of using Japanese citizens for international cooperation purposes. And as recalled by one of his senior aides, the prime minister seriously considered the option of sending Japanese people to the Gulf area in the early stage of the crisis. However, he made it very clear from the outset that the SDF should not be mobilized this time. If there had to be a Japanese presence in the operation, they should be civilian volunteers conducting noncombat duties such as medical or transportation services. Later, as it became obvious that individual volunteers might not be appropriate candidates during a military campaign, Kaifu conceded to set up a peace cooperation corps through new legislation. But he still maintained the no-SDF rule. The maximum effort Japan could make, in his view, was to temporarily discharge SDF servicemen from their posts so that they could be transferred to the peace cooperation corps as civilian officers.[51]

Kaifu's conviction regarding SDF personnel cooperation was not shared unanimously by members of his own party. In a mammoth political party like the LDP that is built upon various factions, it is not rare for party members to hold differing opinions regarding certain policy issues. But even reckoning with this reality, the widely divided views among LDP members on the idea of dispatching SDF personnel to the coalition force were distinctive in the party's history. Among the opponents of the SDF's participation in the coalition, former Chief Cabinet Secretary Gotōda had raised his hand to say no from the very beginning. Borrowing the old Chinese proverb, "A single ant hole causes the dike to crumble," he warned the party that sending the SDF to the coalition force could set Japan on a path toward war.[52] When trying to quash Nakasone's proposal to send minesweepers to the Gulf three years earlier, Gotōda had to fight almost alone within the cabinet. In the autumn of 1990, however, he had plenty of allies. Faction bosses like former

51. Ishihara Nobuo, *Kantei 2668 nichi,* pp. 32–33 and pp. 37–39; Watanabe Akio and Mikuriya, *Shushō kantei no ketsudan,* p. 73; Polomka, *Japan as Peacekeeper,* p. 22.
52. *Asahi shimbun,* August 23, 1990.

JDA Director General Kanemaru Shin or former Prime Ministers Takeshita and Fukuda Takeo, all historical witnesses (as was Gotōda) of the last war, aired similar concern about the use of the SDF as the core of Japan's personnel contribution.[53]

The new leaders of the party, on the other hand, had a totally different opinion. LDP Secretary General Ozawa Ichirō, Chairman of the General Council Nishioka Takeo and Chairman of the Policy Affairs Research Council Katō Mutsuki—all energetic politicians representing the younger generation —found it absurd to exclude uniformed SDF from an international security campaign aimed at assisting the UN to restore peace—not to mention that it would be logistically difficult to control the activities of discharged SDF soldiers acting as civilian individuals, as the prime minister had suggested. Until mid-September, rounds of debate were exchanged inside the party, yet both sides adhered to their original positions. At last, when the Diet session was about to open, Chief Cabinet Secretary Sakamoto Misoji managed to hammer out a compromise draft by mixing the various factions' opinions together. SDF personnel would participate in the cooperation team as "regular public servants" under the command of the prime minister while keeping their posts in their original troops.[54]

But the confusion was just dawning. The proposed legislation, as reflected by its name, "The UN Peace Cooperation Bill" (UNPCB), contained more provisions pertaining to Japan's participation in UN PKO than to its contribution to the US-led coalition force in the Middle East. This puzzling outcome was elaborately designed by the LDP leadership.

If the proposed UNPCB merely recommended cooperation with the coalition force, it would undoubtedly brush against a legal problem— the constitutionality of the right of collective self-defense—that the LDP and the government had evaded for decades. The constitution, in accordance with the government's formal interpretation, forbids the exertion of the collective self-defense right. Therefore, SDF troops could not join overseas operations with a military ally even if only en-

---

53. *Mainichi shimbun,* September 11, 1990; *Yomiuri shimbun,* September 12 and October 10, 1990.
54. Matsumoto, *PKO to kokusai kōken,* p. 49; Ishihara Nobuo, ibid., p. 39; *Yomiuri shimbun,* September 23, 1990.

gaging in noncombat duties. SDF's cooperation with the coalition force led by the US was a vulnerable case when considered in that light.

More important, the LDP older generation's reluctance toward the dispatch of SDF troops to the coalition did not exist in the case of UN cooperation. Seasoned leaders like former Prime Minister Suzuki and former LDP Secretary General Nikaidō Susumu cautioned Kaifu that the Japanese cooperation team must be organized within the framework of the UN charter. Even the fiery Gotōda proclaimed that he had no problem with Japan's noncombat participation in UN PKO. What really got on his nerves, he confessed, was the fact that the coalition force was not a UN force at all.[55] Former Foreign Minister Miyazawa Kiichi, another powerful figure belonging to the wartime generation and then recognized as the man closest to the throne of prime minister, made this point even clearer. "The current multinational coalition force is troublesome," he reiterated, "but there's nothing we couldn't do [to help it] if it were a UN force." In his view, the best and perhaps only possible way for Japanese uniformed officers to pursue an international mission would be joining a "UN permanent force" as UN servants instead of Japanese servicemen.[56]

Under such circumstances, the government and LDP policymakers pointedly argued that the bill was designed to cooperate with "activities taken [by the coalition force] as a result of UN resolutions for the sake of peace maintenance."[57] By the same token, they also dismissed the suspicions that this was an attempt to exercise the collective self-defense right, by sticking to the stance that what they would like to do was to make a contribution to the UN, not a military alliance. "It is ridiculous to interpret UN cooperation through the SDF as an action of collective self-defense," Secretary General Ozawa stated at a gathering of young party members in early September. "If UN cooperation equals collective self-defense, we would have no room to do anything at the UN in the first place."[58]

---

55. *Asahi shimbun,* September 27, 1990; *Mainichi shimbun,* October 21, 1990.

56. Matsumoto, *PKO to kokusai kōken,* p. 33; *Yomiuri shimbun,* October 5, 1990; Miyazawa and Tahara, "Nihon no sentaku," pp. 58–59.

57. Matsumoto, ibid., p. 50; *Asahi shimbun,* September 27.

58. *Yomiuri shimbun,* September 9, 1990.

Alongside the need to dodge domestic criticism or to get around a constitutional barrier, a more ambitious goal harbored by some LDP leaders also made the UN an indispensable element in the UNPCB. While the Japanese public's attention was distracted by tensions in the Middle East, their government was quietly contemplating taking its own initiative in international peace maintenance. And there were certain movements among LDP politicians to link the two issues together.

When Foreign Minister Nakayama Tarō announced the government's plan to establish a UN peace cooperation corps as part of the proposed UNPCB in early September, he was apparently talking about something beyond a provisional measure for the Gulf crisis.[59] But it was not until after a group of LDP "defense clique" (*kokubō zoku*) members returned from the US two weeks later that people began to learn that what was behind the Peace Cooperation Corps proposal was SDF's participation in future UN PKOs. The first such mission was supposed to be in war-torn Cambodia. During their stay in Washington, the LDP defense clique delegation was questioned by US officials concerning Japan's long-term plan regarding UN PKO activities, including those in Cambodia.[60] The US government had indicated its interests in the SDF's participation in UN PKO at formal or informal talks with Japan ever since the mid-1960s.[61] The Japanese side consistently handled those requests in a low-key manner, but this time Japan's response was different. On September 15, former Foreign Minister Kuranari, the head of the LDP delegation, went to see Kaifu. After Kuranari reported that the US was interested in learning whether Japan was willing to send personnel to the UN surveillance team in Cambodia, Kaifu said that he was "studying the problem seriously" and would keep it in mind when considering the UNPCB.[62]

The dialogue between the two was soon leaked to the press. Three days later, during an interview with a major daily newspaper, deputy head of the LDP delegation Yamazaki Taku—former JDA director general and an active supporter of the UNPCB—again played the US

---

59. Ibid.
60. LDP, "Hōbei hōkokusho—kaidan yōshi," p. 91.
61. Pan, "Amerika no tainichi seisaku ni okeru kokuren heiwa iji katsudō," pp. 6–8.
62. *Yomiuri shimbun,* September 16, 1990.

card by impressing on the public the extent of the US Congress's "hysterical" Japan-bashing due to the inefficiency of Japan's collaboration during the Gulf crisis. "The fundamental problem," he emphasized, "was whether we could dispatch SDF troops in the event that Article 42 of the UN charter [authorizing military actions] has been introduced. And the UN PKO in Cambodia will be the first test of our willingness."[63] To LDP leaders like Yamazaki, the UNPCB was a warm-up for that test in Cambodia years ahead. As Secretary General Ozawa stated later, the passage of the UNPCB in the Diet would be "one step forward" from Japan's traditional security stance, maintained for half a century. If the bill could not be adopted, he added, "it is at least worthwhile to straightforwardly raise the issue [SDF's cooperation with PKO] so that our people could have a chance to discuss and think about it."[64]

To policy planners' distress, the clumsy approach that the LDP leadership used to link future contributions to the UN PKO and the dispatch of SDF to the coalition force soon kindled protests outside the party. While LDP leaders were trying hard to unify their own opinions, the opposition was already awaiting them in an extraordinary Diet session to discuss the UNPCB. The LDP was not in an advantageous position in the Diet. With fewer than half of the seats in the Upper House, the party needed sympathetic votes from some of its competitors in order to achieve a quick passage of the bill. The JSP and the JCP, both of which had already declared that they would not tolerate any plan involving the SDF, were out of the question in this sense. The DSP was helpful due to its long-cherished position favoring personnel cooperation with PKO, but its seats were far from sufficient unless the CGP's votes could also be secured.

Theoretically, the LDP's chances of gaining the approval of the CGP on the bill were not that low. Having lost quite a few seats during the recent general election, the CGP was beginning to reconsider its previous partnership with the JSP. Its relationship with the DSP rapidly grew close and its attitude toward the conservative LDP became manifestly flexible. Shortly after Iraq's invasion of Kuwait, the CGP's view on Japan's role in the crisis split into two groups. One was represented by Secretary General Ichikawa Yūichi and his followers. At a meeting

---

63. Matsumoto, *PKO to kokusai kōken*, p. 46.
64. *Yomiuri shimbun*, October 13 and 17, 1990.

of the party's Policy Planning Council held in late August, some members of this group suggested that with the precondition of observing the constitution and the UN-first principles, it might be necessary to send unarmed SDF personnel such as medical officers to join international peace endeavors in the Middle East. On August 30 and 31, Ichikawa mentioned twice the need to "further the debate" regarding the feasibility of dispatching unarmed SDF for overseas missions. These movements, however, upset the party's mainstream factions.[65]

While well-known for the instability of its defense policy, the CGP had never made a concession for nearly three decades regarding its opposition toward sending SDF abroad. Many CGP supporters, specifically those from the Sōka Gakkai, were adamant antiwar pacifists who would not acquiesce with any move to alter this traditional stance. Probably aware of these backgrounds, most party leaders, including chairman Ishida Kōshirō, were inclined to keep their distance from Ichikawa's arguments.[66] Like the opponents of the UNPCB inside the LDP, they also used the UN-centric spirit to legitimize their position. "Troops of the coalition force are devoted spontaneously by individual states, while the UN resolutions only asked for economic sanctions," party Deputy Secretary General Futami Nobuaki wrote to a newspaper in mid-September. "If the SDF were sent there [the Middle East], it would be put under the command of the US."[67]

Ichikawa, who forged a semi-partnership with his LDP counterpart Ozawa, managed to quiet such unease through a counterproposal to the UNPCB. According to his plan, the original bill would be narrowed down into "time-limit legislation" solely for the purpose of cooperating with the coalition force, and SDF members of the Peace Cooperation Corps should be discharged from their military posts and be sent out as civilians. In relation to the UN PKO issue, which was another pillar of the bill, Ichikawa acknowledged its significance but preferred to delete it from the current legislation.[68]

---

65. Ibid., September 2, 1990.
66. Ibid.; Kunimasa and Takabatake, "'Hahei kokkai' no butaiura," pp. 32–33.
67. *Mainichi shimbun,* September 17, 1990.
68. *Yomiuri shimbun,* October 10, 1990; CGP, "Kokuren heiwa kyōryoku ni tsuite no kenkai," p. 87.

Ichikawa's proposal did not receive a favorable response from the LDP. Under Ozawa's leadership, the ruling party decided on October 9 to let SDF officers serve "concurrently" as Peace Cooperation Corps staff while retaining the clauses for future PKO cooperation in the draft of the bill. At this point, the fate of the UNPCB was doomed. The CGP stepped down from a potential coalition with the LDP. The DSP, which had no intention of facing negative public opinion alone, followed suit. When the Diet session began to deliberate the bill in mid-October, it was up to the halfhearted Kaifu and Nakayama instead of the assertive Ozawa (who was not a cabinet member) to defend the government's line.

The opposition parties were resolute and confident during the Diet debate because they knew they would have a quick victory. The breakthrough was made in the correlations between the UN and the coalition force. The government was desperately trying to define Japan's personnel contribution to the US-led coalition force through the UNPCB as imperative for cooperating with the UN's resolutions on Kuwait. But no such connection had been acknowledged between the resolutions and the military actions conducted by the coalition troops in the Middle East. (It was not until November 29 that the UNSC authorized the use of "all necessary means" to get Saddam Hussein out of Kuwait.) On October 19, one day after the UNPCB hit the Diet table, JSP Secretary General Yamaguchi Tsuruo asked for the government's opinion on this bizarre situation. Foreign Minister Nakayama was completely caught off guard, and his aides in MOFA were unable to help him out.[69]

The confrontation between Nakayama and Yamaguchi marked the beginning of what would become a nightmare for the government and LDP leaders. Having refused to recognize the legitimacy of the UNPCB's purpose in the first place, the opposition turned the rest of the session into a stage for exposing the loopholes in the bill. Apart from the issue of compatibility with the UN charter and UNSC resolutions, the status of the Peace Cooperation Corps members, their equipment (including weapons), and the bill's correlation with the constitution were all put under severe scrutiny. Kaifu, Nakayama, and

---

69. "Dai 119 kai kokkai shūgiin yosan iinkaigiroku dai 1 gō" (Proceedings of the 119th Diet Session Budget Committee, Lower House, No. 1), October 19, 1990, NDL.

MOFA were the biggest losers in the debacle. Since Secretary General Ozawa was determined to fight until the bitter end, the only things they could do were to slightly change the context of the bill through confusing government interpretations.[70] Not until early November did Ozawa feel it was time to consult their opponents for an alternative draft.[71] But it was too late. Devoid of support from major opposition leaders, the government had to scrap the bill on November 8.

The withdrawal of the UNPCB was a heavy blow to the Kaifu cabinet, yet it was not necessarily a bad thing for LDP promoters of the bill, who at least learned one precious lesson through the fiasco: if they wanted to get rid of domestic regulations on employing Japanese troops overseas, they'd better do it through the UN. Now without the burden of enabling the immediate dispatch of Japanese forces to the coalition, they were free to return to this safer option. On November 5, three days before the government formally decided to give up the UNPCB, Ozawa paid a call to the prime minister's residence, where he told Kaifu that the party was going to consider the establishment of a "UN standby force" such as those held by Nordic nations rather than sticking with the previous Peace Cooperation Corps formula.[72] This was not an abrupt suggestion. Upon abandoning his support of the UNPCB in mid-October, DSP chairman Ōuchi Keigo conveyed a message through the media that a national security system composed of two separate forces—the SDF specializing in territorial defense and a UN standby force for international peacekeeping—seemed more acceptable to his party.[73] On November 4, Ozawa concurred with this idea in a TV interview. His conversation with Kaifu the next day, in this sense, was just a reconfirmation of his interest.

With the LDP and DSP leaders quietly reaching agreements on the direction of future collaboration, the CGP's attitude again became critical. The CGP was not satisfied with the UNPCB's assignment of SDF troops to the Peace Cooperation Corps. But during the deliberation of the bill, instead of joining the progressive opposition parties' campaign

---

70. *Yomiuri shimbun,* October 20, 25 and 27; *Asahi shimbun,* October 23 and 27.

71. *Yomiuri shimbun,* November 6.

72. Ibid.

73. DSP, "Kokuren heiwa kyōryoku hōan mondai ni tsuite no minshatō no taido," p. 88; *Yomiuri shimbun,* October 11.

aimed at burying it, the party merely reiterated the UN-centric principle.[74] This stance made Ozawa's work much easier. By November 9,
the three parties prepared a six-point framework for new legislation.
Largely absorbing the views of the DSP and the CGP, the framework
focused entirely on "cooperation with UN PKO" and other "humanitarian assistance" related to UN resolutions. The organization engaging
in these activities would also be separate from the SDF.[75]

As the LDP, the DSP, and the CGP forged their united front, the
JSP and the JCP had to decide whether they should jump on the bandwagon or remain independent. A counter-coalition was one option, of
course. But in the early 1990s the two parties' mutual antagonism had
reached a degree that eliminated any possibility of such cooperation.
The two had to fight separately against the LDP-led coalition.

Holding very few seats in the Diet, the JCP took an uncompromis-
ing policy against any plans for active personnel cooperation with UN
PKO.[76] The JSP also refrained from supporting the PKO cooperation
plan. But compared to the JCP, the JSP's hesitation was not due to differences in policy ideals but rather its reluctance to follow other opposition parties' initiative. Before the Diet session entered into discussions
on the UNPCB, the JSP published a proposal calling for "civilian cooperation" with PKO through a "UN Peace Cooperation Agency," while
excluding SDF participation.[77] The essence of this proposal was pretty
close to that of the six-point framework concluded by the LDP, the
DSP, and the CGP. Yet JSP leaders were stunned by the clandestine
negotiations that had been going on among other parties concerning
future PKO cooperation without requesting their opinions. On November 9, Secretary General Yamaguchi bluntly refused the invitation
to join the six-point agreement during a four-party secretary general
meeting. "This is the first time ever since I was nominated as the Secre-

---

74. *Yomiuri shimbun,* October 17; *Mainichi shimbun,* October 21.
75. LDP, DSP and CGP, "Kokusai heiwa kyōryoku ni kansuru gōi oboegaki,"
p. 88.
76. Sasaki, "Iraku no Kuweito shinryaku to Nihon kyōsantō no tachiba," p. 28;
Yamazaki, "Iraku no Kuweito shinkō to kokusai rengō," pp. 100–101; Muramatsu, Ueda Kōichirō, Takeda, Tsutsui and Katō, "Gekiron: 'kokuren heiwa
kyōryokutai' o kiru," p. 154 and p. 158.
77. JSP, "'Kokuren heiwa kyōryoku kikō' secchi taikō," pp. 157–59.

tary General that I have attended a four-party secretary general consultation in such a bad mood," he told the press after the meeting.[78]

Despite their initial anger, JSP leaders were soon aware of the disadvantage of letting the other opposition parties shift to the conservative camp. By mid-November, party chairwoman Doi Takako gestured that she favored a more intimate connection with the CGP in working out new PKO legislation. But at that moment, the CGP no longer cared so much what the JSP's position might be. CGP leaders agreed to talk, though they also informed the JSP that the latter's acceptance of their agreement with the LDP would be the prerequisite for the resumption of collaboration. Knowing the best timing was gone forever, the JSP announced on December 4 that it would never yield to the six-point framework and would henceforth give priority to the refinement of its own proposal.[79]

As the opposition parties lost their solidarity, the government and the LDP were in a comfortable position to make another bid for the bill. Before doing so, however, the six-point framework still needed to be polished. The framework ruled out the possibility of using SDF in PKO, a policy that was echoed by many moderate leaders within the LDP.[80] But at the same time, from the very beginning some LDP members saw the six-point framework prohibiting SDF's participation simply as a transitional agreement for the sake of gaining the support of the opposition. Those close to the SDF like JDA Director General Ishikawa Yōzō had no intention at all of accepting it.[81]

The party leadership behaved prudently this time and avoided taking substantial actions to remove the barrier to SDF participation until new developments in the Middle East created an opportunity for them to do so. The UNSC adopted a resolution (Resolution 678) on November 29 authorizing the use of "all necessary means" to repel Iraqi forces from

---

78. CGP, *Ningen shugi "chūdō shugi" no atarashii sentaku,* p. 33; *Yomiuri shimbun,* November 9, 1990.

79. JSP, *Shiryō—Nihon shakaitō no 50 nen,* p. 1083.

80. Muramatsu, Ueda Kōichirō, Takeda, Tsutsui and Katō, "Gekiron: 'Kokuren heiwa kyōryokutai' o kiru," pp. 146–47; Matsumoto, *PKO to kokusai kōken,* pp. 163–64.

81. Ishihara Nobuo, *Kantei 2668 nichi,* p. 65.

Kuwait if they were not withdrawn by January 15, 1991. On January 17, two days after the deadline passed unheeded, the coalition force launched its offensive against the Iraqis. When the operation ended on February 28, not only was Kuwait liberated but part of Iraqi territory was also occupied by the coalition. Having failed to make personnel contributions before and during the war, the LDP leadership grasped at a chance to send SDF minesweepers to clear the high seas near Kuwait in April. While Japanese policymakers insisted that the dispatch was demanded by President George H. Bush, the US ambassador denied the existence of such a request in his memoir.[82] But no matter what exactly happened between the two governments, this epoch-making mission to the Persian Gulf substantially changed the atmosphere of the ruling LDP.

The SDF's minesweeping technology is in the upper echelon among Western navies, and this guaranteed the success of the mission. As Japan's international reputation was enhanced by the performance of these minesweepers, LDP leaders became more confident about the SDF's role in international spheres. Even the once reluctant Kaifu was impressed by the SDF's achievement in the Persian Gulf.[83] But the party did not lose its caution. The dispatch of minesweepers was made by a temporary administrative order from the prime minister and therefore was nothing but an exceptional incident. The royal road toward the SDF's overseas employment still had to be found through the UN.

Due to the sensational news coverage of the Gulf crisis, by the time the coalition force moved to crush Saddam Hussein's troops in Kuwait, a government poll showed that the majority of Japanese people had already come to support the SDF's cooperation with PKO. But such support was granted under a precondition that no military purposes should be involved.[84] A similar trend was observed in the signatories of the six-point framework. Though the DSP backtracked to its previous position in terms of promoting SDF's participation in PKO, both the LDP and the CGP were less keen on moving quickly in this direction. Hinting that SDF personnel might join PKO as civilians while keeping

---

82. Ibid., p. 42; Armacost, *Friends or Rivals?*, p. 124.
83. Ishihara, ibid., p. 65.
84. Prime Minister's Office, *Gaikō ni kansuru yoron chōsa heisei 2 nendo*, pp. 87–92; Prime Minister's Office, *Jieitai, bōei mondai ni kansuru yoron chōsa heisei 2 nendo*.

their posts in original units, the CGP firmly held to its bottom line that the SDF's missions must be "humanitarian" activities based on UN requests or resolutions. Within the LDP, powerful figures like Miyazawa, Gotōda, and Takeshita also opposed letting the SDF go so far as to join peacekeeping forces of a combat nature.[85]

Sympathetic to these arguments, Kaifu attempted to pin down Japan's scope of cooperation by defining PKO in two categories. One was called "Peacekeeping Forces (PKF)" referring to UN forces that might easily be involved in military actions. The other was "PKO" including logistics, transportation, and medical services. In his plan, the new bill regarding PKO contributions (the PKO Law) would exclude PKF-type missions in order to secure the CGP's endorsement. But the party leadership thought this compromise outrageous and insisted on having a law covering all PKO missions. Before the infighting during the early stage of the Gulf crisis could happen again, MOFA found a solution. Borrowing from Switzerland's PKO Law, MOFA suggested that without isolating SDF from PKF Japan could keep its right to unilaterally withdraw from any PKO mission whenever it sensed the danger of being dragged into military conflict. The idea was accepted. In July 1991, the government issued the draft of the PKO Law and planned to submit it to a Diet session scheduled a month later.[86]

If the DSP had not suddenly retracted its support for the law, Kaifu might have gained the credit as the Japanese prime minister opening the door for the SDF's affiliation with PKO. Presumably aiming at impressing the public with his party's independent role, DSP chairman Ōuchi remarked shortly before the Diet session that advance approval of the Diet must be necessary for any decisions regarding PKO participation. If the government did not accept this, he maintained, his party would not support the law.[87] This was a bolt from the blue for the LDP. Faced with Ōuchi's unflinching attitude, deliberations on the law were postponed to another extraordinary Diet session in November. But Kaifu was unable to take part in the debate any longer. The party's big

---

85. Ōuchi, "Jieitai sanka ni yoru PKO soshiki o," pp. 6–9; Matsumoto, *PKO to kokusai kōken,* pp. 107–8; Sakurai, Ozawa and Gotōda, "Jiyū minshutō no kenpō mondai," pp. 130–31.

86. Ishihara Nobuo, *Kantei 2668 nichi,* pp. 66–67.

87. Watanabe Akio and Mikuriya, *Shushō kantei no ketsudan,* pp. 90–91.

bosses felt the necessity for a new face, so he was forced to resign in early November and Miyazawa became his successor.

Miyazawa's method of tackling the PKO Law was no less circumspect than that of Kaifu. Just a few weeks before his election as the LDP president, he expressed his regret yet again about the Kaifu cabinet's failure to tell the international community during the Gulf crisis that the country could not send its people to the coalition force because the mission was not organized by the UN.[88] After he himself was put in the position of overseeing the government's promotion of the PKO Law, however, Miyazawa soon realized how complicated his job was going to be. During the renewed Diet discussion on the law from November, the DSP refused to budge on its request for advance authorization. Moreover, the gap between the LDP and other opposition parties on critical issues (such as weapons used by Japanese personnel and operational control of SDF troops participating in PKO) remained unfilled. Rather than hastening the debate, Miyazawa and his deputy Kanemaru judged that a pause was necessary.[89]

While waiting for the Diet discussion to resume, Miyazawa stepped up the LDP's negotiations with the CGP and the DSP so as to stabilize the cooperative relations among the three parties. In the meantime, in a clever piece of strategy, he used the UN to generate pressure for passage of the law. In late January, during a summit of leaders from all UNSC member states, Miyazawa boldly declared that the PKO Law would be adopted during the forthcoming Diet session.[90] After this unexpected promise, domestic movement regarding the legislation picked up sharply. In early February, CGP Secretary General Ichikawa remarked that the government should "freeze" the enactment of the PKF part in the original draft. Three weeks later, the LDP accepted this idea. At first sight, Ichikawa's suggestion appeared to be aimed at nullifying the PKO Law, since PKF was supposed to be the core of the LDP's proposal. But in fact, it was a tricky device that helped the ruling party to overcome a major hurdle: the DSP's opposition.

On the pretext of strengthening civilian control over the SDF's participation in PKF, the DSP had demanded the advance approval of the

---

88. Miyazawa, "Kaifu san to watashi wa koko ga chigau," pp. 115–16.
89. Matsumoto, *PKO to kokusai kōken,* pp. 139–40.
90. Araki, "Kenshō, PKO hō seiritsu o rīdo shita minshatō," p. 22.

Diet. Now that the government had decided to shelve the proposal of using the SDF in PKF, the DSP could easily resume its cooperation with the LDP by letting the advance approval requirement die with the PKF. DSP chairman Ōuchi understood this benefit quite well. On April 12, he commented in a TV talk show that the CGP's proposal "leaves certain room for negotiation."[91] A few days later, the three parties agreed on a new draft in which the SDF's participation in PKF would be frozen for the present time, and Diet approval was required before this regulation could be removed in the future.

Besides the pressure he himself had forged at the UNSC, Miyazawa received another gift from the UN: the peacekeeping mission in Cambodia (UNTAC). The UNTAC mission headed by Japanese UN senior official Akashi commenced in late March. Shortly before then, Cambodian Prime Minister Hun Sen came to Tokyo to ask for the Japanese government's assistance, specifically the SDF's cooperation, in the UN's efforts. The timing of his visit was crucial, as the progressive opposition parties were determined to deliver a *coup de grâce* to the PKO Law in the Diet session scheduled a month ahead. During his stay, Hun Sen not only talked with LDP leaders and their political allies but also held a meeting with JSP leaders. While JSP chairman Tanabe consistently emphasized constitutional barriers to the SDF's participation, his explanation appeared pale before his earnest Cambodian counterpart.[92]

After Hun Sen's visit, the LDP, the CGP, and the DSP seized the chance to persuade the public that the PKO Law should not be delayed any longer, as the UN desperately needed Japan's help in Cambodia. The JSP also adjusted its position slightly. By this point, debates regarding a possible new stance on the PKO issue had been going on among various JSP factions for almost a year. While all party leaders now agreed that Japan had to send some people to join the UN's peacekeeping efforts, there was no consensus on the role of the SDF. At last, the party leadership decided to ask for the establishment of an independent unit for PKO cooperation whose members may contain police officers but not SDF troops. In November 1991, the party announced this plan

---

91. Ibid., p. 35; Watanabe Akio and Mikuriya, *Shushō kantei no ketsudan,* p. 91.
92. Leitenberg, *The Participation of Japanese Military Forces in UN Peacekeeping Operations,* pp. 21–22.

as a counterproposal to the government's PKO Law.[93] Yet the LDP-CGP-DSP coalition insisted on their original plan. To avoid being perceived as obstructing UNTAC, on April 14, 1992, the "foreign minister" of the JSP's "shadow cabinet," Kubota Manae, issued a ten-point plan for international cooperation in which she urged the ruling and opposition parties to have a supra-partisan talk on personnel cooperation with UNTAC. Party chairman Tanabe also indicated his willingness to accept one-time-only PKO legislation specifically designed for UNTAC.[94] But the ties between the LDP and the two middle-of-the-road opposition parties had by then grown too tight to allow the inclusion of the JSP. "The LDP, the DSP and the CGP had decided all schedules and contents of the Diet discussion . . . . They behaved like one party," JSP chairman Tanabe complained after his party's endeavors ended in vain.[95]

The Diet debate on the PKO Law approached its final stages in early June. By then, the LDP had acquired what it needed for passage. Both the DSP and the CGP were ready to back the LDP and thereby brightened the prospects of the law's passage in the Upper House. Having lost all cards with which they could have trumped the LDP and stopped the law, JSP and JCP members managed to delay the Diet decision for a few days through "ox-walk tactics"—moving at a snail's pace during the voting. But the filibuster brought no difference in the final outcome. On June 15, with the affirmative votes of the LDP, the DSP, and the CGP, the PKO Law was adopted in the plenary session of the Lower House. The JSP did not attend the voting and left a handful of JCP members finishing the last performance of the ox-walk ritual.[96]

The LDP had by no means forgotten the real reason for the success of its effort to grant the SDF a constitutional role in international cooperation. "The prime difference between this law and the UNPCB drafted a couple of years ago is that it does not include cooperation

---

93. Uezumi, *Nihon shakaitō kōbōshi,* pp. 394–406; JSP, "Kokusai heiwa kyōryoku (PKO), kinkyū enjo ni kansuru shakaitō no hōan," p. 145.

94. Kubota, "Kokusai kōken ni kansuru 10 kōmoku teigen," pp. 72–73; Tanabe, "PKO gekitotsu kokkai, kecchaku wa korekara da," pp. 8–9.

95. Ibid., p. 12.

96. JSP, *Shiryō—Nihon shakatō no 50 nen,* pp. 1111–13; Nakamura, "Kaigai hahei soshi, gikaisei minshu shugi tsuranuita Nihon kyōsantō," p. 110–11.

with the so-called multinational coalition force," the party explained shortly after the PKO Law's passage.[97] The government also stressed in Article 1 of the law that this legislation was created to "enable Japan to actively contribute to efforts for international peace centering upon the UN"—words that were found nowhere in the previous UNPCB.[98] Having adopted a common strategy of using the UN to legitimize their policies on national security and SDF issues for more than four decades, it seemed that the conservative government and the ruling LDP eventually gained the upper hand.

---

97. LDP, "Kokuren heiwa iji katsudō to wa nani ka," p. 89.
98. Morrison and Kiras, *UN Peace Operations,* p. 91.

PART III

The UN and Japan's International Status

ᔥ 8 ᔥ
Fighting for Equal Status:
The Road to the UN

The role of the UN in Japan's domestic politics had its roots in the nation's experience of losing the last world war, and in its inability to maintain national interests through military means. But party politics is not the only way in which this historical experience tied Japan to the organization. Japan's defeat in WWII also gave proactive shape to strong attachments to the UN among Japanese people (including foreign policymakers) for the sake of restoring first equal and then superior status in the postwar international community.

The vicissitudes of Japan's international status during the first half of the twentieth century were closely related to two world peace organizations: the League of Nations and the UN. After the end of WWI, Japan was one of the most prestigious nations in the world. The empire's outstanding status was reflected by the fact that it was the only non-Occidental nation that was entitled to a permanent membership in the League of Nations Council. But Japan's splendid career in the League ended abruptly in the early 1930s. In February 1933, after the League Assembly denied Tokyo's claims that its military operation following a feigned explosion at the Japan-owned Southern Manchurian Railway (the so-called "Manchuria Incident") in northeast China was purely defensive, Japan's chief delegate Matsuoka Yōsuke gave a farewell speech to the League and left Geneva for good. This action gained enthusiastic applause from the Japanese public, long indignant at what they saw as intervention from the West in the course of the legal expansion of their empire. Major dailies reported the news under sensational headlines like

"So long, the League!" or "In a rage, our delegate stomped out of the League."[1] And Matsuoka returned home like a national hero. In March, the Japanese imperial government declared the termination of its relationship with the international peace institution.

Japan's withdrawal from the League was dramatic. But it was painful and humiliating when the exhausted empire knocked at the door of the UN some 20 years later and received no positive response from the inside. The glorious days at the League were gone forever and the postwar Japanese government had to rebuild the nation's international status from scratch. Admission to the UN, in this sense, was a crucial first step.

Returning to the International Community through the UN

In the initial days of the postwar era, Japanese officials were appalled at the sharp contrast between their nation's international status before and after the war. One month after Emperor Hirohito broadcast Japan's decision to end its resistance, Shigemitsu, nominated as postwar Japan's first foreign minister, noted in his diary that the government's task of settling the details of the surrender with the Allied Forces was "the most disgraceful scandal in the 3000-year history" of the empire.[2] In another MOFA document prepared during the same period, Shigemitsu's staff lamented the fact that because of the defeat Japan fell from "the ladder of glory and prosperity" and descended to an international status "on par with the Eskimos."[3] Even General Douglas MacArthur, Japan's real ruler during the occupation era, had little doubt about his former enemy's downfall. He told the press in September 1945 that as a result of the war, Japan had been downgraded to a "fourth-rate nation."[4]

The restoration of what Japan had lost was the primary task for those in charge of foreign policymaking within the government. But this was not something that could be achieved overnight. Being barred from all significant international activities, Japan had to first get itself

---

1. *Asahi shimbun* and *Yomiuri Shimbun*, February 25, 1933.
2. Shigemitsu, *Shigemitsu Mamoru shuki*, p. 531.
3. Watanabe Akio, "Taigai ishiki ni okeru 'senzen' to 'sengo,'" p. 242.
4. MOFA, *Nihon gaikō 30 nen*, p. 12; Dower, *Embracing Defeat*, pp. 43–44.

out of the state of isolation and become an equal player in postwar world politics. The UN—the largest global governmental organization—became the best channel to facilitate Japan's efforts.

One of the early connections between postwar Japan's international status and the UN arose from the new Japanese constitution. When composing the blueprint of the constitution in February 1946, SCAP officials created Article 9, prohibiting the use and maintenance of military forces as a tool to settle international conflicts, coupled with a preamble asserting the Japanese people's desire to "occupy an honored place" in international society through their endeavors to preserve world peace.[5] Most Japanese leaders were hardly satisfied with this American-made constitution, which sounded like a mixture of the UN charter and the Gettysburg Address. But this did not prevent them from utilizing the constitution's idealistic flavor to strengthen their appeal for the country's appropriate status in the world. "It is obvious that the spirit of the new constitution is coincident with the ultimate ideals of the UN," stated the chairman of the Diet's Constitution Revision Committee, Ashida Hitoshi. "I, therefore, think that revising the [old imperial] constitution is a precondition for Japanese affiliation with the UN and, to put it plainly, to occupy an honorable status in international society."[6] Prime Minister Yoshida made a similar statement, asserting that Article 9 was inserted in the constitution to make Japan "a leading actor in the international peace organization [the UN]."[7]

But the constitution alone could not automatically turn the defeated nation into that "leading" actor or "honorable" member of the world community. It was up to government policy planners, specifically diplomatic professionals, to finish this arduous job. Like many politicians, MOFA staffers clearly noticed that Japan would have no chance to raise its international status unless it could become a member of the UN family. The opinion of officials at the Treaties Bureau—the cornerstone of the Ministry's decision-making body—regarding this problem was laconically outlined in a July 1947 memo:

---

5. SCAP, "Makkāsā sōan," p. 276.

6. Shimizu, *Chikujō Nihonkoku kenpō shingiroku dai 2 kan,* pp. 298–99.

7. Kasuya Susumu, *Sengo Nihon no anzen hoshō rongi,* p. 17.

Countries like Switzerland can probably be treated like member states even though they do not join the UN. States like Japan and Germany, however, will not be allowed to have any international communication if we remain outside the organization. In order to raise our country's international status, we believe that it is necessary to seize every opportunity to participate in the UN, its special agencies and other non-governmental organizations.[8]

MOFA's observation was solid, yet UN membership or international status was a luxury subject for a Japan that was under occupation and thereby had no right to conduct any diplomatic activities. Notwithstanding their quixotic arguments on the common ground shared by the new constitution and the spirit of the UN, government leaders and senior officials had repeatedly to caution their impatient colleagues at the Diet that the UN affiliation issue was a sticky matter that must be shelved until an arrangement for peace was concluded.[9] What they did not anticipate, however, was that the peace arrangement might not smooth the way toward joining the UN and, as a matter of fact, would even interfere with Japan's efforts to raise its international status.

While the 1951 San Francisco Peace Treaty ended the Allied occupation, it also marked the beginning of Japan's struggle with the Eastern bloc on the stage of the Cold War. As the Soviet delegation (and those of its satellites) walked out of the peace conference, Japan regained its diplomatic rights as an independent sovereign state, albeit only in the realm of the free world. This was not a promising condition for the Japanese government's quest for a seat in the UN.

With negotiations on the peace and security treaties reaching their final stage around 1951, the government felt that the time was ripe to make a serious bid for UN membership—the symbol of equal position in the postwar world community. MOFA officials conducted tentative surveys on the issue. The results, however, were discouraging. The escalation of the East-West confrontation that began in the late 1940s not only impaired the UN's peacekeeping capabilities but also paralyzed other administrative functions of the organization, including the admission of new member states. From 1945 to 1951, twenty-four nations submitted their applications for a UN seat, of which only nine were ap-

---

8. International Cooperation Division, "Kokusai rengō no hanashi," 1947, UTL.
9. Policy Division of the Policy Bureau, *Kokkai ni okeru kōwa rongi*, p. 228 and p. 235; Shimizu, *Chikujō Nihon kenpō shingiroku dai 2 kan*, pp. 93–95.

proved by the UNSC. Holding majority votes at the Council, the US and other Western allies successfully blocked the admission of Soviet satellites into the UN. The Soviets, in retaliation, used their vetoes to shut out pro-Western candidates. By the time Japan was added to the waiting list, the Council's deliberations on new members were dormant. Initially, MOFA policymakers were still in high spirits, hoping that the "efforts of the US and other states concerned" could lead to a solution to this impasse.[10] But when they investigated the situation more thoroughly, the optimism vanished. "The possibility of joining the UN through an affirmative Soviet vote at the UNSC is next to none," they concluded in a report in late 1951. "The sole way to break the deadlock is a political deal between the Soviet and the American camps."[11] Subsequent developments proved the adequacy of this judgment.

An "Associate" UN Membership?

In the preamble of the peace treaty, the Western powers pledged to "welcome" Japan's intention to apply for a membership in the UN. Based on this provision, the Japanese government officially submitted its application to the UN in June 1952—two months after the treaty came into effect. As most Japanese policymakers well knew, any country seeking a seat in the UN had to manage to obtain the endorsement of two key players: the US and the USSR. Without a stable channel to communicate with Moscow, Japan had to start its endeavor through close consultations with Washington. But within a few months, Japanese policy planners found that the assistance extended by the US might not necessarily lead to a quick realization of their dream.

The US paid attention to Japan's affiliation with the UN as early as the occupation era. As the Cold War began to affect the political landscape in the Far East, the US government was compelled to hasten Japan's comeback in the international community as a responsible Western ally. In April 1949, the US informed the Far Eastern Commission (FEC, the official coordination board for the Allied Powers' policies toward Japan) that General MacArthur, "subject to his discretion and

---

10. Treaties Bureau, "Kokusai rengō kanyū mondai to mitōshi" (The prospects of joining the UN), August 14, 1951, B'0014, DRO.
11. MOFA, "Heiwa jōyaku chōingo no gaikō seisaku shingi yōkō," 1951, ibid.

continued control, should permit Japan to participate with other na
tions or groups of nations in such international relations, conventions,
consular arrangements or other bilateral or multilateral accords as Japan
may be invited to enter into, accede to, attend or participate in."[12] The
response of FEC members differed, but this had little impact on Washington's decision. With the help of SCAP and the State Department,
Japan joined UN special agencies such as the International Telecom-
munication Union (ITU), the Universal Postal Union (UPU), and the
UNESCO as a full member state even before achieving its independence. In the meantime, US officials certainly did not forget the significance of Japan's joining the UN main body. But the way they pursued
this goal irritated their Japanese counterparts.

Starting in 1949, in order to pave the way for the admission of its fellow socialist nations, the USSR tried hard to make a bargain with the
US on the issue of UN membership. It offered a so-called "package
deal" suggesting the simultaneous admission of a group of states from
both the Eastern and Western blocs. Upset about the Soviet's intention
to add states such as Mongolia or North Korea into the package, the
US did not take kindly to this proposal. But the Japanese government,
which was determined to achieve its seat at the UN through any available means, was attracted by the package deal formula. MOFA officials
began to inquire of the US about its likely reaction in the event the
USSR offered a package deal including Japan.[13]

Japan's interest in the package deal made policy planners in Foggy
Bottom uneasy. While supporting Japan's bid, US officials always
viewed Japanese membership in the UN as a card in its overall competition with the USSR within the organization. If Japan's application
could improve the US position in the game, they would push it. If it
turned out to be an obstacle, they would not hesitate to knock it down.
The package deal, unfortunately, was a case of the latter. The State Department was alarmed by the connection between the deal and Japan's
moves. Although officials in the Department were also in the process
of reconsidering the feasibility of the Soviets' offer, no final decision

---

12. Department of State, "Japanese Participation in International Conferences,"
1950, Box 19, Lot File 59D237, NA.
13. Araki to Okazaki, June 24, 1952; Okazaki to Araki, July 9, 1952, both in
B'0014, DRO.

had been made by the time they received the inquiry from MOFA. A Soviet package deal including Japan at this stage, therefore, would be an unwelcome scenario from the Department's standpoint.[14] Probably in the hopes of eliminating Japan's illusory hopes, State Department officials consistently refused to give Tokyo an affirmative answer and some of them even told their MOFA colleagues on private occasions that they would not accept the Soviet deal no matter whether Japan was on the list.[15]

In July 1952, the UNSC resumed discussions on the membership question. The result was a great relief to the US. From the outset Soviet Representative Malik denied any willingness on the side of his government to let Japan sit in the UN through a package deal. In September, he buried Japan's membership application with his veto against the ten positive votes cast by other Council members.[16]

Japanese officials were also hardly surprised by the tough Soviet stance. While holding ambiguous expectations toward the package deal idea, the Japanese government was never confident of the prospect of a gentle Soviet policy toward Japan's admission.[17] As no miracle happened, it calmly went on to prepare for a longer race.

One month after the failure of its application, Japan opened an observer's office in New York and appointed Takeuchi Ryūji as the country's first "Permanent Observer to the UN." The mission of Takeuchi's office, according to MOFA, was to cultivate relationships with Western powers, the UN Secretariat, and other membership candidates while "virtually occupying an influential status in international society prior to UN admission."[18] Six months later, the government took another action to strengthen its activities in the UN by nominating former Vice Foreign Minister Sawada Renzō, an expert on international organization affairs, as the new permanent observer. The rank of the observer

---

14. Wainhouse to Hickerson, April 18, 1952, Box 19, Lot File 59D237, NA.

15. Araki to Okazaki, July 8, 9, and August 15, 1952, all in B'0014, DRO.

16. Shimazu to Okazaki, August 22, 1952; MOFA, "Statement of Director of Public Information and Cultural Affairs Bureau in Relation to Japan's UN Membership Application," September 19, 1952, ibid.

17. Nakagawa Susumu, "Nihon no kokusai rengō kamei ni tsuite" (Japan's admission to the UN), June 27 and 29, 1952, ibid.

18. MOFA, "Heiwa jōyaku chōingo no gaikō seisaku shingi yōkō," 1950, ibid.

post was also raised from minister to ambassador. But just when Japan was to step up its campaign in the battle for membership, it found that the US was standing in its way.

Japan was not the only Western, former Axis state whose bid for a UN membership was trapped by the Soviet veto. Italy encountered the same problem, despite the fact that Moscow signed a peace treaty with it promising support for its admission to the UN. Reckoning with the difficulty in evading Soviet opposition, the US government came up with a compromise proposal to offer Italy an "associate member-ship"—a position that could allow participation in UN discussions without voting rights—for the time being. The proposal was shrugged off by the Italians, who believed the commitment made by the USSR in the peace treaty would eventually make the Soviets come to terms with them.[19] While continuing to work on bringing Italy around, the US also tried to sell the idea to Japan. During his trip to Tokyo in April 1951, Dulles, then the US president's special representative to negotiate the Japanese peace treaty, made a reference to the associate membership proposal in a meeting with a group of Japanese politicians.[20] The media in Japan quickly publicized the idea. The Japanese government, how-ever, remained silent. MOFA officials observed in their studies that such an idea was "impossible" to achieve under the current UN sys-tem.[21]

But the US did not give up. On August 27, 1952, one week after the USSR declared its opposition to Japan's admission, US Deputy Repre-sentative to the UN Ernest Gross approached the Japanese minister in Washington, Kamimura Shinichi, to express his "personal opinion" that Japan might need to give the associate membership formula a sec-ond thought. If Tokyo agreed to go with this formula, he explained, it would be possible to adopt a resolution for Japan's participation in the UN without the approval of the UNSC. He also added that once Japan

---

19. Shimazu to Okazaki, August 28, 1952, B'0014; International Cooperation Bu-reau, "Kokuren kamei mondai ni kanshi zaikyō Itaria dairi taishi to kaidan no ken" (Meeting with the Italian chargé d'affaires in Tokyo on admission to the UN), October 1, 1954, B'0040, both DRO.

20. *Mainichi shimbun,* April 22, 1951.

21. MOFA, "Heiwa jōyaku chōingo no gaikō seisaku shingi yōkō," 1950, B'0014, DRO.

began to attend UN sessions as an associate member, the mood among member states to grant Japan a full membership might soon warm up.[22]

Gross's statements caused quite a stir back in Tokyo. The initial response of policymakers within MOFA was relatively positive. Upon receiving the report from Kamimura, the International Cooperation Bureau in charge of UN policies conducted a preliminary study on the issue and concluded that the government should take Gross's advice seriously since under the current circumstances it might allow Japan to "have a say in world affairs" and thereby "raise the status of the independent Japan." The Bureau's recommendation, nevertheless, was made with one prerequisite. "Although we will not oppose the associate membership formula when a considerable number of states agree to join us, we shall not be the only associate member." [23]

On August 29, the International Cooperation Bureau's position was disclosed before officials from other bureaus of the Ministry. During the discussion, one division chief suggested that Japan must take the lead to draft a concrete proposal that would allow the associate members to "behave as if they have already joined the UN." Some officials also argued that the name of "associate member" needed to be changed so as to avoid being criticized as "false advertising." But in the end, they all concurred that this formula could be an optimal chance to promote Japan's international status.[24] Based on these arguments, Foreign Minister Okazaki instructed Japanese Ambassador in Washington Araki Eikichi to notify the US side that he had "great interest" in Gross's offer and asked for further information on the plan.[25]

The State Department was unprepared when the Japanese suddenly got serious about the associate membership formula. US officials were only able to give vague answers to Okazaki's questions and refrained

---

22. Shimazu to Okazaki, August 27, 1952, ibid.

23. First Division of the International Cooperation Bureau, "Kokuren kamei seido ni kansuru kōsatsu" (Study on the admission system of the UN), August 28, 1952, ibid.

24. First Division of the International Cooperation Bureau, "Bei kokuren daihyō Gurosu taishi no 'jun kamei' an ni kansuru tōgi yōshi" (Outline of discussions regarding US UN Delegate Ambassador Gross's "associate member" proposal), August 29, 1952, ibid.

25. Okazaki to Araki, August 30, 1952, ibid.

from providing any written explanations on the issue.[26] From this point, it became clear that even within the Department there was no consensus regarding the value of the associate membership. Certain senior officials including Gross and Dulles might have favored the idea, but those at the Office of United Nations Political and Security Affairs (UNP) were discreet at best. During the coming years, this lack of consistency on the US side would further bewilder their Japanese counterparts, who were desperately looking for a shortcut to a seat in the Assembly Hall.

While US officials were still coming to grips with the associate membership proposal, Japanese policymakers did not sit idly by. Aware of the need for Japan to come forward with its own idea, they drew up a detailed proposal on the feasible outcome of the associate membership idea. The plan was ambitious. "The non-voting participants" (which was the official name coined by the Japanese to supplant the term "associate member"), it read, shall have the right to send to "every session of the General Assembly the same delegation as those of the member states." Except for formal votes, these states might enjoy "all rights of participation in discussion" encompassing "the right to speak, to submit a draft resolution, an amendment, and to submit and withdraw a motion." They could also "receive from the Secretary General all communications and documents pertaining to the General Assembly."[27] Above all, the authors of the plan felt that the composition of the non-voting participants' UN delegation "must not be inferior to that of full members."[28] MOFA presented this plan to the US government in late October with an acknowledgment that it was nothing but "the result of technical study of the problem" and hence "should not be construed as reflecting the decision of the government of Japan to apply for 'Associate Membership.'"[29]

Although it was the US delegates at the UN who had kept urging Japan to think about the formula, the plan submitted by MOFA obvi-

---

26. Wainhouse to Hickerson, October 3, 1952, Box 19, Lot File 59D237, NA.

27. Kamimura to Young, November 4, 1952, ibid.

28. MOFA, "Kokuren jun kamei ni tsuite no hōshiki an to jun kameikoku no gimu ni tsuite" (Proposal on the formula of the UN associate membership and the duties of the associate members), October 10, 1952, B'0014, DRO.

29. Kamimura to Young, November 4, 1952, Box 19, Lot File 59D237, NA.

ously did not fit the original thinking of the State Department, which simply wanted to see more Western allies seated in the UN without any trouble. After going through the draft, UNP officials commented that although the US itself had no problem making an arrangement based on the general points outlined there, it was concerned about the potential opposition of certain member states which might feel the Japanese proposal established "a status too nearly equal to that of [full] members." They therefore concluded that the US "should consult with other members before agreeing to the [Japanese] formula."[30] Following this judgment, the Department told MOFA in December that the associate membership problem would "remain a tentative matter for future study by both governments" while the US did "not propose to take any steps" at the coming UNGA session to promote the plan.[31] But when the Department returned to the plan months later, the situation within Japan had already changed.

The non-voting participant proposal represented only one part of MOFA's investigation. Fearing ending up as the sole country that had to take the inferior associate membership, MOFA instructed overseas posts to sound out the attitudes of all Western and pro-Western candidates for UN membership toward the US's offer. The feedback it received was mostly negative. In particular the Italians, who thought the idea would bring damage to the "dignity" of their country, eagerly imparted to the Japanese side information about how reluctant other states were with respect to the associate membership formula.[32] As a result, the tentative consensus in MOFA fell apart.

By the end of 1953, there were two views among MOFA officials concerning associate membership. While both accented this idea's implications for Japan's status or voice in international society, their evaluation on whether such implication was positive or negative were divided. One group held a position that could be summarized as "all or

---

30. Wainhouse to Hickerson, November 7, 1952, ibid.

31. Young to Kamimura, December 8, 1952, B'0014, DRO.

32. Shima Shigenobu, "Kokuren kamei mondai ni kansuru Itari taishi no mō-shiire ni kansuru ken" (The request from the Italian ambassador on the UN associate membership problem), September 12, 1952; Takeuchi to Okazaki, November 11, 1952; Okumura Katsuzō, "Kokusai rengō ni taisuru jun kamei no ken" (The UN associate membership problem), December 12, 1952, ibid.

nothing." The supporters of this view harbored grave apprehensions about the "second-class nation treatment" accompanying the membership. They also argued that the associate membership would delay Japan's admission to the UN as a full member while forcing the nation to bear moral obligations on UN resolutions it had no chance to vote for or against.[33] With these considerations, Vice Foreign Minister Okumura Katsuzō, the leader of this group, told the Italian ambassador in December 1952 that Japan was "not so enthusiastic about the US's proposal."[34] A few months later, he instructed the director of the Ministry's Public Information and Cultural Affairs Bureau to inform the executive members of the Japan United Nations Association that the government would go along with Italy to oppose the associate membership while continuing its effort to join the UN as a full member.[35] Treaties Bureau Director Shimoda Takezō, also a member of this group, confirmed this stance with even plainer words. "I am not sure," he said at a meeting of the Lower House's Committee on Foreign Affairs in November 1953, "whether it is expedient to let first-class nations like Japan and Italy join the UN with lower ranking status [like the associate membership]."[36]

These negative opinions were countered by another group of officials who tended to see the issue from a "better-than-nothing" point of view. They deemed that "securing a voice at the General Assembly," no matter how, would "contribute to the rise of our country's international status."[37] Of course, they understood that other nations like Italy might feel uncomfortable with the associate membership. Yet they were also

---

33. First Division of the International Cooperation Bureau, "'Kokuren jun kamei' ni kansuru ken" (The "UN associate membership" question), August 21, 1953, ibid.

34. Okumura Katsuzō, "Kokusai rengō ni taisuru jun kamei no ken," ibid.

35. First Division of the International Cooperation Bureau, "'Kokuren jun kamei' ni kansuru ken," ibid.

36. "Dai 17 kai kokkai shūgiin gaimu iinkaigiroku dai 3 gō" (Proceedings of the 17th Diet Session Committee on Foreign Affairs, Lower House, No. 3), November 2, 1953, NDL; First Division of the International Cooperation Bureau, "Zai honpō Beikoku taishikan Donarudo nitō shokikan to no kaidan no ken" (Meeting with Second Secretary of the US Embassy to Japan Donald), November 9, 1953, ibid.

37. First Division of the International Cooperation Bureau, "'Kokuren jun kamei' ni kansuru ken," ibid.

aware of Japan's unique situation. "It goes without saying that Japan's international status is substantially different from that of Italy, which is a European state," Japanese Ambassador in Rome Harada Ken remarked in a June 1953 report, "because I can vividly feel here [in Italy] that Japan has still been isolated from international politics even after its return to international society." In his opinion, "for the sake of Japan's future it is better not to follow the Italians in delaying the solution of the associate membership case." Iseki Yūjirō, director of the International Cooperation Bureau, registered his endorsement of Harada's judgment.[38]

The better-than-nothing group remained a minority within the government until August 1953 when the US reactivated the associate membership proposal. Like what had occurred on the Japanese side, the US government's policy toward this issue also divided after the inauguration of the Eisenhower administration early that year. Officials of the UNP did not lose their discretion in handling the case. On the other hand, standing firm against Soviet vetoes, the new Secretary of State Dulles and US Ambassador to the UN Henry Cabot Lodge, Jr., moved quickly to renew the exploration of the associate membership formula. In February, Dulles's deputy, Walter B. Smith, sent a memorandum to the National Security Council (NSC) laying out the new administration's policy objectives regarding Japan, in which it was suggested that "full consideration" be given to the "possibility of non-voting membership for Japan through a resolution of the General Assembly should the Japanese so desire."[39] On August 8, during a meeting in Tokyo in the presence of Prime Minister Yoshida, Foreign Minister Okazaki, and Secretary Dulles, Ambassador Lodge directly asked the Japanese leaders to reconsider the associate membership. Lodge's statement was made in a very abrupt manner. But as it was brought out at the highest level, the request attracted serious attention from MOFA policymakers.[40]

---

38. Harada to Okazaki, June 4, 1953, ibid.
39. NSC, "A Report to the National Security Council by the Under Secretary of State on United States Objectives and Courses of Action with Respect to Japan," February 19, 1953, Reel 2, *Document of the National Security Council, Fourth Supplement.*
40. First Division of the International Cooperation Bureau, "'Kokuren jun kamei' ni kansuru ken."

Iseki's International Cooperation Bureau responded to Lodge's suggestion by rustling up a proposal to switch back to the associate membership formula in the event that the US lost its confidence regarding Japan's admission as a full UN member. Foreign Minister Okazaki was inclined to accept the idea and ordered the Japanese embassy in Washington to sound out the US position one last time.[41] What he heard, however, were two different voices. Dulles and Lodge told Ambassador Araki that the US government was well prepared to uphold Japanese associate membership since it would be "impossible" for Japan to acquire a regular membership at the UN for a "considerable" period of time. State Department officials, for their part, split between UNP policy planners now ready to give Lodge *carte blanche* on the case and those in the Tokyo embassy who hesitated to press Japan too much. With such internal disarray, the best answer the Department could find for their Japanese counterpart was that it was uninformed about Lodge's proposal and had not yet reached any agreement on the associate membership scheme.[42] Confused by the contradictory messages from Washington, MOFA finally decided to tell Lodge that Japan would like to postpone its decision on the case until the situation became clearer.[43]

But the game was far from over. Having kept in close contact with Lodge and Dulles after arriving in New York in April 1953, Japanese Observer to the UN Sawada began to lean toward the associate membership. Believing that the ultimate goal of admission to the UN was to "establish Japan's status in Asia and to resurrect its reputation in the world," Sawada was not unconcerned about his country's dignity when coping with the membership problem.[44] But like Ambassador Harada in Rome, he was also open-minded to any policy scheme that might get Japan closer to its goal. In December, he submitted a 36-page report on Japan's UN membership quandary to the foreign minister.[45] The report

---

41. Ibid; Okazaki to Araki, August 31, 1953, B'0014, DRO.

42. Araki to Okazaki, September 18 and 22, 1953, ibid.; Popper to McClurkin, September 16, 1953, McClurkin to Popper, September 17, 1953 and Popper to McClurkin through Bacon, September 17, 1953, all in Box 19, Lot File 59D237, NA.

43. Inukai to Sawada, October 9, 1953, B'0014, DRO.

44. Sawada to Shigemitsu, April 28, 1955, B'0040, ibid.

45. Sawada to Okazaki, December 29, 1953, B'0014, ibid.

displayed three alternatives for Japan's next move: first, waiting until the two superpowers worked out a solution; second, making a proactive bid for a full membership; and third, the second alternative plus exploring various measures including associate membership. Sawada immediately dismissed the first option, for it would make other Western powers think Japan was in no particular rush on the issue. The second one was ideal but difficult to pursue given the deadlock between the two blocs within the UN. This naturally narrowed down his choices to the third option.

Foreseeing domestic aversion to associate membership, which was an essential component of the third option, Sawada assigned a lot of space in his report to justifying the formula. He rebutted the argument that joining the UN as an associate member would hinder efforts for a full membership, asserting that if anything Japan's full membership was ultimately determined by the international situation in general, not by what kind of position it currently occupied within the UN. By sending able delegates to the UNGA through the associate membership formula, he continued, "Japan could further improve its prestige within the UN and thereby create an atmosphere favorable to a full membership." The only point that deserved specific attention was the necessity of avoiding the impression that the formula was imposed on Japan by the US. As long as Japan could take the lead to "set up a model" for associate membership, he assumed that even the stubborn Italians might eventually come around.

Sawada's observation matched neatly with the International Cooperation Bureau's views on the issue. In February 1954, his three-option argument appeared in a memorandum issued by the Bureau and was circulated within the Ministry.[46] Back in New York, the ambassador also wasted no time in enacting his proposal, starting with a daring push for Japan's full UN membership. On April 27, he offered Lodge his "private" opinions on a "conciliatory US proposal" for facilitating Japan's admission to the UN with two clear-cut requests. First, he told Lodge it was worthwhile for the US government to seek a chance for the simultaneous admission of all Western and pro-Western nations to-

---

46. First Division of the International Cooperation Bureau, "Kokuren kamei mondai ni tsuite" (The UN associate membership problem), February 9, 1954, B'0040, ibid.

gether with about five candidates from the other side of the Iron Curtain. Second, considering Soviet opposition to the membership of the ROK, South Vietnam, Cambodia, and Laos, the US should retract its bid for these states so that other allies' admission could be approved. In other words, Sawada was telling Lodge and Dulles that they should abandon their longstanding opposition to the Soviet package deal at the expense of some of their closest friends—a demand that could in no way gain a quick approval from Washington.[47] Three weeks later, Lodge's associate informed Sawada of the US's decision to reject the proposal.[48]

Perhaps this was exactly what Sawada wanted to see. While ostensibly cautioning Lodge not to divulge the details of their conversations to the State Department and the US embassy in Japan, Sawada reported to MOFA every word he had exchanged with the US side on the package deal. As Washington had turned down the plan to promote Japan's full membership, Sawada had now snared a sound rationale for embracing the second-best choice: associate membership.

In July, Sawada once again wired Tokyo to promote associate membership.[49] But many MOFA officials were still unwilling to back off and maintained that having already achieved full membership in a number of UN special agencies, Japan should not "beg for a status lower than other member states within the UN." Some also grumbled, "We do not think it will raise our country's international status to allow such discussions about associate membership aimed at receiving an inferior position to continue for so long within the UN."[50] These views, which were certainly not what Sawada had hoped to hear, prompted the ambassador to make a last-ditch effort to turn the tide.

On August 27, US Deputy Representative to the UN James J. Wadsworth received an urgent request from Sawada for an appointment. During the subsequent talk between the two at the US delega-

---

47. Sawada to Okazaki, April 28, 1954 and Sawada, "Japan's Admission to the United Nations," ibid.; Lodge to Key, April 28, 1954, Box 19, Lot File 59D237, NA.

48. Sawada to Okazaki, May 18, 1954, B'0040, DRO.

49. Sawada to Okazaki, July 27, 1954, ibid.

50. International Cooperation Bureau, "Jun kamei hantai ron" (Opposition to the associate membership), July 16, 1954, ibid.

tion's office, Sawada told Wadsworth that although he "personally" was in favor of the associate membership, he had received "official word" from his government stating that Japan was not interested in the formula at this time. "Nevertheless," he continued, he was informed that Foreign Minister Okazaki "had not completely forsaken the idea." He thus suggested that Lodge ask Dulles, who was scheduled to drop by Tokyo on his way back from Manila some days later, to "speak favorably of associate membership with Okazaki." Wadsworth, needless to say, gave assurance to Sawada that his message would be sent to the Secretary of State.[51]

While Dulles was unable to exert American pressure on Okazaki due to the cancellation of his trip, the US government did not let Sawada's venture end in vain. On September 24, Philip W. Bonsal, a senior advisor at the US UN delegation, presented Sawada with a "resident representative" proposal. Besides the main elements of the previous associate membership, the proposal would create opportunities for representatives of states whose membership was rejected by the Soviet veto to have their vote in the UNGA "recorded but not counted" and hence took a half-step forward from the non-voting associate membership formula.[52]

Like the associate membership, the resident representative plan tickled Japan's aspiration for equal status at the UN while escalating the arguments among MOFA policymakers on the issue. Members of the better-than-nothing group were flattered to see the US coming to their aid. Dismissing their opponents' thought that Japan's membership at UN special agencies had brought the nation a sufficiently high position, they contended that Japan's voice in the world community would not be recognized unless it improved its status in the UN's main body. They also rebutted the view that the votes cast by the resident representatives were less influential, noting that "it is better to have some voice than no voice at all," and that the weight of the voice largely depended

---

51. "Associate Membership," memorandum of conversation, August 27, 1954, Box 19, Lot File 59D237, NA.

52. Sawada to Okazaki, September 24 and 30, 1954, B'0040, DRO.

on what it said.[53] Those belonging to the all-or-nothing group, on the contrary, failed to recognize any fundamental difference between the new offer and the associate membership formula. If Japan acquired a resident representative seat under strong pressure from Washington, they warned, "our representative would be regarded as a peculiar baby [of the US] not only by the Soviets but also by other Asian delegates."[54] Torn between the two sides, Foreign Minister Okazaki had to delay his decision while requesting more information from the US side.[55]

Ambassador Sawada in New York was determined not to repeat the rejection of the associate membership. The US had made its offer at an excellent time, whether intentionally or not, just as Prime Minister Yoshida was about to stop by the US on his way to Europe. Sawada seized the chance by privately briefing Yoshida on the resident representative plan when the latter was in New York on September 29. The prime minister, who always treated requests from the US seriously, immediately instructed Sawada to telegram Okazaki his concurrence with the proposal.[56] The word from the chief settled everything. Within 24 hours, Okazaki signed the order to Sawada indicating Japan's acceptance of the resident representative formula under the premises that the government would reapply for full membership simultaneously.[57]

But it seems that any attempt to entitle Japan to a UN position other than full member state may have been destined to fail. Just when the Japanese government made the difficult decision to take the State Department's advice and began to study concrete measures to sway public opinion accordingly, the climate in Washington again turned gloomy. As it was becoming obvious that the interest of other membership candidates in the resident representative proposal was unexpectedly low,

---

53. International Cooperation Bureau, "Kokuren jun kamei an naishi 'Resident Representative' an ni kansuru ken" (Proposals on the UN associate membership and "resident representative"), September 30, 1954, ibid.

54. First Division of the International Cooperation Bureau, "Konji beian no rigai tokushitsu ni tsuite" (The gain and loss regarding this time's US proposal), September 27, 1954, ibid.

55. Okazaki to Sawada, September 28, 1954, ibid.

56. Sawada to Okazaki, September 29, 1954 and Yoshida to Okazaki, September 30, 1954, ibid.

57. Okazaki to Sawada, October 1, 1954, ibid.

US policymakers' tone was no longer confident by mid-October. On October 11, Senator James W. Fulbright, who was serving as US UN delegate in charge of the resident representative agenda, confided in Sawada that the prospects for the new formula were bleak and the US might have to drop the case if it was unable to obtain the endorsement of two-thirds of the UNGA members.[58]

Desperately searching for a way to raise Japan's status, Sawada passed an alternative proposal to the US side suggesting that the UN permit non-member state observers like himself to participate in the Assembly sessions without the right to vote. But State Department officials' response was noncommittal.[59] The final blow came on October 22 when Fulbright officially informed Sawada that the US government had decided not to pursue the resident membership proposal in the forthcoming UNGA session. While Sawada's plan was also "interesting," he commented, it would meet as many difficulties as the US plan would once implemented.[60]

The Japanese side made its last effort on November 4 as Second Secretary Suma Michiaki at the Japanese embassy visited the State Department asking whether the US was going to reconsider the resident representative idea during Prime Minister Yoshida's coming visit to Washington. He received a definite answer. "For the time being," UNP Director David H. Popper told him, "we are letting the matter rest."[61] A month later, Foreign Minister Okazaki delivered the government's farewell to the associate membership idea during an Upper House session of the Diet:

We do not think the associate membership or a recent proposal [the resident representative formula] with a slightly different format is preferable at the moment and would like to go directly to the goal of admission to the UN [as a

---

58. Sawada to Ogata, October 11, 1954; International Cooperation Bureau, "Kokuren kamei mondai" (The UN admission problem), October 12, 1954, both ibid.

59. "Non-member Participation," memorandum of conversation, October 18, 1954; "Membership," memorandum of conversation, October 21, 1954, both in Box 19, Lot File 59D237, NA.

60. Sawada to Ogata, October 22, 1954, B'0040, DRO.

61. "Membership," memorandum of conversation, November 4, 1954, Box 19, Lot File 59D237, NA.

full member]. We have decided to take this course because it is not relevant to ask a powerful nation like Japan to join the UN with certain preconditions. Of course, considering problems in terms of [the Soviet] veto and package deals, the situation is by no means easy. But we will continue to promote it through consultations within the UN.[62]

Compared to the Japanese government, its American counterpart needed more time to let the failure of the associate membership formula sink in. With his passion for the idea intact, Ambassador Lodge insisted in March 1955 that the State Department follow up on the associate membership (or "non-member participation," to use his term) proposal.[63] The suggestion was soon embraced by Dulles and Assistant Secretary of State for International Organization Affairs David Key. As of mid-April, Japan was again on its way to be selected as the most promising potential associate UN member.[64] But this time, developments in the international situation forbade Washington from carrying out this plan.

"The Worst Day of My Life"

When filing its first application for UN membership in June 1953, Japan could only count on Western allies, especially the US, to pave the way for its admission. But by June 1955, two more channels became available. One was directly connected with the USSR. After the Hatoyama cabinet was inaugurated in December 1954, Japan embarked on official talks with Moscow regarding the normalization of diplomatic relations between the two wartime foes. And Soviet support for Japan's seat at the UN was one item on the negotiation's agenda. Another channel was Japan's Asian neighbors. While Lodge and Dulles were dwelling upon the feasibility of reenacting the associate membership scheme, the UN

---

62. "Dai 20 kai kokkai sangiin yosan iinkaigiroku dai 3 gō" (Proceedings of the 20th Diet Session Budget Committee, Upper House, No. 3), December 5, 1954, NDL.

63. Lodge to Dulles, March 31, 1955, in Department of State, *FRUS 1955–57, Vol. XI*, pp. 266–67.

64. Key to Lodge (with a draft for Dulles), April 1, 1955; Lodge to Key, April 11, 1955; "Non-Member Participation Plan–Italy," April 15, 1955, all in ibid., pp. 267–72.

membership issue was raised at the First Asian-Afro Conference (the Bandung Conference) in April 1955. With the concurrence of almost all major Asian and African independent states, the Conference issued a joint communiqué in which the admission of pending AA candidates to the UN, including Japan, was mentioned. Consequently, Japan's UN seat was not an isolated case any more but stood as a component of an appeal from the AA Group.

In addition to new trends on the bilateral and regional stages, there was also a more promising picture regarding UN membership at the global level. In June 1955, with the first East-West Summit at Geneva slated to take place one month later, foreign ministers from UN member states gathered in San Francisco to celebrate the organization's ten-year anniversary. During the ceremony, more than twenty representatives urged the organization in their speeches to find a quick solution to the membership problem. Five of them actually cited Japan's application as a case deserving specific attention. When the tenth session of the UNGA was summoned three months later, the membership question became a common topic in member states' speeches during the general debate.[65]

All these movements fueled Japan's yearning for equal status at the UN. Nearly three years after their first bid for membership, Japanese officials' frustration with their country's lower position in international society approached the point of explosion. MOFA policymakers described the lack of a full UN membership as a "heavy blow" that made Japan's comeback to world affairs "devoid of a finishing touch."[66] Those serving in New York had an even more bitter experience. "That was painful," Ambassador Sawada said later, recalling his service as an observer in the UN. "We had a sense of inferiority and a feeling that we might have to hesitate to enter the Assembly Hall because we were, in one sense, similar to guys attending a party without paying their dues."[67] As the international climate improved, these officials naturally looked upon the tenth UNGA session as a golden chance to change the status quo. Yet before resuming the battle for full membership, Japan

---

65. First Division of the International Cooperation Bureau, *Kokuren dai jū sōkai ni okeru kamei mondai,* pp. 6–8.

66. Tanaka, "Nihon no kokusai chii," p. 17.

67. Sawada, "Kokuren wa wareware no kikan da."

still needed to have a road map in accordance with the three alternative paths: the traditional US-centered strategy, the Soviet route, and the AA Bandung channel.

Long before the Assembly session, Japanese officials had started probing Moscow's will to resolve the problem. Certain breakthroughs were made. In November 1953, Sawada managed to hold an informal talk with Soviet Ambassador to the UN Andrei Vishinsky, who verbally indicated that the USSR might cease to oppose Japan's membership "in the near future."[68] A month later, the Soviet delegate refrained from blocking Japan's admission to the ICJ through an abstention rather than a veto at the UNSC. After the two countries entered into formal discussions for a rapprochement in June 1955, however, the Soviets started using the membership question as a diplomatic card.

Moscow agreed to pledge their endorsement of Japan's admission once the formal relationship between the two countries was revived. But in the meantime, the Soviets refused to phrase their promise in an "unconditional" manner as requested by the Japanese and thereby deliberately reserved the option of linking Japan's UN seat with those of the USSR's satellites. Noticing the danger of increasing Moscow's bargaining power, Foreign Minister Shigemitsu instructed his staff to strictly separate the bid for a UN seat from the category of the bilateral negotiations with the Soviets—a decision that virtually froze the Soviet channel at least for the time being.[69]

In comparison with the stalemate of the Soviet channel, the AA channel seemed more productive. The Japanese government benefited from the Bandung Communiqué soon after the AA Conference. In June 1955, Ceylon (now Sri Lanka), one of the seven candidates for UN membership raised in the Communiqué, volunteered itself to rally the endorsement of members of the AA Group and the British Commonwealth. Indonesia and India immediately offered to assist by courting Moscow for a compromise.[70] In September, the Japanese government

---

68. Sawada to Okazaki, December 9, 1953, B'0014, DRO.

69. Shigemitsu to Kase, September 30, 1955, B'0041, ibid.

70. Kotelawala to Ali, June 6, 1955; Kotelawala to Hatoyama, June 10, 1955; UP, "Kotelawala urges Japan's immediate admission to UN," June 13, 1955; Radio Press International, "Kotelawala asks Eden to push UN membership issue," July 18, 1955; Yuki to Shigemitsu, July 22, 1955, all in B'0040, ibid.

also joined this effort, as Prime Minister Hatoyama told his Ceylonese counterparts that Japan would like to cooperate with the latter through its pipe to pro-Western AA members at the UNSC.[71]

The AA channel was helpful, but it was still not sufficient in accomplishing Japan's goal, since any solution short of the endorsement of the two superpowers could be foiled in an instant. Japanese officials understood that without the capacity to forestall the Soviet veto, the chance of gaining Moscow's support for Japan's individual application was fairly slim. To be sure, it was not totally impossible for the AA Group and some moderate Western nations to press the USSR to accept a package deal including Japan.[72] But in this case, the US opposition to the package deal formula could be very troublesome. MOFA's solution to the dilemma was to ask the US to make a concession. The reason was simple. While it was impossible to counter the Soviet veto, as one report judged, it was at least "comparatively easier" to defeat the veto of the US as long as the Japanese government could come up with an idea to "save the face" of some intransigent Cold Warriors in Washington.[73] This would have been a very successful calculation if the US had acted more efficiently during the tenth UNGA session.

Regardless of Japan's eagerness to be seated in the UN, the US government was not prepared to trade their diplomatic preponderance over the USSR for earlier Japanese admission, even though most other nations in the world were willing to resolve the problem for good through a package deal. In June 1955, the UNP at the State Department composed a position paper recommending that the US accept the package deal if the USSR raised the issue in the coming East-West summit in Geneva.[74] The proposal met fierce opposition from Deputy Assistant Secretary of State for Far Eastern Affairs William J. Sebald,

---

71. Hatoyama to Kotelawala, September 6, 1955, ibid.

72. First Division of the International Cooperation Bureau, "Waga kuni kokuren kamei no hōsaku ni kansuru ken" (Methods for our country's admission to the UN), May 8, 1955, B'0040, DRO.

73. First Division of the International Cooperation Bureau, "Kokuren kamei kōsaku ni kansuru shomondai" (Several problems regarding the UN admission bid), May 22, 1955, ibid.

74. UNP, "Bilateral talks in San Francisco June 1955," Box 6, Lot File 56D679, NA.

who contended that a package deal including Soviet satellites could weaken the US position against Moscow's plot to secure a UN seat for Beijing. Instead, he proposed to submit a resolution at the UN calling for the implementation of the Bandung Communiqué by admitting to the UN seven AA nations, none of which belonged to the Eastern bloc. "If, as anticipated, the USSR vetoes the proposal," he observed, "the free world will have gained by showing an initiative in support of a Bandung suggestion and the USSR will have lost prestige." Worried about a Japanese concession toward a possible Soviet bluff on UN membership, Sebald also thought his proposal could "assist" Japan in its ongoing negotiation with the USSR.[75] The UNP's paper, unsurprisingly, was scrapped by Dulles. But Sebald's plan was not executed either.

Rather than a shrewd proposal to assault the Soviets, UN members attending the tenth session in September were more interested in a win-win game that could satisfy the demands of both Eastern and Western applicants for membership. Prior to the general debate of the Assembly, Canadian Foreign Minister Lester B. Pearson, Canadian UN Representative Paul Martin, and Chairman of the UN Committee of Good Offices on Admission of New Members Victor A. Belaunde (the Peruvian representative), worked out a package deal to approve the application of eighteen pending candidates (including Japan) from both blocs. Soviet Foreign Minister Vyacheslav Molotov submitted a counterproposal made up of two package deals—a sixteen-state deal excluding Japan and Spain or a six-nation deal containing three nations from each bloc but again without Japan. After several behind-the-scenes negotiations, the two sides eventually agreed in early November that the Soviets would cast an affirmative vote for a package deal specifying the names of all eighteen states mentioned in the original Canadian proposal. In other words, by offering its support to Japan and Spain the USSR would be able to secure seats for five of its satellites (Albania, Bulgaria, Hungary, Mongolia and Romania)—not a bad deal for Moscow.

The obstacle set by the Soviets for Japanese admission to the UN was swept away by the eighteen-state deal. But a new obstacle created by the US and the Chinese Nationalist government surfaced in its place. Ever since the eighteen-state deal had begun to be circulated among

---

75. Sebald to Dulles, June 9, 1955, ibid.

UN members, Japanese officials had been anxious to know the reaction of Washington, which usually opposed package deals. The US side, nevertheless, kept asking for more time to study the plan.[76] This was not necessarily an excuse to delay the process, considering the fact that State Department leaders were still resisting substantial compromises with the USSR and that President Eisenhower's physical condition had temporarily prevented him from making prompt decisions on foreign relations.[77] It was not until early November that the President and the Secretary of State made up their minds to accept a package deal, albeit not exactly the eighteen-state deal designed by the Canadians.

On November 5, Dulles told British Foreign Minister Harold Macmillan that while he was disposed to think favorably about the package deal he could not swallow Outer Mongolia being listed in the Canadian package.[78] On the same day, Eisenhower registered his support for the package deal with the assumption that only four communist states other than Mongolia would be accepted.[79] The issue was immediately taken up during a meeting between Dulles and Molotov in Geneva. Dulles suggested that the Soviets drop their reservations against Japan and Spain in exchange for American support for the admission of two or four East European nations. But in any case, he added, Mongolia, which he did not consider an independent state, was not acceptable. Molotov was not moved.[80] He had every reason to stand firm. Dulles had declared a month earlier that the US would not exercise its veto right on admission issues based on the 1948 Vandenberg Resolution of the Congress—a pledge, in Japanese UN Observer Kase's words, that meant that "the Americans voluntarily dropped their guns while the

---

76. "UN Membership; Miscellaneous Items," Memorandum of Conversation, October 6, 1955 and "UNGA Development," October 26, 1955, both in Reel 34, LOTF; Kase to Shigemitsu, September 30, 1955, B'0041, DRO.

77. Kase to Shigemitsu, October 4, 1955; "Japan's Entry into the United Nations," August 22, 1955, Box 7, Lot File 56D679, NA; Sebald to Dulles, August 29, 1955, Department of State, *FRUS 1955–57, Vol. XI*, p. 297.

78. Dulles to Macmillan, November 5, 1955, Department of State, *FRUS 1955–57, Vol. XI*, p. 326.

79. Hoover to Dulles, November 5, 1955, p. 327, ibid.

80. "UN Membership," Memorandum of a Conversation, November 13, 1955, pp. 351–55, ibid.

Soviets still held theirs."[81] Thus, no matter how resolutely Dulles threatened to exclude Mongolia, Molotov understood that his American counterpart's hands were already tied.

Within hours after the Dulles-Molotov meeting, the US announced its decision to accept a package deal formula and unveiled a seventeen-nation deal excluding Mongolia to counterbalance the eighteen-nation proposal.[82] The USSR responded four days later by declaring its endorsement of the eighteen-nation deal, which already enjoyed majority support from UN members.[83] By then, the US was completely isolated on the membership issue. Die-hard anticommunists like Dulles and Sebald were unwilling to give up, while other officials, including Lodge, were aware of the reality that they had lost the game of chicken with the Soviets.[84] In late November, the US backed off, indicating that it would not veto Mongolia if the country were included in a package deal.[85] As the two superpowers agreed to uphold the eighteen-nation deal, Japan seemed closer than ever to its UN seat. But unexpected resistance from Taipei changed everything.

The Chinese Nationalists, especially their leader Chiang, were bothered by the possibility of Mongolia being seated in the UN. Chiang had recognized Mongolia's independence in 1946 when he was still the head of China. But after being exiled to Taiwan in 1949, his regime withdrew that initial recognition as part of an effort to strengthen its anticommunist character. During the tenth Assembly session, the Chinese Nationalist representative, who occupied the China seat at the UNSC, adhered to this position and vowed to cast a veto if Mongolia's admission was put to a vote. Most countries, including Japan and the US, did not take Taipei's warning so seriously, as they thought that Chiang was just

---

81. Kase, *Nihon gaikō no ketteiteki shunkan,* pp. 201–202.

82. Kase to Shigemitsu, November 14, 1955, Membership," memorandum of B'0041, DRO.

83. Kase to Shigemitsu, November 23, 1955, ibid.

84. Kase to Shigemitsu, November 21 and 24, 1955, ibid.; "UN Membership," memorandum of conversation, November 23, 1955, Box 19, Lot File 59D237, NA.

85. Lodge to State Department, November 28, 1955, Department of State, *FRUS 1955–57, Vol. XI,* pp. 406–407.

following the American lead to bluff Moscow.[86] But after Washington ruled out its veto against Mongolia, the situation concerning the Chinese veto turned ominous.

Around late November, the US government started encouraging Chiang to take a constructive attitude in order to avoid endangering his seat at the UN. President Eisenhower also sent a personal message to the generalissimo to urge the latter to change his mind. Meanwhile, many US officials remained optimistic, speculating that the Mongolians would be unable to gain enough affirmative votes for their bid if most UNSC members abstained. Even the Chinese Nationalist Ambassador to the UN Tsiang confirmed that he would cast a veto only when the majority of UNSC members supported Mongolia.[87]

Japan nevertheless grew alarmed as some UNSC members moved to save Mongolia's application rather than kill it. If Mongolia acquired enough votes at the Council and hence triggered the Chinese Nationalists' veto, there was no doubt that the USSR would use its own veto to bury the whole deal. On November 26, MOFA began to put pressure on the Chinese Nationalists through diplomatic channels in Tokyo, New York, and Taipei.[88] But it was too late. Chiang was no longer in a position to act freely. His national legislature had passed a resolution mandating him to prevent Mongolian admission through a veto, which meant he risked damaging his authority if he had to yield to the US or Japan at the last minute. His foreign minister and ambassadors understood the grave consequence of the veto, but none of them was powerful or brave enough to dissuade their leader from the dangerous course.[89]

On December 10, the UNSC started deliberating the eighteen-nation deal. As the Chinese Nationalists continued to demonstrate an unswerving attitude toward Mongolia, Japan and other candidates had to face the music without any guarantee on their seats. The showdown

---

86. Kase to Shigemitsu, November 17 and 19, 1955; Yoshizawa to Shigemitsu, November 18, 1955, B'0041, DRO.

87. Iguchi to Shigemitsu, November 22, 1955; Kase to Shigemitsu, November 24, 1955, ibid.

88. Shigemitsu to Yoshizawa, November 26, 1955, ibid.

89. Kase to Shigemitsu, December 6 and 9, 1955, Miyazaki to Shigemitsu, December 14, 1955, ibid.

took place three days later. After Ambassador Tsiang cast Taipei's negative vote on Mongolia, Soviet Ambassador Arkadii A. Sobolev vetoed all thirteen non-socialist nations, including Japan. The deal was dead. But Japan's bad luck was not yet over.

On December 13, Japan was one of the Western victims of the ill-fated package deal. On December 14, it became the only Western victim of a swift tradeoff among UNSC members. That morning, the Council suddenly announced that an emergency session would be held within the day to discuss a new package deal submitted by the Soviets. At first, there were rumors about a Soviet proposal to revise the eighteen-nation deal by cutting out Mongolia and Spain. But when the session was about to start in the afternoon, it became known that the USSR was going to dump Japan, not Spain, together with Mongolia. This was a dexterous choice for Moscow. While the Spanish were backed by the powerful Latin America Group, the Japanese relied almost entirely on the Western members, making them much easier to discard. Besides, as the bilateral negotiations with Japan were approaching a very delicate stage, it would be better for the USSR to save the UN card for future bargaining.

This was a stunning reversal to Japanese officials, of course. After the session was summoned, the UNSC members soon retreated into a back room to consider the proposal. The Japanese delegates left outside desperately sought the chance to recess the session in the hope that they could secure more time for negotiation. But most member states were not in the mood to listen to Japan's appeal. Within thirty minutes, the session was resumed. Lodge submitted a seventeen-nation deal to preserve Japan, only to see it knocked down by Sobolev's veto. Other delegates, including Pierson Dixon of the UK and Martin of Canada readily accepted the Soviet deal, urging Japan to step aside.[90] With the US, Belgium, and the Chinese Nationalists abstaining, the Soviet's sixteen-nation deal was adopted by the Council.

While the new members of the UN family began to celebrate their victory, Japanese Ambassador Kase was experiencing the "worst day of my life," as he called it. "The ambassadors of the sixteen nations who were my partners until the day before were taking snapshots shoulder to shoulder, opening champagne at the celebration party, whereas I was

---

90. Kase to Shigemitsu, December 15 and 16, ibid.

left alone like a 'defeated general who had no right to talk about battles,'" Kase wrote in a book later.[91] Within days, he sent in his resignation. The fiasco also aroused a dramatic repercussion in Tokyo. The opposition parties filed a motion of nonconfidence against the Hatoyama cabinet at the Diet. MOFA officials were under enormous pressure for their role in the predicament. "I have never seen [Foreign Minister] Shigemitsu look as worried as he did this noon," US Ambassador to Japan John M. Allison reported the day Japan lost the battle. "I believe there is real substance in his fears that he may be forced to assume responsibility and have to leave government."[92] While neither the prime minister nor any senior MOFA officials (including Shigemitsu and Kase) eventually lost their jobs, the incident did force Japanese foreign policymakers to reconsider the feasibility of their strategy for the UN seat.

The End of the Tunnel

Japanese officials had no doubt that their traditional allies had betrayed them. Resentment toward the maladroit stance of the US sometimes escalated into a deep suspicion of Washington's real intention. Ambassador Kase bluntly told State Department officials that the Japanese people were disappointed by the "lack of reliability" of the US. In classified reports to MOFA, he was even more critical. "The US obviously feels that the membership problem is now out of its hands," he bitterly wrote in a telegram, "and therefore it looked rather relieved when the eighteen-nation deal backfired." Other Western powers like Canada were no less guilty in his view because they "sold Japan for the sake of the Soviet tricks."[93] Kase's dissatisfaction was not unique on the Japanese side. In Tokyo, the US embassy was targeted by protests. One week after the UNSC emergency session, Ambassador Allison told the State Department that Japan's "confidence in [the] US has been shaken" over the membership issue, adding, "Embassy officers have been repeatedly hit by [the] charge of US failure to insure UN member-

---

91. Kase, *Nihon gaikō no ketteiteki shunkan,* pp. 224–25.

92. Allison to State Department, December 15, 1955, Department of State, *FRUS 1955–57, Vol. XI,* pp. 453–54.

93. Kase to Shigemitsu, December 18 (two telegrams), 1955, B'0041, DRO.

ship for Japan on [the] part of well-informed Japanese concerned with [the] maintenance of our partnership."[94]

If the Western allies were not trustworthy, the only thinkable channel left for Japan's bid would be the AA Group. In fact, one lesson Japanese officials learned through the package deal debacle was the significance of regional backing. When the Spanish application was facing a Soviet veto, the Latin American Group blackmailed Moscow through their opposition votes against East European candidates at the UNGA. But when Japanese representatives asked for similar assistance from the AA Group, the response was overtly lukewarm.[95] "Given the fact that the sixteen-nation deal could not pass the Council without Spain, whereas the exclusion of Japan aroused no problem, it is undoubted that our international status is not yet established," Kase concluded in his report about the session.[96] This conviction became more widely accepted among MOFA officials as Japan proceeded to draft its strategy to gain admission during the eleventh session of the Assembly.

With the number of pending applications for a UN seat largely decreased after the sixteen-nation deal, the possibility of Japan's case being deliberated individually in the UNSC emerged. This scenario became even more likely in February 1956 when Sudan joined the UN as the first new member since 1949 whose application was approved not as a part of a package deal but purely based on its own merit. A solution other than the package deal formula was preferable for Japan because it could avoid a bizarre combination with Mongolia or the PRC. But Japanese officials had no illusion as they knew that Moscow would not let Tokyo go so easily before the normalization of diplomatic relations. Not to mention that the Soviets had already declared their intention to link Japan's seat with that of Mongolia after the passage of the sixteen-nation deal. Theoretically, Japan could evade the Soviet veto by acceding to the UN with Mongolia. Yet in this case, the Chinese Nationalists' veto again posed a thorny problem. Fully conscious of the dim outlook, MOFA was convinced that Japan's last resort was international opinion,

---

94. Allison to State Department, December 22, 1955, Department of State, *FRUS 1955–57, Vol. XXIII, Part 1 Japan*, p. 144.

95. Kase to Shigemitsu, December 16, 1955, B'0041, DRO.

96. Kase to Shigemitsu, December 18, 1955, ibid.

which the USSR was unable to completely neglect. The main forger of such opinion would be the AA Group.

By the spring of 1956, the assistance of the AA Group was regarded as the pivot of Japan's diplomatic activities concerning its UN admission.[97] From May 1956, MOFA officials launched a campaign to draw sympathy from AA Group members for Japan's position in the UN on two fronts. One was to warm relations with Asian members of the British Commonwealth, such as Ceylon, Pakistan, and India, so that they could join other Western members of the Commonwealth in speaking favorably for Japan's UN admission. This goal was realized during the Commonwealth summit in July that year, where participants unanimously reconfirmed their support of Japan's effort.[98] In the meantime, Ambassador Kase pursued another mission aimed at stabilizing Japan's status among AA nations inside the UN. This was not an easy task because India, the self-styled leader of the group that had a somewhat pro-USSR penchant, did not, at least from the Japanese viewpoint, back Japan's bid wholeheartedly. Kase's objective was membership in the AA Group within the UN. India, as expected, opposed the idea. But Kase earned timely assistance from Turkey—another influential member of the Group. In June, Japan became the only non-UN member state which had a regular membership in the AA Group. As soon as the Japanese representative made his first appearance in the group's meeting, Japan's admission to the UN was brought up as a major issue. India remained ambiguous but was unable to resist the majority opinion of the group. On July 24, the AA members reached an agreement to support Japan's membership no matter what kind of outcome was produced by the Japan-USSR negotiation under way.[99]

---

97. Inoue, "Kokuren to sengo Nihon gaikō," pp. 206–207; Kurino, "Waga kuni no kokuren kamei jitsugen hōsaku ni kansuru ken" (Methods to realize our country's admission to the UN), March 12, 1956, International Cooperation Bureau, "Waga kuni no kokuren kamei ni kansuru ken" (Our country's admission to the UN), May 22, 1956, both in B'0042, DRO.

98. First Division of the International Cooperation Bureau, "Kokuren kamei mondai" (The UN admission issue), May 26, 1956; Kase to Shigemitsu, May 28, 1956; Shigemitsu to Yuki, June 1, 1956; Suzuki to Shigemitsu, July 10, 1956, ibid.

99. Kase to Shigemitsu, July 24, 1956, ibid.; Kokuren kōhō sentā, *Nihon to kokuren*, p. 32; Kase, *Nihon gaikō no ketteiteki shunkan*, p. 226.

Japan's strategy of mobilizing international opinion through the AA Group worked quite well. But prior to the eleventh session of the Assembly, no Japanese policymakers seemed to feel that they were moving closer to their goal. At times even a touch of unease prevailed among them. It was obvious that Soviet representatives' statements on Japanese membership had been sounding more flexible since June. On certain occasions they also stopped reiterating the linkage between the admission of Japan and that of Mongolia. Nevertheless, it was equally true that Moscow never admitted abandoning its previous policies on this issue, which were that, first, both the Japanese and the Mongolians were entitled to a full membership and second, Soviet support for Japan's application did not need to be unconditional.[100]

Plus, the US government continued to test Japan's nerve. US officials were not ignorant about the damage caused by their miscalculations during the sixteen-nation deal deliberation. The US delegate to the UN frankly admitted that throughout the tenth UNGA session "the US abdicated its leadership on the membership issue by failing to have a timely policy that was clear-cut and consistent, appearing to be paralyzed when flexible action was called for, and underlining what appeared to other nations to be our 'righteous hypocrisy' by urging them to dirty their hands to achieve the end we came to share, while trying to keep our own skirts immaculate."[101] But such self-criticism paled before the demands to defeat Soviet diplomatic offensives. In contrast to Lodge's humble offer to "do everything both front-stage and back based on the Japanese government's request," Washington could not help viewing Japan's UN membership agenda through the Cold War lens.[102] Dulles and other State Department leaders kept on reminding the Japanese of the importance of taking a tough stance toward the So-

---

100. Kase to Takasaki, August 6, 1956; First Division of the International Cooperation Bureau, "Waga kuni no kokuren kamei mondai ni kansuru ken" (Our country's admission to the UN), September 24, 1956, ibid.

101. "Report on 'Evaluation of Role of US in 10th General Assembly,'" February 9, 1956, Department of State, *FRUS 1955–57, Vol. XI*, p. 47.

102. Kase to Shigemitsu, April 29, 1956, B'0042, DRO.

viets on the membership problem.[103] US officials also disturbed MOFA by their strenuous suggestions to submit Japan's application to the UNSC before any agreement was worked out between Moscow and Tokyo. "Japan could occupy a rather comfortable position in the resumed negotiations with the USSR if the Soviets used their veto [on Japanese UN membership]," they explained, without appreciating that this was the last thing the Japanese wanted to see.[104]

Japanese policymakers were not unfamiliar with the superpowers' arbitrary stance toward Japan's membership. This time, however, instead of relying on the benevolence of Washington, they chose to find their way to the UN by conquering the Soviets. Despite the official intent to detach UN membership from the negotiations with the USSR, Japanese officials never treated the two factors separately in actual policymaking. Soviet support of a Japanese UN seat was an item in the Japan-USSR negotiations from the very beginning. MOFA officers in charge of UN affairs also considered Japan's strategy regarding the membership issue in the context of Soviet policies toward normalization talks. The formal negotiations between the two sides adjourned in March 1956 leaving a number of delicate issues unsettled. Under tremendous domestic pressure, the government sent Foreign Minister Shigemitsu to the USSR in late July to resume talks. This was not a pleasant trip for the Japanese side, as Soviet leaders made no substantial concessions on major issues, including the membership problem. "Japan, which once threw away her status as a permanent member at the Council of the League of Nations without regret, is now looking to be reinstated as a peaceful nation through admission to the UN but has been foreclosed by the USSR—what a bitter irony of history," MOFA's

---

103. Washington to Tokyo, July 11 and September 14, 1956, Box 40, Japan Post File, NA; "Japan's Entry into the United Nations," September 20, 1956, Box 5, Lot File 59D679, NA.

104. Kitahara to Shigemitsu, July 13, 1956; Teraoka to Shigemitsu, July 13, 1956; Kawasaki, "Kokuren kamei mondai ni kansuru Kawasaki kyokuchō to Mōgan sanjikan to no kaidan yōshi" (Meeting between Director Kawasaki and Counselor Morgan on the UN admission issue), July 13, 1956; Shigemitsu to Kase, July 14 and 18, 1956, all in B'0042, DRO.

Treaties Bureau Director Shimoda, who accompanied Shigemitsu to Moscow, lamented in his memoir.[105]

The failure of the Shigemitsu mission was hard to swallow, but it also convinced Japanese officials that they could no longer afford to bypass the Soviet channel in promoting Japan's admission to the UN. As aptly noted in a September 1956 MOFA memorandum, no matter how lofty the international opinion formulated by the AA Group was, it was unable to cut the Gordian knot of Japan's application: the Soviet intention to tie Japan with Mongolia and the Western group's rejection of a Mongolian seat. "We must understand that admission to the UN is not something that can be achieved by playing low tricks," the memo read. "We have to rebuild the foundation of our diplomacy in order to make efficient efforts to tackle this formidable problem straightforwardly."[106]

An optimal chance to use this "straightforward" approach emerged in early October when Prime Minister Hatoyama, disregarding the opposition from the ruling party, decided to end the prolonged negotiation with the USSR through his own visit to Moscow. Given the prime minister's passion on the issue, MOFA officials judged that the normalization of diplomatic relations between the two countries was not so remote. However, they were not yet sure about the reliability of the Soviet pledge to endorse Japan's UN seat. Some of them, therefore, suggested that if the Hatoyama mission proved successful, Japan could directly ask the USSR to submit a resolution for Japan's admission at the UNSC. The idea was controversial. Its proponents argued that this was a practical way to force the Soviets to take action rather than play with words in advancing Japan's bid. But the opponents cautioned that it was unfitting to "let the Soviets have the credit for Japan's admission" as Moscow might "expect something in return" in the future. Officials were unable to reach a consensus on this matter.[107] But Hatoyama's performance in Moscow put a period on their debates.

---

105. Shimoda, *Sengo Nihon gaikō no shōgen*, pp. 166–67.

106. First Division of the International Cooperation Bureau, "Waga kuni no kokuren kamei mondai ni kansuru ken" (Our country's admission to the UN), September 24, 1956, B'0042, DRO.

107. Yoshimura to Matsumoto, October 5, 1956, ibid.; International Cooperation Bureau, "Waga kuni no kokuren kamei jitsugen hōsaku ni kansuru iken"

After a week of tense meetings with Soviet leaders, Hatoyama somehow achieved a final agreement with the USSR to restore diplomatic relations on October 19. In a joint declaration signed by the two sides, the Soviets formally promised to support Japan's admission to the UN. But with the word "unconditional" still missing, MOFA officials were not immediately liberated from their fear of a Soviet package deal including both Japan and Mongolia. Some even thought that the Soviets were going to block Japan's application for the third time.[108]

It was true that Hatoyama had tolerated the Soviets' request for a less concrete pledge on the declaration. But according to Minister of Agriculture, Forestry and Fisheries Kōno Ichirō, who was a key member of the Hatoyama's mission, the prime minister had also obtained Bulganin's confirmation of a memorandum of conversation in which the Soviet side "specifically and clearly promised to support Japan's application for UN entry in a manner more detailed than set forth in the Joint Declaration."[109] Presumably encouraged by this achievement, from early November Japanese officials became more interested in the procedure of Japan's admission than in its prospects.

While the agreement with the USSR was waiting for Diet deliberation, some MOFA officials, including Foreign Minister Shigemitsu, began to toy with the idea of joining the UN before the ratification of the agreement. In doing so, Japan could not only attend the whole eleventh UNGA session as a full member but get rid of the impression that its admission was the result of the rapprochement with Moscow. But other officials who did not want to push their luck in the face of the

---

(Methods to realize our country's admission to the UN), October 2, 1956, "Waga kuni no kokuren kamei jitsugen hōsaku ni kansuru ken setsumei" (Explanation on methods to realize our country's admission to the UN), September 29, 1956, and "Oboegaki" (Memorandum), October 4, 1956, all in B'0043, DRO; Inoue, "Kokuren to sengo Nihon gaikō," pp. 208–9.

108. "Kawasaki kyokuchō naiwa (kokuren kamei mondai)" (Confidential remark made by Director Kawasaki, the UN admission issue), October 26, 1956, B'0042, ibid.

109. Matsudaira to Shigemitsu, November 6, 1956, ibid.; "Japanese-Soviet Relations," Memorandums of Conversation, October 25 and 26, 1956, Lot File 58D3, NA.

changeable Soviets quashed this move.[110] After careful studies, policy-makers ultimately decided to wrap up their battle in the safest way. Japan would ask the UNSC to consider its application on December 12 after the Diet ratified the Japanese-Soviet agreement.[111] It was not going to request the USSR to submit the draft resolution on its admission. Nor would it ask Lodge or any other Western ambassadors to take the lead. "Since certain members of the Western group occasionally attempt to take advantage of this case [Japanese membership] for antagonistic purposes," MOFA officials asserted, "we must firmly keep any initiative on the issue under our control."[112] The person who could submit the resolution for Japan under these conditions was Ambassador Belaunde of Peru—a neutral figure and the chairman of the UN Committee of Good Offices on Admission of New Members who faithfully assisted Japan's bid.[113]

Japan ran into several other bumps in the road during the last few weeks before the UNSC session resumed. In mid-November, US Undersecretary of State Herbert Hoover, Jr., frightened Tokyo by misleadingly mentioning Japan's membership with those of the ROK and South Vietnam in his speech at the UNGA. The Chinese Nationalists, for their part, made an abrupt request for Tokyo's promise—preferably in the form of a written statement—to support Taipei's seat at the UN and to refrain from developing an official relationship with Beijing in exchange for a positive stance toward Japanese membership. All these

---

110. International Cooperation Bureau, "Waga kuni no kokuren kamei mondai no shori ni kansuru ken" (The handling of our country's admission to the UN), October 22, 1956; "Kokuren kamei mondai no shori ni kansuru ken" (The handling of the UN admission issue), October 30, 1956; Shigemitsu to Kase, November 1, 1956, all in B'0042, DRO.

111. Japan did not give up hope that "if the USSR agreed" they might raise the issue at the Security Council slightly before the exchange of ratifications. This, however, never happened. See Shigemitsu to Kase and Tani, November 28, 1956, ibid.

112. International Cooperation Bureau, "Mosukō kōshō go no kokuren kamei mondai shori hōsaku ni kansuru ken" (Proposals regarding the handling of the UN admission issue after the negotiation in Moscow), October, 1956, ibid.

113. Shigemitsu to Yamada and Teraoka, November 7, 1956, ibid.

problems were promptly resolved. The Japanese ambassador in Washington got word from the State Department that Hoover's statement was nothing more than a "gesture" to show that the anticommunist regimes in Seoul and Saigon were "not forgotten or neglected," though they had "no chance" to join the UN right away. The generalissimo in Taipei also received the written guarantee he needed.[114]

On December 12, the UNSC was summoned to discuss the Peruvian draft resolution on Japan's membership. The statements of Council members were businesslike, and went as scheduled. The point of greatest tension was Soviet Ambassador Sobolev's long speech that had the Japanese representatives sweating until he concluded with a favorable tone concerning the application. At noon, a unanimous vote made Japan the eightieth member state of the UN. The whole process was completed in about three hours with no turbulence, perfectly matching the wish of the Japanese delegation: "simple, short and smooth."[115]

For more than three years, Japan had worked hard on the UN membership issue. Though it had experienced twists and turns aroused by what appeared to be shortcuts (the associate membership formula and the package deal), it eventually walked into the UN on its own merits. Some people, like former Prime Minister Yoshida, criticized the government for its use of the Soviet channel to hustle Japan's UN admission, seeing this as undignified.[116] But the majority of the people, particularly those involved in Japan's endeavor, felt relieved as postwar Japan's journey to restore its citizenship in the international community finally reached its destination. "It was an emotional moment for MOFA officials, who had put their whole heart and soul into this diplomatic mission," Director Shimoda recalled, "and ordinary citizens tasted the sense of liberation and excitement as if their construction of a long tunnel had finally reached the end."[117]

114. Tani to Shigemitsu, November 17, 1956; Horiuchi to Shigemitsu, November 11 and 13, 1956; Shigemitsu to Horiuchi, November 12, 1956, ibid.

115. Kase to Shigemitsu, December 11, 1956, ibid.; Kase, *Nihon gaikō no ketteiteki shunkan,* pp. 231–32.

116. *Mainichi shimbun,* November 13, 1956.

117. Shimoda, *Sengo Nihon gaikō no shōgen,* p. 168.

As soon as Tokyo received the voting result of the UNSC, Foreign Minister Shigemitsu issued an official statement describing the admission as a "great leap in our country's international status" and "a fruit of the nation's effort for eleven years after the end of the war."[118] Six days later, after the Assembly approved Japan's membership, Shigemitsu, who was then designated to head the nation's first delegation to the UNGA, declared before a group of reporters that what had just happened inside the Assembly Hall not only demonstrated Japan's "comeback as a partner of international society" but also "put an end to the turmoil in Japan ever since the 1931 Manchuria Incident" that had caused the Japanese Empire's withdrawal from the League of Nations.[119] MOFA Senior Advisor Sawada, the former observer to the UN, made one of the tersest comments on the event. "The Japanese people harbor a sort of inferiority complex toward the outside world," he stated in a newspaper interview, "but with this [admission to the UN] it is time for us to graduate from this stage."[120] As we will see in the next chapter, Sawada's words can be seen as half correct. He was right that the Japanese people, including foreign policymakers within the government, were sensitive about the gap between their international status and that of other nations (in particular, the big powers). But a seat in the UN alone was insufficient to eliminate such a feeling. The UN membership was nothing but a pass to the town meeting of the postwar international community, where Japan's status remained undetermined. The battle for equality was over. The race for superiority was about to begin.

---

118. "Anzen hoshō rijikai no Nihon kamei kankoku ketsugi saitaku ni tsuite no Shigemitsu gaimu daijin danwa" (Foreign Minister Shigemitsu's statement in the aftermath of the adoption of the UNSC resolution recommending Japan's admission), December 13, 1956, B'0042, DRO.

119. *Asahi shimbun,* December 19, 1956.

120. Sawada, "Kokuren wa wareware no kikan da."

~ 9 ~
Seeking the Highest Status: The Battle for UNSC Permanent Membership

From the late 1950s on, the Japanese government's efforts to win higher status inside the UN were impressively successful. By the year 2006, it was neck and neck with Brazil for the record as the most frequently elected non-permanent member of the UNSC and semi-permanent member of the Economic and Social Council (ECOSOC). Outside New York, Japanese candidates were elected to hold crucial posts in many major UN affiliated agencies. Four Japanese figures—Nakajima Hiroshi, Ogata Sadako, Matsuura Kōichirō and Utsumi Yoshio—were nominated to head the World Health Organization (WHO), UNHCR, UNESCO, and ITU respectively. Any of these achievements seems big enough to intoxicate a small nation. But Japan, despite its handicap as a latecomer to the UN, was not satisfied so easily. As we will see in this chapter, Japanese policymakers have set their long-term objective at the highest level: permanent membership in the UNSC. Although this ambition is more salient since the end of the Cold War, it has affected Japan's UN diplomacy in one way or another throughout the nation's career as a full member of the organization.[1]

---

1. Until very recently Japan's policy regarding a permanent membership at the UNSC did not earn much attention from students of postwar Japanese foreign policy. Reinhard Drifte's *Japan's Quest for a Permanent Security Council Seat: A Matter of Pride or Justice?* published in 2000, is a long-awaited pioneering work. But as Drifte himself admitted, due to the lack of first-hand documents, all he could do at that point was to piece together a story based on interviews and other reliable secondary sources. "Later generations of researchers," he wrote in the book's introduction, "will have to compare these findings with the

The Awakening of Ambition

Japan's aspiration toward a permanent seat in the UNSC has been no secret in the inner circle of UN members ever since its admission to the organization in 1956.[2] In January 1957, only a few weeks after acceding to the UN, Japan declared before members of the AA Group that it was seeking the opportunity to be a UNSC permanent member and was willing to make concessions regarding the veto power.[3] Such movement was contingent on an ongoing trend toward charter revision within the UN. Having been in effect for over a decade, the UN charter entered into its first revision period in 1955. The big powers were resistant to changing the current charter. Smaller nations, on the other hand, were eager to seize this opportunity to bolster their influence. The AA Group was competing with the Latin American Group in hammering out a proposal to increase the number of UNSC members. India led the pack on the AA side and harbored intentions of crowning itself a permanent member. Japan's display of a similar interest at this moment was therefore a defensive measure so as not to lag behind once a deal for UNSC reform was done.

The Japanese government took no further actions on the UNSC permanent seat matter for the rest of the 1950s. But the topic resurfaced in the early 1960s as Japan moved beyond recovering from the ravages of the last war and advanced into a new age of unprecedented high economic growth. Motivated by his nation's accomplishment, Prime Minister Ikeda invested more energies than his predecessors in restoring Japan's status as a world power in international affairs. He was the person who introduced the term "equal partnership" to redefine the asymmetric

---

documentary evidence which will then be available." No substantial progress has been made on the Japanese side, as numerous files of the case are still locked in MOFA's storage for understandable reasons. Yet thanks to the release of US and UK documents concerning these two countries' talks with Japan on the permanent membership problem, we are now able to paint a more detailed, if not impeccable, picture on this less scrutinized aspect of Japan's UN diplomacy. See Drifte, *Japan's Quest for a Permanent Security Council Seat,* p. 7.

2. "Japan on the Security Council," Action Memo, September 3, 1971, Subject-Numeric Files 1970–73, Box 3181, NA.

3. New York to Tokyo via Washington, January 14, 1957, Japan Post File, Box 40, ibid.

US-Japan alliance, and he was convinced that Japan must be treated as one of the three key players (along with the US and West Europe) in world politics. The government's UN policy was susceptible to his zeal.

Ikeda was enthusiastic about expanding Japan's presence in the UN. He tossed around plans to recruit a UN ambassador from among celebrities outside the government or to create a ministerial post for UN affairs.[4] In a casual talk with MOFA UN Bureau Director Tsuruoka, he even joked that the Japanese delegation to the UN should be as big as the MOFA headquarters in Tokyo in order to implement the country's UN-centrism principle.[5] When Secretary of State Rusk referred during an official meeting in 1961 to Japan's "increasing willingness to take the initiative" within the UN, Ikeda confidently replied that this was "attributable in part to the growth of Japan's real power."[6] A permanent membership at the UNSC, needless to say, could be a suitable symbol for such "real power."

In March 1961, Kosaka (Ikeda's foreign minister) stated in an Upper House committee that the UNSC's composition needed to be "reconsidered" since the Council was "attaching too much importance" to big powers "particularly in regard to the permanent membership system."[7] While containing no concrete suggestions as to how the P5's predominance could be corrected, this was the first public statement made by a Japanese foreign minister that indicated Japan's dissatisfaction with the P5 formula. Over the next few months MOFA backed up Kosaka's words by reactivating the claim in New York for a permanent UNSC seat together with India, Nigeria, and some other AA members.[8]

In the second half of 1961, the UN slipped into the most turbulent period of its history with the tragic loss of Secretary General Ham-

---

4. Drifte, *Japan's Quest for a Permanent Security Council Seat,* pp. 16–17; *Asahi shimbun,* February 21, 1961.

5. Kokuren kōhō sentā, *Nihon to kokuren,* p. 89.

6. Memorandum of Conversation, November 3, 1961, in Department of State, *FRUS 1961–63, Vol. XXII: Northeast Asia,* p. 711.

7. "Dai 38 kai kokkai sangiin yosan iinkaigiroku dai 8 gō" (Proceedings of the 38th Diet Session Budget Committee, Upper House, No. 8), March 6, 1961, NDL.

8. "Predictable Major Issues in the 16th General Assembly of the United Nations," August 1961, NS Files, Box 310A, JFKL.

marskjold in the jungle of the Congo and the exacerbated East-West conflicts running the gamut from West Berlin to Cuba. But the political turmoil surrounding the UN seemed to have little impact on Japanese leaders' fervor concerning a UNSC permanent membership. In November 1962, Ikeda paid a visit to British Prime Minister Macmillan and Foreign Minister Douglas-Home at the Admiralty House in London as part of his tour of Western Europe. The meeting went smoothly until Douglas-

Home mentioned the British government's support of the PRC's seat in the UN. Apparently confusing the UN with the UNSC, Ikeda was fairly upset about the British foreign minister's remark. While agreeing that it was "absurd" to let the Chinese Nationalists occupy the UNSC permanent seat, Ikeda rebutted that he was "by no means satisfied" to see the PRC's displacement of the Nationalists' position at the Council because Beijing's "national power" was "no different than India's." He then suggested that India had "at least as good a claim to permanent representation on the Council, and Japan a better one." In his view, "[t]he composition of the Council should reflect the changing world situation, and the permanent members should be those countries who contributed most to world affairs."[9]

Both Douglas-Home and Macmillan made no response and swiftly turned to other topics. But officials at the British Foreign Office were somewhat taken aback by Ikeda's improvised comments. From December 1962 to March 1963, notes on this issue were exchanged among officials in London and the relevant overseas posts. The conclusion drawn from these discussions, however, appeared to indicate that Japan's UNSC permanent seat was not a worrisome problem under the current circumstances. "I cannot myself see Japan replacing China," one official at the Foreign Office's UN Department wrote, "nor do I see any real chance of Japan getting a permanent seat on the Council even in the event of expansion." The judgment was based on a very ra-

---

9. "Record of Conversation between the Prime Minister and the Prime Minister of Japan at Admiralty House at 3 p.m. on November 12, 1962," November 12, 1962, FO 371/164976, Reel III, PRO; MOFA, "Ikeda sōri to Makumiran shushō tono kaidan yōshi (dai 1 kai)" (Outline of the meeting between Prime Ministers Ikeda and Macmillan, the first meeting), November 12, 1962, A'0363, DRO.

tional reason: Since the UN members were too selfish to control their individual aspirations toward a UNSC seat, it was "extremely unlikely" that a provision would be made "in any scheme" of expansion for the number of permanent members "any higher than it is now."[10]

In a more prudent manner, Ambassador Oscar Morland in Tokyo presented a similar view of Ikeda's statement. Morland admitted that the claim for permanent membership could be a "logical consequence" if Japan's economic strength increased further. Yet he found no reason to fear that "Mr. Ikeda's reference to this possibility was intended to be taken very seriously at present" because "Japan has hitherto shown little inclination either to assume the leadership which her economic power would justify or to become involved in the Cold War to the extent which a more prominent role in the United Nations would involve."[11] While somewhat underestimating the extent of the Japanese government's passion, these observations generally fit Japan's situation in the mid-1960s.

Like Ikeda, some Japanese leaders in the ruling LDP did find it psychologically difficult to acquiesce in the idea of seating the PRC in the UNSC. In a March 1964 Upper House session, for instance, the chairman of the party's Foreign Policy Commission, Kajima Morinosuke, argued that if Japan was left behind as a regular UN member in the wake of Beijing's takeover of Taipei's UNSC permanent seat, the nation would be put in an "inferior status against Communist China politically, economically and socially." According to Kajima, "As this could in no way uphold the esteem of our people and the interests of our country, Japan should secure its position as a UNSC permanent member at least before the Chinese Communists obtain theirs."[12]

In contrast to the sensational tone of Kajima and Ikeda's statements, foreign policymakers inside the government behaved more cautiously. Director of MOFA's UN Bureau Hoshi Bunshichi publicly dismissed

---

10. "Answers question raised as a result of the Japanese Prime Minister's visit to the United Kingdom," December 20, 1962, Reel 109, FO 371/164964, PRO.

11. Morland to Douglas-Home, December 20, 1962, ibid.

12. "Dai 46 kai kokkai sangiin yosan iinkaigiroku dai 8 gō" (Proceedings of the 46th Diet Session Budget Committee, Upper House, No. 8), March 6, 1964, NDL.

the possibility of accomplishing this goal in the foreseeable future.[13] And Ikeda's new foreign minister, Ōhira, answered Kajima's foregoing inquiry in the same Diet session by remarking that the government felt the timing of its effort was crucial. It wanted to wait until it had "the support of the majority of the (member) states," and it felt that for the time being it was more appropriate to "substantially reinforce Japan's contribution to UN activities."[14]

MOFA's caution was reasonable given the situation within both the UN and the Japanese government. The process of increasing UNSC seats through a charter review was painstakingly protracted in the first place. The charter revision was raised at the UNGA as early as 1953. The initial idea to carry out the revision through a "General Conference of the members of the United Nations" as stipulated in Article 109 of the charter was thwarted by Soviet opposition. As the second-best solution, the Latin American Group suggested in 1956 that it was easier to ask for a partial amendment to the charter exclusively for the sake of expanding the UNSC and ECOSOC, which, according to Article 108 of the charter, did not need to be done through a General Conference of the UN members. But the deliberation of this proposal was again delayed by the reluctance of the great powers, in particular the USSR.

The situation did not get better after Japan joined the UN. The Japanese delegation was one of the most ardent promoters of the revision. The agenda was mentioned, and in some cases emphasized, in almost every speech delivered by Japanese foreign ministers in the UNGA general debates until 1965. Meanwhile, Japan was also a rational player in the game. In spite of its membership in the AA Group, for instance, the Japanese delegation liked to act with the Latin American Group, whose solidarity cast more influence on the balance of power within the UN, in pursuing the bid.[15]

With the admission of a large number of new members in the wake of decolonization in Asia and Africa, major powers (except for the USSR) eventually agreed to discuss the problem during the eighteenth

---

13. Hoshi, "Nijū shūnen o mukaeta kokuren," p. 8.

14. "Dai 46 kai kokkai sangiin yosan iinkaigiroku dai 8 gō," March 6, 1964, NDL.

15. MOFA, "Kokusai rengō kenshō no kaisei ni kansuru setsumeisho" (Interpretations of the revision of the UN charter), January, 1965, MOFAD.

UNGA in 1963. But as pointed out in the British Foreign Office note mentioned above, this time the egoism of the seekers of the UNSC seats impeded further progress in the negotiations. The Latin American Group drafted a plan to add two non-permanent seats to the UNSC, equally divided between Asian and African states. The AA Group, however, needed more. But Japan could not wait any longer. Sympathetic to the Latin American draft, it proceeded to look for a compromise from the AA side. Japanese delegates presided over several rounds of meetings to coordinate positions among AA members. In the end, the Group came up with a counterproposal to create four more seats at the Council. The Latin American and West European members were averse to the proposal at the beginning but finally accepted it as the AA Group promised to give them one extra seat each in the ECOSOC. The AA resolution was adopted at the UNGA in December 1963, though it took another two years for the P5 to ratify the expansion.[16] The charter was amended but only to add four non-permanent seats to the UNSC, leaving Japan's permanent membership a remote dream.

In addition to the charter review, which was directly linked to the UNSC membership matter, Japan also did not forget to raise its overall status in the UN through other approaches. But as late as the mid-1960s, its achievements in that area were meager. One such approach was to expand Japan's influence through economic and financial means. As reflected in Ikeda's arguments, Japan was used to resting its demand for a UNSC permanent seat upon its distinguished accomplishments in beefing up "national power." And for well-known reasons, in Japan's case the term "national power" referred exclusively to economic and political powers, rather than military might.

MOFA officials set their sights on the role of economic power in enhancing Japan's fame at the UN long before the era of the so-called "Japanese miracle." In 1955 when Japan had not yet won UN admission, Ambassador Sawada already contended that it was meaningless to calculate the short-term cost of supporting the UN financially without reckoning with the long-term gain in raising a nation's "national prestige" in the organization.[17] Two years later, shortly after Japan joined the UN, a MOFA International Cooperation Bureau memorandum

---

16. Ibid.; Iguchi, *Nihon gaikōshi 32,* pp. 85–87.

17. Sawada to Shigemitsu, April 28, 1955, B'0040, DRO.

presented another interesting argument on the nation's current status in the UN from an economic viewpoint. "If economic power is the representative element of national power and each member state's share of the UN budget is a barometer of its economic power," the memo read, "then there is no doubt that our country whose share of the UN budget will be ranked number eight,—only behind the P5, Canada and India— shall take on international responsibility and acquire appropriate influence as a first-class nation."[18]

The correlation between status and money might have looked logical to MOFA policymakers. But this view was not shared by those who held the government purse strings. The scale of Japan's financial contributions to the UN and other international organizations is not determined by MOFA within the government. This is an issue completely falling under the purview of the Ministry of Finance (MOF). Compared to MOFA, the MOF, whose chief concern is the health of economic and financial policies, found no reason to waste the nation's precious economic resources in hunting for hollow fame in the international community. This attitude put MOFA in an ironic position within the UN. Despite their willingness to show Japan's generosity, MOFA officials, pushed by the MOF, had to cross swords with delegates of other UN members in order to save every last cent in payments. As a matter of fact, when the UN recommended Japan's first assessment scale in November 1958, which would make the newcomer the eighth largest donor to the organization's budget as MOFA expected, Japanese Ambassador Matsudaira had to express "deep disappointment" rather than satisfaction at the Fifth Committee (in charge of budgeting issues) of the UNGA because the scale exaggerated his country's economic capability.[19] This response set the tone for Japan's position at the committee from then on as MOFA officers continued to find fault with the UN's budgetary plans, more or less speaking for their MOF colleagues.

However, Japan did not—likely could not—resist the assessments to the bitter end since they are imposed on member states as part of their duties set forth in the charter. No matter how reluctant they were dur-

---

18. International Cooperation Bureau, "Kokuren ni okeru Nihon" (Japan in the UN), February 9, 1957, B'0042, ibid.

19. United Nations Bureau, *Statements Delivered by Delegates of Japan during the XIII Regular Session of General Assembly*, p. 102.

ing the debates, Japanese delegates swallowed all recommendations on Japan's assessment scale, and its percentage in the UN budget kept rising during the decade after 1957. The real problem, nevertheless, was in Japan's attitude toward voluntary contributions to UN projects and missions. In the late 1950s and early 1960s Japan made active commitments to resolving critical UN agendas such as peacekeeping efforts in the Middle East (for instance, Egypt, Lebanon) and Africa (the Congo) or the crisis caused by the USSR's default.[20] But when it came to discussions on the division of financial burdens, Japan was much more reluctant.

In 1959, due to the MOF's opposition, Japan failed to go along with the UN's decision to strengthen the financial basis of the UNEF deployed in Egypt, despite Japanese delegates' earnest support of the mission when it was founded.[21] The same thing took place in 1961 when the UN called for financial contributions from member states to the ONUC in the Congo. As a recipient of the UN technical assistance program, Japan was eligible for a 50 percent rebate on its ONUC assessment. The US encouraged Japan to pay the full amount of the assessment, underlining that such a gesture could "redound to [the] prestige" of Japan as a responsible power supporting the peace and security operations of the UN. MOFA officials, including Foreign Minister Kosaka, were fascinated by this suggestion. But it was flatly discarded by the MOF.[22]

A year later, the two ministries clashed on a proposal to purchase UN bonds to help the organization out of its financial crisis. MOFA, which was eager to quickly settle on Japan's pledge, used every possible means to pressure the MOF. This time, the MOF tried to make some compromise and agreed to buy $4.5 million in bonds, the equivalent of Japan's annual assessment in the UN budget. But MOFA was dissatisfied. Ambassador Okazaki told MOF officials that it could be a "seri-

---

20. See Chapters 2 and 3.

21. "Japanese Views on Certain General Assembly Items," memo of conversation, July 22, 1957, Box 12, Lot File 61D68; Washington to Tokyo, October 31 and December 1, 1959, Tokyo to Washington, November 7, 1959, all in Box 59, Japan Post File, NA.

22. Washington to Tokyo, March 1, 31, 1961 and Tokyo to Washington, March 2, 7, 31, 1961, all in Box 59, Japan Post File, ibid.

ous blow to Japan's prestige" if the government could not make a commitment above its payment to the regular budget. After more than three months of bargaining, MOFA won the game by squeezing five million dollars from the MOF's pocket.[23]

During the next few years, MOFA's insistence, coupled with pressures from the US, enriched Japan's contributions to a number of UN agencies, including the UN Relief and Works Agency for Palestine Refugees (UNRWA) and the UN Children's Fund (UNICEF).[24] But the progress again reached a deadlock in 1965 when Japan was asked by the UK to join the latter's plan of ameliorating the UN's debt situation through voluntary payments. Using Japan's percentage payment of the UN budget as a yardstick, MOFA recommended that the government make a contribution of three million dollars on the condition that other members would do the same thing. Unsurprisingly, the MOF deemed the payment outrageous and refused to approve it. MOFA, meanwhile, could not afford to back down given the efforts it had put in to avoid the collapse of the UN system. The standoff lasted for more than a year until October 1966 when MOFA finally got the fund.[25] Though this was of course a victory for MOFA, it did not imply any fundamental change in the difficult domestic wrangling inside the government related to UN financial cooperation. When determining the amount of the voluntary contribution requested by the UK, the MOF wasted no time in cutting the scale of the proposed $3 million to $2.5 million. MOF officials also

---

23. Tokyo to Washington, March 30, April 20, May 29, 1962, Washington to Tokyo, April 9, 1962, all in Box 84, ibid.; MOFA, *Waga gaikō no kinkyō 1963,* p. 45.

24. Washington to Tokyo, December 11, 1963 and Tokyo to Washington, December 13, 1963, both in Box 100, Japan Post File; "Japanese Contributions to UN Agencies," January 10, 1964, Box 3335, Subject-Numeric File 1964–66, NA; "Background Paper: Near East Situation," January 4, Reel 5, Asia & Pacific (First Supplement), LBJL.

25. Tokyo to Washington, August 4, 1965, DDRS; Political Division of the UN Bureau, "Daijin hōō yō hatsugen yōryō, kokuren zaisei mondai" (Materials for the minister's statements during visit to Europe, the UN financial problem), July 1, 1965 and West European Division, "Dai 1 kai Nichii teiki kyōgi" (The first Japanese-Italian periodical consultation), July 28, 1965, both in A'0387, DRO; Memo from P.H. Gore-Booth, June 24, 1965, FO 371/181082, Reel 134, PRO; New York to Washington, January 19, 1966, Box 3321 and New York to Washington, October 15, 1966, Box 3322, both in Subject-Numeric File 1963–66, NA.

remained unconvinced, questioning the necessity to participate in "genuine aid programs abroad" when Japan was "so capital hungry."[26]

Just like its performance in achieving a good reputation through economic power, Japan's attempts to raise its status in the UN by using political power also reached their limit around 1966. One example was for Japan to occupy senior posts at the UN Secretariat and affiliated agencies so as to magnify Japan's voice in the organization from within. By the late 1950s, Japan made several pitches for positions like USG or deputy executive secretary of the UN Economic Commission for Asia and the Far East (ECAFE) with no success.[27] By 1964, only one Japanese citizen had been promoted to the director class (D-1) at the UN Secretariat, with 20 others working as junior staff.[28] MOFA officers had tried their best to increase the number of Japanese UN servants in higher ranks, yet the problem was not easy to resolve. The UN personnel officers' preference during recruitment could be one reason. But more essentially, as admitted by Japanese Ambassador Matsui himself, it was difficult for the government to "find Japanese who have the executive talent" and who could "make themselves understood in English and/or French."[29] As long as this weak point existed, there seemed to be little hope for a drastic expansion in the scale of Japanese senior employees in UN organizations.

Another political approach to seeking higher status was to maintain a good record during elections at various UN agencies. The Japanese government impressed the international community with its passion and skill to win those elections even before acceding to the organization. In early 1956, an ICJ judge post became vacant due to the death of Chinese judge Hsu Mo. Based on a gentleman's agreement guaranteeing the permanent presence of the P5 in the ICJ, Hsu's seat was supposed to be occupied by another Chinese candidate. But Japan, then a new member of the Court, ignored this convention by announcing Supreme Court Judge Kuriyama Shigeru's candidacy for the seat. The P5 were thrown into consternation over this action. The US, which was

26. Tokyo to Washington, January 9, 1965, Reel 4, DOS 1963–66.
27. "Japan's interest in secretariat posts," February 13, 1959, Box 59, Japan Post File, NA.
28. Hoshi, "Saikin no kokuren," p. 23.
29. Geneva to Washington, July 24, 1964, Reel 43, DOS 1963–66.

ready to support Ambassador V. K. Wellington Koo of the Chinese Nationalist government, asked Japan to give up its bid. Japan, instead, rejected Washington's plea in an emotional memorandum. "For political reasons, the permanent membership on the Security Council might be given to the 'Great Powers,'" the memo stated, "[but] historically and statutorily, the assertion that every permanent member of the Security Council should be represented on the Court cannot be justified in any way."[30] During the subsequent election, the UNGA and UNSC produced different voting results favoring the two candidates respectively. Kuriyama eventually lost the election to Koo during the revote in January 1957, but the election was legendary: the UN members had to vote nineteen times to get a winner.[31]

Once seated in the UN as a full member state, Japan accelerated its election campaign within the organization. In early 1957, the Japanese government began exploring the possibility of gaining a non-permanent membership in the UNSC.[32] This was another bold plan for a member state that had just commenced its career at the UN a couple of months earlier. But it received a positive reaction from the US. Alert to Tokyo's intention to adopt a more independent stance at the UN, State Department officials concluded that "the best way of keeping Japan on [the] US side" was to help the LDP regime "stay strong" vis-à-vis domestic left-wing opposition parties and to "be of assistance to it in achieving what Japanese regard as Japan's rightful place of importance in international life." Besides, without Japan's presence, the potential winner of the UNSC election that year would have been Czechoslovakia or Ceylon—either of which, in their view, could have been "much worse than Japan."[33]

Yet when US officials approached their Japanese counterparts on the issue, they were taken aback by Japan's appetite. The UNSC offer,

---

30. MOFA, "Observations of the Japanese Government concerning the election of Judges of the International Court of Justice," November 1, 1956, Box 43, Lot File 60D113, NA.

31. Iguchi, *Nihon gaikōshi 32*, pp. 115–6.

32. "Considerations involved in possible U.S. support of Japan for the Security Council," May 3, 1957, Box 3, Lot File 59D19, NA.

33. McNutt to Martin and Osborn to Martin, May 3, 1957, Box 12, Lot File 61D68, ibid.

of course, was welcomed, though the Japanese had more in mind. For example, they were still zeroing in on the Chinese judge's seat in the ICJ and were preparing to let Kuriyama renew his challenge against Koo, whose term was coming to an end later that year. They also considered a proposal to run for the vice president of the coming UNGA session. After all, what Japan needed was not one but a number of honorable seats in the UN simultaneously.[34] Loath to accept all these requests, each of which could be accompanied by an energy-consuming race, the US took more than a month to persuade Japan to narrow down its list to one post. Finally, the Japanese government stepped down from the ICJ and UNGA elections in exchange for the US promise to "campaign on Japan's behalf" for the UNSC seat.[35] In October, Japan acquired its first term as a non-permanent member of the Council.

Despite the triumph in the 1957 UNSC election, Japan's score in elections for critical political positions at the UN was still mediocre in the mid-1960s. Since 1959, Japan had run for UNGA president, vice president, or ICJ judge several times.[36] Apart from the 1960 ICJ election where former Tokyo University professor Tanaka Kōtarō won a seat, Japan had withdrawn its candidacy in most cases.[37] And Japan showed no sign of trying again on the UNSC non-permanent membership for more than five years after finishing its term in 1959. The reasons were complex. Regarding the UNGA posts, Japan never had a unified policy

---

34. "Japanese Desire for Seat on Security Council and International Court of Justice," memo of conversation, June 17, 1957, Box 2, Lot File 59D19; "Japan's Candidacy for the Security Council," June 21, 1957, Box 44, Lot File 60D113, ibid.

35. "Japan's Security Council Candidacy," memo of conversation, July 26, 1957, Box 12, Lot File 61D68, ibid.

36. Washington to Tokyo, August 22, 1959, Box 59 and Washington to Tokyo, April 27, 1962, Box 84, both in Japan Post File; "Japanese Probing on Chirep; Peacekeeping Views; Japanese Candidacies," February 3, 1964, Box 3305, Subject-Numeric Files 1964–66, ibid.

37. Japan did manage to trade its withdrawal for other states' support during elections in non-political UN organizations on some occasions. See "Japanese Positions on Principal Items at the 13th UNGA," September 5, 1958, Washington to Tokyo, August 20, 1959, both in Box 59, Japan Post File; New York to Washington, August 17, 1965, Box 3320, Subject-Numeric File 1964–66, ibid.

on this matter. A typical example was found in the 1962 election for UNGA president. Prime Minister Ikeda was enthusiastic to see Japan take the position because of the "prestige it could bring [to] Japan," as MOFA officials put it.[38] Ambassador to the UN Okazaki and MOFA policymakers, on the other hand, had a different view. Since the UNGA presidency was usually saved for small nations, they considered it irrelevant for Japan to fight for the post. Moreover, if Japan competed with AA members on this race, it would hurt Japan's chance to gain sufficient endorsements during other more important elections. Thus, in disregard of Ikeda's intention, MOFA made a deal with Pakistan, its rival in the election, to give up Japan's candidacy in exchange for Pakistani support for Japanese membership in the ECOSOC.[39]

Japan's reluctance to run for the UNSC non-permanent member position stemmed from more political considerations. Having served two years in the Council, Japan understood the risk as a UNSC member of involving itself in international disputes that had no direct implication for it. And the turbulence occurring within the UN around 1960 forecast an even more difficult time for the Council in the coming decade. In addition, Japan's two-tiered identity as both an Asian and an industrialized country complicated its position. For Japan's election to the Council in 1957, it had mainly counted on the votes of the Latin American or Middle Eastern nations, many of which belonged to the pro-Western moderate group of developing countries. But after 1960, it was no longer easy to get into the Council without the majority support of the AA Group members.[40] Around 1963, MOFA appears to have adopted a wait-and-see stance to avoid colliding with the AA Group for the sake of UNSC membership. "We are not going to stretch ourselves too much," Foreign Minister Ōhira said, "but we would like to see Japan's power or ability recognized by the international community in an unaffected manner and naturally reflected in our status within the

---

38. New York to Tokyo via Washington, April 28, 1962, Box 84, Japan Post File, ibid.

39. *Asahi shimbun,* August 4, 1962; New York to Tokyo via Washington, April 27 and May 17, ibid.

40. Matsudaira, "Nihon no kokusaiteki chii to sekinin," pp. 11–16.

UN."[41] This attitude, which was in itself reasonable and high-minded, was soon ruined by the international political trend in the UN, which rapidly widened the gap between Japan and its AA brothers. "We moved from underdeveloped to industrialized country by hard work on the part of our own people," Japanese Ambassador to the UN Matsui once claimed, "and would appreciate more recognition by other countries now trying to do the same."[42] But no such recognition had been paid by the time Japan was going to run for a second UNSC appointment.

Japan's decision to enter the UNSC non-permanent member election in 1965 was engendered by the attempt to secure one of the four seats created during the 1963 charter revision that should be reserved for a "genuine Asian country."[43] But it was a hard race from the outset. As mentioned in Chapter 3, many African nations were determined to impede Japan's candidacy in retaliation for Tokyo's close relationship with South Africa. The repercussion of that movement was so devastating that some Western allies like the US started doubting whether "Japan could make it."[44] The Japanese government was also uncertain about its chance to win. But once they made up their mind, MOFA officers behaved resolutely, swearing to "fight to [the] end even without African Group endorsement."[45] Skillfully consolidating the support of Asian members, Japan obtained just enough votes to let it be included as one of the four new members.[46]

But there was another hurdle lying ahead. In accordance with the arrangement made during the charter revision, only half of the four seats had two-year terms; the rest were restricted to a term of one year. After

---

41. Kobayashi, "Keishari tōsen to Nihon no chii," p. 48; for a similar statement made by MOFA senior officer, see Saitō, "Dai 18 kai kokuren sōkai o kaerimite," p. 18.

42. Geneva to Washington, July 24, 1964, Reel 43, DOS 1963–66.

43. Cheke to Falle, June 17, 1965, FO 371/181112, Reel 136, PRO.

44. New York to Washington, October 1, 1965, Box 3306, Subject-Numeric File 1964–66, NA.

45. New York to Washington, June 10, 1965, Box 3306; New York to Washington, October 1, Box 3321, ibid.

46. New York to Washington, August 17, 1965, Box 3320; Washington to Tokyo, October 29, 1965, Box 3305, ibid.

tense negotiations, it was agreed that a second vote must be taken to decide which winners would get the longer terms. Among the four elected nations, Nigeria took the first two-year post thanks to the solidarity of African members. The other three—Japan, New Zealand, and Uganda   failed to get the required support after three rounds of voting. When the election adjourned for the weekend, Japan waged a ravenous campaign to increase votes. It not only courted Asian member states but also tried to squeeze its way into rival camps. New Zealand, for instance, had long expected to resolve the case through talks with Japan. The Japanese delegate did pay a visit, though not for talks but to ask New Zealand to withdraw its candidacy. While this request was sternly rejected, Japan went on to seize votes from the Western European Group, New Zealand's base camp.[47]

On December 13, 1965, Japan's restless canvassing was rewarded by its election as a UNSC non-permanent member with two-year tenure. Yet many Japanese officials were not relieved by the victory, which was won by an incredibly narrow margin in the runoff. "Looking back," a Japanese delegate concluded later, "this election has made it clear that our country, unfortunately, is not in a position to be proud of its status as a big power and feel relaxed during [UN] elections."[48]

The Economic Superpower's Demand

The Japanese government's campaign for a UNSC permanent membership was neither provocative nor proactive throughout the first decade after joining the UN. But compared to the late 1950s, Japan in the late 1960s seemed to have enough reason to make a stronger claim to that status. The country's high economic growth was approaching its climax. In 1968, the Japanese gross national product (GNP) eclipsed that of West Germany, an epoch-making record that made Japan literally one of the three pillars of the world economy. The 1964 Olympic Games held in Tokyo and the scheduled 1970 Osaka International Exposition further strengthened Japan's image as a big economic power in the world community. With this background, it was not surprising that the

---

47. Amō, *Takokukan gaikōron,* pp. 334–7; New York to Washington, November 30, 1965, Box 3306, ibid.
48. Amō, ibid., p. 338.

"rising sun" wanted a post in the UN commensurate with its national power. The only problem was when and how it would make that wish known.

Prime Minister Satō, who came into office in late 1964, was preoccupied with two bilateral diplomatic issues: the normalization of relations with the ROK and the restoration of Japan's governance over then US-occupied Okinawa. Meanwhile, he was also a well-known "pro-UN" politician who had given the maiden speech by a Japanese premier at the UNGA and made a critical contribution to establishing the United Nations University in the early 1970s. But unlike his predecessor Ikeda, Satō was a discreet player in terms of UN diplomacy and tended to shy away from any audacious remarks on the UNSC permanent membership issue. This, however, did not mean that he and his administration were indifferent to the bid. The prime minister had actually acquiesced in the initiative of his foreign ministers and MOFA policymakers on this case. And it was under his administration that Japan revved up its campaign for the permanent membership after years of silence.

It started with a seemingly routine personnel change. Having served in the UN for almost five years, Ambassador Matsui was relieved of his post in July 1967. While keen about the need to maintain Japan's presence at the UNSC, Matsui, a faithful student of "quiet diplomacy," was prone to avoid showy means in pursuit of this goal.[49] His successor, Tsuruoka—a former director of MOFA's UN Bureau who had also worked at the Japanese mission to the League of Nations—made no secret from the outset that he planned to enact a totally different type of strategy concerning the permanent seat. Pointing out that Japan would be the sixth largest contributor to the UN budget in 1968, Tsuruoka told the press upon departing for New York that "if our country wants to gain a voice appropriate to this [contribution]" it will then have to attain the status of "a big power" like the P5, who in his words were all "victors of the last war" and needed to be "replaced, considering that 22 years have passed since the end of the war." He added, "This may not be achieved during my tenure, but I would like to turn

---

49. Matsui, "Sōritsu nijū nen o mukaeta kokuren," pp. 30–31; *Asahi shimbun*, July 28, 1967.

international opinion in that direction by informally consulting the delegates of other nations."[50]

Before Tsuruoka started the consultations with other UN members, his boss, Foreign Minister Miki, had already sent up a trial balloon in Tokyo. In September, during a meeting with US Ambassador to the UN Goldberg, Miki touched upon Japan's "hope" to be a UNSC permanent member. The statement was very brief and Miki recognized that there could be difficulties in relation to the charter review.[51] But instead of shelving the agenda for another few years as they had done before, this time Japanese officials continued to demonstrate their eagerness before foreign audiences. In November, a UN Bureau officer expressed his "completely personal viewpoint" to British officials that "considerations should be given to the reelection every 20 years of UNSC permanent members."[52] From June to July 1968, Tsuruoka and Miki resumed dialogues with the US concerning the possibility of Japan's acquisition of a permanent seat.[53] In October, Tsuruoka asserted in a public speech on a college campus in New York state that since Japan had abandoned its "old image" of "a country famous for its scenic beauty and traditional culture" and become the second largest industrial power in the West, it is "now entitled to claim a permanent seat in the Security Council so that we may be able to contribute fully all that is in our power to the search for peace through the United Nations."[54]

More active moves were witnessed in 1969. Following Miki's resignation, Aichi Kiichi took office as foreign minister in December 1968. The new MOFA chief appeared to be the consummate salesman for Japan's appeal. On February 12, 1969, when questioned during a Diet session by an LDP member about his view on the permanent membership bid, Aichi replied that he thought it was "preferable" to "see Japan's posi-

---

50. *Asahi shimbun,* July 30, 1967.

51. New York to Washington, September 22, 1967, Box 3189, Subject-Numeric Files 1967–69, NA.

52. Goulding to Denson, November 28, 1967, FCO 21/274, Reel 145, PRO.

53. New York to Washington, June 15, 1968, Box 2249; Tokyo to Washington, July 26, 1968, Box 3193, both in Subject-Numeric Files 1967–69, NA.

54. *The New York Times,* October 18, 1968; Drifte, *Japan's Quest for a Permanent Security Council Seat,* p. 26.

tion reflected in places like the UNSC."[55] With the media reporting the statement as a remarkably forward-looking stance toward the permanent seat, politicians from both opposition and ruling parties came to ask Aichi for more concrete explanations during the subsequent weeks. At first, the foreign minister was careful in selecting words. But as time passed, his circumspection was supplanted by an increasingly confident attitude.[56]

By late March, Aichi began declaring that, given Japan's high assessment in the UN budget and its "unique" anti-nuclear weapon policy, "Japan has the desire to achieve a voice as a UNSC permanent member."[57] Six months later, he took a step forward by indirectly indicating Japan's desire for the seat in his speech at the UNGA general debate: "I believe that, in order to make the Security Council most effective, it would be desirable, in view of its importance, that it be an organ composed of member states which, as clearly provided in the charter, are in a position to render the most effective contributions to the maintenance of international peace and security and also are truly representative of various regions of the world."[58] There was no direct reference to "Japan" in the speech, though the delegates gathering in the Assembly Hall had little problem in understanding who was in Aichi's mind when he enumerated the criteria for a qualified UNSC member.

Apart from the permanent membership bid, Japan continued its efforts to win a non-permanent seat at the UNSC during this period. The only difference was that now Japanese officials were prepared to make

---

55. "Dai 61 kai kokkai shūgiin yosan iinkaigiroku dai 9 gō" (Proceedings of the 61st Diet Session Budget Committee, Lower House, No. 9), February 12, 1969, NDL.

56. "Dai 61 kai kokkai shūgiin gaimu iinkaigiroku dai 6 gō" (Proceedings of the 61st Diet Session Committee on Foreign Affairs, Lower House, No. 6), February 17, 1969; "Dai 61 kai kokkai shūgiin naikaku iinkaigiroku dai 4 gō" (Proceedings of the 61st Diet Session Committee on Cabinet, Upper House, No. 4), February 25, 1969; "Dai 61 kai kokkai sangiin yosan iinkaigiroku dai 16 gō" (Proceedings of the 61st Diet Session Budget Committee, Upper House, No. 16), March 20, 1969, ibid.

57. "Dai 61 kai kokkai sangiin yosan iinkai daiichi bunkakaigiroku dai 1 gō" (Proceedings of the 61st Diet Session Budget Committee, Upper House, No. 1), March 29, 1969, ibid.

58. New York to London, September 20, 1969, FCO 21/573, Reel 149, PRO.

the frequency of their country's appearances in the UNSC a bit closer to that of the P5. When Japan's second non-permanent tenure terminated in late 1967, the government decided to reenter the race for the seat in 1968 so that its representatives could return to the Council in 1969. There was no legal barrier for doing so since even if Japan won the election in 1968 it would not be an "immediate" reelection, which was prohibited by the charter. But Japan's decision was an abnormal gesture that neglected the principle of rotation concerning the non-permanent memberships.[59] Ambassador Tsuruoka explained his government's position on the basis of the conviction that the Council was "the best place in which Japan as a major economic power could play [a] more important role in world affairs than it could as just another member of [the] UNGA."[60] Speaking more frankly, the Japanese minister in London, Kimoto Saburō, told his counterparts at the British Foreign Office that Japan's real intention was to occupy a UNSC seat "semi-permanently."[61]

MOFA officers seemed to believe that this semi-permanent membership would not be difficult to achieve because Japan's competitor this time within the AA Group was Nepal, a modest South Asian state. But their confidence was soon shattered as the Nepalese started rallying support from India, Malaysia, and other AA Group members. By February 1968, it was crystal clear that the majority of the AA members would not allow Japan to win the race. After Tsuruoka's last effort to ask for Nepal's withdrawal ended in vain, Tokyo declared the postponement of its candidacy for another two years.[62]

The abandonment of the candidacy did not mean that Japanese policy planners had given up their efforts to gain the semi-permanent

---

59. Up to that point, only Brazil and Turkey had managed to reappear in the UNSC just one year after their latest tenure. Both cases happened in 1954 when there were only 60 UN members—less than half of the 1968 number.

60. New York to Washington, December 28, 1968, Box 3182, Subject-Numeric File 1967–69, NA.

61. "Record of a meeting between Sir D. Greenhill and the Japanese Minister at the Foreign Office at 4.00 p.m. on Monday, 5 February, 1968," February 5, 1968, FCO 21/256, Reel 143, PRO.

62. New York to Washington, February 1, 6 and 22, March 20 and 30, 1968, Box 3205, Subject-Numeric File 1967–69, NA.

membership. Shortly after backing off from the 1968 UNSC race, Tsuruoka proceeded to sound out the opinions of member states on a proposal to reshuffle the AA Group. Viewing the complicated composition of the group a chief hurdle to Japan's ambition, he suggested the establishment of a "Pacific Group" including Asian states "east of Burma" as well as Australia and New Zealand. Tsuruoka emphasized that this "culturally powerful" new group could make Japan's work at the UN "much easier" than the current AA Group. But as observed by US officials, a more important objective behind this thought was to make Japan "the bigger fish in a small pond" so as to override the resistance from states like India toward Japan's bid for a semi-permanent UNSC seat.[63]

Around 1969, Japanese officials put forth another two scenarios for the semi-permanent membership. The first one was to share the seat between Japan and an influential Asian power (presumably India) so that both could be elected to the Council "every other term." If this did not work, they had a secondary plan to rotate one of the AA seats at the UNSC among a handful of states—namely, Japan, India, Indonesia, and Pakistan. But none of these proposals gained sufficient backing within the UN due to the reluctance of AA states to treat Japan or India as a special case during elections.[64]

As the plan to promote the semi-permanent membership option through the AA Group broke down, Japanese officials moved to cultivate the idea from a different angle: the veto power. Japan's attitude toward the veto issue was ambiguous. Japanese officials despised the P5's abuse of their veto rights. Yet many of them also looked at the privilege of the veto as a necessary evil which kept the major powers' support of the UN system.[65] Regarding the correlation between Japan's permanent seat and the veto power, the government's policy was very

---

63. New York to Washington, June 15, 1968, Box 2249 and "Japan-United Nations: Implication of Japan's 1970 Security Council Candidacy," May 11, 1970, Box 3181, ibid.; Tsuruoka, "Kokusai kaigi zakkan–kokuren gaikō no keiken o tōshite," pp. 31–32.

64. "Japan-United Nations: Implication of Japan's 1970 Security Council Candidacy," ibid.

65. Drifte, *Japan's Quest*, pp. 31–32; Tsutsumi, "Nijūgo shūnen o mukaeru kokusai rengō," p. 98.

flexible. Anticipating the P5's passion toward their vested interests, Japan hinted on several occasions after 1970 that it might be willing to accept a semi-permanent status short of veto. "If [discussions on] the veto problem have to be avoided, then it may be possible to increase member states receiving semi-permanent member treatment," Foreign Minister Aichi stated during a Diet session in April of that year.[66] However, it was not easy to make the big powers accept a compromise like this because of its implications for charter amendments.

Aside from frequent presence at the Council, Japan also perked up its financial and personnel contributions to the UN in the early 1970s. Throughout the 1960s, the chronic financial crisis crippled the UN's daily management and its peacekeeping abilities. The situation got even worse after 1970 as the US demanded a further reduction in its contribution to the organization. As US funding was no longer reliable, Japan—the world's third largest economic superpower—was naturally expected by the UN to take on more bills. Japanese officials were very adept at manipulating that expectation to push Japan's UNSC bid. They did not lodge a serious protest when the UN recommended a 1.62 percent increase, the largest for any member state, in Japan's assessment for the organization's regular budget in 1970. Japanese diplomats at the UN actually considered this increase quite satisfactory and indicated that their government would "not take any prominent position on UN budget restraint" during the coming UNGA session.[67]

This cooperative stance was not adopted unconditionally, however. As a consequence of the big jump, Japan surpassed Nationalist China as the fifth largest donor to the UN. And there was a good chance that its rank would rise again since the US was contemplating cutting more money from its UN allotment. In October, Tsuruoka told the US delegation officers that Japan was more concerned with the "political" rather than the "financial" aspect of its assessment percentage and would "have to demand a permanent seat" at the UNSC "particularly if" its percentage exceeded those of the UK and France in the next as-

---

66. "Dai 63 kai kokkai sangiin yosan iinkaigiroku dai 12 gō" (Proceedings of the 63rd Diet Session Budget Committee, Upper House, No. 12), April 1, 1970, NDL; *Asahi shimbun,* March 30, 1970.

67. New York to Washington, March 3, 1970, Box 3188; New York to Washington, May 27, 1970, Box 3172, both in Subject-Numeric File 1970–73, NA.

sessment scale.[68] As we will see, Tsuruoka's statement was not a mere bluff.

One of Japanese officials' favorite idioms when displaying their position on the UN financial problem was "no taxation without representation." With the steady increase of Japan's share in the UN budgetary assessment scale, Tokyo's demand for more Japanese UN employees became incrementally stronger. In August 1968, the government set up an inter-ministerial liaison conference to coordinate policies encouraging Japanese citizens to work for the UN and other international organizations. Programs to strengthen the language capacity of candidates were set in motion and the Diet also adopted a law to smooth the dispatch of government officials to the UN. Consequently, the number of Japanese staff at the UN Secretariat almost doubled within less than five years.[69] But as before, most Japanese employees were below the D-1 class. The government had a clear-cut idea of the kind of post it was looking for. In 1967, a director post for trusteeship affairs became available for Japan. MOFA, however, passed up the opportunity because it was holding out for the more influential directorship in charge of security affairs or the assistant secretary-generalship (ASG)—the third highest ranking in the UN bureaucratic echelon. Japanese foreign ministers seized every chance to bring this matter up before UN Secretary General U Thant. But it was not until U Thant was replaced by the more pragmatic Kurt Waldheim in 1972 that Japan finally received an offer from the Secretariat to send an ASG to chair the Office of Public Information.[70]

The ASG appointment was a consolation for Japan's relentless effort but was far from satisfactory to many officials involved in the case. "The result of four years of hard work was a pitiful two posts for Japanese citizens out of the total 270 UN staff above the D Class," a March 1972 MOFA document complained. "This is literally a world of difference with the PRC—a UNSC permanent member which acquired the

---

68. New York to Washington, September 11, 1970, Box 2407, ibid.

69. MOFA, *Kokuren jōhō dai 3 kan,* p. 28 and p. 30.

70. Kokuren kōhō sentā, *Nihon to kokuren,* pp. 158–63; Political Division of the UN Bureau, "Aichi gaishō, U Tanto kokuren jimusōchō kaidan kiroku" (Record of the meeting between Foreign Minister Aichi and UN Secretary General U Thant), April 21, 1970, MOFAD.

position of USG for Political and Trusteeship Affairs within six months after acceding to the UN."[71] Once again, the reality of the UN hierarchy reinforced for Japan just how attractive a permanent seat at the UNSC could be.

The scarcity of their compatriots occupying senior UN posts was not the sole source of distress for Japanese officials coping with the question of personnel contribution. Since the mid-1960s, the sensitive subject of sending Japanese military personnel to the UN PKO had also been closely linked with Japan's UNSC permanent membership scheme. In previous chapters, we found that the SDF's participation in PKO was a hot topic during defense policy debates between the ruling LDP and opposition parties. If we take a close look at the history of the policymaking regarding this issue inside the government (in particular MOFA) after the mid-1960s, however, it is not difficult to identify a conspicuous emphasis placed on Japan's international status.

Discussions among government officers on the issue were ignited in 1964 by movements in the USSR and some Nordic nations to reshape the UN's peacekeeping forces. In the summer of that year, MOFA and the CLB conducted an investigation into the possibility of legalizing the SDF's role in PKO through a UN cooperation law.[72] Japan's election to the UNSC in December 1965 accelerated this study. In January 1966, MOFA produced a draft for legislation called the UN Cooperation Law. "Since our domestic legislation is not sufficient in taking actions to meet the UN's requirements of its member states, so far our country's UN cooperation is hardly satisfactory," the introduction of the draft read. "However, with the remarkable growth of our national power based on economic strength during recent years, expectations toward our fulfillment of international responsibility in conjunction with national power have naturally emerged within and outside the country, and our election

---

71. MOFA, *Kokuren jōhō dai 3 kan,* p. 580.
72. Yoshida Nagao, "Kokurengun to Nihon," p. 43; *Tōkyō shimbun,* February 23, 1966; Kotani to Ishii, August 1, 1964, Political Division of the United Nations Bureau, "Kokuren kyōryoku tokureihō (kashō) dai 1 ji shian" (The first draft proposal of the special legislation on UN cooperation, provisional name), January 5, 1966, CLB, "Iwayuru kokurengun to wagakuni kenpō" (The so-called UN forces and our country's constitution), September 3 and October 11, 1965, all in MOFAD.

to the UNSC non-permanent membership this time has further increased our duty." In view of such observations, the draft proposed that the government should adopt new legislation to allow Japanese personnel to take part in "non-combatant" UN peacekeeping missions.[73]

This argument regarding possible external pressure with respect to Japan's allegedly insufficient PKO cooperation was repeatedly raised by MOFA officials thereafter and became more distinctive as Japan articulated its ambition to attain a UNSC permanent membership.[74] In February 1969, MOFA's UN Bureau Councilor, Ogiso Motoo, set forth a revised version of the UN cooperation law that directly linked Japan's participation in PKO with the nation's bid for a UNSC permanent seat. While viewing the demand for the seat a "reasonable" long-term objective "if our country is going to occupy a leading position in the international community not only economically but also politically," Ogiso speculated that "the extent of Japan's contribution to UN peacekeeping activities might pose a problem" in pursuance of this goal. "If we could not even participate in UN PKO activities such as truce surveillance," he wrote in a memo, "suspicions about the merit of turning Japan into a [UNSC] permanent member will probably arise among UN members." In his opinion, the best way to improve Japan's performance in this connection without domestic backlash was to issue a law permitting the use of Japanese military staff in PKO in the form of a "UN Cooperation Force" rather than part of the SDF as the 1966 draft legislation suggested.[75]

This observation regarding the interaction between the UNSC bid and the PKO cooperation issue was soon revealed in public statements. Together with his controversial appeal for permanent membership,

---

73. Sairenji, "Nihon no kokuren heiwa iji katsudō sanka mondai," p. 26; Political Division of the UN Bureau, "Kokuren kyōryoku hōan ni tsuite" (The draft proposal of the UN cooperation law), January 27, 1966, untitled memo, January 21, 1966, both in MOFAD.

74. Yoshida Nagao, "Kokurengun to Nihon," p. 38; Hoshi, "Nihon no kokuren katsudō no jisseki to kadai," p. 97.

75. Sairenji, "Nihon no kokuren heiwa iji katsudō sanka mondai," pp. 32–33; Ogiso, "Kokuren kyōryokuhō ni kansuru mondaiten" (Points regarding the UN cooperation law), February 12, 1969, MOFAD. (This author would like to thank Mr. Sairenji Hiroki for providing this document.)

Foreign Minister Aichi, for instance, proclaimed in his 1969 UNGA speech Japan's willingness to "participate actively" in PKO as part of the country's new UN policy known as "Struggle for Peace." The foreign minister did not explain the correlation between the two, but some MOFA officials confessed openly before the press that cooperation with UN PKO was one element of their strategy to achieve a permanent seat in the Council.[76]

This was followed up when the strengthening of international security (SIS) became a major topic in UNGA discussions. The SIS question was originally raised by the USSR in 1969 as an extension to its earlier proposals regarding the intensification of the UN's security function. But Japan soon became a prime promoter of this agenda in the UN. In 1970, it joined Italy, Canada, Belgium, and some other medium-size Western powers to submit a draft resolution on the issue at the UNGA. The resolution was unique in its reference to using the contributions of member states of the United Nations to the maintenance of international peace and security as a gauge to evaluate the candidates for UNSC memberships.[77] During the following two years when the SIS matter was deliberated at the UNGA and the UN Peacekeeping Committee, Japanese delegates relentlessly urged other member states to pay attention to this linkage between member states' contributions to the UN's peace function and the composition of the UNSC. In June 1972, when UN Secretary General U Thant asked the UNSC members to provide their opinions on the SIS issue, the Japanese delegation circulated a paper in which, rather than discussing the SIS per se, it asked Council members to reflect Japan's arguments on the expansion of UNSC permanent membership in their report to the Secretary General.[78]

Alongside these attempts to tackle the permanent seat problem through indirect approaches, the early 1970s also bore witness to some noteworthy developments in Japan's direct challenge of the P5's pre-

---

76. Drifte, *Japan's Quest,* p. 30; *The Japan Times,* September 22, 1969.

77. Akashi, "Japan in the United Nations," pp. 32–33.

78. Tokyo to Washington, October 26, 1972, Box 3177 and New York to Washington, June 20, 1972, Box 3199, Subject-Numeric Files 1970–73; Letter from Thayer to Shoesmith, December 8, 1972, Box 9, Office of Japanese Affairs Subject Files 1960–75, NA.

dominance in the UNSC. The revision of the UN charter remained the optimum shortcut to alter the composition of the Council. Since the last charter revision took effect in July 1965, Japan had to find a sound reason to bring the agenda back to the UNGA table. Thanks to a motion tabled by the Colombian foreign minister, the feasibility of the current charter was discussed at the 1969 UNGA and a resolution calling for reconsidering the issue in the Assembly's Sixth Committee was adopted soon afterwards. Japan jumped on the bandwagon and cosponsored the resolution. At the 1970 UNGA, the Japanese delegation took further actions to bolster the Colombian initiative. It joined Colombia and the Philippines to draft a resolution mandating a formal debate on charter review. The resolution passed the Assembly due in part to Japan's success in rallying the AA Group's support.[79]

While assisting other countries' efforts, the Japanese government was also conscious of the importance of linking the charter revision effort with its own historical experience. The deletion of the "Enemy States Clauses" was one such example. As recognized by Japanese officials, UN charter articles against former Axis Powers (that is, the Enemy States Clauses) had long lost their relevance to current international relations and thereby were no threat to Japan's national interests.[80] By criticizing the existence of these antiquated clauses, however, Japan could not only erode the UN's legacy as an organization for the victors of WWII but also make its own argument against the UNSC's bias toward old military powers more persuasive before other member states.

"We Will Fight You and Beat You"

The endeavors to make Japan the sixth permanent member of the UNSC through amendments to the charter or the SIS/PKO issue all ended fruitlessly. Like what had happened to earlier PKO proposals

---

79. Iguchi, *Nihon gaikoshi,* pp. 85–87.
80. "Dai 63 kai kokkai sangiin yosan iinkai dai ni bunkakaigiroku dai 1 gō" (Proceedings of the 63rd Diet Session Budget Committee, Upper House, No. 1), April 13, 1970, and "Dai 71 kai kokkai shūgiin gaimu iinkaigiroku dai 2 gō" (Proceedings of the 71st Diet Session Committee on Foreign Affairs, Lower House, No. 2), March 23, 1973, NDL.

composed by the hawkish cliques within the ruling party, government leaders were reluctant to acknowledge the relationship between the permanent seat in the UNSC and the sensitive issue of using Japanese personnel in the UN's peacekeeping missions.[81] Inside the UN, having seen through Japan's intention to bring in the permanent seat question, the big powers also swiftly countered Japanese proposals regarding the SIS. Japan resisted but had no chance to win as some of its erstwhile comrades on this issue, such as Belgium, changed sides.[82]

The charter review effort encountered a similar problem in 1971. The majority of the member states preferred to be bystanders rather than supporters of Japan's ambition. The UN Secretariat understandably maintained its neutrality, except for Secretary General U Thant who frankly commented that the charter review Japan requested "would not be realistic for a long time to come."[83] A handful of states such as Italy, Nigeria, Brazil, Colombia, and the Philippines did echo Japan's initiative. But the endorsement of these nations, most of which either harbored similar ambitions or became interested in the issue for totally different purposes, did not make the prospects for Japan's endeavor any brighter.

Among all these negative signs, the most frustrating problem for Japanese policy planners was probably the attitude of current permanent members. Four of the P5 members were either negative or reluctant toward Japan's endeavor. The UK, which had considered Tokyo's UNSC permanent membership a remote event, was appalled when it

---

81. "Dai 63 kai kokkai sangiin yosan iinkaigiroku dai 11 gō" (Proceedings of the 63rd Diet Session Budget Committee, Upper House, No. 11), March 31, 1970; "Dai 63 kai kokkai sangiin yosan iinkaigiroku dai 12 gō" (Proceedings of the 63rd Diet Session Budget Committee, Upper House, No. 12), April 1, 1970; "Dai 63 kai kokkai sangiin gaimu iinkaigiroku dai 6 gō" (Proceedings of the 63rd Diet Session Committee on Foreign Affairs, Upper House, No. 6), April 7, 1970, ibid.

82. New York to Washington, June 15 and 24, 1972, Box 3199; New York to Washington, July 28 and October 27, 1972, Box 3200, Subject-Numeric Files 1970–73, NA.

83. Political Division of the UN Bureau, "Aichi gaishō U Tan kokuren jimu sō-chō kaidan kiroku," MOFAD; Geneva to Washington, April 15, 1970, Box 3181, Subject-Numeric File 1970–73, ibid.

learned during the 1969 UNGA session that the Japanese government might be interested in gaining a permanent seat by reconstructing the current Council system. One British official underlined the section regarding UNSC reform in the manuscript of Aichi's UNGA speech, scribbling: "The China seat? Or the Japanese claim that Britain and France should lose their status and Japan be given it?"[84] Even after figuring out that Japan was merely demanding its own right to be a new permanent member, British Foreign Office policy planners still concluded that their government must avoid taking up this topic during bilateral consultations with the Japanese side.[85] When British Prime Minister Edward Heath was going to meet his Japanese counterpart Satō in New York in October 1970, his aides advised him to respond reservedly if Satō brought up the charter revision or the UNSC permanent membership issue. "It is unlikely that in the near future the provisions of the charter on permanent membership can be altered," they explained, "nor do we want them to be."[86]

Fearing the spillover effect of Japan's ambition to other AA nations, France was also unsupportive. The French government, when consulted by Japan on the issue, took a polite attitude.[87] But seeing the US show more sympathy toward Japan's cause in late 1972, France wasted no time in ringing the alarm bell. "We are aware of your support for [a] Japanese [UNSC permanent] seat," a French UN delegate warned his American colleagues, "but you should try to explore avenues which do not open up [a] Pandora's Box on [the] rest of [the] charter or stimulate Italian, Indian, Nigerian, Brazilian, etc. demands."[88]

The Chinese and Soviet governments' reactions were even more dramatic. Perhaps worried about repercussions for its own representation at the UN, the Chinese Nationalists had traditionally opposed the

---

84. New York to London, September 20, 1969, FCO 21/573, Reel 149, PRO.

85. "Anglo-Japanese Ministerial Consultations Tokyo: April 1970 Item III: Other International Issues Japanese Candidature for the Security Council," April, 1970, FCO 21/739, Reel 153, ibid.

86. "Visit of the Prime Minister to the United Nations 19–24 October 1970," October 13, FCO 21/744, 1970, ibid.

87. Washington to New York, August 30, 1972, Box 3174, Subject-Numeric Files 1970–73, NA.

88. New York to Washington, November 23, 1972, Box 3200, ibid.

enlargement of the UNSC permanent membership through charter revision. The situation changed after the PRC took the China seat. Criticizing the superpowers' (specifically the Soviet's) dominance in the UNSC, the PRC was the only one in the P5 that openly supported amending the current charter.[89] The USSR had been another fervent opponent of charter revision. But after the anti-Soviet PRC adopted a policy favoring the revision, Moscow softened its stance. In early 1972, the Soviet UN delegate told Japanese officers that his government had "never opposed" adding Japan to the UNSC. The same view was aired by Foreign Minister Gromyko, who told Japanese Foreign Minister Fukuda Takeo, that rather than the opposition of the USSR, the PRC's attitude might pose more difficulties to Japan's permanent membership.[90]

Japanese policymakers were soothed by these seemingly positive signs for a while, but things took a downhill turn when the UNGA started considering a draft resolution concerning the establishment of an ad hoc committee for charter review in 1974. During the debate, the USSR once again refused to yield on the charter revision problem. The PRC, for its part, vehemently attacked the Soviets' negative stance and kept pressing for revision. Yet by that point, it was very clear that Beijing was not interested in Japan's quest but was primarily attempting to offset the influence of the big powers' hegemony by creating extra permanent seats for Third World member states.[91]

With the other permanent members turning their back on Japan's appeal, the US attitude became extremely critical in determining Tokyo's fate. Until 1972, the US government—one of the most adamant filibusterers against the charter review—was not excited about Japanese permanent membership in the UNSC. The Kennedy administration determined in the early 1960s that Japan's request for an additional UNSC permanent seat was dangerous because it would raise the question of

---

89. New York to Washington, October 16, 1972, Box 3220; "Atmosphere at 27th UN General Assembly," memo of conversation, December 27, 1972, Box 3175, ibid.

90. New York to Washington, June 24, 1972, Box 3199, ibid.

91. *Official Records of the General Assembly Twenty-Ninth Session, Sixth Committee, Legal Questions, Summary of Records of Meetings 18 September-9 December 1974*, pp. 291–93; *Official Records of the General Assembly Twenty-Ninth Session, Plenary Meetings, Volume III*, pp. 1546–47, UND.

Chinese representation.[92] The Johnson administration's response was also very negative, largely because of its reluctance toward charter review if not Japan's permanent presence at the UNSC per se.[93] The Nixon team inherited this stance. "The US favors regular Japanese membership on the Council," a May 1970 Sate Department memorandum stated, "but it would have serious reservations about any move which could require amendment of the charter and raise broader questions about the scope and even the desirability of permanent membership."[94]

Japan took various measures to draw the US into its court. Understanding that Washington desperately wanted to ease its financial burden in the UN, some Japanese officials tried to trade the increase in Japan's contribution to the UN budget for American support of Japan's permanent seat at the UNSC.[95] Likewise, when the US's efforts to keep the PRC outside the UN were no longer enough to resist the diplomatic campaigns of pro-Beijing member states, Japanese officials approached US delegates with an offer to "neutralize" the PRC's stance at the UNSC in the future by adding Japan to the permanent members' family.[96] The US, nevertheless, stood firmly by its original policy.

It was not until the summer of 1971 that the State Department began to consider a possible endorsement of Japan's permanent representation in the UNSC. The change was not a result of Japan's lobbying but stemmed from anxiety over a more serious problem in the long run: the likely emergence of an economically powerful Japan beyond US control in the political and military spheres. The US government had felt nervous about the increased nationalistic tendency in Japanese domestic

---

92. "Predictable Major Issues in the 16th General Assembly of the United Nations," 1961, Box 310A, NS Files, JFKL.

93. Tokyo to Washington, July 26, 1968, Box 3193, Subject-Numeric Files 1967–69, NA.

94. "Japan-United Nations: Implications of Japan's 1970 Security Council Candidacy," May 11, 1970, Box 3181, ibid.

95. New York to Washington, October 23, 1967, Box 3198, ibid.; New York to Washington, September 11, 1970, Box 2407, Subject-Numeric Files 1970–73, ibid.

96. New York to Washington, August 3, 1971, "Japan-United Nations," May 11, 1970, Box 3181, ibid.; *The Japan Times,* September 21, 1969.

politics and foreign policymaking ever since the mid 1950s.[97] During the 1950s, in the eyes of US policy planners, Japanese nationalism, with its strong penchant for neutralism, was instigated by left-wing politicians or communists who longed to estrange Japan from the Western bloc. In this sense, it was not so different from the anti-American nationalism observed in other developing countries at that time.

The situation changed after the early 1960s, however. In conjunction with the decay of US economic strength in relative terms and the miraculously high growth of the Japanese economy, Washington's fear shifted to the possibility of a nationalistic Japan that was inclined to take independent policies in fields ranging from foreign trade to military buildup. Under the Johnson administration, such unease was limited to a group of officials, most of whom were Japan or Asia specialists, at the State Department. After the inauguration of the Nixon administration, it spread into higher levels of the government as a result of the change in US policies toward Asia and the stalemate in its negotiations with Japan regarding Okinawa and trade disputes.[98]

In April 1971, President Nixon's advisor on national security affairs, Henry Kissinger, signed a document known as the National Security Study Memorandum 122 (NSSM122) in which he instructed the secretaries of state and defense as well as the director of the Central Intelligence Agency to update the administration's policy guidelines regarding Japan.[99] In early August, in their initial response to the NSSM122, State Department officials admitted that the US was caught on the horns of a dilemma in relation to its Japan policy. "[W]e have an ambivalent view of Japan," it read. "On the one hand, it is regarded as a friendly and allied power in Asia that is not utilizing its resources to 'do more' for our common security interests. On the other hand, there are residual fears that Japan may, in 'doing more,' adopt courses of military preparedness and diplomatic action that are inimical to our interests." To get the US

---

97. "Memorandum of Discussion at the 244th Meeting of the National Security Council, Washington, April 7, 1955," in Department of State, *FRUS 1955–57 Vol. XXIII*, pp. 40–48; Nakajima, "Amerika no higashi Ajia senryaku to Nihon (1955–1960)."

98. Pan, " 'Keizai taikokuka' to kokusaiteki chii," pp. 178–79.

99. "National Security Study Memorandum 122," memo from Kissinger, April 15, 1971, *Presidential Directives on National Security from Truman to Clinton*, NSAW.

out of this catch-22, they recommended that Washington reinforce its security alliance with Tokyo, avoid new major sources of potential conflict and nuclear proliferation in Asia, and strengthen its commitments to other allies in the region. These policies were supposed to be acted out under a set of five guidelines, of which a strategy to "channel Japan's nationalism and desire for recognition as a great power into constructive areas" stood at the top. One of these "constructive areas" was the UNSC permanent membership.[100]

The authors of this draft memo agreed that Japan's desire for a permanent seat at the Council was "a major component of" its quest for "recognition as a front-ranking power," and that such a demand would become more urgent after Beijing assumed the Chinese permanent membership because it could be "very hard" for Tokyo to "play Asian second fiddle" in the UN. At the same time, they also acknowledged the menacing charter review problem incidental to Japan's membership. But they still suggested that the government support Japan's bid. "A permanent seat for Japan would be a clear demonstration that it could attain great power recognition without nuclear or great conventional military power," these officials claimed.[101]

Just as the study of NSSM122 reached its final stage, President Nixon startled the international community on July 15, 1971, by announcing his plan to visit the PRC. This incident—"the Nixon Shock," as the Japanese called it—added more unstable elements into the US relationship with Japan, which was kept in the dark when Nixon and Kissinger were pursuing their secret diplomacy with Beijing. From late August to early September, the State Department produced several supplementary reports concerning the NSSM122 in light of this new situation, all of which reconfirmed the merits of awarding Japan a UNSC permanent membership.[102]

---

100. "NSSM-122, Policy toward Japan," August 1971, Fiche 219, NSA.

101. In the same vein, the authors also espoused "a more prominent" Japanese role in the UN Secretariat, the UNGA, the specialized agencies, the Organization for Economic Cooperation and Development (OECD), "great power political conferences" and bilateral security policy coordination. Ibid.

102. "Japan," memo for Peterson, August 14, 1971; "NSSM 122," memo for Kissinger, August 24, 1971, both in Box 7, White House Central Confidential Files, NPM.

But there was still one question that needed to be resolved. Despite the general agreement on Japanese permanent presence on the Council, US officials failed to reach a conclusion on how to grant Japan the title it sought while keeping the Pandora's box of charter revision sealed. This formidable problem was discussed in a joint report submitted by Assistant Secretaries of State Marshall Green (for East Asian and Pacific Affairs) and Samuel De Palma (for International Organizations) to Secretary of State William P. Rogers on September 3 prior to the visit of Japanese Foreign Minister Fukuda to Washington. Emphasizing the benefits of accommodating Japan's growing desire for international recognition "without forcing it to acquire a major military establishment," both Green and De Palma recommended articulate US support of a Japanese permanent seat in the UNSC. Yet on the flip side of the coin, they also asked the secretary to tell Fukuda that the US "would regard it as important that the Security Council not be too unwieldy and that its membership be as responsible as possible."[103]

Although he approved the report, Rogers did not convey the message of US support to the Japanese foreign minister partly because the UNSC problem was not on the agenda for the meeting between the two. But, more important, it seemed that the US government was not prepared to move one step forward to the final engagement. In particular, policymakers from the NSC were skeptical about the State Department's assessment of the cost of US support for a permanent Japanese seat. In late August, NSC staffer John H. Holdridge, a leading critic of the Department's studies, stressed in a memo to Kissinger that such an endorsement would "stimulate resentment among other nations such as India which believe they also have a claim to [a UNSC permanent seat]."[104] A few days later, the same question was brought up in an NSC senior decision-making meeting regarding NSSM122. The State Department's representative at the meeting, Undersecretary of State for Political Affairs U. Alexis Johnson, was unable to give a confident an-

---

103. "Japan on the Security Council," action memo for Rogers, September 3, 1971; "Japan's Desire for a Permanent Security Council Seat," memo for Nixon, September 7, 1971, both in Box 3181, Subject-Numeric Files 1970–73, NA.

104. "SRG Meeting on NSSM 122: Policy Toward Japan," memo from Holdridge and Hormats to Kissinger, August 25, 1971, Box H-059, NSC Institutional Files, NPM.

swer to it. "We can say we support in principle a Japanese [UN]SC seat," he said, "but we can't do anything about it." In the end, nothing definitive resulted from the meeting except for Kissinger's decision to let the State Department continue its studies on the issue as well as other policy items regarding Japan.[105] While giving serious attention to Japan's quest for UNSC permanent membership in the course of preparing for a formal response to NSSM122, Washington took no further actions on the bid for the subsequent ten months, and US diplomats in New York and Tokyo merely adhered to their role as patient listeners to Japan's claim.

Despite the silence on the US side, Japan gradually began to speak out. As American officials had speculated, Beijing's displacement of the Chinese Nationalists' permanent seat in the UNSC in October 1971 deeply hurt Japan's pride. The Japanese government displayed its anguish in a rather oblique way. A few days after the PRC's debut at the Council, for instance, Foreign Minister Fukuda indicated his chagrin during a Diet session by focusing on the nuclear stance of the current P5. "With China's participation in the UN, all the nuclear powers in the world have become the permanent members of the UNSC by chance," he said. "But considering today's international situation I feel it is irrelevant to fill the permanent membership with great military powers and believe that better operation and results can be achieved by adding major economic or cultural powers as permanent members."[106] When the Diet resumed four months later, Fukuda again took up this issue. This time, coupled with attacks against the predominance of nuclear powers, he mentioned Japan's ability to arm itself with nuclear weapons. In his view, states like Japan, which decided not to acquire nuclear weapons regardless of its technical capability to do so, would be most appropriate to serve as a permanent member in the Council.[107]

---

105. "Talking points: Japan policy—NSSM 122," August 27, 1971, ibid.

106. "Dai 67 kai kokkai sangiin Okinawa henkan kyōtei tokubetsu iinkaigiroku dai 2 gō" (Proceedings of the 67th Diet Session Special Deliberation Committee on the Okinawa Reversion Agreement, Upper House, No. 2), December 8, 1971, NDL.

107. "Dai 68 kai kokkai sangiin yosan iinkaigiroku dai 11 gō" (Proceedings of the 68th Diet Session Budget Committee, Upper House, No. 11), April 4, 1972; "Dai 68 kai kokkai shūgiin gaimu iinkaigiroku dai 19 gō" (Proceedings of the

Japanese diplomats at the UN also hardened their stance toward Washington. At first, they tried to warn the Americans that Japan might not concur with Washington's position that the US share of the UN budget should be lowered.[108] But when the US continued to turn a deaf ear to their arguments, a harsher voice arose on the Japanese side.

On April 6, 1972, the Japanese UN delegation's councilor for political and security affairs, Yoshida Nagao, invited two officials from the US mission to an informal consultation on UN-related issues. This was supposed to be a businesslike discussion, but the atmosphere turned sour during the last quarter of the meeting when Yoshida started grumbling about the US's decision to alter its China policy without informing Japan. This unhappy memory soon pushed him onto another sensitive topic: the NPT. "Why should the government of Japan sign it?" he questioned. "The US government [has] adduced no persuasive reason, and the government of Japan should not feel compelled to sign [the] NPT just because [the] US won the war 25 years [sic] ago." When he finally reached the topic of the UNSC permanent seat issue, his tone and manner became "tense and accusatory" (using the words of his American guests). Trying to calm him down, one US official asked for his opinion on the extent of the enlargement of the UNSC permanent memberships. But Yoshida was already on the brink of explosion. He not only refused to inform the US side of Japan's tactics for UNSC reform or charter review but declared that Washington was not Japan's friend on this issue and until and unless the US prepared to discuss this matter seriously, there would be no negotiations in advance with the Americans. His statement ended with a passionate oath that Japan would "fight you and beat you" to keep charter revision on the agenda and to ensure Japan's permanent place in the UNSC.[109]

It was unclear whether Yoshida made these antagonistic comments intentionally or simply on the spur of the moment. But the impact of this episode on US policymakers was unmistakable. Usually records of routine conversations among UN delegates do not catch so much at-

---

68th Diet Session Committee on Foreign Affairs, Lower House, No. 19), May 31, 1972, ibid.

108. New York to Washington, March 8, 1972, Box 3174, Subject-Numeric Files 1970–73, NA.

109. New York to Washington, April 6 and 8, 1972, Box 3181, ibid.

tention from senior policy planners at the State Department. In this case, however, the reaction was different. Stunned by Yoshida's hostility, the two US officials wired Washington right away to report his remarks at the meeting, which they described as "blunt" and "almost brutal."[110] Two days later, they submitted a second report with more details, together with an additional comment stating that they did understand that Yoshida's attitude could be partly attributed to his character, but even taking this into consideration, "his tone and words on this matter were strong and bitter."[111] The State Department's reply arrived on April 11. While cautioning against direct response to Yoshida's "intemperate exposition," the Department ordered the UN delegation to assure the Japanese side that the US "fully appreciate[s]" Japan's desire for the seat and would like to have a "full discussion of this question" before the next UNGA session started.[112]

In contrast to Yoshida's acrimony, most Japanese officials, when sounded out by the US delegates, showed cooperation and understanding. Some said that they were looking for a minimum expansion of the UNSC. Others reassured the US side that they would not wage an "all-out campaign" for the permanent seat. Even Yoshida later told the US that his government believed the new permanent members would not have the veto power of the current P5.[113] Favorable opinions for Japan's bid also mounted within the Department. The US mission to the UN was inclined to take actions to support Japan's permanent membership in line with the 1971 Green / De Palma memo.[114] Wary of the deterioration of the US-Japan relationship since the Nixon Shock, Ambassador to Tokyo Robert S. Ingersoll also suggested in a long telegram that the UNSC permanent seat question was an issue "on which we can gain greatly in psychological but nevertheless tangible ways" because US endorsement "will have demonstrated in [a] public way to [the]

110. New York to Washington, April 6, 1972, ibid.

111. New York to Washington, April 8, 1972, ibid.

112. Washington to New York, April 11, 1972, ibid.

113. New York to Washington, April 12 and May 10, 1972, Box 3181; New York to Washington, May 17, Box 3220, ibid.

114. New York to Washington, April 27, 1972, Box 3181, ibid.

GOJ [the government of Japan] and [the] people of Japan that we are on their side."[115]

In late May, the State Department ultimately approved a decision to formally notify the Japanese government of US support for Japan's permanent presence at the UNSC. On May 27, Undersecretary of State Johnson instructed the US embassy in Tokyo to execute this new policy. The Department composed the instruction in a very reserved manner leaving no room for illusions that Japan could obtain its goal in a short period of time.[116] But the Japanese government was still delighted by this news. On June 10, Ambassador Ingersoll delivered the message to Foreign Minister Fukuda and a small number of MOFA officials in a secret meeting held at an annex to the Ministry's headquarters. Fukuda was "wholeheartedly grateful" for the US offer, stating that "international developments have eliminated any need to continue to differentiate in the UNSC between defeated nations and victor powers" from WWII and that the "time has come to restudy UNSC composition in terms of promoting peace and development by considering a permanent seat for a nation which possesses only great economic power and poses no military threat." He also concurred with the US position that "over-representation would dilute the devotion of UNSC permanent members" to the purpose of the Council.[117]

The Fukuda-Ingersoll meeting was a milestone in Japan's UN diplomacy. But it did not entirely change the situation concerning Tokyo's endeavor to secure its status at the highest level of the UN's decision-making system. The lack of efficient communications between Tokyo and Washington was at least part of the reason. Outwardly, everything looked good. Soon after Ingersoll's visit to MOFA, Japanese and American officials began exchanging information regarding their strategies for coping with the UNSC enlargement and charter review problems. In late August, President Nixon reconfirmed the US's support at his meeting with Japanese Prime Minister Tanaka in Hawaii.[118] In mid-September, Secretary Rogers made this commitment public by men-

---

115. Tokyo to Washington, April 21, 1972, ibid.

116. Washington to Tokyo, May 27, 1972, ibid.

117. Tokyo to Washington, June 10, 1972, ibid.

118. "Plenary Session of US-Japan Summit Meeting," memorandum of conversation, August 31, 1972, Box 2407, ibid.

tioning it during his speech at the UNGA general debate. Yet the two sides apparently had difficulty in understanding the real motivation behind their counterparts' activities. Unaware of the US's grave concern about Japan's independent diplomatic stance, many Japanese officials continued their ardent drive for charter revision. Worried about this tendency, US officials opposed Japan's idea of establishing an ad hoc committee for charter review at the UNGA. Instead, they suggested in July that Japan leave the agenda to an existing committee for the arrangement of charter review based on Article 109. Knowing that the proposed committee had been paralyzed for more than a decade, Japanese officials rejected the US suggestion, calling it an "elegant form of burial for charter review."[119]

Presumably in an effort to avoid further collision with the US, Japan offered a compromise plan in mid-September by agreeing to discuss the UNSC issue at the Sixth Committee of the UNGA rather than immediately setting up a new ad hoc committee. MOFA also accepted the State Department's request to keep its canvassing within the UN low-key.[120] But Rogers's UN speech reignited Japanese officials' suspicion of US intentions. The State Department felt that the Secretary of State's announcement of US support would "make it difficult for other permanent members to be equivocal in their responses to private Japanese soundings." The Japanese government, which did not want to expose itself to domestic and international pressures in this early stage, viewed the issue in a different way. Rather than appreciating Washington's good will, MOFA officials visited the US delegation in New York to remind the latter of their previous decision to pursue the case quietly.[121]

US-Japan cooperation on the UNSC enlargement question rapidly lost its dynamics after the Rogers speech incident. The Japanese government began spending more time in negotiations with UN members other than the US. Frustrated by Japan's silence, US officials, who had expected more proactive demands from Tokyo, also started suspecting the motive of their counterparts. By July 1973 when Nixon and Tanaka

---

119. New York to Washington, July 28, 1971, Box 3200; Washington to New York, June 19, 1971, Box 3220; Washington to New York, July 5, 1972, Box 3174; New York to Washington, August 17, 1971, Box 2408, ibid.

120. Tokyo to Washington, October 5, 1972, Box 3181, ibid.

121. Washington to Tokyo and New York, October 7, 1972, ibid.

were about to have their second summit meeting, the US government had concluded that "the Japanese do not seem to be giving high priority to this matter."[122] While Washington maintained its verbal commitment to Japan's permanent UNSC seat for another few years, consultation between the two countries on the issue was relinquished before getting any concrete results.[123]

While Japanese officials were busy rallying the support of the P5, the overall movement among UN member states toward charter revision reached a critical watershed. Although Japan behaved prudently in advancing the agenda due to its agreement with the US, many developing countries did not hesitate to table more radical resolutions at the UNGA. Around November 1972, the Philippines put forward a draft resolution to establish an ad hoc committee for charter revision. Having received no advance consultation, Japan was caught by surprise and to some degree embarrassed by Manila's initiative. Yet it had no choice but to cosponsor the resolution so as to protect its reputation as the leading force for charter review.[124] After the draft resolution was put under consideration at the UNGA Sixth Committee in December 1974, the Japanese delegation worked hard to forge a unified international opinion on the issue, only to be overwhelmed by the thrust and parry of the PRC and USSR. The resolution was adopted with the majority votes of the Third World, but the opposition of four of the P5 foretold the buffeting it would face thereafter.[125]

---

122. "Nixon-Tanaka Summit Background Paper—XI: Some Multilateral Issues," June 29, 1973; "Japan's Desire for a Permanent Security Council Seat," July 1973, both in Fiche 275, NSA.

123. Nixon reiterated his support for Japan's UNSC seat in the joint communiqué after the 1973 summit and so did Kissinger in his UNGA speech shortly thereafter. In 1977, President Jimmy Carter made a similar remark before Japanese Prime Minister Fukuda when the latter visited Washington. "Memoranda of the President's Conversation with Japanese Prime Minister Tanaka on July 31 and August 1, 1973," Fiche 281, ibid.; Drifte, *Japan's Quest,* p. 44; "Revised Policy Statement for 1975 Japan PARA," 1974, Box 10, Office of Japanese Affairs Subject Files 1960–75, NA.

124. New York to Washington, November 1, 1972, Box 3220; New York to Washington, November 29, Box 3177, Subject-Numeric Files 1970–73, NA.

125. *Official Records of the General Assembly Twenty-Ninth Session, Sixth Committee, Legal Questions, Summary of Records of Meetings 18 September-9 December 1974,* pp.

The Revival of the Bid

By the mid-1970s, the likelihood for a quick victory in Japan's UNSC permanent seat campaign died out as the big powers consolidated their resistance toward a drastic change in the Council's composition. During the last few years of the decade, most Japanese government leaders were predisposed to keep their distance from this issue. The only exception was Kosaka Zentarō, who in the course of his brief second tenure as foreign minister in 1976 tried to revive the bid. But even he toned down his voice after finding out that the situation at the UN was far more intricate than he had assumed.[126] On the other hand, MOFA policymakers also recognized the need to soften their approach while remaining faithful to their dream. Noticing the discomfort aroused in some permanent members by the proposal to rewrite the charter articles related to the UNSC, they at one stage made plans to start the revision from the easier Enemy States Clauses. To their disappointment, it was impossible to generate a consensus among member states even on this relatively minor issue. Consequently, all they could achieve at the moment was to renew the endless debate in the ad hoc committee for charter revision.[127]

The setback to Japan's UNSC bid occurred in areas other than charter review as well. The Japanese government's strategy to raise its status in the Council by winning a non-permanent seat was again hindered by the AA Group. Japan was elected as a non-permanent member in 1970. After finishing its term in December 1972, the government decided to reenter the race in 1974. This was a very tough battle, as it was simultaneously running for a seat in the ECOSOC. Under the leadership of Ambassador Saitō, a seasoned UN diplomat, Japan won both seats, albeit with the lowest votes among five new members of the UNSC.[128]

291–93; *Official Records of the General Assembly Twenty-Ninth Session, Agenda Item 95 Annexes, Document A/9950, Report of the Sixth Committee, December 13, 1974; Official Records of the General Assembly Twenty-Ninth Session, Plenary Meetings, Volume III,* pp. 1546–47, all UND.

126. *Yomiuri shimbun,* September 30, 1976; Kosaka, "Kuni no ue ni kuni o tsukurazu," p. 31; Kosaka and Takubo, "Kokuren sōkai to Nihon gaikō," p. 15.

127. Drifte, *Japan's Quest,* p. 38.

128. Saitō, *Kokuren no mado kara,* p. 129.

But MOFA tried to push its luck even further by announcing Japan's candidacy in the 1978 non-permanent member election. This time, the magic did not work. Devoid of the AA Group's backing, Japan lost the contest to Bangladesh.

Unable to move forward in gaining either permanent or non-permanent seats in the UNSC, the Japanese government lost its vitality in tackling the issue at the turn of the 1980s. The philosophy of "no taxation without representation" was aired in a rather coarse way when a Japanese delegate bluntly pointed out at a 1979 UNGA session that there was an "incongruity between the increasingly heavy financial responsibility Japan is being asked to bear and the weight its voice carries, its position, and the number of Japanese staff members in the organization."[129] Japan's resentment also targeted the P5. In 1979, it refused to join other Western powers in voting against a resolution aimed at reforming the veto right. "It is necessary to show by actions the fact that Japan has joined the UN after the charter system was fixed and therefore is neither a founder of the organization nor a state which has to protect its vested rights by exalting the charter to a sacred principle, but belongs to those willing to elasticize the charter to fit the times," MOFA's UN Bureau Director Kaya Harunori explained his government's position weeks after the vote.[130]

Japan's dejection over its status as a "have-not" within the UN was mitigated by a landslide victory in the 1982 UNSC non-permanent member election. In 1986, Japan again joined the non-permanent member race and beat Nepal, the country that had forced Japan to drop out of the 1967 UNSC election during a competition for the endorsement of the AA Group. Weeks later, it won the seat despite the rumor that the African members might oppose Japan's membership due to Tokyo's alleged pro-South African trade policy. The race was won by an extremely narrow margin, but it allowed Japan to replace India and Brazil as the most frequently elected non-permanent member.[131]

---

129. MOFA, *Statements Delivered by Delegates of Japan during the XXXIVth Session of the General Assembly of the United Nations*, p. 319.

130. Kaya, *Kokuren to Nihon gaikō*, pp. 16–17.

131. Seisaku kenkyū daigakuin daigaku COE ōraru seisaku kenkyū purojekuto, *Kikuchi Kiyoaki ōraru histori: gekan*, pp. 213–14.

Certain progress was also made in the effort to increase senior staff in the UN Secretariat by the mid-1980s, with more Japanese officers being promoted to higher ranks in the UN headquarters, including the prestigious post of USG. Despite these developments, it took a long time for Japanese policymakers to renew their pursuit of the bid for the permanent seat in the UNSC. Some of them did not even bother to refer to this objective during most of the 1980s. Japanese Ambassador to the UN Nishibori asserted shortly after his retirement in 1983 that if Japan wanted to become a UNSC permanent member it would have to fight another world war. "But we will no longer wage such a war," he added, "so it is impossible for us to get a permanent seat."[132]

In comparison with government officials' circumspection, Japanese political leaders had been more and more outspoken on this issue since the mid-1980s. Prime Minister Nakasone, who assumed office in 1983, was a persistent critic of Japan's inferior status in international society and proclaimed on the nation's biggest TV network that since Japan's contribution to the UN budget was ranked at number two among UN members, second only to the US, he would "feel guilty" before the Japanese people if Japan could not gain "a voice on par with the US" in the international community.[133] From the early days of his term, Nakasone attempted to implant this perspective into the government's UN policies regarding two issues: the abolition of the Enemy States Clauses and a permanent membership for Japan. Without efficient backup from MOFA and other leading UN members like West Germany, he obtained no concrete results on either issue.[134] But this did not discourage him from speaking his mind. Shortly before the termination of his tenure in 1987, he became the first Japanese prime minister who brought up the UNSC enlargement issue at the G-7 Summit.[135]

Probably influenced by Nakasone's enthusiasm, the chairman of the ruling LDP's Policy Research Council, Fujio Masayuki—another assertive nationalist leader—set out to ask for Southeast Asian nations' support for Japan's UNSC permanent seat during an official tour to the re-

---

132. Nishibori, "Saikin no kokuren to Nihon," p. 22.

133. Sekai heiwa kenkyūjo, *Nakasone naikaku shi: shiryō hen,* p. 405.

134. Drifte, *Japan's Quest,* pp. 48–49; Nakasone, *Tenchi ujō,* pp. 469–70; *Yomiuri shimbun,* August 17, 1985.

135. Drifte, *Japan's Quest,* p. 50.

gion in May 1985. He first touched on this topic in his meeting with Indonesian President Suharto, arguing that a permanent membership at the UN could not only fortify Japan's voice before the two superpowers but might allow the Japanese government to magnify Asia's position in the world. Suharto remained reticent, while the Indonesian media was extremely suspicious about Japan's motivation for the seat.[136] But Fujio did not care. Throughout the rest of his journey, he rattled on to Asian leaders about the need to correct the UN's bias as an organization of victorious powers.[137] "I wanted to cause a little commotion [on the UNSC membership matter] since people from our government all avoid this topic," he told MOFA officials after returning to Tokyo.[138]

The move to reopen the UNSC and charter revision debates was not limited to members of the cabinet or the LDP leadership. The Enemy States Clauses were a favorite topic for many politicians from both ruling and opposition parties, who had been pressing the government in the Diet ever since the early 1960s to do something to erase these humiliating articles from the UN charter. The UNSC permanent seat question was more complicated. From the mid-1970s to the mid-1980s, the left-wing opposition parties were not so excited about taking up this issue. The conservative and middle-of-the-road opposition parties, on the contrary, gave lots of attention to the bid. And more times than not, they tended to link Japan's UNSC permanent presence with the country's personnel contribution to the UN's military activities. The DSP's position was that if Japan was wholeheartedly looking for either a permanent or non-permanent seat in the Council, then it must relinquish its policy of banning military personnel from the PKO or the UN force postulated in the charter.[139] The CGP also underscored the con-

---

136. Mutō to Abe, May 6, 1985, MOFAD.

137. Tachibana to Abe, May 9, 1985, ibid.

138. Second Southeast Asia Division of the Asian Affairs Bureau, "Kanbōchō no Fujio seichō kaichō ōhō" (The director of the secretariat's visit to Policy Affairs Research Council Chairman Fujio), May 15, 1985, ibid.

139. "Dai 80 kai kokkai shūgiin naikaku iinkaigiroku dai 6 gō" (Proceedings of the 80th Diet Session Committee on Cabinet, Lower House, No. 6), March 10, 1977; "Dai 80 kai kokkai shūgiin naikaku iinkaigiroku dai 18 gō" (Proceedings of the 80th Diet Session Committee on Cabinet, Lower House, No. 18), May 24, 1977; "Dai 93 kai kokkai shūgiin anzen hoshō tokubetsu iinkaigiroku dai 4 gō"

nection but with a different nuance. Rather than urging the dispatch of the SDF to UN missions it simply asked the government to take this problem into account before raising its hand to request UNSC permanent membership.[140]

The ruling LDP and the government were not necessarily reluctant about the idea of sending the SDF to participate in PKO during this period. But like what took place in the 1960s and 1970s, they did have certain reservations against publicly admitting that PKO cooperation was a prerequisite to UNSC permanent membership. This was a rational attitude because it was meaningless to double the difficulty by tying two unresolved cases together. However, the situation could change when the government was prepared to modify its stance regarding either of these two cases. This was what happened in the last two years of the 1980s. Compared to their predecessors, Japanese leaders in the 1980s paid more attention to their country's "responsibility" in international society. Prime Minister Takeshita's "International Cooperation Initiative" in 1988 was an expression of such a new trend. In Chapter 4 we examined this policy from a security viewpoint, but its implication for Japan's fight for a higher international status was also profound.

The Takeshita Initiative put the government in a more comfortable position to cultivate its plans on security cooperation with the UN for PKO participation. And this in turn revived the idea of using the PKO card to promote the UNSC bid among government and LDP leaders. In May 1989, Hamada Takushirō, a young LDP politician who served as

---

(Proceedings of the 93rd Diet Session Special Committee on Security, Lower House, No. 4), November 5, 1980; "Dai 102 kokkai sangiin gaikō sōgō anzen hoshō ni kansuru chōsa tokubetsu iinkai gaikō mondai shōiinkaigiroku dai 3 gō" (Proceedings of the 102nd Diet Session Subcommittee on Foreign Affairs of the Special Investigation Committee on Foreign Affairs and Comprehensive Security, Upper House, No. 3), May 29, 1985; "Dai 102 kokkai sangiin gaikō sōgō anzen hoshō ni kansuru chōsa tokubetsu iinkai gaikō mondai shōiinkaigiroku dai 5 gō" (Proceedings of the 102nd Diet Session Subcommittee on Foreign Affairs of the Special Investigation Committee on Foreign Affairs and Comprehensive Security, Upper House, No. 5), June 12, 1985, NDL.

140. "Dai 80 kai kokkai shūgiin naikaku iinkaigiroku dai 16 gō" (Proceedings of the 80th Diet Session Committee on Cabinet, Lower House, No. 16), May 19, 1977, ibid.

the parliamentary vice foreign minister during the preparation of the Takeshita Initiative, fired the first shot in the Diet by asking for Foreign Minister Uno Sōsuke's comments on the thought that if Japan was sincerely determined to enact Takeshita's international cooperation proposal the country had to become a permanent member at the UNSC. Uno responded positively, indicating that one way to achieve the permanent seat could be "active contributions" to the UN PKO. Hamada promptly agreed but reminded the foreign minister that if that was the case, Japan should at least take part in the UN peacekeeping forces. Uno's reply left latitude for imagination: "For the moment we would like to cooperate with the PKO through civilian personnel, but as the Diet and the public may want to see more Japanese contributions to world peace, we would also take notice of these opinions so as to figure out the appropriate stance with respect to our peace contribution."[141]

In June 1990, Hamada again challenged the government in the Diet with the same question on the correlation between a UNSC seat and PKO cooperation. This time, he did not earn the expected answer from Prime Minister Kaifu, who was not keen on the idea.[142] Yet unlike the early 1970s, when MOFA's attempt to link the two factors was buried by the cautious LDP leadership, the international situation in the early 1990s, specifically the outbreak of the Persian Gulf crisis, soon pushed the government in the direction suggested by Hamada.

After the Diet started deliberating the government's plan to send SDF to the Middle East through the UNPCB in late 1990, the UNSC permanent membership became one of the major methods for the ruling LDP to justify the bill. Representatives of the party anticipated that the adoption of the UNPCB would bring Japan an "honorable status" in the world community and "appropriate treatment at the UN commensurate with our country's international power."[143] In doing so, they

141. "Dai 114 kai kokkai shūgiin gaimu iinkaigiroku dai 3 gō" (Proceedings of the 114th Diet Session Committee on Foreign Affairs, Lower House, No. 3), May 24, 1989, ibid.

142. "Dai 118 kai kokkai shūgiin gaimu iinkaigiroku dai 10 gō" (Proceedings of the 118th Diet Session Committee on Foreign Affairs, Lower House, No. 10), June 15, 1990, ibid.

143. "Dai 119 kai kokkai sangiin honkaigiroku dai 2 gō" (Proceedings of the 119th Diet Session Plenary Session, Upper House, No. 2), October 17, 1990;

believed, the permanent seat question at the UNSC or the deletion of the Enemy States Clauses would also be resolved much more smoothly. Such arguments were so widespread that even cautious government leaders like Foreign Minister Nakayama joined the chorus.[144] The same phenomenon occurred after the PKO Law was put on the discussion table a year later.[145]

Using the PKO issue as a vehicle, debates on the UNSC permanent seat question quickly heated up inside Japan by late 1991. The next step would be the renewal of the bid in the international arena. To be sure, while acting circumspectly, MOFA officials never diverted their attention throughout the 1980s from the aim of securing a seat for Japan in the Council. In the summer of 1986, a group of Japanese ambassadors stationed in international organizations signed a letter addressed to Foreign Minister Kuranari stressing the significance of boosting Japan's influence in accordance with the "rise in our international status"

"Dai 119 kai kokkai shōgiin kokusai rengō heiwa kyōryoku ni kansuru tokubetsu iinkaigiroku dai 4 gō" (Proceedings of the 119th Diet Session Special Committee on Peace Cooperation with the UN, Lower House, No. 4), October 26, 1990; "Dai 119 kai kokkai shūgiin kokusai rengō heiwa kyōryoku ni kansuru tokubetsu iinkaigiroku dai 5 gō" (Proceedings of the 119th Diet Session Special Committee on Peace Cooperation with the UN, Lower House, No. 5), October 29, 1990, ibid.

144. "Dai 119 kai kokkai shūgiin kokusai rengō heiwa kyōryoku ni kansuru tokubetsu iinkaigiroku dai 4 gō" (Proceedings of the 119th Diet Session Special Committee on Peace Cooperation with the UN, Lower House, No. 4), October 26, 1990; "Dai 119 kai shūgiin kokusai rengō heiwa kyōryoku ni kansuru tokubetsu iinkaigiroku dai 7 gō" (Proceedings of the 119th Diet Session Special Committee on Peace Cooperation with the UN, Lower House, No. 7), October 31, 1990, ibid.

145. "Dai 121 kai kokkai shūgiin kokusai heiwa kyōryoku ni kansuru tokubetsu iinkaigiroku dai 3 gō" (Proceedings of the 121st Diet Session Special Committee on International Peace Cooperation, Lower House, No. 3), September 25, 1991; "Dai 121 kai kokkai shūgiin kokusai heiwa kyōryoku ni kansuru tokubetsu iinkaigiroku dai 6 gō" (Proceedings of the 121st Diet Session Special Committee on International Peace Cooperation, Lower House, No. 6), October 1, 1991, ibid.

through frequent election to the UNSC.[146] MOFA officials also em braced the view that more comprehensive cooperation with PKO could have a positive effect on Japan's international status. In fact, just five months before the 1990 Persian Gulf crisis, a MOFA conference on peace cooperation concluded that since Japan's "status in international society is rising remarkably" based on its economic power, it was time to make a "substantial engagement" in the international political sphere by strengthening its financial and personnel contributions to UN PKO.[147]Aside from these arguments shared with political leaders, many MOFA policymakers seemed to believe that it was not wise to make the goal of a higher status too prominent.

Rather than directly seeking recognition of Japan's superior status in the organization through the permanent membership debate, MOFA chose to commence its endeavor with the Enemy States Clauses, on which it was easier to gain supporters. In the autumn of 1990, Foreign Minister Nakayama mentioned the obsolescence of these articles in his UNGA speech and called for the "endorsement and understanding" of UN members to abolish them "as soon as possible."[148] The appeal became more straightforward in the 1991 UNGA session where he described the articles as "utterly inappropriate historic relics which should be promptly deleted."[149] Along with his vocal appeal, Nakayama also discussed this problem with the foreign ministers of the permanent members. All agreed in principle that the clauses were no longer applicable, but none of them pledged to embrace Japan's plan to accomplish its goal through charter revision.[150] Through the strenuous canvassing of the government, Japan went as far as acquiring a UNGA resolution

---

146. Shuyō kokuren kikan taishi renraku kaigi, "Sekkyokuteki kokuren gaikō no suishin," pp. 17–18.

147. MOFA, "'Heiwa no tame no kyōryoku' misshon: hōkoku yōshi" (The mission of "cooperation for peace," outline of the report), March 1990, MO-FAD.

148. MOFA, *Waga gaikō no kinkyō 1991*, p. 401.

149. MOFA, *Diplomatic Bluebook 1992*, p. 389.

150. US Secretary of State James Baker actually asked Nakayama not to touch charter articles other than those related to former enemy states. See "Dai 120 kai kokkai shūgiin gaimu iinkaigiroku dai 9 gō" (Proceedings of the 120th Diet Session Committee on Foreign Affairs, Lower House, No. 9), April 12, 1991, NDL.

supporting the deletion of the Enemy States Clauses in December 1995. But the resolution has not yet been put in force, since the UN members are still seeking a common ground regarding charter review, which is the prerequisite for the deletion of any clauses of the current charter.

As for the UNSC permanent seat, Nakayama seemed to be encouraged by the attitude of some UN members (such as Italy and Portugal), who suggested that Japan run for the position.[151] But opinions among MOFA policy planners remained diverse. Officials such as Ambassador to the UN Hatano Yoshio were no less zealous than political leaders in championing Japan's right to be seated in the UNSC shoulder to shoulder with the P5 and sometimes even set a timetable for their goal.[152] The majority of the Ministry, on the other hand, was uncertain about the odds of success for a full-scale campaign. This suspicion matched the initial reaction of the big powers, especially the US.

The US government was very nervous about the Japanese UN delegation's vigorous campaign in New York. Ambassador Armacost in Tokyo was instructed to tell MOFA that Washington expected Japan to develop a "plausible" strategy for achieving its objective "without inadvertently undermining" the Council's usefulness. During a trip to Tokyo, US Ambassador to the UN Thomas Pickering also warned the Japanese government that "opening the door to unrestrained logrolling among many other countries that coveted a permanent seat" was the last thing Washington wanted to see. By late 1992, Japanese leaders including Prime Minister Miyazawa had consulted their American counterparts on the issue on several occasions and received the same answer every time.[153]

Japanese officials certainly understood what these words meant. But in order to keep the bid alive, they could not stay idle either. The only available option, therefore, was to keep Japan's request on record in a

---

151. "Dai 120 kai kokkai sangiin gaikō sōgō anzen hoshō ni kansuru chōsakaigiroku dai 2 gō" (Proceedings of the 120th Diet Session Investigation Committee on Foreign Affairs and Comprehensive Security, Upper House, No. 2), February 18, 1991; "Dai 120 kai kokkai shūgiin yosan iinkaigiroku dai 20 gō" (Proceedings of the 120th Diet Session Budget Committee, Lower House, No. 20), March 7, 1991, ibid.

152. Drifte, *Japan's Quest*, p. 117; Armacost, *Friends or Rivals?*, p. 159.

153. Armacost, *Friends or Rivals?*, p. 160; Drifte, *Japan's Quest*, p. 138.

relatively modest manner. In early 1992, serving as a non-permanent member at the time, Japan sent Prime Minister Miyazawa to the summit to deliver a speech before the heads of governments of other UNSC members. In one section of the speech, Miyazawa stated that Japan was "prepared to take an active part" in the process of "thoroughly" adjusting the Council's "functions, composition, and other aspects so as to make it more reflective of the realities of the new era."[154] This statement was in essence a replication of those made by Foreign Minister Aichi in 1969 and 1970. "It was not a declaration of our candidacy for the permanent membership," as one of its authors indicated later, "but it did contain a far-reaching meaning."[155]

While waiting for the opportune timing for the campaign within the UN, the government also managed to cool the zeal of politicians at the Diet who consistently prodded MOFA to pick up its pace. Both Miyazawa and Foreign Minister Watanabe played an important role in this respect. "It's not expedient to let our bid be held up by those countries who themselves are hunting for a permanent seat," Miyazawa admonished his Diet colleagues in early 1992, "and we will seriously think about it [the bid] only when blessed by all nations."[156] Watanabe made this point even clearer in one statement by cautioning the supporters of the bid that "there are not so many states in the world which are ready to endorse our permanent seat." He noted that "it would of course be a good thing if our country could be a UNSC permanent member, but I feel we have to do this in a cautious and natural way."[157]

Developments in the international situation proved the Japanese government's strategy to be worthwhile. Dreams of becoming a new permanent member were not limited to developed countries such as

---

154. MOFA, *Diplomatic Bluebook 1992*, p. 401.

155. Shinyo, "Kokuren no saikasseika o motomete," p. 6.

156. "Dai 123 kai kokkai shūgiin yosan iinkaigiroku dai 5 gō" (Proceedings of the 123rd Diet Session Budget Committee, Lower House, No. 5), February 20, 1992, NDL.

157. "Dai 123 kai kokkai shūgiin yosan iinkai dai ni bunkakaigiroku dai 2 gō" (Proceedings of the 123rd Diet Session Second Subcommittee of the Budget Committee, Lower House, No. 2), March 12, 1992; "Dai 123 kai kokkai sangiin yosan iinkaigiroku dai 12 gō" (Proceedings of the 123rd Diet Session Budget Committee, Upper House, No. 12), April 3, 1992, ibid.

Japan and Germany. The Third World nations, which were the majority of the UN family, also made a strong case for their permanent representation at the Council. In the 1992 UNGA session, a draft resolution regarding UNSC reform composed by these nations was put to a vote. Like what it did in the late 1960s (in the case of the Colombian resolution on UNSC enlargement), Japan quietly followed the initiative of the Third World nations and ended up as one of two developed nations (along with Germany) that cosponsored the draft.[158]

While the Third World resolution passed the Assembly in December, it had little effect in terms of promoting Japan's permanent seat bid. Based on the resolution, UN member states submitted their official opinions regarding the Council's reform to the UN Secretary General in the summer of 1993. A year later, discussions on this matter were set in motion inside a UNGA working group. But all these moves did not change the overall picture. In fact, in the middle of the 1990s, Japan faced a situation akin to that in the mid-1970s when it had been forced to pull back from the race. The big powers were either negative or lukewarm at best to the demand for reform, whereas the challengers could not reach a consensus on who might go first. Despite the end of WWII and the Cold War, Japan is still fighting the battle for the crown it threw away in the international peace organization more than seven decades ago.

---

158. Yoshida Yasuhiko, *Yameru kokuren,* pp. 46–47.

Conclusion

For the nearly five decades after 1945, Japan astonished the international community by miraculously rising from the wreckage of the war to become one of the world's most affluent states. The UN, on the other hand, followed an opposite course during the same period. Called into existence as the guardian of world peace, the organization became crippled in the course of the Cold War and was later discarded even by some of its founding fathers. Yet the relationship between the rising sun and the sinking world peace organization is far more complex than it appears on the surface.

Like other member states, Japan had lost its faith in the UN's military security function and had set out to look for alternative guarantees for its safety even before acquiring its membership. But the fragility of the UN did not prevent Japanese policymakers from believing in the organization's positive role in maintaining their nation's security in a broad sense, beyond territorial defense. At the beginning, the idea was rather vague and sometimes marked by an idealistic tinge, as can be seen in terms like "a shared forum transcending the Cold War," "a tool for international democracy," or "a bridge between the Orient and the Occident." Not until the late 1950s did Japan eventually figure out that what it expected the UN to do in the security area was to serve as an arena for world opinions, or to put it more straightforwardly, an escape valve through which international tensions could be released before reaching the point of a disastrous blowout. This became more significant after the early 1960s when Japan emerged as a new industrial power bearing grave concerns about the safety of its economic interests amid a surging anti-Western penchant in the Third World.

Apart from these economic reasons, Japan also cherished the usefulness of the UN as the sole forum for its participation in debates on international security problems alongside great military powers from both the Eastern and Western blocs. To be sure, Japanese leaders and policy planners were not enthusiastic about getting involved in international conflicts; nor did they wish to take advantage of the UN to offset the influence of the big powers. Their request was a modest one aimed simply at keeping themselves well-informed on critical decision-making that had a substantial impact on Japan's national security. Consequently, while maintaining a low profile during UN debates on political and security matters, Japan was eagerly trying to keep certain issues like the nuclear disarmament problem under the UN's jurisdiction. It also never looked on idly when some UN members, no matter how powerful they were or which bloc they were from, took actions that could jeopardize the existence of the organization per se.

While the UN did not completely lose its value in Japan's national security policy in a broader sense, it is also evident that the Japanese government's modest expectations demanded nothing more than occasional efforts when something fundamental was going wrong. Besides, as Japan itself was targeted by the AA nations for its pro-Western stance in the UN during the 1960s and 1970s, the world peace organization was hardly efficient at meeting even Japan's modest security needs. In this sense, if broad national security concerns had been the sole underpinning of Japan's relationship with the UN, the manifest frequency of the organization's appearance in the nation's security and foreign policymaking process would be a very curious phenomenon. Such ubiquity of the UN could not be explained without reckoning with elements at the domestic political and psychological levels.

As discussed at the beginning of this book, ever since the late 1940s Japanese political parties have been engaging in heated debates on sensational topics such as war and peace or the nation's identity as a member of Asia and the Western industrial club. The opposition parties' prime objective was to find a method through which they could demonstrate that by binding Japan with the US and the West, the conservative regime was leading the country down a path toward annihilation.

Uneasy about the impact of such arguments on the pacifist, pro-Asian public's opinion, the government and the ruling parties were compelled to erase the bellicose image of their foreign and security policies through a sound political cause. For both sides, the UN, which was adored by the Japanese people as the symbol of world peace and justice, was a convenient tool to achieve their objectives.

Using the slogan of UN-centrism or UN-first, the leadership of the ruling party and policy planners inside the government proficiently adorned their policies on controversial agendas ranging from the recognition of the PRC to the overseas deployment of SDF with internationalist hues. The opposition leaders had even more reasons to emphasize the significance of the UN. In an active sense, the government's blunders in handling onerous UN agendas like the AA-Western collision and the Chinese representation issue certainly provided the opposition leaders with plenty of munitions to attack their conservative rivals. But a more important role of the UN in the opposition's strategy was actually rather passive. Aware of the difficulty of finding a practical security scheme other than the alliance with the US, Japanese opposition parties were wont to consign the unresolved problems of their security counterproposals to the mirage of a UN-centered international order that was supposed to take full responsibility for maintaining world peace some time in the future. Finally, all major Japanese political parties had used the UN as the greatest common denominator to glue fragmented opinions of different factions inside their organizations into unified policy packages. The bargain between left-wing and right-wing JSP leaders regarding the peace and security treaties in the early 1950s and discussions among LDP factions on SDF cooperation with PKO since the mid-1960s were perfect examples of this strategy.

The correlation between the UN and Japan's national security or domestic party politics is by and large determined by decision-makers' rational calculation of gain and loss. But it is not always so easy to make a rational judgment regarding gain and loss in relation to international status, which is closely connected to the psychology of national prestige. "Prestige" is originally a very sentimental and personal concept. "We state something [about] someone when we say that he possesses prestige; but our statement is not clear, and the predicate cannot be distinguished from the subject," as the social theorist Lewis (Lajos) Leopold put it. "We are unable to localize it [prestige] otherwise than in a person and are bound to refer it to a whole individual."[1]

Regardless of the individual connotations of the word "prestige," students of international politics have attempted to widen its usage with the term "national prestige." Scholars of the realist and neorealist schools managed to rationalize the term "national prestige" so that it could be used like "national security" or "national interests." Carefully avoiding touching the definition of prestige from a personal or individual perspective, Hans J. Morgenthau argued in his *Politics Among Nations* that prestige "is rarely the primary objective of foreign policy." In his opinion, states usually pursue prestige "in support of a policy of the status quo or of imperialism," and a "policy of prestige is, therefore, an indispensable element of a rational foreign policy."[2] Taking a slightly different approach, Waltz—the champion of the neorealist school— also believes that as rational players of international politics, great economic powers are destined to obtain status as great military powers. If they do not, the public's desire for prestige may force them to do so. "Pride knows no nationality," he declared.[3]

But does Japan fit these assumptions? Based on what we have seen in this study, Japanese policymakers' quest for equal or higher international status through the UN looked more like a policy of prestige for its own sake. Despite its frequent election to the prestigious UNSC non-permanent membership, Japan was by no means a proactive participant in the Council's discussions on major security agendas. Instead of seeking the post as another military superpower, Japanese leaders enshrined their appeal for a UNSC permanent seat in an argument based on Japan's identity as an economic power without strong military capacities. Meanwhile, some government officials did from time to time deny the existence of a causal linkage between national prestige and their passion for more influential status in the UN. Yet this position looked wan before statements made by other members of the government who had participated in policymaking related to the UN. A MOFA division chief, for instance, once commented that elections in-

---

1. Leopold, *Prestige,* p. 21.
2. Morgenthau, *Politics among Nations,* pp. 80–81.
3. Waltz, "Emerging Structure of International Politics," p. 66.

side the UN were like a "sumo match" and Japan's success in them was a method for the country to raise its rank from "sekiwake class" (the third-highest rank in sumo wrestling) to "ōzeki class" (the second-highest rank).[4] Yet what did Japan hope to do after becoming an "ōzeki class" power in the UN? One of the chief's senior colleagues offered his view on this question years later. When asked whether Japan should seek UNSC membership, former UN Ambassador Nakagawa answered: "Although things could become very busy once we get a seat at the UNSC, other nations will come to ask for our help regarding various issues. So it is better to obtain the membership considering the substance of the work and our nation's prestige."[5] Given these public statements, it seems that the following criticism made by UN senior official Akashi was not overly cynical: "Japan behaves too much like a status-seeker in international society, when what is important is learning how to use such status for the sake of Japan and the world."[6]

However, it is not the intention of this study to dismiss Japan's aspiration for a respectable position in the UN as irrational or as the desire of "foolhardy egocentrics," to use Morgenthau's words.[7] What matters here is not whether Japan has had a strong interest in higher international status but how it has attempted to achieve such status.

Postwar Japan is no longer considered a great military power and is prohibited from reinforcing its position in the world through military means. But compared to other foreign policy areas, Japan's UN diplomacy was influenced little by these restrictions. The UN is the symbol of world peace and its institutional mechanism matches perfectly with Japan's understanding of international hierarchy. The fact that the UN was established by the same Allied Powers that defeated the Japanese Imperial Army and Navy in the last world war also spurred Japan's earnest desire to gain a respectable position in the organization and thus stand alongside those victory powers once again in the international community. Moreover, in the UN and its affiliated bodies, the voice of a member state is dependent on whether it is a member of major councils and committees. And most of these titles can be won by elections,

---

4. Amō, *Takokukan gaikōron*, pp. 276–77.
5. Kokuren kōhō sentā, *Nihon to kokuren*, p. 153.
6. Akashi, *Kokuren kara mita sekai*, p. 167.
7. Morgenthau, *Politics among Nations*, p. 81.

which do not demand the strong military capacities or nuclear weapons that are unavailable for postwar Japan. Even in the case of the highest rank in the UN (permanent membership in the UNSC, currently held by the nuclear powers), Japan (and Germany as well) can still ask for a similar title by revising the UN charter or contributing small PKO forces without arming itself with nuclear weapons. Given these benefits, it is in no way surprising to see Japanese decision-makers choose the UN as a valuable channel to wage their campaign for first-class nation status. In sum, Japan's decision to use the UN as a major arena to promote its international status has shown that although national prestige per se may know "no nationality," the ways in which national prestige is pursued do in fact differ among nations.

The coexistence of three different policy objectives guaranteed the ubiquity of the UN in Japan's foreign policymaking. But it also brought about the negative aspects of Japan's UN diplomacy. The UN did not play a central part in the government's security policy. In most cases, unless the existence of the organization was severely threatened, Japan had no motivation to take the initiative to strengthen the influence of the UN in the international political and security spheres. In addition, the UN's function in party politics had little direct impact on Japan's behavior inside the UN. While political leaders from the ruling and opposition parties were earnest in impressing the public with their UN-first position, their interest in the UN was shaped not by international factors but by domestic considerations. Therefore, the ruling LDP was able to continue reinforcing its bilateral security pact with Washington outside the UN framework while reiterating in public that its fundamental object was to perfect the UN's collective security system. In the same manner, the opposition parties could underscore the intimate relationship between their security plans and the UN-centric international order without taking any substantive measures to assist the organization's peacekeeping efforts. The protracted bid for higher international status has induced the Japanese government to make more contributions, of both money and personnel, to bolster the UN's capacity to maintain international peace. Yet we should not forget the other side of the story. In trying to use its financial wealth in exchange for a UNSC permanent seat, Japan can also harden its attitude toward the UN when its strategy does not bring the desired results; not to mention that the outcome of the diplomatic game regarding Japan's status in the UN usually depends more on bilateral talks with individual member states, and achievements in terms of UN cooperation only have secondary importance.

Policy objectives pertaining to broader national security, domestic party politics, and international status or national prestige might not in themselves always benefit the UN substantially. Yet the combination of these purposes has closely connected postwar Japan's foreign and security policymaking with the world's biggest peace body. In a speech delivered at the forty-second UNGA general debate, Japanese Prime Minister Nakasone cited a stanza in English from the American poet Henry W. Longfellow's "A Psalm of Life": "Let us, then, be up and doing, with a heart for any fate; still achieving, still pursuing, learn to labor and to wait."[8] The poem was used as a message to other member states which were getting increasingly impatient about the lack of progress in the UN's peace enterprise, but it also suits nicely Japan's own relationship with the organization. Insofar as the economic superpower remains heavily dependent on a peaceful international environment, its politicians continue to engage in their endless infighting on foreign and security courses, and the gap between its national power and status in the world community does not vanish, the UN will always be a crucial, if not central, arena where Japanese policymakers and political leaders have to keep on achieving, pursuing, and laboring while calmly waiting for the full bloom of their endeavors.

---

8. Nakasone, "Kokuren o shin ni kokuren tarashimeru tame ni," p. 10.

Reference Matter

Bibliography

The titles of Japanese sources were translated by this author, except for those having an English title made by the original authors.

Abbreviations Used in the Footnotes

DDEL: Dwight D. Eisenhower Library

DDRS: *Declassified Documents Reference System*

DOS: *Confidential US State Department Central Files*

DRO: Diplomatic Record Office, MOFA (Nihon gaikō bunsho)

FRUS: *Foreign Relations of the United States*

FRUSF: *Foreign Relations of the United States: Microfiche Supplement*

JFKL: John F. Kennedy Library

LBJL: *The Lyndon B. Johnson National Security Files*

LOTF: *Confidential US State Department Special Files: Japan 1947–1956, Lot Files*

MOFAD: Documents declassified in accordance with the Freedom of
   Information Act

NA: National Archives II

NDL: National Diet Library

NPM: Nixon Presidential Materials

NSA: National Security Archive, ed. *Japan and the United States*

NSAW: National Security Archive website

PRO: Public Record Office (*Foreign Office File for Japan and the Far East*)

PSI: Research Institute for Peace and Security

UND: UN Documents

UTL: Faculty of Economics Library, Tokyo University

Unpublished Sources

Diplomatic Record Office, MOFA, Tokyo.

—. Nihon gaikō bunsho (Documents on Japanese foreign policy), micro-films/CD-ROMs.

Division for the Access to Government Information of the Minister's Secretariat, MOFA, Tokyo

—. Documents declassified in accordance with the Freedom of Information Act.

Dwight D. Eisenhower Library, Abilene, Kansas.

—. DDE Diary Series.

Faculty of Economics Library, Tokyo University, Tokyo.

—. Treaties Bureau. "Kokusai rengō sanka mondai kankei shiryō" (Documents on Japan's admission to the UN).

Higuchi Toshihiro. "Educating about the Fear—The U.S. Nuclear Test Policies, Japan, and World Public Opinion." M. Phil. diss., University of Tsukuba, 2002.

John F. Kennedy Library, Boston, Massachusetts.

—. National Security Files (NS Files).

—. Papers of James C. Thomson, Jr.

—. Roger Hilsman Papers.

Matsudaira Kōtō. "Nihon no kokusaiteki chii to sekinin: Kokuren gaikō ni tsuite" (Japan's international status and responsibility: UN diplomacy). Record of lecture, Kōchikai, June 1961.

National Diet Library, Tokyo.

—. Asanuma Inejirō monjo (Papers of Asanuma Inejirō).

—. Ashida Hitoshi monjo (Papers of Ashida Hitoshi).

—.Ishibashi Mashi monjo (Papers of Ishibashi Masashi)

—. Wada Hiroo monjo (Papers of Wada Hiroo).

National Archives II, College Park, Maryland.

—. Subject-Numeric Files 1964–73.

—. Office of Japanese Affairs Subject Files 1960–75.

—. Lot Files.

—. Japan Post Files.

Nixon Presidential Materials, College Park, Maryland.

—. National Security Council Files (NSC Files).

—. White House Central Confidential Files.

Research Institute for Peace and Security, Tokyo.

—. Dōba Hajime monjo (Papers of Dōba Hajime).

Microformed and Internet Sources

Confidential U.S. State Department Central Files: Japan, Internal Affairs and International Affairs, 1960–January 1963. Bethesda, MD: University Publications of America, 1997.

Confidential U.S. State Department Central Files: Japan, Internal Affairs and Foreign Affairs, February 1963–1966. Bethesda, MD: University Publications of America, 1998.

Confidential U.S. State Department Special Files: Japan 1947–1956, Lot Files. Bethesda, MD: University Publications of America, 1990.

Declassified Documents Reference System, published on the Primary Source Media website, www.galegroup.com (subscription required).

Foreign Office File for Japan and the Far East: Series Two: British Foreign Office Files for Post-War Japan, 1952–1980 (Public Record Office Class FO 371 & FCO 21, Part 1–7). Marlborough, Wiltshire: Adam Matthew Publications, 1998–2002.

Foreign Relations of the United States 1958–1960, Volume 11, Lebanon and Jordan: Microfiche Supplement. Washington, DC: Department of State, 1992.

Kesaris, Paul, ed. *Document of the National Security Council, Fourth Supplement.* Frederick, MD: University Publications of America, 1987.

Kokkai kaigiroku kensaku shisutemu (Full-text database system for the minutes of the Diet), published on the National Diet Library website, http://kokkai. ndl.go.jp (free access).

National Security Archive, ed. *Japan and the United States: Diplomatic, Security and Economic Relations, 1960–1976.* Ann Arbor: Bell & Howell Information and Learning, 2000.

Presidential Directives on National Security from Truman to Clinton, published on the National Security Archive website, http://nsarchive.chadwyck.com (subscription required).

The Lyndon B. Johnson National Security Files 1963–1969: United Nations. Frederick, MD: University Publications of America, 1988

The Lyndon B. Johnson National Security Files 1963–1969: Asia and the Pacific, First Supplement. Bethesda, MD: University Publications of America, 1996.

Newspapers and Periodicals

Ashahi jānaru

Asahi shimbun

Mainichi shimbun

Nihon keizai shimbun

The New York Times

The Japan Times

Tōkyō shimbun

Tōyō keizai shinpō

Yomiuri shimbun

Published Sources

Adachi Toshiaki. *Shinsei suru kōmeitō* (The revitalized CGP). Daiwa shobō, 1971.

Aichi Kiichi. "The United Nations and Japan's Position." In *Japan in Current World Affairs,* ed. Kajima heiwa kenkyūjo, pp. 26–39. Japan Times Ltd., 1972.

Akashi Yasushi. "Japan in the United Nations." *The Japanese Annual of International Law* No. 15 (1971): 23–37.

——. *Kokuren kara mita sekai* (The world viewed from the UN). Saimaru shuppankai, 1992.

Amō Tamio. *Takokukan gaikōron* (A talk on multilateral diplomacy). PMC shuppan, 1992.

Anzen hoshō kenkyūkai. "Nihon no anzen hoshō seisaku" (Japan's security policy). *Kakushin* (Feb. 1981): 152–75.

Arakawa Kazuaki. "Hankaku heiwa no kyōdō o kyohisuru bōgaisha" (The saboteurs rejecting the unification for anti-nuclearism and peace). *Zenei* (Aug. 1968): 126–35.

Araki Shirō. "Kenshō, PKO hō seiritsu o rīdo shita minshatō" (Inspection: DSP taking the lead to adopt the PKO Law). *Kakushin* (Aug. 1992): 22–27.

Armacost, Michael H. *Friends or Rivals? The Insider's Account of US-Japan Relations.* New York: Columbia University Press, 1996.

Asai Yoshiyuki. "Kaku haizetsu e aratana ketsui o!—ima koso gentaiken o wasurezu kokusai yoron no kesshū o" (Renewed determination toward nuclear abolishment: it is time to rally international opinion without forgetting our original experience). *Kōmei* (Oct. 1976): 74–84.

Asakai Kōichirō. *Shoki tainichi senryō seisaku: Asakai Kōichirō hōkokusho (jō)* (Initial policy on the occupation of Japan: report by Asakai Kōichirō, Vol. 1). Mainichi shimbunsha, 1978.

Asukata Ichio. "Hikaku heiwa chitai secchi o suishin shiyō" (Promoting the establishment of NFZs). *Gekkan shakaitō* (July 1982): 14–17.

Benton, Barbara, ed. *Soldiers for Peace: Fifty Years of United Nations Peacekeeping.* New York: Facts On File, Inc., 1996.

CGP. "Nichibei anpo taisei no dankaiteki kaishō no hōto anzen hoshō kōsō" (The way to gradually abolish the US-Japan security system and proposal for security). *Zenei* (Apr. 1969): 361–68.

—. "Kōmeitō no anzen hoshō seisaku" (The CGP's security policy). *Kōmei* (Dec. 1981): 53–64.

—. "Kōmeitō no gaikō seisaku" (The CGP's foreign policy). *Kōmei* (Jan. 1982): 50–58.

—. "Kokuren heiwa kyōryoku ni tsuite no kenkai" (Opinions on peace cooperation with the UN). *Zenei* (Jan. 1991): 87–88.

—. *Ningen shugi 'chūdō shugi' no atarashii sentaku: 90 nendai kōmeitō no shihyō* (Humanism, the new choice of "centrism": the CGP's goal in the 90s). Kōmeitō kikanshikyoku, 1991.

Chen Zhaobin. *Sengo Nihon no Chūgoku seisaku—1950 nendai higashi Ajia kokusai seiji no bunmyaku* (Japan's policy in the context of East Asian international relations in the 1950s). Tōkyō daigaku shuppankai, 2000.

Cohen, Warren I. *The Cambridge History of American Foreign Relations, Volume 4: America in the Age of Soviet Power, 1945–1991.* New York: Cambridge University Press, 1993.

Department of State. *Foreign Relations of the United States, 1955–1957, Volume 11, United Nations and General International Matters.* Washington, DC: United States Government Printing Office, 1988.

—. *Foreign Relations of the United States, 1955–1957, Volume 23, Part 1, Japan.* Washington, DC: United States Government Printing Office, 1991.

—. *Foreign Relations of the United States, 1964–1968, Volume 1, Vietnam 1964.* Washington, DC: United States Government Printing Office, 1992.

—. *Foreign Relations of the United States, 1961–1963, Volume 22, Northeast Asia.* Washington, DC: United States Government Printing Office, 1996.

Dower, John W. *Embracing Defeat: Japan in the Wake of World War II.* NY: W. W. Norton & Company/The New Press, 1999.

Drifte, Reinhard. *Japan's Quest for a Permanent Security Council Seat: A Matter of Pride or Justice?* London: Macmillan, 2000.

DSP. "Shōwa sanjūhachi nendo gaikō seisaku" (Foreign policy of 1963). *Seisaku to tōron* (Jan. 1963): 139–43.

—. "Bōei to anzen hoshō narabini heiwa no tame no hōsaku" (Measures for defense, security and peace). *Seisaku to tōron* (July 1963): 15–16.

—. "Anzen hoshō to bōei ni kansuru waga tō no kihon hōshin" (Our party's basic policies on security and defense). *Seisaku to tōron* (Oct. 1966): 14–20.

—. "1978 nendo gaikō hōshin—anzen hoshō to kokusai kyōryoku" (Diplomatic principles in 1978: security and international cooperation). *Kakushin* (May 1978): 193–97.

—. "Heiwa to anzen hoshō mondai ni tsuite no shinpojiumu kanren shiryō" (Materials related to the symposium about peace and security issues). *Seisaku to tōron* (Dec. 1980): 26–36.

—. "Kakugunshuku to anzenhoshō o ikani hakaru ka: chūritsu ni nareba heiwa ni naru to iu no wa gensō da" (How to pursue nuclear disarmament and security: it is a fantasy to think that peace will come if we go neutral). *Kakushin* (June 1982): 20–28.

—. "Minshatō no kangae wa kō da" (This is the DSP's thought). *Kakushin* (Dec. 1983): 18–30.

—. *Minshatō seisaku handobukku'84* (DSP policy handbook for 1984). Minshatō kyōsenkyoku, 1984.

—. *Minshatō sanjūgo shūnen shi* (A history of the DSP for the past 35 years). DSP, 1996.

Finger, Seymour Maxwell. *American Ambassadors at the UN: People, Politics, and Bureaucracy in Making Foreign Policy.* New York and London: Holmes & Meier, 1988.

First Division of the International Cooperation Bureau, ed. *Kokuren dai jū sōkai ni okeru kamei mondai* (The admission issue at the tenth UNGA session). First Division of the International Cooperation Bureau, 1956.

—. *Kokusai rengō gaikan* (The outline of the UN). First Division of the Public Information and Culture Bureau, MOFA, 1956.

Fuwa Tetsuzō. "Nihon no chūritsuka to anzen hoshō" (Japan's neutralization and security). *Zenei* (July 1968): 10–31.

Gaimushō hyakunenshi hensan iinkai, ed. *Gaimushō no hyakunen* (100 years of MOFA). Hara shobō, 1969.

Gotōda Masaharu. *Sei to kan* (Politicians and bureaucrats). Kōdansha, 1994.

Hatano Sumio. *Taiheiyō sensō to Ajia gaikō* (The Pacific War and Asian diplomacy). Tōkyō daigaku shuppankai, 1996.

Hayase Sōichi. "Hankyō yatō no anpo seisaku no hensen" (The transition of the anticommunist opposition parties' security policies). *Zenei* (Nov. 1980): 70–89.

Hayashi Jōji. "Sekai no jiyū kokka to tomoni" (Together with the world's liberal states). *Kaizō* (Nov. 1952): 112–14.

Herring, George C. *America's Longest War: The United States and Vietnam, 1950–1975.* Third Edition. New York: McGraw-Hill, Inc., 1996.

Higuchi Toshihiro. "Kakujikken mondai to Ikeda gaikō: 'sengo Nihon' zō no kyojitsu to 'hibaku keiken'"(The nuclear experiment issue and Ikeda cabinet's diplomacy: the truth and fiction of the image of "postwar Japan" and "the experience of being A-bombed"). In *Ikeda, Satō seikenki no Nihon gaikō* (Japanese foreign policy under the Ikeda and Sato cabinets), ed. Hatano Sumio, pp. 199–233. Kyoto: Mineruba shobō, 2004.

Hirose Hidehiko, ed. *Tōyō daigaku shakaigaku kenkyūjo kenkyū hōkokusho dai 4 shū* (Research report of the sociology institute of Tōyō University, Volume 4). Tōyō daigaku shakaigaku kenkyūjo, 1988.

Hoshi Bunshichi. "Nijū shūnen o mukaeta kokuren" (The UN upon its twentieth anniversary). *Sekai no ugoki* (Sept. 1965): 7–11.

——. "Nihon no kokuren katsudō no jisseki to kadai" (The achievements and themes of Japan's activities within the UN). *Kokusaihō gaikō zasshi* (Aug. 1966): 73–100.

Hoshijima Nirō. "Kōwa kaigi o mae ni shite" (Prior to the peace conference). *Saiken* (Dec. 1950): 10–16.

Ichikawa Yūichi. "Shin anzen hoshō seisaku 20 mon 20 tō—'risō' to 'genjitsu' o ryōritsu saseru sentaku" (20 questions and answers on the new security policy: a choice making 'ideal' and 'reality' compatible). *Kōmei* (Dec. 1981): 35–52.

Ide Hiroshi. "Kakuheiki haizetsu e no michi—daiikkai kokuren gunshuku tokubetsu sōkai kara dainikai sōkai e" (The path toward the abolishment of nuclear weapons: from the UN SSD I to SSD II). *Zenei* (Aug. 1981): 50–64.

Iguchi Sadao, ed. *Nihon gaikōshi dai 32 kan: kōwago no gaikō (III)—kokusai rengō.* (Japanese diplomatic history, vol. 32, diplomacy after the peace III: the UN). Kajima kenkyūjo shuppankai, 1972.

Ikeda Ichirō. "Kokuren de sōten to sareta Chūgoku daihyōken mondai" (The Chinese representation problem considered a point of controversy in the UN). *Zenei* (Jan. 1966): 243–46.

Ikeda Naotaka. "Senryōki gaimushō no anzen hoshō mondai kenkyū" (The Japanese Foreign Ministry and its studies on national defense during the American occupation). *Kikan gunjishigaku* (Mar. 1999): 52–65.

Ikei Masaru and Horie Fukashi, ed. *Nihon no seitō to gaikō seisaku—kokusaiteki genjitsu to no rakusa* (Japanese political parties and foreign policy: the gap with international reality). Keiō tsūshin, 1980.

Inoue Juichi. "Kokuren to sengo Nihon gaikō" (The UN and postwar Japanese diplomacy). In *Nenpō kindai Nihon kenkyū: sengo Nihon gaikō no keisei* (Journal of modern Japanese studies: the making of postwar Japanese diplomacy), ed. Kindai Nihon kenkyūkai, pp. 189–214. Yamakawa shuppan, 1994.

Iokibe Makoto. *Seijishi II—Nihon seiji gaikōshi* (Political history II: Japanese political and diplomatic history). Hōsō daigaku kyōiku shinkōkai, 1985.

Iriye Akira. *Nihon no gaikō: Meiji ishin kara gendai made* (Japan's diplomacy: from the Meiji restoration to the present day). Chūō kōronsha, 1966.

Ishibashi Masahi. "Hibusō chūritsu kenpō o sekai no kenpō ni" (Making the demilitarized neutral constitution the constitution of the world). *Gekkan shakaitō* (Jan. 1970): 24–37.

——. "Gojūgo nen taisei" uchigawa kara no shōgen ("The 1955 system": a testimony from inside). Tabata shoten, 1999.

Ishihara Iwane. *Kōmeitō no seiji, kokkai kisha no me* (CGP's politics: from the eyes of a journalist in the Diet). Daikōsha, 1969.

Ishihara Nobuo. *Kantei 2668 nichi—seisaku kettei no butaiura* (2,668 days at the prime minister's official residence: the backstage of decision-making). Nihon hōsō shuppan kyōkai, 1995.

Ishii Osamu; Gabe Masaaki and Miyasato Seigen, eds. *Amerika gasshūkoku tainichi seisaku bunsho shūsei dai 9 ki Nichibei gaikō bōei mondai 1965 nen dai 9 kan* (Documents on United States policy toward Japan IX: documents related to diplomatic and military matters, 1965, Vol. 9). Kashiwa shobō, 2001.

Isomura Eiichi. "Gunshuku, kakkin o mezashite—kokuren 'gunshuku tokubetsu sōkai' ni sankashite kanjita koto" (Toward disarmament and nuclear abandonment: impressions gained during participation in the UN "SSD"). *Kakushin* (July 1978): 81–85.

JCP. *Chika sennyū no taisei o totonoeta Nihon kyōsantō no bunkenshū (zokuhen)* (Collection of documents of the JCP, a party ready to go underground, supplement). Nikkan rōdō tsūshinsha, 1951.

——. "Kokuren no genjitsu to Nihon jinmin no tōsō" (The reality of the UN and the Japanese people's struggle). *Zenei* (June 1965): 84–91.

——. "Nihon no shin no anzen o mamoru tame ni—Nihon kyōsantō no anzen hoshō seisaku" (To maintain Japan's real security: JCP's security policy). *Zenei* (Mar. 1967): 84–97.

——. "Anpo jōyaku hantai to Okinawa henkan o mezasu, zen minshu seiryoku no tōitsu to, minshu rengō seifu no taigai seisaku" (Opposing the security treaty and fighting for the reversion of Okinawa: the united front of all democratic factions and the foreign policy of the democratic coalition government). *Zenei* (Aug. 1968): 113–15.

——. "Nihon no chūritsuka to anzen hoshō ni tsuite no Nihon kyōsantō no kōsō" (JCP's proposal on Japan's neutralization and security). *Zenei* (Sept. 1972): 42–44.

——. "Nihon no heiwa to chūritsu, shin no dokuritsu o kachitoru" (Japan's peace and neutrality: winning the real independence). *Zenei* (Sept. 1972): 24–32.

——. "Sangiin senkyo de no sōten to Nihon kyōsantō no yondai kihon seisaku" (Points at issue during the Upper House election and the JCP's four basic policies). *Zenei* (Aug. 1974): 28–75.

——. "Shōwa nijūichi nen roku gatsu, Nihon kyōsantō chūō iinkai kenpō iinkai happyō no 'Nihon kyōsantō kenpō sōan' ni tsuite" ("The JCP draft proposal for constitution" published by the Constitution Committee of the JCP Central Committee in June 1946). *Gekkan jiyū minshu* (Jan. 1981): 304–10.

——. "Shin no heiwa kōryō no tame ni" (For the real peace platform). *Zenei* (Sept. 1981): 25–62.

——. Central Committee ed. *Nihon kyōsantō no rokujū nen 1922–1982* (60 years of the JCP 1922–1982). Nihon kyōsantō chūō iinkai shuppankyoku, 1982.

——. "Hidōmei chūritsu, jiei no seisaku kōsō Nihon no heiwa to anzen o hoshō suru michi: Nihon kyōsantō no shuchō to teian" (A policy of nonalignment, neutrality and self-defense is the real way to guarantee Japan's peace and security: the JCP's arguments and proposals). *Zenei* (Mar. 1984): 83–99.

——. "Kyōdō seimei—Miyamoto Kenji gichō o danchō to suru Nihon kyōsantō daihyōdan to K. U. Cherunenko shokichō o danchō to suru Soren kyōsantō daihyōdan no kaidan ni tsuite" (Joint communiqué: regarding the meeting between the JCP delegation led by Chairman Miyamoto Kenji and the USSR communist party delegation led by General Secretary K. U. Chernenko). *Zenei* (Feb. 1985): 53–55.

Johnson, U. Alexis. *The Right Hand of Power: The Memoirs of an American Diplomat.* Englewood Cliffs, NJ: Prentice-Hall, Inc., 1984.

JSP. "Asukata hōōdan kaidan, komyunike" (Meetings and communiqués of the Asukata mission to Europe). *Gekkan shakaitō* (June 1982): 195–222.

——. Mission to Europe. "Hankaku, gunshuku no tatakai no kyōka o—tō hōō daihyōdan no igi to seika" (Intensifying the struggle for non-nuclear disarmament: the meaning and achievements of the party's mission to Europe). *Gekkan shakaitō* (June 1982): 188–94.

——. "Kakushin bundan ni te o kasu Nihon kyōsantō no dokuzenshugi" (The JCP's self-righteousness, which is helping the split of revolutionary factions). *Gekkan shakaitō* (June. 1980): 86–95.

——. "1988 nendo undō hōshin" (Policies for activities in 1988). *Gekkan shakaitō* (Apr. 1988, extra): 18–78.

—. *Nihon shakaitō seisaku shiryō shūsei* (A collection of documents on the policies of the JSP). Nihon shakaitō chūō honbu kikanshikyoku, 1990.

—. "'Kokuren heiwa kyōryoku kikō' secchi taikō—kokuren chūshin no heiwa kyōryoku no suishin ni tsuite" (Outline of the establishment of a "UN peace cooperation agency": regarding the promotion of UN-centered peace cooperation). *Gekkan shakaitō* (Jan. 1991): 157–59.

—. *Shiryō—Nihon shakaitō 50 nen* (Materials: 50 years of the JSP). Nihon shakaitō chūō honbu kikanshi kōhō iinkai, 1995.

Kadota Shōzō. "Kokuren to Nihon" (The UN and Japan). *Kokuren* (Aug. and Sept. 1983): 13–16.

Kameda Tōgo. "Amerika teikokushugi no nimen seisaku—sono ikutsuka no tokuchō" (The two-faced policy of American imperialism: some of its characteristics). *Zenei* (Jan. 1964): 79–90.

Kamijō Sueo. "Minshatō kihonseisaku no hensen" (The transition of the DSP's basic policies). *Kaikakusha* (Jan. 1972): 44–51.

Kamiyama Shigeo, ed. *Nihon kyōsantō sengo jūyō shiryōshū dai 1 kan* (Collections of important JCP documents from the postwar era, Vol. 1). Sanichi shobō, 1971.

Kaneko Mitsuhiro. "Gensuikin undō tōitsu e no dōhyō" (Milestones on the way to the unification of the anti-nuclear movement). *Zenei* (July 1977): 14–27.

—; Nakajima Atsunosuke and Niihara Shōji. "Kakuheiki o meguru jōsei to kakuheiki kinshi undō" (The situation regarding nuclear weapons and the anti-nuclear bomb movement). *Zenei* (Aug. 1979): 20–50.

—. "Gensuikin undō no tōmensuru kihon mondai" (Basic problems facing the anti-nuclear movement). *Zenei* (Aug. 1984): 30–48.

—. "INF zenpai jōyakugo no sekai no hankaku, heiwa undō no hōkō" (The direction of the world's anti-nuclear and peace movements in the aftermath of the INF arrangement). *Zenei* (June 1988): 34–45.

Kase Toshikazu. *Nihon gaikō no ketteiteki shunkan* (The decisive moments of Japan's diplomacy). Nihon keizai shimbunsha, 1965.

— and Kiuchi Nobutane, "Kokuren ni tsukai shite" (Dispatched to the UN). *Bungei shunjū* (June 1957): 74–82.

Kasuya Susumu. *Sengo Nihon no anzen hoshō rongi—kenpō 9 jō to Nichibei anpo no genten* (The security debates in postwar Japan: Article 9 and the origin of the US-Japan security alliance). Shinzansha, 1992.

Katsumata Seiichi. "Kōwa mondai to kōwa go no mondai to o kubetsu seyo" (Separate the peace problem from the problems after the peace). *Sekai* (Apr. 1951): 89–94.

—. "Yongensoku no jūyōsei wa izen to shite kawaranu" (The significance of the four principles remains unchanged). *Sekai* (Oct. 1951): 144–48.

Kawamura Shigemitsu. "Tōitsu mondai o meguru byūron" (Erroneous arguments on the unification problem). *Zenei* (Oct. 1977): 30–48.

Kawakami Tamio. "Kakugunshuku to hikaku busōchitai secchi no suishin o" (Promoting nuclear disarmament and the establishment of nuclear-free-zones). *Gekkan shakaitō* (Apr. 1982): 38–45.

Kawabe Ichirō. *Kokuren to Nihon* (The UN and Japan). Iwanami shoten, 1995.

Kaya Harunori. *Kokuren to Nihon gaikō* (The UN and Japan's diplomacy). Kokumin gaikō kyōkai, 1980.

Kimura Toshio. "Saikentōki no Nihon gaikō: nani o kaketeirunoka" (Japan's diplomacy in the revision period: what is missing?). *Sekai* (Feb. 1979): 40–52.

Kitaoka Shinichi. *Jiminō—seikentō no 38nen* (The Liberal Democratic Party—The 38 years as a ruling party). Yomiuri shimbun sha, 1995.

Kōno Masaharu. *Wahei kōsaku* (Peace moves). Iwanami shoten, 1999.

Kokuren kōhō sentā, ed. *Nihon to kokuren no 30 nen: Rekidai kokuren taishi ga kataru gendaishi no naka no Nihon* (30 years of Japan and the UN: UN ambassadors talk about Japan in contemporary history). Kōdansha, 1986.

Komori Yoshio. "Gensuikin undō o henshitsu saseru bunretsu rosen—Sōhyō, 'kin' burokku no shuchō to kodō hihan" (The split course that is degenerating the anti-nuclear movement: criticizing the arguments and behaviors of the Sōhyō, "Gensuikin" bloc). *Zenei* (Sept. 1984): 26–41.

Kosaka Zentarō. "Waga kuni no kokuren kyōryoku no sho mondai" (Problems in our country's cooperation with the UN). *Kokuren* (May 1966): 22–27.

——. "Wareware wa nani o kokuren ni kitai subeki ka" (What shall we expect from the UN?). *Kokuren* (Oct. 1969): 33–39.

——. "Kuni no ue ni kuni o tsukurazu" (Do not make one nation superior to another). *Economisto* (Nov. 9, 1976): 30–33.

—— and Takubo Tadae. "Kokuren sōkai to Nihon gaikō" (The UNGA and Japanese diplomacy). *Kokuren* (Dec. 1976): 8–15.

——. *Giin gaikō 40 nen—watashi no rirekisho* (A Diet member's diplomacy for 40 years: my resume). Nihon keizai shimbunsha, 1994.

Kōzai Shigeru. *Kokuren no heiwa iji katsudō* (The UN PKO). Yūhikaku, 1991.

Kubota Mane. "Kokusai kōken ni kansuru 10 kōmoku teigen" (A ten-item proposal on international contributions). *Gekkan shakaitō* (June 1992): 71–76.

Kunimasa Takeshige and Takabatake Michitoshi. "'Hahei kokkai' no butaiura" (Backstage at the "Diet session for military dispatch"). *Sekai* (Dec. 1990): 22–39.

Kuriyama Takakazu. "Gekihen suru sekai jōsei to Nihon gaikō no shinro" (The drastically changing international situation and the course of Japanese diplomacy). *Sekai keizai hyōron* (Apr. 1990): 8–19.

——. *Nichibei dōmei: hyōryū kara no dakkyaku* (The Japan-US alliance: from drift to revitalization). Nihon keizai shimbunsha, 1997.

Kurosaki Akira. "Satō seiken no kakuseisaku to Amerika no 'kaku no kasa'" (The Satō administration's nuclear policy and the American "nuclear umbrella"). *Prime*, 110. 17 (Mar. 2003): 73–93.

Kusunoki Ayako. "Senryōka Nihon no anzen hoshō kōsō—Gaimushō ni okeru Yoshida dokutorin no keisei katei, 1945–1949" (Japanese security conceptions during the occupation: the Foreign Ministry and the formation of the "Yoshida doctrine"). *Rokkōdai ronshū* 45, no. 3 (Mar. 1999): 1–55.

LBP. "Jiyūtō, kenpō kaiseian o happyō" (The LBP publishes its proposal for the revision of the constitution). *Saiken* (Sept. 1954): 58–60.

LDP. *Jiyū minshutō shi: shiryō hen* (The history of the LDP: data volume). LDP, 1987.

——; DSP and CGP. "Kokusai heiwa kyōryoku ni kansuru gōi oboegaki" (Memorandum on the agreement regarding international peace cooperation). *Zenei* (Jan. 1991): 88.

——. "Kokuren heiwa iji katsudō to wa nani ka" (What is UN PKO). *Gekkan jiū minshu* (Aug. 1992): 86–96.

Leitenberg, Milton. "The Participation of Japanese Military Forces in UN Peacekeeping Operations." *Maryland/Tsukuba Papers on U.S.-Japan Relations* (June 1996): 1–62.

Leopold, Lewis. *Prestige: A Psychological Study of Social Estimates*. London: F. Unwin, 1913.

Masuda Kaneshichi. *Masuda Kaneshichi kaisōroku: Yoshida jidai to watashi* (Memoirs of Masuda Kaneshichi: the Yoshida era and I). Mainichi shimbunsha, 1984.

Matsui Akira. "Sōritsu nijū nen o mukaeta kokuren to Nihon no yakuwari" (The UN upon its twentieth anniversary and Japan's role). *Kokuren* (Aug. 1965): 26–31.

——. "Kokuren gokanen no omoide" (Recollections of the five years in the UN). *Seisaku geppō* (Nov. 1967): 38–48.

Matsumoto Tatsuya. *PKO to kokusai kōken* (PKO and international contributions). Kenpakusha, 1994.

Meisler, Stanley. *United Nations: The First Fifty Years*. New York: The Atlantic Monthly Press, 1995.

Miyagi Taizō. *Sengo Ajia chitsujo no mosaku to Nihon: "umi no Ajia" no sengoshi, 1957–1966* (Japan and Southeast Asia in the quest for order: the cold war, decolonization, and development, 1957–1966). Sōbunsha, 2004.

Miyamoto Kenji. "Kakuheiki kinshi wa shōbi no kyū" (Nuclear weapon abandonment is a crying need). *Zenei* (Sept. 1977): 269–73.

Miyazawa Kiichi. *Tōkyō—Washinton no mitsudan* (Secret negotiations between Tokyo and Washington). Jitsugyō no Nippon sha, 1956.

— and Tahara Sōichirō. "Nihon no sentaku—Miyazawa Kiichi rongu intabyū" (Japan's choice: a long interview with Miyazawa Kiichi). *Chūō kōron* (Sept. 1991): 48–67.

—. "Kaifu san to watashi wa koko ga chigau" (This is where Mr. Kaifu and I are different). *Bungei shunjū* (Dec. 1991): 114–24.

MOFA. *Waga gaikō no kinkyō* (The present condition of our nation's diplomacy). MOFA, 1957–92.

—. "Kokuren sōkai ni okeru ugoki" (Movements of the UNGA). *Sekai no ugoki* (Nov. 1957): 18–23.

—. "Waga gunshuku teian hiketsu saru—11 gatsu no kokuren no ugoki" (Our country's disarmament proposal rejected—the movements of the UN in November). *Sekai no ugoki* (Dec. 1957): 8–19.

—. "Kokuren dai jūsan tsūjō sōkai owaru" (The end of the thirteenth UNGA Plenary Session). *Sekai no ugoki* (Jan. 1959): 28–29.

—. "Gaimushō anpo seisaku kikakui bunsho (zenbun)" (Document of the MOFA Security Policy Planning Council, full text). *Zenei* (Oct. 1980): 107–13.

—. Gaimushō sengo gaikōshi kenkyūkai, ed. *Nihon gaikō 30 nen—sengo no kiseki to tenbō 1952–1982* (Japan's diplomacy for 30 years: path and perspective of the postwar era 1952–1982). MOFA, 1982.

—. *Diplomatic Bluebook: Japan's Diplomatic Activities.* Info Plus Inc., 1991–92.

—. *Nihon gaikō bunsho: Heiwa jōyaku no teiketsu ni kansuru chōsho: dai 1 satsu–dai 4 satsu* (Documents on Japanese foreign policy: records related to the conclusion of Treaty of Peace with Japan, vols. 1–4). MOFA, 2002.

Morgenthau, Hans J. *Politics Among Nations: The Struggle for Power and Peace.* New York: Knopf, 1973.

Morikawa Jun. *Minami Afurika to Nihon—kankei no rekishi, kōzō, kadai* (South Africa and Japan—The history, mechanism and agendas of the relationship). Dōbunkan shuppan kabushikigaisha, 1988.

Morrison, Alex and James Kiras, eds. *UN Peace Operations and the Role of Japan.* Clementsport, NS: Canadian Peacekeeping Press, 1996.

Motono Moriyuki. "Oitsukigata gaikō no shūen" (The end of catching-up diplomacy). *Gaikō fōramu* (Oct. 1988): 34–40.

Moynihan, Daniel Patrick. *A Dangerous Place.* New York, Boston, and Toronto: Atlantic-Little, Brown, 1978.

Muller, Joachim W. *The Reform of the United Nations, Volume 1, Report.* New York, London, and Rome: Oceana Publications, 1991.

Murakami Tomoaki. "Kishi naikaku to kokuren gaikō—PKO gentaiken toshite no Lebanon kiki" (The Kishi cabinet and the UN: the Lebanon crisis as the original experience shaping the PKO commitment). *Journal of International Cooperation Studies,* vol. 2, no. 1 (Sept. 2003): 141–63.

Muramatsu Takeshi; Ueda Kōichirō; Takeda Gorō; Tsutsui Nobutaka and Katō Kōichi. "Gekiron: 'Kokuren heiwa kyōryokutai' o kiru—Kaifu naikaku no kuniku no chūtō kōkensaku o meguru sanpi ryōron" (Heated discussions: analyzing the "UN Peace Cooperation Corps": the pros and cons of the Kaifu cabinet's desperate measures to make contributions in the Middle East). *Bungei shunjū* (Dec. 1990): 146–58.

Murasawa Maki. "Seisaku shōiinkai hōkoku" (Report of the policy subcommittee). *Gekkan shakaitō* (Apr. 1969, extra): 259–63.

Murata Kiyoaki: *Kokuren nikki: Supponwan no kaisō* (The UN diary: recollections of Turtle Bay). Hara shobō, 1985.

Murata Ryōhei. "Kawariyuku kokusai jōsei to Nihon gaikō no kadai" (The changing international situation and matters for Japan's diplomacy). *Sekai keizai hyōron* (July 1988): 8–26.

—; Honma Nagayo; Tabuchi Mamoru and Kasuya Kazuki. "'Kokuryoku' ni ōjita aratana bijon no keisei ni mukete" (Toward the formation of a new vision congruent with "national power"). *Gaikō fōram* (Oct. 1988): 10–25.

Nagano Nobutoshi. *Gaimushō kenkyū* (A study on MOFA). Saimaru shuppankai, 1975.

Nakahira Noboru. "Kongo no waga kuni gaikō to kokuren" (Our country's diplomacy from now on and the UN). *Keizai to gaikō* (Jan. 1987): 11–13.

—. "Nihon to kokuren" (Japan and the UN). In *Saikin no kokusai jōsei* (The recent international situation), ed. Domestic Public Information Division of the Minister's Secretariat, pp. 97–105. MOFA, 1987.

Nakajima Shingo. "Amerika no higashi Ajia senryaku to Nihon (1955–1960)—Nihon o meguru direnma to chōwaten no mosaku" (Japan in American East-Asian strategy, 1955–60: America's quest for stable relations with Japan). *Kikan gunjishigaku* (Mar. 2000): 20–40.

Nakamura Nobuo. "Kaigai hahei soshi, gikaisei minshu shugi tsuranuita Nihon kyōsantō—dai 123 tsujō kokkai no hōkoku" (The JCP, which prevented overseas military dispatch and adhered to parliamentary democracy: report on the 123rd Diet Plenary Session). *Zenei* (Aug. 1992): 102–11.

Nakasone Yasuhiro. "Kokuren o shin ni kokuren tarashimeru tame ni" (To make the UN like it should be). *Kokuren* (Nov. 1987): 2–10.

—. *Tenchi ujō: gojūnen no sengo seiji o kataru* (The sentience of the heavens and the earth: talking about 50 years of postwar politics). Bungei shunjūsha, 1996.

Narita Satoshi and Takebayashi Nobuo. "Nakasone naikaku, shakōmin no bika wa hankaku heiwa undō o bōgaisuru" (The idealization of the Nakasone cabinet and the JSP-CGP-DSP bloc will obscure the anti-nuclear peace movement). *Zenei* (Sept. 1987): 42–66.

Nakayama Yoshihiro. "Senzen kara sengo e" (Before and after the war). *Gaikō fōram* (1995): 16–20.

Nihon kōhō kyōkai, ed. *Sōrifu, kokuritsu yoron chōsajo, yoron chōsa hōkokusho, dai 7 kan* (Report of the National Institute on Public Opinion Polls at the Prime Minister's Office, Vol. 7). Nihon kōhō kyōkai, 1992.

Nihon kyōshokuin kumiai, ed. *Kōwa mondai shiryō* (Materials on the peace problem). Nihon kyōshokuin kumiai shuppanbu, 1950.

Nishibori Masahiro. *Japan Views the United Nations*. Public Information and Culture Bureau, MOFA, 1970.

—. "Saikin no kokuren to Nihon" (The recent UN and Japan). *Kokuren* (May 1983): 19–22.

Nishihira Shigeki. *Yoron chōsa ni yoru dōjidaishi* (A contemporary history based on public opinion polls). Burēn shuppan, 1987.

Nishimura Kumao. "Nichibei anzen hoshō jōyaku no seiritsu jijō" (The conclusion of the US-Japan Security Treaty). In *Nihon no anzen hoshō* (Japan's security), eds. Nihon kokusai mondai kenkyūjo and Kajima kenkyūjo, pp. 199–227. Kajima kenkyūjo shuppankai, 1964.

—. *Nihon gaikōshi dai 27 kan: Sanfuranshisuko heiwa jōyaku* (Japanese diplomatic history, Vol. 27: the San Francisco Peace Treaty). Kajima kenkyūjo shuppankai, 1971.

Nishitani Yutaka. "Gensuikin undō wa dō arubeki ka" (How should the anti-nuclear movement be). *Gekkan shakaitō* (Oct. 1984): 80–90.

Ogata Sadako. "Nihon no kokuren gaikō no hensen" (Transition in Japan's UN diplomacy). In *Kokuren o kaizō suru* (Reforming the UN), ed. Satō Eisaku kinen kokuren daigaku kyōsan zaidan, pp. 281–306. Sekai no ugokisha, 1986.

Ōhira Masayoshi and Takemura Kenichi. "80 nendai o hiraku: kokusaika e 'nōryoku shigen' ikasō" (Paving the way toward the 80s: using the "resources of talent" for internationalization). *Gekkan jiyū minshu* (Nov. 1979): 32–39.

Ōta Hiroshi. "1980 nendai no Nihon gaikō" (Japan's diplomacy in the 1980s). *Gaikō jihō* (Feb. 1980): 5–14.

Ōuchi Keigo. "Jieitai sanka ni yoru PKO soshiki o" (Creating a PKO organ with the participation of the SDF). *Kakushin* (July 1991): 6–9.

Oka Yoshitake. *Meiji seijishi, Oka Yoshitake chosaku shū, dai 1 kan* (Political history of the Meiji era: collection of Oka Yoshitake's works, Vol. 1). Tōkyō daigaku shuppankai, 1992.

Okazaki Katsuo. "Kokusai rengō to Nihon" (The UN and Japan). *Kokuren* (Nov. 1964): 18–27.

Ōmori Minoru. "Dokuritsu jūnen Nihon gaikō no naimaku" (A decade after independence: the inner side of Japan's diplomacy). *Chūō kōron* (Sept. 1962): 36–51.

Ostrower, Gary B. *The United Nations and the United States: The Fragile Relationship.* New York: Twayne Publishers, 1998.

Ōtake Hideo. *Sengo Nihon bōei mondai shiryōshū dai 1 kan* (Documents on postwar Japan's defense issues, Vol. 1). Sanichi shobō, 1991.

Owada Hisashi. "Kokuren ni yoru heiwa iji to kokusai kyōryoku" (The UN's peacekeeping activities and international cooperation). *Kokuren* (July 1973): 21–28.

——. "1992 nen no sekai jōsei to Nihon gaikō" (The international situation in 1992 and Japan's diplomacy). *Sekai keizai hyōron* (Apr. 1992): 8–26.

Pan Liang. "The Formation of Japan's UN Policy in the Early Postwar Era 1946–57." *Kokusai seiji keizaigaku kenkyū*, no. 4 (Sept. 1999): 17–42.

——. "Amerika no tainichi seisaku ni okeru kokuren heiwa iji katsudō sanka mondai" (Japanese participation in the United Nations Peacekeeping Operations and the US Policy toward Japan during the Johnson and Nixon Administrations). *IPE Discussion Paper* 4 (2002): 1–16.

——. "'Keizai taikokuka' to kokusaiteki chii: anpori jōnin rijikokuiri mondai o meguru Nichibei kankei" (Economic power and international status: Japan's bid for a UNSC permanent membership and US-Japan relations). In *Ikeda, Satō seikenki no Nihon gaikō* (Japanese foreign policy under the Ikeda and Sato cabinets), ed. Hatano Sumio, pp. 167–97. Kyoto: Mineruba shobō, 2003.

Policy Division of the Policy Bureau. *Kokkai ni okeru kōwa rongi* (Debates on the peace at the Diet). MOFA, 1951.

Policy Studies Bureau, CGL, ed. *Yakushin suru kōmeikai no seisaku—taishū no fukushi o mezashite* (The advancing policies of the CGL: for the welfare of the people). Kōmei seiji renmei kikanshikyoku, 1964.

Polomka, Peter. *Japan as Peacekeeper: Samurai State, or New Civilian Power.* Canberra: Strategic and Defense Studies Center, Research School of Pacific Studies, The Australian National University, 1992.

Prime Minister's Office. *Gaikō ni kansuru yoron chōsa* (Public opinion poll on foreign policies). Prime Minister's Office, 1977–92.

——. *Jieitai, bōei mondai ni kansuru yoron chōsa Heisei 2 nendo* (Public opinion poll on the SDF and defense, 1990). Prime Minister's Office, 1992.

Public Information and Culture Bureau. *Kokuren gunshuku tokubetsu sōkai: sono seika to waga kuni no shuchō* (The UN SSD: its achievements and our country's arguments). MOFA, 1978.

Public Information Division. *Our Position in the Korean Conflict.* MOFA, 1950.

Rōyama Michio and Yano Junya. "72 nen ni okeru Nihon no sentaku" (Japan's choice in 1972). *Komei* (Jan. 1972): 20–31.

Sairenji Hiroki. "Nihon no kokuren heiwa iji katsudō sanka mondai—bunkan haken ni itaru made" (Japan's participation in the UN PKO: up to the dispatch of civilian officers). *Seiji keizai shigaku*, no. 434 (Oct. 2002): 23–47.

——. "Nihon no kaku jikken mondai e no taiō" (Japan and nuclear test ban problems). *Kikan kokusai seiji*, no. 136 (Mar. 2004): 3–17.

Saitō Shizuo. "Dai 18 kai kokuren sōkai o kaerimite" (Reviewing the eighteenth UNGA session). *Kokuren* (Feb. 1964): 13–18.

——. *Kokuren no mado kara* (From the window of the UN). Japan Association for the UN, 1976.

——. "Anpori senkyo haiboku riyū no bunseki" (Analyzing the reason for the defeat in the UNGA election). *Kokuren* (Nov. 1978): 18–20.

——. "Kokuren kenjin kaigi to Nihon" (The UN eminent persons conference and Japan). *Kokuren* (Aug. and Sept. 1986): 20–27.

——. "Kokuren gyōzaisei kaikaku no sono go" (After the UN administrative and financial reform). *Kokuren* (Oct. 1987): 2–5.

——. "Iran Iraku funsō shūketsu no kyōkun" (The lesson of the end of the Iran-Iraq War). *Kokuren* (Aug. and Sept. 1988): 2–8.

——. *Gaikō* (Diplomacy). Saimaru shuppankai, 1991.

Sakaguchi Kiyoshi. "Sengo Nihon no anzen hoshō to kokuren 1945–1952 nen" (Conceptions of postwar Japanese security policy and the United Nations 1945–1952). *Kokusai kōkyō seisaku kenkyū* vol. 3, no. 1 (1999): 63–92.

Sakamoto Kazuya. *Nichibei dōmei no kizuna: anpo jōyaku to sōgosei no mosaku* (The bonds of Japan-US alliance: searching for the reciprocity of the security treaty). Yūhikaku, 2000.

Sakurai Yoshiko; Ozawa Ichirō and Gotōda Masaharu. "Jiyū minshutō no kenpō mondai: kaiken? goken? kaishaku kaiken?" (The LDP's constitution agenda: defending the constitution, revising the constitution, or revising the constitution through interpretations?). *Shokun* (May 1992): 122–36.

Sasaki Mutsumi. "Iraku no Kuweito shinryaku to Nihon kyōsantō no tachiba—mondai no kōsei, binsoku na kaiketsu no tame ni" (Iraq's invasion of Kuwait and the JCP's position: for a fair and prompt solution to the problem). *Zenei* (Oct. 1990): 26–39.

Satō Hiroyuki. *Nihon no seitō kōryō* (Platforms of Japanese political parties). Minshu shakaishugi kenkyū kaigi, 1977.

Satō Isao. "Dai kyū jō no seifu kaishaku no kiseki to ronten (ge)—dai kyū jō no seiritsuji kara saikin no kokurengun sanka rongi ni itaru made" (The course and arguments of the government's interpretation of Article 9, vol. 2: from the enactment of Article 9 to recent discussions on participation in the UN forces). *Jurisuto* (June 1, 1992): 38–50.

Satō Seizaburō. "The Foundations of Modern Japanese Foreign Policy." In *The Foreign Policy of Modern Japan*, ed. Robert A. Scalapino, pp. 367–89. Berkeley: University of California Press, 1977.

Satō Susumu. "Reisen, kokuren, 'tōzai no kakehashi'—Chūtō mondai e no Nihon no taiō (1956–1958)" (Japanese policy towards the Middle East in the late 1950s: a mediator between "Orient and Occident"?). *IPE Discussion Papers* 3 (2001): 1–29.

Sawada Renzō. "Kokuren wa wareware no kikan da: Nihon mo sekkyokutekini hatsugenshiyō" (The UN is our organization: Japan should also actively speak out). *Asahi shimbun* (Dec. 19, 1956).

SCAP. "Makkāsā sōan" (MacArthur's draft proposal). *Gekkan jiyū minshu* (Jan. 1981): 276–91.

Seisaku kenkyū daigakuin daigaku COE ōraru seisaku kenkyū purojekuto. *Kikuchi Kiyoaki ōraru historī: gekan* (Oral history: Kikuchi Kiyoaki, vol. 2). Seisaku kenkyū daigakuin daigaku, 2004.

Sekai heiwa kenkyūjo, ed. *Nakasone naikaku shi: shiryō hen* (The history of the Nakasone cabinet: materials volume). Sekai heiwa kenkyūjo, 1995.

Sekiguchi Kanobu. "NGO to kongo no gensuikin undō no kadai—kokuren gunshuku tokubetsu sōkai ni sankashite—" (NGOs and the agenda for the anti-nuclear movement in the future: attending the UN SSD). *Gekkan shakaitō* (Aug. 1978): 118–32.

——. "Ikanishite kaku gunshuku o tassei suru ka—dai ni kai kokuren gunshuku tokubetsu sōkai ni sanka shite" (How to accomplish nuclear disarmament: attending the UN SSD II). *Gekkan shakaitō* (Aug. 1982): 28–39.

Shigemitsu Mamoru. *Shigemitsu Mamoru shuki* (Notes by Shigemitsu Mamoru). Chūō kōronsha, 1986.

——. *Zoku Shigemitsu Mamoru shuki* (Notes by Shigemitsu Mamoru, supplement). Chūō kōronsha, 1989.

Shimizu Shin. *Chikujō Nihonkoku kenpō shingiroku dai 2 kan* (A record of the article-by-article deliberations on the Japanese Constitution, Vol. 2). Hara shobō, 1976.

Shimoda Takezō. *Sengo Nihon gaikō no shōgen (jō)* (A testimony of postwar Japan's diplomacy, Vol. 1). Gyōsei mondai kenkyusho, 1984.

Shinyo Takahiro. "Kokuren no saikasseika o motomete—P5 to G7 wa dō chōwasuru ka" (Calling for the revitalization of the UN: how to harmonize the P5 with the G-7). *Kokuren* (July 1992): 2–10.

Shuyō kokuren kikan taishi renraku kaigi. "Sekkyokuteki kokuren gaikō no suishin" (Actively promoting UN diplomacy). *Kokuren* (Nov. 1986): 17–18.

Soeya Yoshihide; L. William Heirich, Jr.; and Shibata Akiho, eds. *UN Peace-Keeping Operations: A Guide to Japanese Policies.* Tokyo, New York, and Paris: United Nations University Press, 1999.

Sōgō anzen hoshō kenkyūkai, ed. *Economisto ga kaita sōgō anzen hoshō no kōzu* (The mechanism of comprehensive security from the viewpoints of economists). Nihon seisansei honbu, 1981.

Sone Eki. "Foreign Policy of the Japan Socialist Party." In *Japan's Foreign Policy: Conservative and Socialist Views,* eds. Ashida Hitoshi and Sone Eki, pp. 18–33. Japan Institute of Pacific Relations, 1958.

SPSC. "Waga kuni no anzen hoshō seisaku" (Our country's security policy). *Seisaku geppō* (Sept. 1973): 40–56.

Stockwin, J. A. A. *The Japanese Socialist Party and Neutralism.* Melbourne: Melbourne University Press, 1968.

Suzuki Tetsu. "Kokuren heiwa iji katsudō to Nihon" (UN PKO and Japan). *Kokuren* (Jan. 1990): 2–6.

Takashima Masuo. "Kokuren kaisō, sono nerai" (The purpose of reshuffling the UN). *Sekai shūhō* (Oct. 11, 1960): 32–35.

Takenaka Yoshihiko. "Kokusaihōgakusha no 'sengo kōsō'—'daitōa kokusaihō' kara 'kokuren shinkō' e" (Postwar visions of the international lawyers in wartime Japan: from the pursuit of the Greater East Asian International Law to the idealization of the United Nations). *Kikan kokusai seiji,* no. 109 (May 1995): 70–83.

Tanabe Makoto. "PKO gekitotsu kokkai, kecchaku wa korekara da" (A serious collision on PKO at the Diet: the showdown is yet to come). *Gekkan shakaitō* (Aug. 1992): 6–21.

Tanaka Mitsuo. "Nihon no kokusai chii" (Japan's international status). *Jikei* (Nov. 1954): 16–19.

Tanuma Hajime; Yoshida Yoshikiyo and Tachiki Hiroshi. "Kokuren gunshuku tokubetsu sōkai to Nihon no gensuikin undō" (The UN SSD and Japan's anti-nuclear movement). *Zenei* (Aug. 1978): 136–53.

Tatebayashi Chisato. "Jieitai o ikani kaishō suru ka—iwayuru 'iken gōhō ron' o meguru giron no seiri" (How to abolish the SDF: laying out the arguments on the so-called "unconstitutional lawfulness theme"). *Gekkan shakaitō* (May 1984): 24–40.

Terasawa Hajime; Kuroyanagi Akira and Nakagawa Yoshimi. "Kokuren Ajia Kyokutō chiiki honbu no secchi o isoge" (Hurry up and establish the UN Asian Far Eastern headquarters). *Kōmei* (June 1970): 38–45.

Tobe Ryōichi. "Gaikō ni okeru 'shisōteki rikyo' no tankyū: Shiratori Toshio no kōdō gaikōron" (Kōdō diplomacy in the thought of Shiratori Toshio). *Kikan kokusai seiji*, no. 71 (Aug. 1982): 124–40.

Tomizuka Mitsuo. "Hankaku, gunshuku, heiwa: kōdōsuru nijūni nin iinkai" (Anti-nuclearism, disarmament, peace: the committee of twenty-two people in action). *Gekkan shakaitō* (Aug. 1984): 22–31.

Tsugawa Hisayoshi. "Gensuikin undō tōitsu no honryū to shōgai" (The general trend toward unification of the anti-nuclear movement and the obstacles to it). *Zenei* (Aug. 1981): 65–75.

Tsuruoka Senjin. "Kokuren no hatten to Nihon" (The development of the UN and Japan). *Sekai shūhō* (Jan. 10, 1961): 42–45.

——. "Kokusai kaigi zakkan—kokuren gaikō no keiken o tōshite—" (Miscellaneous thoughts on international conferences: through the experience of UN diplomacy). *Sekai no rōdō* (May 1976): 26–36.

Ueda Kōichirō; Kaneko Mitsuhiro and Tanuma Hajime. "Jidai yurugasu hankaku undō no nami" (The surge of the anti-nuclear movement shaking the times). *Zenei* (Aug. 1982): 92–123.

——. "'Sangiin senkyo no sōten to Nihon kyōsantō no seisaku' no tokuchō to kihonten" (The characteristics and basic points of the document, "The JCP's policy and the points at issue in the Upper House election"). *Zenei* (June 1980): 10–39.

Ueda Seikichi. "Shūdan anzen hoshō to gunji dōmei—Nichibei anpo jōyaku to kokuren kenshō gojūichi jō narabini gojūni jō" (Collective security and military alliance: US-Japan Security Treaty and Articles 51 and 52 of the UN charter). *Zenei* (Nov. 1959): 51–60.

Ueki Mitsunori. *Nihon no seizon—sōgō anzen hoshōron* (Japan's survival: opinions on comprehensive security). Kokusho kankōkai, 1987.

Uezumi Mitsuhiro. *Nihon shakaitō kōbōshi* (The history of the rise and fall of the JSP). Jiyūsha, 1992.

UN Bureau, ed. *Statements Delivered by Delegates of Japan during the Regular Session of General Assembly.* MOFA, 1959–91

——. *Kokuren jōhō dai 2–3 kan* (UN information, vols. 2–3). MOFA, 1971–72.

United Nations. *Official Records of the General Assembly Twenty-Ninth Session, Agenda item 95 Annexes, Document A/9950, Report of the Sixth Committee, December 13, 1974.* New York: UN, 1974.

——. *Official Records of the General Assembly Twenty-Ninth Session, Plenary Meetings, Vol. 3.* New York: UN, 1974.

—. *Official Records of the General Assembly Twenty-Ninth Session, Sixth Committee, Legal Questions, Summary of Records of Meetings 18 September-9 December 1974.* New York: UN, 1974.

Wada Haruo. "'Jiei' no hyōgen o kaeta tō kōryō" (The party platform that changed the expression of "self-defense"). *Kakushin* (Jan. 1980): 98–101.

Waltz, Kenneth N. *Theory of International Politics.* New York: Random House, 1979.

—. "Emerging Structure of International Politics." *International Security* vol. 18, no. 2 (1993): 44–79.

Watanabe Akio. "Taigai ishiki ni okeru 'senzen' to 'sengo'" (International awareness in modern Japan before and after WWII). In *Kindai Nihon no taigai taido* (Modern Japan's attitude toward the outside world), eds. Satō Seizaburō and Roger Dingman, pp. 225–74. Tōkyō daigaku shuppankai, 1974.

—. "Kōwa monndai to Nihon no sentaku" (The peace arrangement issue and Japan's choice). In *Sanfuranshisuko kōwa* (Peace in San Francisco), eds. Watanabe Akio and Miyasato Seigen, pp. 17–56. Tōkyō daigaku shuppankai, 1986.

— and Mikuriya Takashi, eds. *Shushō kantei no ketsudan—naikaku kanbō fukuchōkan Ishihara Nobuo no 2600 nichi* (The decision of the prime minister's official residence: the 2,600 days of Deputy Chief Cabinet Secretary Ishihara Nobuo). Chūō kōronsha, 1997.

Watanabe Ichirō. "Kokuren Ajia honbu secchi no igi—sono hassō to gutaisaku o ronzu" (The significance of establishing the UN Asian headquarters: discussing the idea and concrete measures). *Kōmei* (Mar. 1969)

—. "'Kokuren Ajia honbu' secchi no igi" (The significance of establishing the "UN Asian headquarters"). *Kōmei* (Dec. 1969): 18–25.

—. "Gaikō ni okeru risō to genjitsu—Kōmeitō no iu tōkyori chūritsu heiwa gaikō koso riarizumu to aidearizumu tōitsu eno michi da!" (Ideals and realities in diplomacy: the equidistant neutral peace diplomacy argued by the CGP is the real way to unify realism and idealism!) *Kōmei* (July 1978): 45–53.

—. "Issenman shomei undō ni atatte" (In the campaign for ten million signatures). *Kōmei* (Mar. 1982): 14–20.

—. "Hankaku, gunshuku undō to kōmeitō no tatakai: 'Hankaku, gunshuku, ima koso heiwa o' tēma ni tasaina undō" (Anti-nuclear and disarmament movements and the struggle of the CGP: various campaigns under the title of "anti-nuclearism and disarmament, now is the time for peace now"). *Kōmei* (Aug. 1984): 66–70.

Watanabe Ryōjirō, ed. *Sonoda Sunao gaimu, kōsei daijin nitteihyō* (Schedules of Foreign Minister and Health and Welfare Minister Sunoda Sunao). Nichibei bunka shinkōkai, 1990.

Watanabe Yōzō and Okakura Koshirō, eds. *Nichibei anpo jōyaku—sono kaisetsu to shiryō* (The US-Japan Security Treaty: interpretations and materials). Rōdō junpōsha, 1968.

Yamaguchi Fusao. "Shakaitō gaikō rosen o jiko hihan suru" (A self-criticism of the JSP's diplomatic policy). *Chūō kōron* (Apr. 1966): 108–19.

Yamane Takashi. "Jieitai kaigai hahei eno shōdō—Nihon no kokurengun sanka sakudō no kidō o miru" (The drive toward sending SDF overseas: tracing the scheme for Japan's participation in UN forces). *Zenei* (May 1987): 103–13.

Yamasaki Shinji. "Iraku no Kuweito shinkō to kokusai rengō" (Iraq's invasion of Kuwait and the UN). *Zenei* (Dec. 1990): 89–102.

Yamashita Masako. "Hitorihitori no fujin ga jikakushite tachiagaru: kokuren gunshuku sōkai ni fujin no daihyō toshite" (Each woman should become self-aware and stand up: Being a woman representative to the UN SSD). *Gekkan shakaitō* (August 1982): 19–21.

Yano Junya. "Kongo no tatakai no hōkōsei ni tsuite—jakusha no tachiba ni tesshikitta katsudō o" (Future directions of struggle: taking action entirely from the standpoint of the underdog). *Kōmei* (Sept. 1981): 14–23.

— and Ichikawa Yūichi. "Ima tōnai de rongi shiteiru koto" (Things being discussed inside the party). *Kōmei* (Oct. 1981): 82–98.

Yoshida Kisaburō and Otaka Tomoo. *Kokusai rengō to Nihon* (The UN and Japan). Yūhikaku, 1956.

Yoshida Nagao. "Kokurengun to Nihon" (The UN force and Japan). *Kokusai mondai* (May 1966): 36–43.

Yoshida Shigeru. *Kaisō jūnen dai san kan* (Recollection of the decade, Vol. 3). Tokyo shirakawa shoin, 1983.

Yoshida Yasuhiko. *Kokuren kōhōkan* (An UN public information officer). Chūō kōron sha, 1991.

— *Yameru kokuren: Nani o dō kaikaku subeki ka* (The sick UN: what to reform and how). Bungei shunjūsha, 1995.

Yoshioka Yoshinori. "Nihon no shin no anzen hoshō no michi—dokuritsu, heiwa, chūritsu, jiei no seisaku tenbō" (The real course of Japan's security: policy prospects for independence, peace, neutrality and self-defense). *Zenei* (Dec. 1980): 6–35.

Yoshizawa Seijirō, ed. *Nihon gaikōshi dai 29 kan: kōwago no gaikō I—tai rekkoku gaikō (ge)* (Japanese diplomatic history, vol. 29, diplomacy after the peace I: relationship with nations, vol. 2). Kajima kenkyūjo shuppankai, 1973.

Index

Harvard East Asian Monographs
(*out-of-print)

Harvard East Asian Monographs

181. Soon-Won Park, *Colonial Industrialization and Labor in Korea: The Onoda Cement Factory*

182. JaHyun Kim Haboush and Martina Deuchler, *Culture and the State in Late Chosŏn Korea*

183. John W. Chaffee, *Branches of Heaven: A History of the Imperial Clan of Sung China*

184. Gi-Wook Shin and Michael Robinson, eds., *Colonial Modernity in Korea*

185. Nam-lin Hur, *Prayer and Play in Late Tokugawa Japan: Asakusa Sensōji and Edo Society*

186. Kristin Stapleton, *Civilizing Chengdu: Chinese Urban Reform, 1895–1937*

187. Hyung Il Pai, *Constructing "Korean" Origins: A Critical Review of Archaeology, Historiography, and Racial Myth in Korean State-Formation Theories*

188. Brian D. Ruppert, *Jewel in the Ashes: Buddha Relics and Power in Early Medieval Japan*

189. Susan Daruvala, *Zhou Zuoren and an Alternative Chinese Response to Modernity*

190. James Z. Lee, *The Political Economy of a Frontier: Southwest China, 1250–1850*

191. Kerry Smith, *A Time of Crisis: Japan, the Great Depression, and Rural Revitalization*

192. Michael Lewis, *Becoming Apart: National Power and Local Politics in Toyama, 1868–1945*

193. William C. Kirby, Man-houng Lin, James Chin Shih, and David A. Pietz, eds., *State and Economy in Republican China: A Handbook for Scholars*

194. Timothy S. George, *Minamata: Pollution and the Struggle for Democracy in Postwar Japan*

195. Billy K. L. So, *Prosperity, Region, and Institutions in Maritime China: The South Fukien Pattern, 946–1368*

196. Yoshihisa Tak Matsusaka, *The Making of Japanese Manchuria, 1904–1932*

197. Maram Epstein, *Competing Discourses: Orthodoxy, Authenticity, and Engendered Meanings in Late Imperial Chinese Fiction*

198. Curtis J. Milhaupt, J. Mark Ramseyer, and Michael K. Young, eds. and comps., *Japanese Law in Context: Readings in Society, the Economy, and Politics*

199. Haruo Iguchi, *Unfinished Business: Ayukawa Yoshisuke and U.S.-Japan Relations, 1937–1952*

200. Scott Pearce, Audrey Spiro, and Patricia Ebrey, *Culture and Power in the Reconstitution of the Chinese Realm, 200–600*

201. Terry Kawashima, *Writing Margins: The Textual Construction of Gender in Heian and Kamakura Japan*

202. Martin W. Huang, *Desire and Fictional Narrative in Late Imperial China*

203. Robert S. Ross and Jiang Changbin, eds., *Re-examining the Cold War: U.S.-China Diplomacy, 1954–1973*

204. Guanhua Wang, *In Search of Justice: The 1905–1906 Chinese Anti-American Boycott*

205. David Schaberg, *A Patterned Past: Form and Thought in Early Chinese Historiography*

206. Christine Yano, *Tears of Longing: Nostalgia and the Nation in Japanese Popular Song*

Harvard East Asian Monographs

256. Jonathan W. Best, *A History of the Early Korean Kingdom of Paekche, together with an annotated translation of* The Paekche Annals *of the* Samguk sagi

257. Liang Pan, *The United Nations in Japan's Foreign and Security Policymaking, 1945–1992: National Security, Party Politics, and International Status*